Global Media Ethics and the Digital Revolution

This volume responds to the challenges posed by the rapid developments in satellite TV and digital technologies, addressing media ethics from a global perspective to discuss how we can understand journalism practice in its cultural contexts.

An international team of contributors draw upon global and non-Western traditions to discuss the philosophical origins of ethics and the tension that exists between media institutions, the media market and political/ideological influencers. The chapters then unveil the discrepancies among international journalists in abiding by the ethics of the profession and the extent to which media ethics are understood and applied in their local context/environment. Arguing that the legitimacy of ethics comes not from the definition per se, but from the extent to which it leads to social good, the book posits this should be the media's raison d'être to abide by globally accepted ethical norms in order to serve the common good.

Taking a truly global approach to the question of media ethics, this volume will be an important resource for scholars and students of journalism, communication studies, media studies, sociology, politics and cultural studies.

Noureddine Miladi is Professor of Media and Communication at Qatar University. He is former head of the Department of Mass Communication and President of the Arab Media and Communication Network (AMCN.online). He is editor of JAMMR, the first peer-reviewed English journal in Arab media and society.

Routledge Research in Journalism

For more information about this series, please visit:
https://www.routledge.com/Routledge-Research-in-Journalism/book-series/RRJ

Global Media Ethics and the Digital Revolution

Edited by
Noureddine Miladi

Routledge
Taylor & Francis Group

LONDON AND NEW YORK

First published 2022
by Routledge
2 Park Square, Milton Park, Abingdon, Oxon OX14 4RN

and by Routledge
605 Third Avenue, New York, NY 10158

Routledge is an imprint of the Taylor & Francis Group, an informa business

© 2022 selection and editorial matter, Noureddine Miladi; individual chapters, the contributors

The right of Noureddine Miladi to be identified as the author of the editorial material, and of the authors for their individual chapters, has been asserted in accordance with sections 77 and 78 of the Copyright, Designs and Patents Act 1988.

All rights reserved. No part of this book may be reprinted or reproduced or utilised in any form or by any electronic, mechanical, or other means, now known or hereafter invented, including photocopying and recording, or in any information storage or retrieval system, without permission in writing from the publishers.

Trademark notice: Product or corporate names may be trademarks or registered trademarks, and are used only for identification and explanation without intent to infringe.

British Library Cataloguing-in-Publication Data
A catalogue record for this book is available from the British Library

Library of Congress Cataloging-in-Publication Data
A catalog record has been requested for this book

ISBN: 978-1-032-06214-3 (hbk)
ISBN: 978-1-032-06724-7 (pbk)
ISBN: 978-1-003-20355-1 (ebk)

DOI: 10.4324/9781003203551

Typeset in Sabon
by Taylor & Francis Books

To my parents

Contents

Illustrations

Figure

Tables

Contributors

Andrew Pilkington is Professor of Sociology at The University of Northampton, UK and a Fellow of the Royal Society of Arts. His research has especially focused on issues relating to race and ethnicity, and he has published widely in this area, including *Racial Disadvantage and Ethnic Diversity in Britain* (Palgrave, 2003) and, with Shirin Housee and Kevin Hylton, an edited collection, *Race(ing) Forward: Transitions in Theorising Race in Education* (HEA, 2009). A particularly influential book is *Institutional Racism in the Academy: A Case Study* (Trentham, 2011) in which he compares the response of universities and the police to legislative measures and policy initiatives designed to promote equality and diversity.

Sylvia Harvey is a Visiting Professor in the School of Media and Communication, University of Leeds (UK). She obtained her doctorate from the University of California, Los Angeles, returning to Britain to teach film studies and then broadcasting policy from 1975 to 2009. She chaired the Citizen's Coalition for Public Service Broadcasting (2009–10), was a founder member of the Sheffield International Documentary Festival (Doc/Fest) and is a trustee of the Voice of the Listener and Viewer. Her publications include *May '68 and Film Culture*, articles on cultural history, Channel 4 Television, broadcasting regulation and impartiality, spectrum allocation and the importance of public service and free-to-air television. Her most recent work is on the impact of subscription video on demand on public service broadcasting: 'Broadcasting in the Age of Netflix: When the Market is Master', in *A Companion to Television*, 2nd edition, ed. J. Wasko and E. Meehan (2020). She has made regular policy submissions to the UK regulator Ofcom and to government and parliamentary inquiries.

Noureddine Miladi is Professor of Media and Communication and former Head of Department of Mass Communication, at Qatar University. He is Editor of the *Journal of Arab and Muslim Media Research (JAMMR)*, an international peer-reviewed journal specialized in Arab and Middle Eastern Media and Society, www.intellectbooks.com/journal-of-arab-muslim-media-research. He is co-editor of *Routledge Handbook of Arab Media* (Routledge, 2021). He is also co-author of *Media and the Democratic Transition in the Arab World* (2019) *and Mapping the Al Jazeera Phenomenon 20 Years*

On (2017). He supervises MA and PhD researchers in social media and social change, media and democracy, youth, identity and social media networks, media ethics, Arab media, Al-Jazeera and global media and public opinion.

Mazhar Al-Zo'by is Associate Professor of culture and politics in the Department of International Affairs at Qatar University. His interests, both in research and teaching, focus principally on the politics of representation, identity and social change in the context of globalization. While his work is comparative in nature, his area of focus is the Muslim world in general and the Arab world in particular. Among the critical issues on which his teaching and writing have concentrated are the role of culture in the production of hegemony, media and identity, social movements, colonial discourse and the world system.

Daya Thussu is Professor of International Communication at the Hong Kong Baptist University. For the academic year 2018–2019, he was Distinguished Visiting Professor and Inaugural Disney Chair in Global Media at Schwarzman College, Tsinghua University in Beijing. For many years, Professor Thussu was Professor of International Communication and Co-Director of India Media Centre as well as research advisor to the China Media Centre at the University of Westminster in London. Professor Thussu is the Founder and Managing Editor of the Sage journal *Global Media and Communication*. Author or editor of 18 books, among his main publications are *Electronic Empires; International Communication: Continuity and Change*, 3rd edition; *Media on the Move: Global Flow and Contra-flow; News as Entertainment: The Rise of Global Infotainment; Internationalizing Media Studies; Media and Terrorism: Global Perspectives; Communicating India's Soft Power: Buddha to Bollywood; Mapping BRICS Media* (co-edited) and *China's Media Go Global* (co-edited).

Fethi B. J. Ahmed holds a Ph.D. in Sociology (2003) and an MA in Islamic Studies (1997). He is former Assistant Professor at the International Islamic University in Malaysia, International Student Advisor at the University of Auckland, Academic Director with the Saudi Arabian Cultural Mission in New Zealand, and Research Coordinator with Hamad Bin Khalifa University in Qatar. Dr Ahmed authored a number of refereed as well as general and online publications in sociology, ethics and Islamic studies.

Noureddine Khadmi is Professor of Islamic Studies and Head of the Research Unit at the College of Sharia, Qatar University. He formerly served as Minister of Religious Affairs in Tunisia, and President of the Tunis International Center for the Purposes of Sharia and Jurisprudence. He is member of the Board of Trustees of the World Federation of Muslim Scholars. In terms of his scholarly output, Prof Khadmi has authored more than 60 published books and dozens of research articles. He is a member of various scientific institutions and jurisprudence bodies. He has numerous TV and radio educational programmes on Islamic culture. He is winner of various international scientific awards.

Jamel Zran is Professor of media and communication at the Institute of Journalism and Information Sciences, University of Manouba, Tunisia. He previously worked at Qatar University and served as Editor-in-Chief and Director of the Tunisian Cultural Radio (public radio) in 2012. His research interests include social media networks in the Arab world, media ethics and Arab media issues in the new communication environment. He co-edited various books, including *Media and Democratic Transition in the Arab World* (2019), with Dr Noureddine Miladi, and the *History of Journalism in the Mediterranean Countries* in 2014. Dr Jamel Zran was awarded a major grant from the Qatar National Research Fund (QNRF) to study 'Media and national identity in Qatar, case study: *Al Rayyan* channel and its audience'.

Suzana Žilič Fišer, is Associate Professor and head of the Institute of Media Communication at the University of Maribor. She spent ten years in the media the industry as a journalist and an executive producer. She conducted research as the Chevening scholar, and worked as a visiting lecturer at various universities in Europe. In her research, she mainly focuses on journalism, broadcasting, media management, culture and public interest. She has published various books, chapters and articles in international scientific journals. From 2011 to 2013 she served as the Director General of the European Capital of Culture, Maribor 2012. She was designated by the European Commission for two mandates (2013–2019) as a member of the selection panel for the European Capital of Culture.

Irena Lovrenčič Držanič is a Researcher and PhD student at the Institute of Media Communication at the University of Maribor. Her research focuses on Media Ethics, Fake News, Journalism, and Digital Platforms. Currently, she is involved in research work for multiple Erasmus+ projects, as well as conducting research for scientific papers and book chapters. She is also active in national projects funded by the Slovenian Research Agency. Her PhD work focuses on platformization and its effects on the media organizations and audiences.

Moez Ben Messaoud is Associate Professor in the Department of Mass Communication, College of Arts and Sciences, Qatar University. He got a PhD from the Sorbonne University in France and served previously as Head Department of Communication at the Institute of Journalism and Information Sciences (IPSI), University of Manouba, Tunis. Ben Messaoud served also as Editor-in-Chief of the Tunisian *Journal of Communication Sciences*, and coordinated various research projects in both Manouba University, Tunisia, and Qatar University. His research interests include social media networks and social change, public service broadcasting, and media and democratic transition. He has authored several refereed articles, books and book chapters of which the most recent is 'Social Media Networks and Democratic Transition in Tunisia: From Censorship to Freedom' in the *Routledge Handbook on Arab Media* (2021).

Hala A. Guta is Associate Professor of Mass Communication, Qatar University. Her research interests include international media and communication, feminist media studies, communication for social change, and the intersection of communication, culture, and identity in the global South. Her publications and conference presentations include papers on the role of culture in communication, communication role in peace building in societies emerging from conflict, and the role media and other cultural institutions play in social change and the identity politics, as well as digital communication.

Jairo Lugo-Ocando is Professor in Residence and Director of Executive and Graduate Education at Northwestern University, Qatar. Born in Venezuela, he is author of several books, journal articles and other academic publications. Over the years he has received over US$ 1.1 million in external research grants funding from a diversity of institutions and organizations from around the world and was recipient of the Theodore C. Sorensen Fellowship from the John F. Kennedy Library and was a visiting fellow at the National University of Singapore. Before becoming an academic, he worked as a journalist, correspondent and news editor for several media outlets in Latin America.

Steven Harkins is a lecturer in Communications Media and Culture at the University of Stirling. His research interests sit at the intersection between journalism studies, political communication and social theory. His most recent research examined news framing of poverty and inequality.

Ibrahim N. Abusharif, PhD, is Associate Professor at Northwestern University in Qatar, in the journalism and strategic communication program. He has a post-graduate degree in journalism and a doctorate in religious and Islamic studies. His academic interests include the intersections of religion and media, particularly digital media and religious authority. He also researches the origins, promulgation and effects of key journalistic framing terminologies used in prominent Western print news sources in covering Middle East and North African events and ongoing affairs.

Abdulfatah Mohamed is Senior Research Fellow in the Centre for Conflict and Humanitarian Studies and an Adjunct Assistant Professor at Hamad Bin Khalifa University in Doha, Qatar. He has more than 30 years of experience working in various disciplines and sectors, from being advisor to government institutions to an independent advisor to The United Nations Office Humanitarian Affairs (UNOCHA) during the consultation process leading to the World Humanitarian Summit. He has worked with major corporations and NGOs, in the Middle East, Europe and Africa. Mohamed has lectured and wrote numerous articles on Islamic charities. He holds PhD in Middle East Politics and International Studies from University of Exeter, United Kingdom.

Winston Mano is Reader and a member of the University of Westminster's top-rated Communication and Media Research Institute (CAMRI). He is also Course Leader for the MA in Media and Development and the Founder/

Editor-in-Chief of the *Journal of African Media Studies*. Mano joined the University of Westminster's Communication and Media Research Institute (CAMRI) from the University of Zimbabwe in 2000 where he was a Senior Lecturer in Media and Communication. He studied in Zimbabwe, Norway and Britain. Among his publications are *Routledge Handbook of African Media and Communication Studies* (2021) (with viola c. milton); *Social Media and Elections in Africa* (2020) (with Martin N. Ndlela), vols 1 and 2 (2019) and *International Media Development: Historical Perspectives and New Frontiers* (with Nicholas Benequista, Susan Abbott, Paul Rothman). Link to his publications: https://www.westminster.ac.uk/about-us/our-peop le/directory/mano-winston.

Introduction

Global digital media explosion and the question of ethics

Noureddine Miladi

The renewed debate on media ethics is a valid discussion and remains ever needed due to the unprecedented developments in global communication technologies and its impact on society. For decades, globalization has firstly meant a growing sense of interconnected and fast movement of information due to satellite technology and Internet social media platforms. Recent developments in media and communication technologies have had impact on the everydayness of people around the world. The unremitting global reach of satellite and mobile technology, the Internet and social media have meant blurring of geographical boundaries and shrinking of time and space through which the media message can travel. It can indiscriminately penetrate and affect every culture and tradition.

Secondly, such technological developments have also meant resistance of the local and a resilience to sustain native identity in face of the global homogenizing forces. Thirdly, the developments of digital platforms on the Internet and the explosion of global communication have entailed mounting challenges with regard to controlling disinformation on the web and upholding basic ethos of media ethics and responsible journalism.

Such unprecedented developments in the global media and communication scene invite philosophical responses from all disciplines in order to come up with a holistic view about ethics and the media. The temporal changes on a global scale beg global considerations for a media ethics approach that appreciates the sophistication of the global. Stark discrepancies in diverse worldviews concerning what constitutes ethics in journalism is more evident nowadays than ever before. Not least, the unmissable differences that exist between the East and the West in what constitutes responsible journalism and whether free speech should have limits or not. For instance, the Islamic perspective regarding limits to free speech especially when it comes to the sacred compared to the unlimited scope of freedom of expression in the Western context is a case in point. However, this is not in my view the only problem. What increases tension and misunderstanding is the inability of marginalized voices to be heard and appreciated. Also, what adds to the clash of values are the double standards in some parts of the world in applying rules about freedom of expression and controlling hate speech in the media.

DOI: 10.4324/9781003203551-1

For example, president Macron's claim in October 2020 (The Telegraph, 2020) that insulting the Prophet Muhammad is a matter of free speech reminds us that morality in some parts of the world has reached the end of the tunnel. We are witnessing the demise of the ethical, what Nietzsche (2014) calls moving beyond good and evil. In his philosophical views, Nietzsche (2019) overemphasized the agency of the individual above the group. He attributes an absolute freedom to man, giving him a total subjective morality, which goes beyond the boundaries of religion. This view is in line with the growing criticism to the Enlightenment rationalism, which 'has been exposed as imperialistic, oppressive of non-western perspectives' (Christians, 2010: 7). Nietzsche call the Christian morality as herd morality as they obstruct the individual's 'will to power'. That is why he revolted against the European puritanical values of the time and instead called to destroy all moral values and promote Nihilism as a solution. Man according to him should then break away from the Christian devalued morality and create their own value system. One may argue that the French approach as a symptom of ethics in crisis seems caught in this juncture of a nihilistic stance, which does not appreciate ethical moral values stemming from other cultures or faith groups.

Moving beyond this debate, globally there has been growing interest in academic research in recent years about ethics in the media. What has been termed in the work of Garber, Hanssen and Walkowitz (2000) as 'The Turn to Ethics' in social science disciplines has also dominated public debates especially in liberal democracy. The media coverage of the invasion of Iraq in 2003, coverage of humanitarian crises, as well as coverage of ethnic minority communities on Western media received lots of criticism during the last few decades (Hall, 1973; Zulaika and Douglass, 1996; Said, 1997; Poole, 2002; Richardson, 2004; Shaheen, 2009; Morey and Yakin, 2011) among scores of other studies. Also, debates about the media and social responsibility are as old as mass media itself. However, French President, Emanuel Macron, repeated defence of offensive Charlie Hebdo cartoons on Prophet Muhammad in October 2020 yet again ignited the debate on free speech and social responsibility. The echo of Macron's stance regarding Islam and French cartoons moved beyond the French context and took a global scale.

In this global debate on media ethics, an important precursor is the work of Clifford Christians. Christians (2010) suggests that in the pursuit of global media ethics we should develop global media values, which he calls 'ethics of universal being'. These universally shared values encompass truth, human dignity and non-violence. He writes that these values should be primarily 'grounded in the sacredness of the human life' (2010: 6). A credible ethics, argues Christians (2010: 6), 'must be transnational in character'.

In this book

Global Media Ethics and the Digital Revolution appears at a strategic time when debates about the ethical practices in journalism and the challenges of digital platforms are becoming of a global nature. Approaches to ethics in relation to global cultural diversity and considerations of what sensitivities we should be aware of are paramount (Miladi, 2021).

This book recognizes the fact that global collective ethics standards are farfetched. Diversity in the world of journalism across cultures, worldviews, political/ideological interpretations makes a solidly defined and encompassing set of codes accepted by all is almost impossible. However saying this, it is not unrealistic to come to a shared ground of respect and understanding.

The challenges of global media outreach entail a global understanding/ approach of ethics. On the one hand, Internet and social media platforms have been employed by various right-wing and extremists groups around the world to spread hate speech content. For instance, Apple, Google, Facebook and Spotify rightly removed material posted by right-wing sites like conspiracy theorist Alex Jones, or such extremist groups like Al-Qaida and Daesh. Alex Jones Infowars on social media channels has been considered a platform to 'spread dark and bizarre theories, such as that the Sandy Hook school shooting was a hoax and that Democrats run a global child-sex ring' (Nicas, 2018).

On the other hand, Facebook, Twitter, and YouTube have been criticized of playing a gatekeeping role when it comes to manipulating social media content to serve their agendas. Fukuyama (2018) asserts that such digital platforms '… craft algorithms that determine what their users' limited attention will focus on, driven (at least up to now) not by any broad vision of public responsibility but rather by profit maximization, which leads them to privilege virality'. Further examples show that Facebook for instance was accused of allowing Cambridge Analytica to access its data to help the Trump presidential campaign in October 2020 (Cadwalladr, 2020).

In light of the above challenges, this edited volume attempts to give voice to the often neglected perspectives of media ethics. It offers a platform where these various voices expressed and debated. Through a wide range of international experts, this work broadens the scope and contributes to the enrichment of the discussion in this regard. Chapters in this edited volume zoom into particular local contexts where ethics interact with the social, political and philosophical realms.

This book was partly funded through a research grant by Qatar National Research Fund (QNRF), Grant #: CWSP16-W-0310-19062. This funding support thankfully helped kick start the book project with an international symposium in February 2020 on global media ethics.

Book outline

In Chapter 1, Andrew Pilkington discusses political correctness in a global age and the ethical implications of a hegemonic discourse. The concept of political correctness, or more accurately, anti-political correctness, argues Pilkington, has re-emerged in the last decade as a major interpretive framework in the media. Populist politicians such as Trump in the US and Farage (a key advocate of Brexit) and Johnson in the UK for example routinely draw upon a discourse featuring political correctness as a bête noire. Pilkington adopts a Foucauldian analysis to argue in this chapter that such an anti-political correctness discourse has become hegemonic and is frequently routinely reproduced by journalists. This chapter critically examines the arguments mounted by critics of political correctness and argues that they are not only flawed but that they also constitute an ideology which delegitimizes an agenda concerned to promote equality, diversity and inclusion.

Sylvia Harvey (Chapter 2) discusses the principles of 'impartiality' and 'fairness' as developed in British and American broadcasting, taking as a brief case study the 'Suez' incident of 1956 when a British Conservative Government attempted to regain control of the Suez Canal following its nationalization by the President of Egypt, Gamal Abdul Nasser. At that time both the BBC and its new commercial rival, Independent Television (ITV), faced the challenge of representing sharply opposing views as Britain began to move slowly beyond the age of empire.

Harvey suggests that the 'home' of impartiality lies within the nation state and that the implementation of the principle is significantly affected by perceived national interests. She also argues that attachment to the journalistic value of an even-handed representation of competing beliefs has survived the abolition in 1987 of the Fairness Doctrine in the United States. Some ten years later saw the launch in the Arab world of the satellite channel Al Jazeera with a commitment to representing 'the opinion and the other opinion'. Thus, a new lease of life has been given to the principle – once strongly advocated in the US – of a 'due regard for the opinions of others'.

Noureddine Miladi (Chapter 3) discusses the notion of freedom of expression and social responsibility and considers the contested worldviews in this matter. He approaches the debate through analysing two examples from the cartoons controversies about Prophet Muhammad from the French newspaper Charlie Hebdo and Danish newspaper Jyllands-Posten. These cases, which ignited cross-culture differences regarding the boundaries of free speech and received inevitably global impact and wide criticism. Miladi's chapter explores the roots of such problem of misunderstanding and engendered in the systematic French attitude towards Muslims. Although the proponents of absolute free speech may argue that both cases are local in nature and they reflect the fundamental value of free speech, Miladi contends that their impact have proven global in its outreach. The repercussions of such media content have been dramatic in light of the outbreak of dissent from affected communities.

This chapter further analyses these two examples in relation to the controversial responses received and the contested debates about free speech and social responsibility. It engages with the questions of where should the media draw the line between the sacred value of free speech and respect of sacred religious symbols? Should freedom of speech have limits? Does social responsibility come first, or does freedom of the individual supersede all other benefits?

Worldviews regarding this, argues Miladi, have obviously been divergent. However, in this chapter he suggests that political cartoons as a form of satire should not be different from any other journalistic genre when it comes to raising ethical considerations. The right to freedom of expression should also not mistaken with the right to freedom of opinion, thought and religion. Freedom of expression is a right with outward reach and public scope that might well interfere with the rights of others.

Mazhar Al-Zo'by (Chapter 4) analyses what he terms as the ideology of difference and Eurocentrism. He argues that the advent of capitalist modernity in its transnational mass-mediated digital forms has clearly inspired a critical discussion about the universal ethical virtues of media in modern history. At the heart of this discussion, he argues, is the emergence of an ideological and epistemological formation of a hegemonic Western account of media ethics that is enshrined in Eurocentric philosophical values and professed as the exclusive domain of European liberal tradition. Conversely, and afflicted by the doctrinal complicities of colonial and orientalist representations, the non-Western is presumed to be constrained by the imperatives of cultural irrationality, and therefore is unable to symbolize in universal reason. In order to analyse this intrinsic and complex interplay between universalization and localization in the global media ethical discourse, Al-Zo'by seeks to examine the foundation of universal ethical principles to illustrate its Eurocentric discursive character. Therefore, to him, in order to disrupt and transform this prevailing narrative of media ethical ideology, it is insufficient to simply investigate its polemical Western site of production – additionally, one also has to seek its fundamental deconstruction and reproduction. More specifically, he asserts in this chapter that universal ethics must be shaped within the realm of cultural differences, yet should never remain an exclusive domain of Western cultural hegemony.

Daya Thussu (Chapter 5) rethinks global media ethics for a 'Post-American' world. In the era of digitized and globalized 24/7 media, the one-way vertical flow of media and communication from the West to the Rest has given way to multiple and horizontal flows, in which Asian countries play an increasingly significant role. While the US-led Western domination of the global media and communication hard and software continues, new actors, harnessing the potential of digital globalization, have emerged in the past decade to challenge and contest the Western hegemony in the 'post-American' world. In this chapter, Thussu suggests that the change in communication environments warrants a re-evaluation of how we define the global media and its ethics. The global communication order, shaped and structured by major Western powers – notably the United States, is undergoing a transformational change. This change triggered by the relative decline of the West and the growth of large non-Western nations such as China and India, together with the exponential expansion of digital connectivity. China is already the world's largest user of the Internet, followed by India. Apart from being the world's two most populous countries and fast-growing large economies, both China and India are also civilizational powers, with old and distinctive cultures and aspirations for a greater role in a multipolar world. The Asian giants also have the world's two largest diasporas, increasingly connected with their countries of origin and acting as a bridge between cultures. Thussu further contends that the notions of ethics based on Confucian ideas of 'harmony' and old Indian concept of *Vasudhaiva Kutumbakam* ('the world is one family') are also potential alternatives to the Western definition of media ethics. Given the scope and scale of change in these two countries, he suggests that a new world communication order may be evolving for the digital age. The chapter ultimately asks about the possible implications that such digital connectivity will have for global media and communication flows, media ethics and broader communication agendas? His chapter suggests that the ascent of Asia contributes to further internationalizing of media and its study.

Fethi Ahmed (Chapter 6) discusses the relationship between freedom of speech, responsibility and human rights in Islam. Traditional methods of communication, he argues, have declined in popularity and new media channels that rely essentially on digital technology have emerged. However, numerous problems have appeared due to this including the wrong perception and practice of freedom of speech and lack or absence of social responsibility. For instance, numerous social media users believe that freedom of speech is without limitation and thus they fall into unethical practices such as breach of privacy, hate speech, racism and defamation. Besides, other social media users, he argues, have been influenced by funding, political power and ideological influences to serve certain agendas. These unethical problems in new media have become very complicated due to many factors particularly globalization, the high Internet speed and frequency mechanisms that digital technology offers.

Therefore, Ahmed's chapter examines the correlation between freedom of speech, responsibility and human rights from an Islamic perspective within the context of new global media ethics. Ahmed offers a multidisciplinary approach, which includes media studies, sociology, ethics, human rights, Islamic legal maxims, and higher objectives of *Sharia* (Islamic law). He finally asserts that freedom of speech is a crucial value in Islam, guaranteed for all creations and tied to responsibility and liability.

Noureddine Khadmi (Chapter 7) analyses the philosophical roots of ethics in the Islamic tradition. His chapter attempts to discuss the Islamic worldview of what values should characterize journalism work. These summarized in few principles such as honesty, truth-telling, efficiency, free will, integrity and positive neutrality. They also include non-targeting of individuals, protecting privacy, public order, support of freedom and human rights, rigour in confronting foreign occupation and internal tyranny/corruption.

The functional Islamic view represents a significant framework, argues Khadmi, for guiding media performance. He suggests that this vision has three levels. Firstly, the philosophical vision which is concerned with the belief system and aims of human existence. This is based on the *raison d'être* of the human life on earth, upholding one's faith, the protection of human beings, and pro- tection of dignity. Hence, media ethics should reflect awareness and protection of these universal values. Secondly, the Islamic jurisprudence vision which is concerned with the science of *Sharia*. It is the science of judgements on the one hand, framing the media moral act, and assigning it to its legal provisions.

Thirdly, the operational Islamic vision, which is concerned with summoning the practical side of the Islamic philosophical and scientific vision of media ethics, in terms of institutional and procedural work, taking into account diversity in contexts.

Jamel Zran (Chapter 8) discusses ethics of investigative journalism. Zran argues that journalism ethics relate to how to distinguish between the public interest, the individual and society's right to be informed and a journalist's right to access information. The judgement depends on the ethics of any decision, on the ethical framework used to justify it, and on the values adopted in this context. Ultimately, what journalists and editors need to decide is to determine who will benefit from the publication of his/her investigative reports in the first place.

Zran also asks if the press is committed to the democratic accountability of officials, the question to be asked is whether or not the citizen will benefit fairly from the publication of newspaper investigations. Whose interest does investigative journalism serve when publishing a specific news story? Does the press fulfil its social responsibility to reveal corruption for instance? Who will be affected? And whose rights, can be violated?

Most discussions on the ethics of investigative journalism, further argues Zran, have focused on whether there is an ideal method which can be useful in exposing the wrong behaviour of officials? Is resorting to deception considered legitimate when the aim of the journalist is to tell the truth? Finally, is it permissible for journalists to use false identities, lying or forging documents in order to obtain information which is difficult to unblock?

Suzana Žilič Fišer and Irena Lovrenčič Držanič (Chapter 9) discuss fake news as a challenge to media credibility. In this fast transforming digital world, they argue, the media industry is facing increasing economic, social and technological challenges, as well as changing media consumption habits. Social media consumers, also termed in this chapter the 'digital natives', tend to spend most of their time on social media and multimedia platforms. They are inclined to substitute traditional media with social media and other online services. In this chapter, Fišer and Držanič argue that despite these significant transformations and the growing standing of online media, online users still perceive traditional media to be more credible sources of information than user-generated content on social media. Social media networks, they contend, enable a breadth of 'fake news', which brings the overall perception of media into a different perspective. The phenomenon of misinformation and mistrust could be a new indicator of a crisis in the media that led to the post-truth era. Fišer and Držanič also suggest that due to the profound negative impact of fake news on individuals and society, various detection tools can be applied. Their chapter illustrates the challenges for society and modern democracy that arise from changing media consumption habits regarding credibility and trust issues.

Moez ben Messaoud (Chapter 10) discusses media ethics and the challenge of transitional democracy in Tunisia. After decades of authoritarian control, the Tunisian media witnessed a window of freedom and openness post the 14 January 2011 revolution that it had never experienced before. Despite this, he argues, the traditional media sector seems so far unable to keep pace with the changes that accompanied the democratic transition phase in Tunisia. This reality has contributed to the development of social media activism as a counter hegemonic form in light of the development of the flow of information on these media and the growing power of the public. This situation has led to various manifestations of falsehood, fabrication of news, false headlines, disguised advertising, contempt, defamation, violent rhetoric.

Based on the above, Ben Messaoud sought to highlights the fragile media regulatory frameworks and the challenges of establishing a solid culture of journalism ethics given the transitional nature and sometimes instability of political frameworks in the country. He eventually attempts to signpost to the development of a solid foundation for professional ethics to protect the public and freedom of expression in the public sphere.

Hala Guta (Chapter 11) discusses in her piece journalism ethics and conflict-sensitive reporting by analysing Al Jazeera network as a case study. Considering its importance as a global media player, and its claims of providing an alternative model of journalism, Guta's chapter interrogates Al Jazeera's coverage of the Syrian conflict taking peace journalism as a frame of reference. It attempts to establish the ethical standards that guide Al Jazeera in its coverage and investigates if Al Jazeera brings an alternative point of view when it comes to conflict-sensitive reporting. Through employing a framing analysis method, Guta revealed that both Al Jazeera Arabic and Al Jazeera English focused on human suffering and high human cost of the conflict. Guta concludes that Al Jazeera demonstrated that conflict-sensitive reporting can indeed be achieved without falling into the trap of sensationalism and propaganda or compromising journalism ethics. Yet both channels, she argues, fell short in giving agency and voice to the victims as elite sources dominated the voices represented on both channels. Direct violence dominated the news discourse and little consideration was given to the structural and cultural aspects of the reported conflict.

Jairo Lugo-Ocando and Steven Harkins (Chapter 12) discuss the deontology in news coverage of poverty in the digital age and ask the question why objectivity is bad when reporting on inequality. Their chapter looks at how initial promises around the Internet for a more participatory and inclusive type of journalism have never been met. Also, why the digital revolution actually had very little impact upon the ethics and deontology of Western journalists when it comes to the news coverage of poverty. In their view, the practices, aesthetics and overall approach to poverty in the newsroom remain unaltered by the technological change in the media landscape. The authors argue that this is because the deontology of journalism in relation to poverty remains linked to prevalent professional normative aspirations such as 'objectivity', which impede the incorporation of structuralist notions, concepts and worldviews into the narrative of poverty in the news. Their analysis calls for a move away from the parochial and traditional ways of understanding journalism ethics and argues for a more comprehensive framework that challenges the values and goalposts set by the liberal and positive traditions of journalism in the West.

Ibrahim Abusharif (Chapter 13) discusses the culture of framing terminologies vis-à-vis global media ethics. He argues that academic research has shown that there are uneven usages of key journalistic framing terminologies applied in the Western coverage of public acts of violence, namely 'terror' and 'terrorism' ('domestic' and 'international'), which seem to be based on religious or racial categories of the perpetrators of the acts. While engaging in a critical evaluation of journalistic practices is valuable, it also has limits because such evaluations do not include sufficient consideration of the broader ideologies and epistemic imaginaries that have permeated the public sphere of a given society, in which journalistic practices have been established. In this chapter, Abusharif, argues that journalistic practices are best assessed in close colloquy with broader discursive trends and public discourses, which recently have attracted significant attention and that have linked news media practices with extra-journalistic phenomena, such as Islamophobia, racism, Orientalism, and calls for decoloniality. Guided by van Dijk's conceptual principle of 'news as discourse', the chapter also argues that it is critical to situate news processes within a larger 'macrosociology' and the social and political climates in which they exist.

Abdulfatah Mohamed (Chapter 14) discusses in this chapter securitization, global media and agenda setting. He argues that a new global political regime was instituted in the aftermath of the 11 September 2001 attacks in the United States. Launched in response to the attacks, the so-called 'War on Terror' increased securitization at the global, regional, and national levels, and this, it is argued, had significant impact on the global media discourse, as well as on refugees and non-governmental organizations (NGOs).

In this chapter, Mohamed analyses the speech acts of the securitization process that have set and framed the agendas, narratives and discourses of global media conglomerates. Theoretical frameworks of Copenhagen School of securitization have been analysed through what is known as the *speech act* to produce securitization outcomes. Even though the *speech act* securitization does not demonstrate clearly how it gets to the audience, yet the political communication messages securitized quite often. Speech act means that expressions are understood in terms of their performative rulings. Mohamed further debates that the far-reaching impacts of securitization and the War on Terror have detrimental effects on Islamic NGOs and on refugees in many parts of the world, as highlighted in the findings of several reports, academic papers and case studies. The author asserts that the securitization discourse is curtailing the operations of Islamic NGOs, with devastating effects on vulnerable people, whilst negative depictions of refugees by the mainstream media are driving policies with often grave consequences.

Winston Mano (Chapter 15) discusses what he terms as Afrokology, Afriethics and African journalism in the digital age. His chapter deploys Afrokology in a double gesture: first, Afrokology is positioned in a way that underpins a critical engagement with remnants of colonial epistemes as well as to unmask the incompleteness of dominant global North journalism ethical frameworks. Secondly, Afrokology demands a commitment towards journalism ethics from an African standpoint, reimagining journalism ethics from an

African/global South perspective. In essence, Afrokology as deployed in Mano's chapter is underpinned by key values of conviviality and incompleteness, with emphasis on accommodating so-called 'other' knowledges and ethical norms from an African standpoint. Mano argues that the main objective is to build a resonant framework for ethical values and behaviour of African journalism. His chapter further reviews debates about ethics of African journalism and builds on Francis Kasoma's concept of Afriethics. Mano openly calls for a de-colonial approach to African journalism ethics. Afrokology according to him helps centre African ethics, derived from African lived experiences, in their own right not as appendages or mere add on to global ethics. In sum, the author contends that the digital age has amplified both the volume of vendetta journalism and its impact on society in African society. Such necessary corrective builds on Kasoma's Afriethics and proposes Afrokology as a viable heuristic tool for more relevant journalism ethics in Africa in the digital age.

References

BBC News (2005), 'French court bans Christ advert'. Retrieved from: http://news.bbc.co.uk/2/hi/europe/4337031.stm. Accessed: 3 November 2020.

Cadwalladr, C. (2020), 'Fresh Cambridge Analytica leak "shows global manipulation is out of control"'. *The Guardian*, 4 January 2020. Retrieved from: Fresh Cambridge Analytica leak 'shows global manipulation is out of control' | Cambridge Analytica | The Guardian. Accessed: 23 May 2021.

Christians, C. (2010), 'The Ethics of Universal Being', in S. Ward and H. Wasserman (eds), *Media Ethics beyond Borders: A Global Perspective*. London: Routledge.

Cohen-Almagor, R. (2001), *Speech, Media and Ethics: The Limits of Free Expression*. Basingstoke: Palgrave.

Feinberg, J. (1984), *Harm to Others: The Moral Limits of the Criminal Law*. New York: Oxford University Press.

Fukuyama, F. (2018), 'Social media and censorship'. *The American Interest* (6 August). Retrieved from: https://www.the-american-interest.com/2018/08/08/social-media-and-censorship/. Accessed: 10 April 2021.

Garber, M. B., Hanssen, B. and Walkowitz, R. L. (2000), *The Turn to Ethics*. New York: Routledge.

Guyer, J. (2015), 'Political cartooning after the Charlie Hebdo attacks'. *Nieman Reports*, Winter 2015 2015.

Hall, S. (1973), *Encoding and Decoding in the Television Discourse*. Birmingham: Centre for Contemporary Cultural Studies.

Hanafi, S. (2009), 'Cultural difference or cultural hegemony? Contextualizing the Danish cartoon controversy within migration spaces'. *Middle East Journal of Culture and Communication* 2, 136–152.

Hanafi, S. (2020), 'Macron's populism and Islam The election strategy that forges a new populism through its conceptualization of freedom of expression and "political Islam"'. *Open Democracy*, 2 November 2020. Retrieved from: https://www.opendemocracy.net/en/openmovements/macrons-populism-and-islam/. Accessed: 3 November 2020.

Miladi, N. (2021), 'The discursive representation of Islam and Muslims in the British tabloid press'. *Journal of Applied Journalism and Media Studies*, 10(1), 117–138.

Morey, P. and Yakin, A. (2011), *Framing Muslims: Stereotyping and Representation after 9/11*. Cambridge and Massachusetts: Harvard University Press.

Nicas, J. (2018), 'Alex Jones and Infowars content is removed from Apple, Facebook and YouTube'. *The New York Times*, 6 August. Retrieved from: https://www.nytimes.com/2018/08/06/technology/infowars-alex-jones-apple-facebook-spotify.html. Accessed: 10 April 2021.

Nietzsche, F. (2014), *Beyond Good and Evil*. London: Millennium Publication.

Poole, E. (2002), *Reporting Islam: Media Representations of British Muslims*. London: I. B.Tauris.

Richardson, J. (2004), *(Mis)Representing Islam: The Racism and Rhetoric of British Broadsheet Newspapers*, Amsterdam and Philadelphia: John Benjamins Publishing.

Riddle, K. (2014), 'The Case of Media Violence: Who is Responsible for Protecting Children from Harm?', in M. Drumwright (ed.), *Ethical Issues in Communication Professions: New Agencies in Communication*. Abingdon: Routledge, pp. 65–84.

Said, E. (1997), *Covering Islam: How the Media and the Experts Determine How We See the Rest of the World*. New York: Vintage Books.

Shah, N. A. (2017), 'Charlie Hebdo: Testing the limits of freedom of expression'. *Muslim World Journal of Human Rights*, 14(1), 83–111. https://doi.org/10.1515/mwjhr-2017-0007

Shaheen, J. (2009), *Reel Bad Arabs: How Hollywood Vilifies a People*. New York: Olive Branch Press.

The Telegraph. (2020), 'Emmanuel Macron on Prophet Mohammed cartoons: It is not my role to limit freedom of speech'. *The Telegraph*, 1 November. Retrieved from: https://www.youtube.com/watch?v=Vu0JRs1KrAk. Accessed: 8 August 2021.

Zulaika, J. and Douglass, W. V. (1996), *Terror and Taboo: The Follies, Fables, and Faces of Terrorism*. New York: Routledge.

Part 1
Media ethics revisited

1 Political correctness in a global age

The ethical implications of a hegemonic discourse

Andrew Pilkington

Introduction: What is political correctness?

We are continually being reminded that we live in a world where political correctness is pervasive. And yet the concept itself remains unclear and indeed contested. A few writers embrace the term to signal their belief in the importance of being inclusive, especially in language, and their concern to redress the disadvantages faced by minority groups: 'PC fosters civility between diverse humans and ... at its best, is sensitivity to the feelings and needs of others' (Alibhai-Brown, 2018: 11, 21). More commonly, however, the term is used in a disparaging way to mock what is seen as a ludicrous attempt to avoid the real issues (see Ridler below) or warn us of the dangerous new culture threatening free speech and plain honest speaking (see Hitchens below). In the process a contrast is often drawn between political correctness and common sense: 'Voters seek return to common sense in revolt against political correctness' announces a headline in one broadsheet (Shipman, 2020).

> Political correctness does not address the real problem faced by ethnic minorities, says head of the National Black Police Association ... Andrew Gaye, an inspector with the Police Service of Northern Ireland told the Sunday Telegraph that this sensitivity may have gone 'too far in some stages' such as leaving people unable to call a black coffee black coffee. (Ridler, 2020)
>
> I fear anyone who dissents from today's pervasive culture of political correctness will be visited by the Thought Police ... so how long until anyone who writes an article like this is dragged away in handcuffs. (Hitchens, 2020)

In 2017 Trevor Phillips, the first Chair of the Equality and Human Rights Commission, presented a documentary on British television entitled, 'Has political correctness gone mad?'. This question is commonly asked and answered in the affirmative (as in Bond, 2018). I shall restrict myself here to two examples where this common refrain is evident: the lampooning of an analysis of a children's book (Brown, 2019) and the response of a supermarket to a complaint (Young, 2019).

DOI: 10.4324/9781003203551-3

World's gone PC mad … Snowflakes: Mr Clever is a sexist … Flakes have slammed 'sexist' Mr Men character Mr Clever for 'mansplaining' an iconic bridge to 'stupid' blonde Little Miss Curious. (Brown, 2019)

Waitrose has apologized for selling 'racist' chocolate Easter ducklings after it received complaints that the dark one was named 'ugly' … Many Twitter users have reacted angrily to the supermarket's decision to remove the chocolate ducklings suggesting it has given in to excessive political correctness. PC gone mad … yet again one person wrote. (Young, 2019)

These two examples clearly ridicule and belittle political correctness but the invocation of the common refrain, PC gone mad also in a sense brings the positive and negative usages of the concept together. A narrative is constructed which suggests that at one stage PC was indeed progressive in promoting social justice for minorities but that it has gone too far so that now 'people are becoming frightened of saying the wrong thing, using the wrong language about a pretty wide range of opinion' (Parris, 2019). This view is widely shared: 'The progressive movement, that has done so much to tackle inequality and unfairness, has been captured by ultras who demand absolute conformity with every article of their faith' (Phillips, 2020a). Another journalist, further right on the political spectrum, concurs. The decline of religion and subsequently secular ideologies has left a vacuum which has been filled by social justice zealots. Failing to acknowledge the success of previous human rights campaigns in righting historical injustices relating to race, gender and sexuality, new theories emerged 'to suggest that things had never been worse. Suddenly – after most of us had hope it had become a non-issue – everything seemed to have become about race' (Murray, 2020: 6). A crusading desire to right perceived wrongs has entailed the creation of 'a set of tripwires laid across the culture … What everyone does know are the things that people will be called if their foot ever nicks against these freshly laid tripwires. "Bigot", "homophobe", "sexist", "mysognist", "racist" and "transphobe" are just for starters' (Murray, 2020: 7).

There is little doubt that political correctness now typically carries negative connotations. Few people consequently identify themselves as supportive of PC and when they do, they sound on the defensive (Johnson, 2017; Alibhai-Brown, 2018). More typically, those who are sympathetic to the causes associated with PC will studiously avoid defining themselves as advocates of PC. The same is also true of a related concept, 'woke' which, though initially coined to refer to awareness of racial injustice 'has been weaponised, used in conservative media circles as an insult' (Hunt, 2020; Hirsch, 2019). Two examples will suffice: 'The woke left is the new Ministry of Truth … Good people are silenced in an Orwellian nightmare where a tyrannical minority decide what we're allowed to say (Turner, 2020). And 'The march of wokeism is an all-pervasive new oppression' (Phillips, 2020b).

Both political correctness and woke are rarely defined. Instead they are used to depict the Other in a disparaging way and often to suggest that there are powerful forces suppressing inconvenient truths and steadily eroding our freedom. One journalist claims that 'the thought police are spiraling out of control' (Street-Porter, 2020), while another believes that we need to wake up before it's too late: 'We've become a timid, mute, fearful society in which everyone must walk on constant eggshells for fear that they will be next for the social media pile-on and politically correct execution' (Morgan, 2020: 327). This characterization of PC and woke is highly influential and clearly resonates with many people. A 2018 YouGov poll found that nearly half the respondents believe that '"there are many important issues these days when people are simply not allowed to say what they think", 13 points more than the 35 per cent who believe people are generally "free to discuss what they think"'. In addition, 'by two to one – 67 per cent to 33 per cent – Britons believe "too many people are too easily offended these days over the language that others use" as against the view that care with language is needed "to avoid offending people with different backgrounds"' (Clark, 2019). A 2020 CSS poll presents a broadly similar picture, with 'six in ten' agreeing 'that political correctness gives "too much power to a small minority of people who like to take offence"' and nearly eight in ten agreeing 'that "you have to walk on eggshells when speaking about certain issues these days"' and over eight in ten agreeing 'that "too many people are easily offended these days"' (Shipman, 2020). The media in short portray political correctness in a derogatory fashion and most people buy this picture.

Origins of political correctness

The term political correctness, unlike woke, has a long history. While there is general agreement that it originated in left-wing circles, 'an important historical shift seems to have occurred in the 1980s when the term increasingly came to be used by the political right, particularly in the US ... to denigrate left wing political opponents' (Lea, 2009: 11; 74). An influential article in the *New York Times* entitled 'The rising hegemony of the Politically Correct' (Bernstein, 1990) popularized the term and set in train a wave of stories about the threats posed to universities by cultural relativism, challenges to the canon and changing admissions policies. Such stories drew upon and reinforced a series of critiques mounted by conservative writers who espoused an avowedly elitist position in defence of high culture and criticized multiculturalism as a threat to Western civilization. The philosopher, Allan Bloom was the first out of the tracks with his book *The Closing of the American Mind* (Bloom, 1987) but he was quickly followed by other critics (Kimball, 1990; D'Sousa, 1991). 'Decrying the influence of the campus left', these writers were scathing about what they saw as its censoriousness, in the process enabling conservatives, 'traditional supporters of censorship ... to present themselves' anew 'as opponents of censorship' and in favour of free speech (Sparrow, 2017). They attacked what they saw as the politicization of higher education, but they were themselves just as political as their liberal opponents, with their work 'funded by networks of conservative donors' (Weigel, 2016).

The term crossed the Atlantic in the early 1990s, carrying with it similar negative connotations. As the first book addressing the debate put it: 'PC is a dirty word in modern Britain. To call someone PC is less a description than an insult carrying with it accusations of everything from Stalinism/McCarthyism to (even worse?) having no sense of humour' (Dunant, 1994; vii). What paved the way for the campaign against political correctness in the UK in the 1990s was not, however, as in the US a critique of higher education but rather a campaign mounted by the right-wing press against the Labour Party, 'popularly referred to as *Loony Leftism* at the time' (Lea, 2009:158).

The contemporary derogatory meaning of political correctness goes back to this period. While some people have subsequently tried to put a positive gloss on the concept and reclaim it, this has not been successful (Ackroyd and Pilkington, 2007). The upshot is that those who continue to 'embrace the causes most often associated with the term – the use of enlightened language; the promotion of multicultural forms of curriculum; and forms of affirmative action' – typically feel 'that they should avoid it and distance their behaviour from its connotations' (Lea, 2009: 8).

Political correctness in a digital age

While concern with political correctness has ebbed and flowed, there is little doubt that in the last decade it has again become a critical concept in the rightist lexicon. Universities continue to be seen as posing a central threat in the US and, with the expansion of higher education in recent decades, universities in the UK also have received renewed attention, increasingly being characterized, along with their American counterparts, as controlled by a liberal elite and pervaded by political correctness. The ideas that inform social justice zealots and thus underpin PC have their roots within the humanities and social science departments of universities, it is argued, and these ideas are dangerous. Thus, despite the radical reduction of social injustice, the theories and texts (purportedly) pervading the academy 'express with absolute certainty, that all white people are racist, all men are sexist … seeking' in this way 'to divide humans into marginalized identity groups and their oppressors', fuelling tribalism and threatening to reverse the manifest progress made in reducing incidents of racism, sexism and homophobia (Pluckrose and Lindsay, 2020: 183; 258). In the absence of serious issues relating to race, gender and sexuality, attention is paid to trivial matters: 'Cambridge University set new standards of political correctness this week with its announcement of an inquiry into the way it benefitted from the slave trade' (Biggar, 2019), an inquiry lampooned by another critic as 'virtue signaling on steroids' (Lyons and Yorke, 2019).

Despite continuities in perceptions of the threat posed by PC, the rediscovery of political correctness in the last decade takes a somewhat different form from that predominant in the 1990s and early 2000s. The distinctiveness of PC in its modern guise is twofold: a belief that freedom of speech, which should be absolute, is under grave threat, and a belief that younger generations (notably

millennials, and especially their successors, generation z, the Internet generation) are fragile 'snowflakes' and keen to be protected from offensive speech
(Symons, 2018).

The threat to free speech is deemed so severe that in the UK a Free Speech
Union has recently been created which sets out its manifesto in the following
terms: 'Free speech is the bulwark on which all our other freedoms rest, yet it is
currently in greater peril than at any time since the second world war' (Dabhoi-
wala, 2020). This verdict is shared by the two most prominent proponents of
absolute free speech in North America, notably Jordan Peterson and Niall Ferguson. Peterson, who came to prominence for his vehement opposition to a
change in Canadian anti-discrimination legislation obliging people to refer to
transgender people by their preferred pronoun, contends that legislation on hate
crime threatens freedom of speech (Fry, Peterson, Dyson and Goldberg, 2018).
Ferguson concurs and in a series of interventions is highly critical of social media
companies regulating access, a development which he argues puts free speech at
peril (Ferguson, 2019b). In the UK an Internet magazine, *Spiked* (see Monbiot,
2018) and an influential conservative think tank, Civitas, have taken up the cud-
gels in promoting libertarianism, highlighting what they see as the dangers to
freedom of speech of a culture of victimhood (Green, 2019) and harassment
policies in universities (Civitas, 2000). Hate crime laws and the equality legislation should in its view be abolished and legislation passed instead to establish an
absolute right to free speech. The latter is crucial since it is only when people are
not censored and are able to speak freely in the public sphere that 'the marketplace of ideas' works effectively to enable truth and superior ideas to win out,
and falsehoods and inferior ideas to wither on the vine.

Alongside the belief that free speech is in peril is the belief that younger
generations are, as a result of being brought up in a safety-first culture, very
fragile and demand to be protected from ideas that they find offensive. Claire
Fox is often credited with being the first person to talk of 'Generation
Snowflake':

> Barely a week goes by without reports of something "offensive" being
> banned from campus ... this all-pervading sense of grievance, displayed by
> so many students, is now beginning to cause serious anguish for older
> commentators, who look on with horror at the increasing evidence that
> young people have become dangerously thin-skinned. (Fox, 2016: xvii)

This conceptualization of millennials and generation z has taken off, with the US
attorney general, for example describing students as increasingly 'sanctimonious,
sensitive, supercilious snowflakes' and their campuses as an 'echo chamber of
political correctness and homogeneous thought, a shelter for fragile egos' (Sessions
quoted in Malik, 2019a: 67).

The most influential proponents of this view are Greg Lukianoff and Jona-
than Haidt in a book entitled 'The coddling of the American mind', a title
echoing Bloom's, 1987 best-seller and like its predecessor an account of what is

going wrong in universities. The authors argue that the Internet generation who first went to university in 2013 has been brought up in a safety-first culture. Overprotected and brought up without experiencing free play, these young people often lack the resilience of previous generations and indeed experience more anxiety when they arrive at university. 'Requests for safe spaces and trigger warnings' along with 'the "disinvitation" of guest speakers' spread because of the prevalence of the 'idea that college students should not be exposed to "offensive" ideas' (Lukianoff and Haidt, 2019: 31; 47–48). The response of college authorities 'to protect students by creating bureaucratic means of resolving problems' reinforces the safety-first culture (Lukianoff and Haidt, 2019: 212). In this culture a belief that 'straight white males' comprise 'the main axis of oppression' spreads along with 'the development of a "call out culture" and a corresponding sense among students that they are walking on eggshells, afraid of saying the wrong thing ... out of fear that they themselves will be called out by a mob on social media' (Lukianoff and Haidt, 2019: 70–72). A similar picture of universities has been presented in the UK. The current generation of students has been brought up in an overprotective way where safety is paramount and emotional security takes precedence over other values. This process of socialization is inimical to resilience with the result that students now are less grown up than those in the past when they go to university and do not expect to be challenged. Emotions have in the process become weaponized, with students increasingly being unwilling to be open to new ideas; feeling offended has taken the place of disagreement. The response of universities in a context where students are seen as customers has been paternalistic with the result that freedom has become trumped by a concern to promote diversity, safety and not give offence (Furedi, 2016).

The free speech crisis exacerbated by the advent of the snowflake generation entails, according to those critical of PC, cancel culture, a modern form of ostracism whereby people who speak out against fashionable left-wing positions are abused online and may even lose their jobs. Peterson and Ferguson take this line and are adamant that it is the left, or 'political correctness types' as Peterson puts it (Buncombe, 2019), who comprise the main threat and that conservatives are their targets. 'In every case the pattern is the same. An academic deemed to be conservative gets "called out" by a leftist group or rag. The Twitter mob piles in. Mindless mainstream media outlets amplify the story. The relevant authorities capitulate' (Ferguson, 2019a).

While the latest iteration of the political correctness gone mad refrain has distinctive features, we must not exaggerate its novelty. Here is President George Bush in 1991 on PC and free speech:

> The notion of political correctness has ignited controversy across the land. And although the movement arises from the laudable desire to sweep away the debris of racism and sexism and hatred, it replaces old prejudice with new ones ... It declares certain topics off limits, certain expressions off limits, even certain gestures off limits. What began as a crusade for civility

has soured into a cause of conflict and even censorship. (Bush quoted in Malik, 2019a: 61–62; and Alibhai-Brown, 2018: 30)

And here is another critic in 1992 on PC and current students: 'We are miseducating a generation of students to run to Daddy Dean and Mummy President for paternalistic protection when someone offends them' (Dershowitz quoted in Lea, 2009: 165).

Nonetheless, the belief that free speech is in peril and that generation snow-flake is intolerant, entailing the advent of a dangerous cancel culture, has given the attacks on PC renewed venom. The critics share a disgust with identity politics by which they mean movements foregrounding identities based on eth-nicity, gender and sexuality. The focus on these identities, it is claimed, divides people unnecessarily and encourages tribalism. An individualistic perspective is preferred instead, with some of the key players even espousing self-help man-uals (Peterson) and cognitive therapy (Lukianoff and Haidt). Many of the most prominent figures are on the right of the political spectrum (Peterson, Ferguson and Murray for example) but there are also people who identify themselves as further left on the political spectrum (Haidt, Fox, Furedi, Pluckrose and Morgan for example) who share the same concerns and believe that many of those purportedly promoting social justice have imbibed a new religion (informed by postmodernism and/or Marxism) which is illiberal, entails 'virtue signaling', threatens free speech and is antithetical to reasoned debate. While there is an acknowledgement that societies face threats from the right as well as the left, the focus for PC critics is on the threat from the left arising from social justice warriors.

Contesting contemporary critics of PC

I shall address below each of the claims mounted by PC critics in turn: the arguments relating to freedom of speech; the arguments relating to university students; and the claims relating to cancel culture.

Free speech under threat?

Free speech is indeed vital. There is a strong liberal case, following John Stuart Mill (2010), to tolerate speech even when it is offensive, but there is an impor-tant caveat. For Mill, we also need to take account of the harm principle and curb speech when it directly entails violence to others. In other words, we should not support absolute freedom of speech. Indeed, to do so would be contradictory since absolute free speech would drown out the right of each of us to free speech. Even the US first amendment, which prevents hate speech laws found in other democracies, does not support absolute free speech and 'has not protected, for example, libel, slander, perjury, false advertising, obscenity and profanity, solicitation of a crime, or "fighting" words' (Malik, 2019a: 107). The right to free speech is an important principle but principles may collide, for example the right to freedom of speech and the right to life and we may be forced to choose between them (Monbiot, 2021). The prohibition against shouting fire in a crowded theatre is uncontroversial; the suppression of misinformation about vaccines in a pandemic is more contentious.

Free debate is also vital, a sine qua non of a healthy democracy and critical for scientific progress and the development of innovative new technologies. The notion that the arena for debate comprises a marketplace of ideas is, however, misleading because in practice 'the market is skewed and not all ideas receive equal representation' (Malik, 2019a: 112). Oligopolies such as Fox Corporation hold sway and the voices of white middle class men tend to be privileged. Given this, it is somewhat obfuscatory to dismiss a perspective which acknowledges group affiliations and power differences in favour of a wholly individualistic approach.

It is distinctly odd to argue that there is a free speech crisis since the rise of digital platforms means that 'speech has never been freer than it is today, including speech that is hostile, emotional and potentially extreme. The traditional barriers and gatekeepers that used to restrict access to the public sphere and intellectual canon are losing power' (Davies, 2018). The result is that a wider range of voices can be heard. The sense that there is a crisis is partly explicable in terms of shifting cultural norms (Why can't I use the N word or talk of picaninnies?). It partly reflects a sense of grievance by cultural elites that they are losing authority and are increasingly being challenged, sometimes in an abusive way; the moral panic over free speech on this reading is a conservative response to 'this messier less predictable world' and an attempt 'to restore a traditional cultural order' (Davies, 2018). And it partly conflates the right to speak with the right to speak with impunity. It is perfectly legitimate, for example, to protest against hate speech and to brand this as 'silencing' is itself an assault on free expression (Malik, 2019a: 107).

The outrage at infringements to free speech, in pointing to PC gone mad, is highly selective. The British government's Prevent strategy entails a legal obligation on universities to prevent people being drawn into terrorism. Guidelines stipulate the need to vet external speakers and this does have 'serious consequences for freedom of speech' (Titley, 2020: 73)). And yet this and other cases which challenge freedom of speech, such as the banning of materials from anti-capitalist groups in schools, tend to be overlooked. The same was true of the BBC ruling (later rescinded by the Director General) that Naga Munchetty had broken the corporation's guidelines in her response to President Trump's tweet that four congresswomen (all people of colour) 'should go back to the totally broken and crime-infested places from which they came'. Manchetty speaking from her own experience of being told 'as a woman of colour, to go back to where I came from' commented that this phrase was racist and that she well understood why people would be furious with Trump. This comment was deemed to have transgressed the principle of impartiality (Hirsch et al. 2019). While this judgement is highly problematic and later was recognized as such by the Director General, the point I wish to make here is that the case was not taken up as an example of PC gone mad.

The case I wish to turn to now was taken up as an example and is illustrative of a general point: 'the right to express racist ideas … is increasingly marked out as what is most at stake in relation to freedom of speech' (Titley, 2020: 11) so that 'calling out' racism is summarily dismissed as PC gone mad. Take for example the cartoon of Serena Williams published in an Australian newspaper. Many saw the cartoon as an example of 'glaring bigotry', but the newspaper dismissed this reaction as 'PC BS', with the critics labelled as 'oversensitive'. In an editorial the following day,

> the paper blamed the "social media hordes" for attempting to defeat car-
> tooning – and satire – with a politically correct barrage. It also published
> the cartoon again on the front page … with the headline "Welcome to PC
> World", a label "Satire free zone" and the words: "If the self-appointed
> censors … get their way on this Serena Williams cartoon, our new politi-
> cally correct life will be very dull indeed". And so it is that we once again
> enter the culture wars … with aggressors posing as victims, bigotry mas-
> querading as satire, free speech condemned as censorship, and any calls for
> sensitivity, historical context, moral responsibility, equality, accuracy,
> decency, fairness or accountability dismissed as "political correctness".
> (Younge, 2018)

There is widespread agreement that digital platforms are increasingly significant and that they raise issues that did not arise with old media. They are not seen as publishers and therefore are not subject to the same regulations. This means that dangerous misinformation can spread like wildfire and online abuse can go viral. The latter can be, at least partially, addressed when it constitutes criminal behaviour such as threats to kill, but the former is currently a more intractable problem. Facebook, Google and Twitter recognize that there is an issue and employ content moderators, but it is questionable whether companies 'as big and ubiquitous' as these should have such power to censor what is objectionable (Ferguson, 2019b). What seems incontrovertible is that some kind of regulation of big tech is needed to allow any possibility for a public sphere where there can be reasoned debate between diverse views (Monbiot, 2021: D'Ancona, 2017).

Universities in crisis?

I shall now turn to the claims mounted by PC critics in relation to university students. The first point to make is that it is not unusual for an older genera-tion to hanker back to a golden age – typically 20 years earlier – when young people behaved appropriately and civility flourished (Pearson, 1983). That is exactly what is going on when reference is made to the snowflake generation. Despite the congruence in the picture of young people presented by PC critics, much of the evidence is anecdotal. The authors of the book which has been most influential in conceptualizing young people in this way acknowledge themselves that 'most students are not fragile, they are not "snowflakes" and

---

they are not afraid of ideas' (Lukianoff and Haidt, 2019: 268). This is borne out by a YouGov survey in 2018 which does not point to greater 'sensitivity' or disbelief in the value of 'free speech' among young people or students compared to 'the general population' (Murray 2018–19: 46–47).

As for what is happening in universities, the claims by *Spiked* and Civitas that campus censorship is rife are deeply misleading. Upon closer analysis, the scores produced suggesting that the situation is so bad that it requires legislation arise from collating a wide range of disparate variables including 'human resources policies and codes of conduct, of a sort now standard in most large organisations and often required by law' (Malik, 2019a: 119). These policies and codes of conduct turn out to be the main examples of censorship identified in universities. The purported campus censorship is thus an artefact which stems from a belief in absolute free speech and antipathy to the 'cumbersome legal obligations' exemplified by the Equality Act, which entail a need to balance the duty to promote freedom of speech with other obligations (Civitas, 2020: 20). There is little evidence in fact that academic freedom is under threat (Watkins, 2020). On the contrary, BBC reality check

> found that since 2010 there had been: seven student complaints about course content being in some way offensive or inappropriate – four have resulted in action being taken; six occasions on which universities cancelled speakers as a result of complaints and no instances of books being banned or removed. We picked these measures as ones that would reveal restrictions at an institutional level regarding what students are learning. And of the 136 universities and more than two million higher education students in the UK, the number of incidents is small. (Schraer and Butcher, 2018)

A Parliamentary cross-party investigation in the same year came to a similar judgement: 'press accounts of widespread suppression of free speech are clearly out of kilter with reality' (Titley, 2020: 80). Despite this, the government are introducing new measures to strengthen free speech at universities, even creating a role called 'Free speech and academic freedom champion' (Oluwole, 2021).

'Safe spaces', 'trigger warnings' and 'no-platforming' … have been heralded as proof that we are educating a new generation of 'snowflake' students' and comprise the main indicators of a safety-first culture. In fact, both the policies relating to safe spaces and trigger warnings

> are aimed at being as inclusive as possible and allowing as many people as possible to participate in conversations. Trigger warnings … do not stop anybody from being allowed to say anything; rather they help people who might be affected negatively by that speech to prepare themselves or choose not to expose themselves to that material. Safe spaces prevent people from speaking about a topic in a particular setting, but they do not prevent people from having these conversations in other places, and they only exclude people in order to better enable vulnerable groups to speak freely. (Riley, 2021: 10)

Unlike safe spaces and trigger warnings, no-platforming, a policy which entails refusing to provide a platform for a speaker because of their views or affiliations, is not new, with the National Union of Students having had such a policy since 1973. It should be noted that 'the fundamental act of not inviting a speaker is not itself an assault on free speech' (Riley, 2021: 11). Only six organizations known to hold racist or fascist views are currently proscribed: 'three of these groups promote Islamic extremism, while the other three promote far right English nationalism and fascism'. What is more, 'no platforming has been used very sparingly: 'there were only twelve institutions that banned controversial speakers or events in the 2014–17 period, according to the free speech absolutists, Spiked Online' (Santivanez in Riley, 2021: 213–214).

Safe spaces, trigger warnings and no-platforming are exceptional. Far from threatening free speech, safe spaces and trigger warnings enhance it. No-platforming by contrast does not. Nonetheless there is a case for exceptionally refusing a platform to a speaker. 'The mission of the university includes discriminating between ideas on the basis of disciplinary norms and intellectual expertise, and foregrounding some ideas while actively neglecting those which have been discredited and disproven' (Titley, 2020: 124–125). There are, however, some ideas that are not only obsolete ... but also undermine the university's functioning' (Baer, 2019: 41). One such idea is the supremacy of the white race, which

> does not merit debate on campus ... By positing that some human beings are inherently inferior to others, white supremacists and virulent racists materially undermine the equal conditions of participation for certain students ... The point is not about students feeling safe, welcome, and not offended, but it is a matter of all students, regardless of their group belonging, having the equal right to participate. (Baer, 2019: 42; 46)

We need to distinguish freedom of speech and academic freedom. The right to free speech means that white supremacist and racists should not be banned from a public space such as a street, but academic freedom demands that they are banned from the university 'since they undermine the very purpose of education, which depends on the equal participation of all members of the community regardless of background and race' (Baer, 2019: 69). Academic freedom in short does not demand the freedom to debate discredited ideas, but it does demand that everyone can participate in debate on equal terms. No-platforming is justified therefore in exceptional circumstances.

In addition to safe spaces, trigger warnings and no-platforming, PC critics have pointed to two other phenomena which are seen as threats to free speech, namely witch hunts of staff, on the one hand, and, intimidation and violence on campus, on the other hand. According to Lukianoff and Haidt, the first has been evident since 2015, while the latter has developed since 2017. These phenomena are clearly disturbing, but they are exceptional. It is revealing that a very limited number of examples are rehashed, with Lukianoff and Haidt and

Murray for example identifying the same three witch hunts to illustrate their argument. Both phenomena arguably are more indicative of a deeply polarized society than an overprotective upbringing. What is noteworthy here are increased provocation from far-right groups' emboldened by the advent of Trump as President and growing anger felt by students 'since by 2015 most people had seen videos of police officers shooting or choking unarmed black men' (Lukianoff and Haidt, 2019: 97; 103).

It is interesting to explore the implications of conceptualizing universities as riven by an assault on free speech by snowflakes for racial inequality. There is now a considerable literature pointing to the persistence of racial inequality in the academy (Arday and Mirza, 2018; Pilkington, 2020). While PC critics differ in their approach, there is a tendency for them to be sceptical about such evidence. Since, in their view, the battle for race equality has been virtually won, the question arises as to why race has resurfaced as an issue. One reason put forward is that young people, or at least snowflakes, have adopted 'a new religion of social justice' and interpret the world through this lens (Murray, 2020: 245). It 'assumes racism is everywhere' and because there has in fact been 'a radical reduction of social injustice ... deeper and deeper readings of situations and texts and increasingly complicated Theoretical arguments have been required to detect them' (Pluckrose and Lindsay, 2020: 132; 211). Interpreting the world in the most negative light i.e. catastrophizing results. Unintentional slights for example are interpreted as microaggressions, 'fostering feelings of victimization, and anger and hopelessness in ... students' who 'will come to see the world – and even their university – as a hostile place' where things never seem to get better. (Lukianoff and Haidt, 2019: 46). While they are careful not to claim that we live in a post racial society, PC critics believe that new religion of social justice exaggerates the problem. It's not surprising therefore that they are so critical of many of the measures proposed to promote race equality. Some wish to see the Equality Act repealed since the legal obligations, including harassment policies, threaten freedom of speech (Civitas, 2020). Others believe that equality and diversity officers 'wield' far too much 'institutional, social, and cultural power' and challenge the requirements to sign up to any 'statement of diversity, equality and inclusion, or mandatory diversity or equality training' (Pluckrose and Lindsay, 2020: 216; 264). And others are insistent that any 'social justice activism' should be resolutely liberal, i.e. concerned only with fair procedures and not fair outcomes (Lukianoff and Haidt, 2019: 231). Clearly those who frame the crisis on campus as racism rather than free speech would take a markedly different approach (Malik, 2019b).

Cancel culture as a problem?

While the claim that free speech is in peril and the contention that generation snowflake exacerbates the danger are found to be wanting, the same is not true of cancel culture. There does indeed exist a modern form of ostracism which can entail online abuse, public shaming and in extreme cases the loss of a job. It is important nonetheless to qualify the view of cancel culture presented by PC critics.

Cancelling itself is not a new phenomenon but social media have eroded the distinction between private and public space so that cancelling can go viral. Goldberg puts it well: 'We all live now in this terrible crowd sourced panopticon that makes you worry that any straight phrase you utter might be used to defame you' (Fry et al. 2018: 92). There is little doubt that panic at the fear of denunciation is common which is why 152 writers of different ideological persuasions in 2020 signed a letter to Harper's decrying the stifling of debate. Public shaming can be based on slip-ups or errors that in a predigital age would probably have been forgotten over time, but 'today, people may be followed by their doppelganger wherever they go in the world' (Murray, 2020: 179).

At the same time, we should recognize that the alleged cancellers include marginalized voices who would not otherwise be heard (Malik, 2020a). It is helpful in this context to distinguish our response to individuals and their beliefs. We may not be able to respect certain ideas and indeed even find them repellent, but we can tolerate them. When it comes to people, however, respect should be the order of the day. Some trans activists fundamentally disagree with some feminists, but that should not entail dismissing the latter as transphobes. Malik puts it well; 'A moral right to express unpopular opinions is not a moral right to express those opinions in a way that silences the voices of others, or puts them in danger' (Malik, 2019a: 133).

We should know that cancelling does not mean silencing. Indeed many of the well-known writers on the right, such as Jordan Peterson and Toby Young, who have been 'cancelled' use newspaper columns, television appearances and online media to complain about being cancelled (Foster, 2019) and in this way garner more publicity (Titley, 2020). They present themselves as victims but have certainly not been silenced. And in fact it is extremely rare, at least in the UK for individuals to lose their job as a result of being cancelled (Lawson, 2020).

Ironically, cancel culture which is often equated with PC (Malik, 2020c), has been blamed for making the most famous advocate of absolute free speech and scourge of snowflakes a victim, and this despite the fact that it is usually the left who are pilloried for sanctifying victimhood.

> Martyr for free speech Jordon Peterson is the professor vilified by the left for his crusade against political correctness. Now he is seriously ill his close friend Douglas Murray reveals the very high price he's paid.
>
> Peterson has bravely battled the political correctness ninjas harder than anyone else. In an age of newly imposed, often suffocating dogmas, he said what people know to be true about a whole range of issues ... But there was a very great cost to pay for being the cause celebre of telling the truth. Becoming Public Enemy, No 1 may have helped lead him to where he is today ... in intensive care in Russia following a dependence on anti- anxiety pills. (Murray, 2020a)

Contrary to the view propagated by PC critics, cancel culture is by no means a purely left-wing phenomenon.

Cancel culture exists, fueled by political intolerance and the toxic anonymity of social media. The great myth about cancel culture … is that it exists only on the left. For the past 40 years, rightwing newspapers have ceaselessly fought to delegitimize and ultimately cancel our national broadcaster … Likewise, recent attacks on museums, universities and the National Trust were launched … to intimidate other institutions and encourage them to cancel projects they might have been considering: to investigate their own historical links to parts of Britain's past that our leaders and much of our press feel should be jettisoned or left unexamined, in particular our historical role in colonialism and slavery. (Olusoga, 2021)

Right-wing cancel culture is arguably a much more potent threat for the simple reason that the right is more powerful and therefore has more clout. When President Trump, for example used Twitter to tell his followers that four Congress women (all people of colour) should 'go back to their country', he was effectively cancelling them (Beckcom, 2020).

An anti-PC campaign?

We should note that the attack on PC is often part of a sustained campaign waged by conservatives and integral to the culture wars they believe play well with many people (Beckett, 2020). Donald Trump is a proficient exponent, presenting himself as a crusader against PC and frequently identifying PC as a pervasive phenomenon to be eschewed and replaced with common sense: 'They [the political establishment] have put political correctness above common sense, above your safety, above all else. I refuse to be politically correct'. And when challenged about his treatment of women, he retorted, 'I think the big problem this country has is being politically correct. I've been challenged by so many people. I don't frankly have time for political correctness. And to be honest with you, this country doesn't have time either' (Trump quoted in Weigel, 2016). The campaign against PC in the US has often been well funded and has included as part of its armoury, as we have seen, many academic critiques. Unlike earlier conservative critics such as Bloom, the populist call, however, is no longer to educate the elites (who are now seen as irredeemably liberal) but to replace them. Trump was unsuccessful in winning a second term, but the campaign against PC continues, with conservatives eager to find a more competent leader to replace him:

No national candidate has ever calumniated political correctness with such contempt, and yet no president has ever permitted political correctness to tighten its hold so much on the lives of citizens. The intimidation of common people as sexists and racists grew under Trump. After the #MeToo movement, mandatory anti-sexism workshops proliferated. After last summer's riots over the death of George Floyd, anti-racism slogans were painted over football fields … By the end of Trump's term his tweets were being censored, and so were the Facebook accounts of supporters who even mentioned the slogan 'Stop the steal'. (Caldwell, 2021)

On this side of the Atlantic in the UK, academics have been quieter, but the right-wing press has waged a long campaign against PC (or its surrogates such as wokeness and cancel culture) which has provided fertile ground for Boris Johnson's brand of populism and helped contribute to the decision for Britain to leave the European Union (Brexit). Boris Johnson as both a right-wing journalist and politician has not been averse to speak disparagingly of people of colour, and in his tweet on the Duke of Edinburgh's retirement from royal duties extolled him in these terms: 'What a fantastic servant of the UK. One of the last bastions of political incorrectness. They don't make them like that anymore' (Johnson quoted in Moore, 2017). What I wish to focus on here is his response as Prime Minister to Black Lives Matter (BLM), a movement which initially was distinctly American and a response to police brutality towards Black people but grew in 2020 into a global movement after the killing of George Floyd, a Black man by White police officers was caught on camera. Floyd's murder prompted widespread demonstrations in solidarity with victims of racial injustice across the world, which entailed in the UK the removal of a statue of a slave trader in Bristol and reflection by a number of cultural institutions about their historical role in colonialism and slavery. Nigel Farage, a central figure in the Brexit campaign, like Trump, was highly critical from the start of a movement he castigated as a threat to the British way of life. He prodded Johnson: 'I'm afraid Boris Johnson and the government have gone along with this PC woke agenda' (Farage quoted in Zindelka, 2020). Provoked by Farage, Johnson used a Conservative conference speech to nail his mast to the wind: 'We are proud of this country's culture and history and traditions; they [Labour] literally want to pull statues down, to rewrite the history of our country, to edit our national CV to make it look more politically correct' (Johnson quoted in Beckett, 2020). This speech is part of a wider campaign waged by the right-wing press and increasingly by the government against PC. The 'war on woke' entails identifying different threats to our way of life and lampooning institutions for their virtue signalling capitulation to PC (Malik, 2020b; Hirsch, 2020). One example relates to the initial decision of the BBC to perform an orchestral rather than choral version of two patriotic songs at the Last Night of the Proms:

> Right-wing newspapers seized on the story ... with the Sun running the story under the headline 'Land of woke and glory'. They saw the lack of singing as a surrender – not a practical decision that reflected the difficulties of putting on a prom during a pandemic. Cue the intervention of the Prime Minister: 'I think it's time we stopped our cringing embarrassment about our history, about our traditions, and about our culture and we stopped this general fight of self-recrimination and wetness. (Johnson quoted in Waterson and Bakare, 2020)

In some cases, there have been veiled threats of funding cuts and proposed new laws. The Culture Secretary announced to museums and funding bodies: 'The government does not support the removal of statues or other similar objects ... You should not be taking actions motivated by activism or politics' (Dowden quoted in Hicks, 2020). The Communities Secretary has subsequently proposed new laws to protect 'statues, plaques, memorials or monuments ... from being removed "at the hands of the flash mob, or by the decree of ... town hall militants and woke worthies"' (Jenrick quoted in Hope, 2021). Meanwhile the Education Secretary summarily dismissed calls for changes to the history curriculum in schools to incorporate Britain's colonial past and involvement in slavery: 'We have an incredibly rich history, and we should be incredibly proud of our history because time and time again, this country has made a difference and changed things for the better, right around the world' (Williamson quoted in Duffy, 2020).

But perhaps the most revealing intervention has come from the Minister for women and equalities in a speech where she set out a new approach to equality 'based on "Conservative values"' and 'pledged that equality will now be "about individual dignity and humanity, not quotas and targets, or equality of outcome"'. The UK had focused too much on 'fashionable' race, sexuality and gender issues:

> We will not limit our fight for fairness to the nine protected characteristics laid out in the 2010 Equality Act, which includes sex, race and gender reassignment ... the focus on protected characteristics has led to a narrowing of equality debate that overlooks socioeconomic status and geographic inequality. This means some issues – particularly those facing white working class children – are neglected. (Truss quoted in *Independent* editorial 2020)

In a year when we had become more aware of racial injustice and ethnic disparities in outcomes, the Minister seemed be 'play[ing] to the culture wars gallery and to be pitting the needs of minorities against those of the working class, when neither of them have been properly addressed' (Malik, 2020). Challenged about this, 'Home Secretary Priti Patel [who described the Black Lives Matter protests as "dreadful"] backed Ms Truss's plans: "We're focusing on the people's priorities – we shouldn't be indulging in fashionable issues of political correctness"' (Bulman and Oppenheim, 2020).

In the US the attacks on PC have clearly been orchestrated. 'Most of the conservative books and articles ... repeat the same stories, use the same terms and [are] largely funded by bodies known to have right-wing leanings' (Lea, 2009: 59). And, not surprisingly in a global world, something like that is evident now in the UK, with the recycling of the same themes, the same examples and indeed the same purported intellectual roots in postmodernism/cultural Marxism. The examples are typically 'exaggerated or fabricated in some way'. Famous examples in an earlier period include the story that 'local councils in London had banned black coffee and black bin liners on the grounds that they were racist' (Lea, 2009: 159) and the story that you could no longer celebrate Christmas in Birmingham because the city council had replaced it with Winterval, a story the *Daily Mail* later acknowledged to be false in 2011. On examination 'almost all claims that "political correctness has gone mad" turn out to be based on hokum and hot air' (O'Brien, 2018: 117; see Alibhai-Brown, 2018 and Johnson, 2017 for further examples). This unfortunately does not mean that they are not believed even years after first being aired. The campaign 'by the conservative right in the US [has been] very successful' in creating a PC bogeyman and stigmatizing the Left (Lea, 2009: 261) and there is evidence that it is making significant headway in the UK (O'Hagan, 2020). Irrespective of whether there has been an orchestrated campaign waged against political correctness, there is no doubt that PC or rather than anti-PC has re-emerged in the last decade as a major interpretive framework in the media uncritically reproduced by many journalists.

Is the threat from the left as serious as the threat from the right?

Critics of PC focus on what they see as a threat from the Left, whether it is conceived as comprising social justice activists, PC idealists or the 'equality, diversity and inclusion mob'. There is no doubt that the equality, diversity and inclusion mob, to use Jordan Peterson's preferred terminology, has 'many flaws and idiocies' as someone sympathetic to PC acknowledges. These flaws and idiocies include being overly prescriptive on what is acceptable language, being sanctimonious, 'hiding inconvenient truths' and sometimes making 'excuses for miscreants ... because they come from groups that are discriminated against' (Alibhai-Brown, 2018: 11; 145). At the same time, however, we should note the progress that this mob [*sic*] helped initiate in jettisoning racist, sexist and homophobic slurs and reducing unfair discrimination (Goldberg in Fry et al., 018).

It's worth looking back at what was considered annoyingly, outrageously, politically correct in the 1980s ... You know adding women or people of colour to the Western Civilization curriculum, or not making gay jokes or using 'retard' as an epithet. I get it: new concepts, new words stick in your throat. The way we're used to talking and thinking seems natural and normal, by definition. And then the new terms, new concepts that have social utility stick, and those that don't fall away (Goldberg in Fry et al., 2018).

What felt like uncomfortable intrusions at one time are now more or less taken for granted.

Much more serious in my view than any purported threat from the Left is the threat from the Right. Here can be found, initially in the US but increasingly in the UK, the perpetrators of dangerous conspiracy theories and serious violence. The US paedophile cult conspiracy theory has now taken root in Europe, with 'one in four people in the UK now believing in conspiracy theories propagated by QAnon' (Sommerlad, 2021). And far-right terrorism is now a much more significant threat than terrorism by other perpetrators.

In 2018 far right convictions in the UK surpassed those of Islamic terror organisations for the first time. In the US, white-orchestrated terrorism claimed more lives on US soil than any other identity-based terrorism since 9/11 ... but the threat such white identity politics poses is often trivialised. (Malik, 2019a: 138–139)

We recognize Black Lives Matter as an example of identity politics, which seeks to secure rights denied to people because of their identity, but we should also acknowledge that whiteness is an identity and that white identity politics played a role in Brexit and the election of President Trump, and can take dangerous forms.

Conclusion

At the risk of provoking the wrath of PC critics, by referring to their major bête noire, what I have been arguing is that an anti-PC discourse has become the dominant discourse in a Foucauldian sense (Foucault, 1980). It comprises a particular way of talking about and thinking about the world which in turn shapes how the world is understood and how things are done in it. It does not merely reflect the world, but re-presents it. It constructs political correctness so that those subject to the discourse can see its pervasiveness and discover it all around them. Alibhai-Brown (2018), describes this discourse as an anti-PC orthodoxy and Hirsch (2019), as an anti-woke orthodoxy.

This discourse has proved very persuasive and underpinned the success of the Brexiteers in the EU referendum and the advent of Trump to the American Presidency. This has given succour to those who wish to go back in time and conjure up an imaginary past (Take back control for the Brexiteers; Make American great again for the Trump supporters).

I have argued that the distinctiveness of this discourse in its most recent iteration is twofold: a belief that freedom of speech, which should be absolute, is under grave threat, and a belief that fragile younger people demand to be protected from offensive speech. Both these beliefs turn out on inspection to be deeply flawed. This has not, however, prevented the discourse becoming hegemonic and indeed a campaign being mounted to spread the word and reinforce the message. The world is in the process turned upside down, with anti-racism (and feminism) seen as the problem rather than racism (and sexism), and, despite the manifest evidence on racial (and gender) disparities to the contrary, white men seen as victims. Black Lives Matter (and the #MeToo) movements are the latest casualties, being transmogrified from movements seeking social justice to become 'symbols of censorship and reverse discrimination' which threaten our way of life (Malik, 2020c). The upshot is that attempts to promote equality, diversity and inclusion become presented as

sabotage, as attacks on a society that is fundamentally good and not in need of reform ... [But] the PC myth does not only work to dampen efforts for change by repackaging these efforts as assaults, it also works to absolve people for their prejudices … being used as 'coded cover' for those who 'still want to say Paki, spastic or queer'. (Malik, 2019: 60; 84; 91)

In other words, the anti-PC discourse comprises an ideology which delegitimizes a social justice agenda and gives people permission to remain locked in their prejudices. As such it is inherently unethical.

References

Ackroyd, J. and Pilkington, A. (2007), '"You are not allowed to say that": Minefields and political correctness'. *Caribbean Quarterly*, 53(1–2), 49–62.

Alibhai-Brown, Y. (2018), *In Defence of Political Correctness*. London: Biteback Publishing.

Arday, J. and Mirza, H. (eds) (2018), *Dismantling Race in Higher Education*. London: Palgrave.

Baer, U. (2019), *What Snowflakes Get Right*. New York: Oxford University Press.

Beckcom, B. (2020), 'Rightwing cancel culture is the real threat: Why are we ignoring it?'.13 July. Retrieved from: Right Wing Cancel Culture Is the Real Threat—Why Are We Ignoring It? | by Brian Beckcom | Medium. Accessed: 9 February 2021.

Beckett, A. (2020), 'The Tories' culture war is a reminder that the right isn't as fearless as it seems'. *The Guardian*, 9 October. Retrieved from: The Tories' culture war is a reminder that the right isn't as fearless as it seems | Society | The Guardian. Accessed: 9 February 2021.

Bernstein, R. (1990), 'The rising hegemony of the politically correct'. *New York Times*, 28 October. Retrieved from: IDEAS & TRENDS; The Rising Hegemony of the Poli tically Correct – The New York Times (nytimes.com). Accessed: 10 February 2021.

Biggar, N. (2019), 'Cambridge is lost in a cloud of leftist virtue signalling'. *The Times*, 3 May. Retrieved from: Cambridge is lost in a cloud of leftist virtue-signalling | News | The Times. Accessed: 11 February 2021.

Bloom, A. (1987), *The Closing of the American Mind*. New York: Simon & Schuster.

Bond, K. (2018), 'PC gone mad? Piers Morgan slams teacher who banned kids for touching snow'. *Daily Star*, 28 February. Retrieved from: PC gone mad? Piers Morgan slams tea cher who BANNED kids touching snow – Daily Star. Accessed: 10 February 2021.

Brown, A. (2019), 'Snowflakes brand Mr Men books degrading to women'. *Daily Star*, 8 May. Retrieved from: Snowflakes brand Mr Men books DEGRADING to women – Daily Star. Accessed: 11 February 2021.

Bulman, M. and Oppenheim, M. (2020), 'Backlash as ministers vow to ditch focus on "fashionable" fight against inequality'. *The Independent*, 17 December. Retrieved from: Backlash as ministers vow to ditch focus on 'fashionable' fight against inequa lity | The Independent. Accessed: 25 February 2021.

Buncombe, A. (2019), 'Jordan Peterson: Controversial philosopher claims Cambridge university buckled to "political correctness types"'. *The Independent*, 20 March. Retrieved from: Jordan Peterson: Controversial philosopher claims Cambridge Uni versity buckled to 'political correctness types' | The Independent | The Independent. Accessed: 11 February 2021.

Caldwell, C. (2021), 'Trump was inept – but his instincts weren't wrong'. *Sunday Times*, 17 January. Retrieved from: Donald Trump was inept—but his instincts weren't wrong | World | The Sunday Times (thetimes.co.uk). Accessed: 22 February 2021.

Civitas (2020), 'Academic freedom in our universities: The best and the worst'. Retrieved from: Academic-Freedom-in-Our-Universities.pdf (civitas.org.uk). Accessed: 15 February 2021.

Clark, T. (2019), 'Free speech? New polling suggest Britain is "less PC" than Trump's America'. *Prospect Magazine*, 16 February. Retrieved from: Free speech? New polling suggests Britain is 'less PC' than Trump's America – Prospect Magazine. Accessed: 16 February 2021.

Dabhoiwala, F. (2020), 'Frees speech wars review – from censorship to cancel culture'. *The Guardian*, 3 December. Retrieved from: The Free Speech Wars review – from censorship to cancel culture | Essays | The Guardian. Accessed: 16 February 2021.

D'Ancona, M. (2017), *Post-Truth*. London: Ebury Press.

Davies, W. (2018), 'The free speech panic: How the right concocted a crisis'. *The Guardian*, 26 July. Retrieved from: The free speech panic: how the right concocted a crisis | Freedom of speech | The Guardian. Accessed: 9 February 2021.

D'Sousa, D. (1991), *Illiberal Education: The Politics of Race and Sex on Campus*. New York: The Free Press.

Duffy, N. (2020), 'Gavin Williamson rejects calls to "decolonize" history curriculum, saying Britons should be "proud of our history"'. *inews*, 19 June. Retrieved from: Gavin Williamson rejects calls to 'decolonise' history curriculum, saying Britons should be 'proud of our history' (inews.co.uk). Accessed: 11 February 2021.

Dunant, S. (ed.) (1994), *The War of the Words: The Political Correctness Debate*. London: Virago.

Ferguson, N. (2019a), 'Join my NATO or watch critical thinking die'. *Sunday Times*, 14 April. Retrieved from: Join my Nato or watch critical thinking die | Comment | The Sunday Times (thetimes.co.uk). Accessed: 11 February 2021.

Ferguson, N. (2019b), 'Free speech is in free fall in Silicon valley'. *Sunday Times*, 9 June. Retrieved from: Free speech is in free fall in Silicon Valley | Comment | The Sunday Times (thetimes.co.uk). Accessed: 16 February 2021.

Foster, D. (2019), 'Niall Ferguson isn't upset about free speech. He's upset about being challenged'. *The Guardian*, 15 April. Retrieved from: Niall Ferguson isn't upset about free speech. He's upset about being challenged | Freedom of speech | The Guardian. Accessed: 11 February 2021.

Foucault, M. (1980), *Power/Knowledge*. Brighton: Harvester.

Fox, C. (2016), *I Still Find That Offensive*. London: Biteback Publishing.

Fry, S., Peterson, J., Dyson, M. and Goldberg, M. (2018), *Political Correctness Gone Mad?*London: Oneworld Publications.

Furedi, F. (2016), *What's Happened to the University? A Sociological Exploration of its Infantalisation*. London: Routledge.

Green, D. (2019), 'We're nearly all victims now'. Civitas. Retrieved from: werenearlyallvictimsnow.pdf (civitas.org.uk). Accessed: 16 February 2021.

Hicks, D. (2020), 'Museums are being drawn into a fake culture war'. *The Guardian*, 16 October. Retrieved from: The UK government is trying to draw museums into a fake culture war | Museums | The Guardian. Accessed: 10 February 2021.

Hirsch, A., Henry, L., Lester A., Guru-Murthy, K.*et al.* (2019), 'You can't be impartial about racism – an open letter to the BBC on the Naga Munchetty ruling'. *The Guardian*, 27 September. Retrieved from: You can't be 'impartial' about racism – an open letter to the BBC on the Naga Munchetty ruling | BBC | The Guardian. Accessed: 12 February 2021.

Hirsch, A. (2019), 'The struggle for equality is real. The "woke police" are a myth'. *The Guardian*, 26 September. Retrieved from: The struggle for equality is real. The 'woke police' are a myth | LGBT rights | The Guardian. Accessed: 10 February 2021.

Hirsch, A. (2020), 'Boris Johnson does have a strategy on racism after all. It's called a 'war on woke''. *The Guardian*, 17 June. Retrieved from: Boris Johnson does have a strategy on racism after all. It's called a 'war on woke' | Black Lives Matter movement | The Guardian. Accessed: 10 February 2021.

Hitchens, P. (2020), 'I fear anyone who dissents from today's pervasive culture of political correctness will be visited by the Thought Police'. *Mail Online*, 15 March. Retrieved from: PETER HITCHENS: I fear anyone who dissents from PC will be visited by Thought Police | Daily Mail Online. Accessed: 9 February 2021.

Hope, C. (2021), 'Statues and monuments given safeguard from "baying mobs"'. *The Telegraph*, 16 January. Retrieved from: https://www.telegraph.co.uk/politics/2021/01/16/historic-statues-get-official-protection-baying-mobs-tough-new/?li_source=LI&li_medium=liftigniter-onward-journey. Accessed: 23 February 2021.

Hunt, K. (2020), 'How the world woke up'. *The Guardian*, 21 November. Retrieved from: How 'woke' became the word of our era | Society books | The Guardian. Accessed: 12 February 2021.

Independent Editorial (2020), 'A dangerous game is being played with equality'. *The Independent*, 18 December. Retrieved from: Liz Truss and the government are playing a dangerous game when it comes to equality | The Independent. Accessed: 25 February 2021.

Johnson, A. (2017), 'In defence of political correctness'. 24 June. Retrieved from: In Defense of Political Correctness | by Adam H. Johnson | Medium. Accessed: 10 February 2021.

Kimball, R. (1990), *Tenured Radicals: How Politics Has Corrupted Our Higher Education*. New York: HarperCollins.

Lawson, D. (2020), 'US cancel culture puts ours in the shade'. *Sunday Times*, 19 July. Retrieved from: US cancel culture puts ours in the shade | Comment | The Sunday Times (thetimes.co.uk). Accessed: 12 February 2021.

Lea, J. (2009), *Political Correctness and Higher Education*. London: Routledge.

Lukianoff, G. and Haidt, J. (2019), *The Coddling of the American Mind*. London: Penguin.

Lyons, I. and Yorke, H. (2019), 'Cambridge University inquiry into slave trade connections is "virtue signalling" on steroids'. *The Telegraph*, 30 April. Retrieved from: Cambridge University inquiry into slave trade connections is 'virtue signalling on steroids'. Trevor Phillips says (telegraph.co.uk). Accessed: 11 February 2021.

Malik, K. (2020), 'The Tory "class agenda" is a culture war stunt that will leave inequality untouched'. *The Observer*, 20 December. Retrieved from: The Tory 'class agenda' is a culture war stunt that will leave inequality untouched | Liz Truss | The Guardian. Accessed: 25 February 2021.

Malik, N. (2019a), *We Need New Stories*. London: Weidenfeld & Nicolson.

Malik, N. (2019b), 'There is a crisis on campuses – but it's about racism not free speech'. *The Guardian*, 13 October. Retrieved from: There is a crisis on campuses – but it's about racism, not free speech | Universities | The Guardian. Accessed: 12 February 2021.

Malik, N. (2020a) 'The "cancel culture" war is about old elites losing power'. *The Guardian*, 13 July. Retrieved from: The 'cancel culture' war is really about old elites losing power in the social media age | Social media | The Guardian. Accessed: 12 February 2021.

Malik, N. (2020b), 'The right's culture war is no longer a sideshow to our politics – it is our politics'. *The Guardian*, 31 August. Retrieved from: The right's culture war is no longer a sideshow to our politics – it is our politics | Politics | The Guardian. Accessed: 9 February 2021.

Malik, N. (2020c), 'Right wing media slurs will not halt Black Lives Matter'. *The Guardian*, 21 September. Retrieved from: Despite being vilified in the rightwing media , Black Lives Matter will endure | Black Lives Matter movement | The Guardian. Accessed 10 February 2021.

Mill, J. S. (2010), *On Liberty*. London: Penguin Classics.

Monbiot, G. (2018), 'How US billionaires are fuelling the hard right cause in Britain'. *The Guardian*, 7 December. Retrieved from: How US billionaires are fuelling the hard-right cause in Britain | Media | The Guardian. Accessed: 16 February 2021.

Monbiot, G. (2021), 'Misinformation kills and we have a duty to suppress it'. *The Guardian*, 27 January. Retrieved from: Covid lies cost lives – we have a duty to clamp down on them | Coronavirus | The Guardian. Accessed: 12 February 2021.

Moore, J. (2017), 'Boris Johnson's tribute to Prince Philip proves that he is the most unsuitable person in the country to be Foreign Secretary'. *The Independent*, 3 August. Retrieved from: Boris Johnson's tribute to Prince Philip proves that he is the most unsuitable person in the country to be Foreign Secretary | The Independent | The Independent. Accessed: 21 February 2021.

Morgan, P. (2020), *Wake up: The World's Gone Nuts'*. London: HarperCollins.

Murray, A. (2018–19), 'Generation snowflake?'. *RSA Journal*, 4, 44–47.

Murray, D. (2020), *The Madness of Crowds*. London: Bloomsbury.

Murray, D. (2020a), 'Martyr for free speech'. *MailOnline*, 15 February. Retrieved from: Jordan Peterson was vilified for his crusade against political correctness and is now seriously ill | Daily Mail Online. Accessed: 10 February 2021.

O'Brien, J. (2018), *How to be Right in a World Gone Wrong*, London: Penguin.

O'Hagan, E. (2020), 'The "anti-woke" backlash is no joke – and progressives are going to lose if they don't wise up'. *The Guardian*, 30 January. Retrieved from: The 'anti-woke' backlash is no joke – and progressives are going to lose if they don't wise up | Race | The Guardian. Accessed: 10 February 2021.

Olusoga, D. (2021), 'Cancel culture' is not the preserve of the left. Just ask our historians'. *The Guardian*, 3 January. Retrieved from: 'Cancel culture' is not the preserve of the left. Just ask our historians | History | The Guardian. Accessed: 10 February 2021.

Oluwole, F. (2021), 'The Conservative Party's free speech reforms are staggeringly hypocritical'. *The Independent*, 22 February. Retrieved from: The Conservative Party's free speech reforms are staggeringly hypocritical (msn.com). Accessed: 24 February 2021.

Parris, M. (2019), 'Let's stop kidding ourselves we're tolerant'. *The Sunday Times*, 25 October. Retrieved from: Let's stop kidding ourselves we're tolerant | Comment | The Times. Accessed: 10 February 2021.

Pearson, G. (1983), *Hooligan*. London: Palgrave.

Phillips. T. (2020a), 'When you erase a nation's past you threaten its future'. *The Times*, 19 September. Retrieved from: Trevor Phillips: When you erase a nation's past, you threaten its future | Comment | The Times. Accessed: 11 February 2021.

Phillips, T. (2020b), 'The march of wokeism is an all-pervasive new oppression'. *The Times*, 7 November. Retrieved from: The march of wokeism is an all-pervasive new oppression | Comment | The Times. Accessed: 10 February 2021.

Pilkington, A. (2020), 'Promoting Race Equality and Supporting Ethnic Diversity in the Academy: The UK Experience over Two Decades', in G. Crimmins (ed.), *Strategies for Supporting Inclusion and Diversity in the Academy*. London: Palgrave.

Pluckrose, H. and Lindsay, J. (2020), *Cynical Critical Theories*. London: Swift Press.

Ridler, F. (2020), 'Political correctness does not address the real problem faced by ethnic minorities, says head of the National Black Police Association'. *Mail Online*, 15 November. Retrieved from: Political correctness 'does not address the real problems faced by ethnic.inorities' | Daily Mail Online. Accessed: 9 February 2021.

Riley, C. (ed.) (2021), *The Free Speech Wars*. Manchester: Manchester University Press.

Schraer, R. and Butcher, B. (2018), 'Universities: Is free speech under threat?' *BBC*, 23 October. Retrieved from: Universities: Is free speech under threat? – BBC News. Accessed: 10 February 2021.

Shipman, T. (2020), 'Voters seek return to common sense in revolt against political correctness'. *Sunday Times*, 24 May. Retrieved from: Voters seek return to common sense in revolt against political correctness | News | The Sunday Times (thetimes.co. uk). Accessed: 9 February 2021.

Sommerlad, J. (2021), 'QAnon: How the US Satanic paedophile cult conspiracy theory took root in Europe'. *The Independent*, 25 February. Retrieved from: QAnon: How the US Satanic paedophile cult conspiracy theory took root in Europe | The Independent. Accessed: 26 February 2021.

Sparrow, J. (2017), '"Political correctness' has no meaning. That's the main appeal'. *The Guardian*, 23 March. Retrieved from: 'Political correctness' has no meaning. That's the main appeal | Australian politics | The Guardian. Accessed: 21 February 2021.

Street-Porter, J. (2020), 'From JK Rowling to "Fawlty towers", the thought police are spiralling out of control'. *The Independent*, 12 June. Retrieved from: From JK Rowling to 'Fawlty Towers'. the thought police are spiralling out of control | The Independent | The Independent. Accessed: 11 February 2021.

Symons, J. (2018), 'Has political correctness gone too far?'. *The Economist*, 10 September. Retrieved from: Open Society: Essay competition winner – Has political correctness gone too far? | Open Future | The Economist. Accessed: 10 February 2021.

Titley, G. (2020), *Is Free Speech Racist?*Cambridge: Polity.

Turner, J. (2020), 'The woke left is the new Ministry of Truth'. *The Times*, 11 July. Retrieved from: The woke left is the new Ministry of Truth | Comment | The Times. Accessed: 10 February 2021.

Waterson, J. and Bakare, L. (2020), '"Trump-like culture war'; Boris Johnson wades into Proms row'. *The Guardian*, 25 August. Retrieved from: 'Trump-like culture war': Boris Johnson wades into Proms row | Proms | The Guardian. Accessed: 24 February 2021.

Watkins, E. (2020), 'Freedom of speech at universities is not under threat – it is actually thriving'. *The Independent*, 17 December. Retrieved from: Freedom of speech at universities is not under threat – it is actually thriving | The Independent. Accessed: 15 February 2021.

Weigel, M. (2016), 'Political correctness: How the right invented a phantom enemy'. *The Guardian*, 30 November. Retrieved from: The right's culture war is no longer a sideshow to our politics – it is our politics | Politics | The Guardian. Accessed: 9 February 2021.

Young, S. (2019), 'Waitrose accused of racism over "ugly" chocolate duckling'. *The Independent*, 10 April. Retrieved from: Waitrose accused of racism over 'ugly' Easter chocolate duckling | The Independent | The Independent. Accessed: 10 February 2021.

Younge, G. (2018), 'The Serena cartoon debate: Calling out racism is not "censorship"'. *The Guardian*, 13 September. Retrieved from: The Serena cartoon debate: calling out racism is not 'censorship' | Race | The Guardian. Accessed: 9 February 2021.

Zindulka, K. (2020), 'Farage: Boris trapped by "PC culture" of Marxist Black Lives Matter mob'. *Breitbart*, 29 June. Retrieved from: https://www.breitbart.com/europe/2020/06/29/farage-bojo-trapped-pc-woke-culture-refusing-stand-up-marxist-blm-mob/. Accessed: 23 February 2021.

2   Impartiality, fairness and the bias of empire

Technologies of freedom or constraint?

Sylvia Harvey

This chapter explores aspects of the concepts of 'impartiality' and 'fairness' in British and American broadcasting and considers the extent to which these concepts might be considered vital for the survival of public service provision and for the development of an informed public in a wider, global context. This concept or principle of impartiality, of open-mindedness and a dedication to presenting a variety of points of view on the big and often controversial issues of the day, is seen here to be of continuing value in the online era. One defender of the regulatory principle of 'fairness' in the United States cited with approval a phrase use by the Federal Radio Commission as early as 1928 that broadcasters should demonstrate 'due regard for the opinions of others' (Johnson, 1988; FRC, 1928: 155). The Arab satellite broadcaster Al Jazeera, launched some 70 years later, adopted perhaps surprisingly similar terminology with its founding motto of 'The Opinion ... and the Other Opinion' (Al Jazeera, 2006; Stanley Foundation, 2006).

However, the implementation of 'fairness' and 'impartiality' principles is also subject to the changing temper of the times, to state and government interests and to geographical location. Thus 'impartiality' in public communication cannot be seen as a simple rule-governed principle; rather it is constrained by the changing requirements of nation states and by what different societies at different times regard as normal and acceptable. In this regard the 'home' of impartiality may be found within the nation state. For example, when the British Broadcasting Corporation (BBC) launched its Empire Service in 1932 and its first Arab language service in 1938, the legitimacy of Britain's imperial ambitions was taken for granted by many and dissenting voices seldom heard. The BBC's first Director General believed that broadcasting provided a 'consolidatory element within the Empire'; and the government apparently trusted the Corporation to do the right thing, removing the 'ban on controversy' in 1928 (Briggs, 1995a: 120). Thus, on the issue of empire and its legitimacy – even when the agents of empire made systematic use of violence to impose order without consent – the absence of even-handed impartiality may be seen in British broadcasting between the two world wars. The point of one example from 1938, given in the following section, is to demonstrate the ways in which the genre of news can find itself closely tethered to taken-for-granted beliefs and national priorities. These priorities were to change as the Suez Crisis of 1956 demonstrates.

DOI: 10.4324/9781003203551-4

Over the last three centuries nation states, rulers, publishing houses, broadcasters, religious leaders and politicians have all attempted to place their stamp on systems of shared and public communication. Autocrats and pluralists had different aims: to create their own echo chambers or to provide the means to enable broader public knowledge and understanding. One of the earliest printing presses in the Ottoman Empire was set up in the city of Aleppo, producing Christian devotional texts in 1706 – evidence, perhaps, of a degree of managed pluralism and religious tolerance (Yale University Library, 2009). However, this empire – imbued with the spirit of Islam – was itself to be disaggregated by those Western Christian nations that emerged victorious at the end of the First World War.

After the war of 1914–18 the winners divided the spoils with the blessing of a wholly new player – the League of Nations – making claims that might also be seen as a form of injurious theft. Thus, in the area that became known by westerners as the 'Middle East', France and the United Kingdom (UK) were to take control of large tracts of formerly Ottoman territory, placing their stamp on this region. The UK would hold the 'mandate' for territory that is now Israel/Palestine, Jordan, Southern Iraq and Kuwait (adding to already significant interests in Iran through, for example, British ownership of the Anglo-Persian Oil Company). France would control the lands that subsequently became Lebanon, Syria and parts of Turkey (Schayegh and Arsan, 2015). These details had already been proposed by France and the UK, agreed at a secret meeting in 1916 and recorded in the Sykes-Picot agreement (Mansfield, 2019; Al Jazeera, 2016a).

By the end of the Second World War a new world power had emerged – the United States – replacing and in some respects challenging the old European colonial powers. While in the Arab world, with the advent of national broadcasting, new and questioning publics were slowly to emerge. From 1953 Nasser's 'Voice of the Arabs' (*Sawat al-Arab*) reached out well beyond the boundaries of Egypt, and was seen as the first transnational and widely influential Arabic radio service. Some 40 years later the advent of trans-frontier satellite television broadcasting would renew that legacy with the launch in 1996 of Al Jazeera, financed and supported by the state of Qatar but allowed a considerable measure of freedom.[1] This broadcaster quickly established a new ethos, supporting detailed and critical investigations, offering frontline coverage of foreign military interventions in Afghanistan and Iraq, publicizing the demands of the Palestinians for a state of their own and offering detailed coverage of the events of the 'Arab Spring' (Sakr, 2001; Lahlali, 2011: 12–15; Al Jazeera, 2018; Lynch, 2006). One contributor to Al Jazeera's output noted the views of an older generation and his father's recollection of the 'dreams of pan-Arabism', fostered by Nasser's ambitious radio service – 'speaking out … against imperialism and in defence of Palestine' (Albaih, 2016: 136–139).

When Iraq invaded Kuwait in 1990 the United States assembled a large multinational force, ostensibly acting with a mandate from the United Nations and embarked on a new and deadly assault on the Muslim world – the 'Gulf War' of 1990–91 (Falk, 1992). The only international satellite news provider at that time was the US-based CNN service, transmitting live reports of the first bombing of Baghdad. However, by the time of the US-led invasions of Afghanistan in 2001 and Iraq in 2003, Al Jazeera was in position and able to provide frontline coverage of events.

The attack on Afghanistan was mounted in response to the deliberate crashing of passenger planes into the World Trade Center in New York and the consequent deaths of some 3,000 civilians. The attack was believed to have been planned and executed by the international Al Qaeda group led by the former Saudi citizen Osama Bin Laden then sheltering – it was believed – in Afghanistan. The 2003 invasion of Iraq was occasioned by the belief that its leader Saddam Hussein was developing a new class of long-range missiles that could prove a threat to Western nations. The numbers of soldiers and civilians killed as a result of these Western attacks on Afghanistan and Iraq was estimated by Brown University to be between 415,000 and 442,000, while the number of displaced persons was estimated at just over 8 million (Crawford, 2018: 1–5).

Al Jazeera's coverage of these conflicts and of Israel's war on Gaza in 2008 brought greatly increased international audiences. However, the significance of the broadcaster within the Arab world was perhaps qualitatively changed by its coverage of the 'Arab Spring' beginning with events in Tunisia and Egypt in 2011. In Cairo's Tahrir Square, for example, the Al Jazeera cameras continued live coverage of the protests despite threats and physical attacks from an angry government. Archbishop Desmond Tutu contrasted the slow pace of change in South Africa in the 1970s with the speed of change made possible by the instant and international transmission of images. Al Jazeera, he said:

> … drew back the curtains and opened the windows. The light streamed in to millions of living rooms across the world – ordinary people telling an extraordinary story of the power of the people to effect societal change – backed by the universal language of pictures … people found courage where there was previously just silence and fear. (Al Jazeera Media Network, 2011: 173)

With such examples the content of news is expanded beyond the coverage of governments and elites and this, in turn, provides a new framework for evaluating the exercise of impartiality.

Western empires and their stories: Some contexts for the exercise of impartiality

As indicated above Britain's imperial interests in the Arab world increased with the defeat of the Ottoman Empire at the end of the First World War. Although as early as 1902 members of the British Parliament – one from Yorkshire in particular – had demonstrated also a strong interest in the neighbouring ancient and powerful state of Persia/Iran. In that year Joseph Walton MP had advocated 'safeguarding the commercial and political interests of the British empire in Persia' (Hansard, 1902). Partly this was about safeguarding the route to India and partly about an emerging interest in the commercial value of oil, recognized as a potentially lucrative new source of energy. By 1909 the British government had become the major shareholder in the Anglo-Persian Oil Company and in 1914 a deal was signed to supply oil for the ships of the British Royal Navy, assisting the preparations for war (Malek, 2020).

In this context it may be appropriate to consider some examples from British broadcasting in the twentieth century as the scenery shifts gradually from the age empire to the age of oil (Hobsbawm, 1987; Mangeri, 2006). The BBC, for example established its Empire Service from the end of 1932 prioritizing the white Dominions of Canada, Australia and New Zealand but also launching its first foreign language service in Arabic in 1938. The broadcasting historian Asa Briggs notes that the area of the interwar British mandate in Palestine accounted for 'more than a quarter of the receiving sets' for this service (1995a: 378). Initially founded as the British Broadcasting Company in 1922 (becoming the BBC Broadcasting Corporation in 1927) its development and expansion overseas was partly driven by a concern that competitor powers like Italy, Germany and Russia were stepping up what were seen as propaganda services directed towards an Arab world of some 40 million potential listeners. The British Foreign Office referred to 'Russian radio propaganda in Palestine and around the Persian Gulf'. Briggs also indicates that research work was making it clear to the BBC that in the Arab world they faced aware and sceptical listeners: 'few could believe that the BBC broadcasts did not have a political purpose' (1995a: 374; 361, footnote 89; 372).

The first BBC Arabic news bulletin of 1938 carried information that presented as unremarkable the exercise of power by the occupying forces, namely 'the execution that morning of a Palestinian Arab on the orders of a British military court'. In response to this item a BBC executive previously in the consular service responded by suggesting that perhaps 'there should be such selection and omission of items as to give a favourable impression of this country to the Arab audience'. However, the producer of the programme replied with a strong defence of the report: 'the *omission* of unwelcome *facts* of News and the consequent suppression of truth runs counter to the Corporation's policy' (Briggs, 1995a: 374). The facts were that the British 'mandated' forces exercised the power of life and death over those whose land they occupied. And whilst there was reflection on whether or not the exercise of these powers should be reported on the radio news there was no questioning of the legitimacy of the actions reported. It was assumed that power, of itself, bestowed authority.

As indicated above the world after the Second World War was to be very different from the previous era. Deeply reliant upon the military resources of the United States (and the Soviet Union) Britain was to emerge from the war as a power in decline, sometimes slow to recognize the growing economic and political pre-eminence of the US. Unsurprisingly, perhaps, the war aims of the UK and the US had been rather different. In August 1941, after Britain's defeat at Dunkirk in June 1940 and before America had entered the war, the leaders of the two countries, President Roosevelt and Prime Minister Churchill, were to draw up an influential agreement: the *Atlantic Charter* (1941; Agar, 1973). The third point of the Charter noted that the two countries would:

> ... respect the right of all peoples to choose the form of government under which they will live; and they wish to see sovereign rights and self-government restored to those who have been forcibly deprived of them.

The final clause of the Charter asserted 'that all of the nations of the world ... must come to the abandonment of the use of force'. Following the defeat of Nazi Germany in May 1945 the document was to become influential in the creation of the United Nations later that year. And – unlike the League of Nations, born out of the victory of European colonial powers – the UN could be seen as a supporter of independence movements and of the new nation states that emerged from these movements. The new rules-based order that followed was designed, at least in theory, to provide justice for all regardless of the extent of a nation's military capacity (Sands, 2005: 8–10).

For Britain, as a military and imperial power in 1941, with extensive colonial possessions in South East Asia, Africa and elsewhere, the inhabitants of these territories had certainly not been able to 'choose the form of government' under which they lived; and, on the contrary, they had been 'forcibly deprived' of their sovereign rights. Much was to change – and quite quickly – in the decades after the war including the independence of India and Pakistan in 1947 as the empire started, slowly, to roll back. Moreover, with the creation of the UN, Britain's various political parties, its citizens and Parliament had increasingly to reflect upon the country's new place in the world. Though male supremacism continued to cast its long shadow since the right to vote or 'universal adult suffrage' was still quite a recent phenomenon with votes for women on equal terms with men only being granted in 1928.

By 1956, the parliamentary debates about the Suez Crisis indicated that the old imperial ways of doing things might no longer be acceptable, that the UN should be recognized as a key player in situations of conflict and that old forms of bullying could no longer be hidden under the claimed mantle of a commitment to 'peace' (Eden, 1956; Gaitskell, 1956).

The Suez Crisis provides a key moment for analysis of Britain's continuing sense of its imperial identity and for consideration of the way in which its broadcasters – the BBC and its newly arrived competitor, Independent Television (ITV) – went about describing and analysing what happened. The incident has also provided a key moment for scholars interested in the fortunes of the impartiality principle – often put at risk when states or other powerful actors deliberately conceal at least part of the truth (Briggs, 1995b; Mills, 2016; Holland, 2006; Barnett, 2011).

In July 1956 President Gamal Abdul Nasser of Egypt announced the nationalization of the Suez Canal, a key transport route for trade moving between East and West (Decree, 1956). By this time the Suez Canal Company had been owned by French and British interests for nearly a century. The British government had already adopted the methods of subterfuge rather than open attack in its covert involvement in the 1953 coup that removed Mohammad Mossadegh, Prime Minister of Iran. (Lynch, 2017). In response to Nasser's action the British Conservative Prime Minister Sir Anthony Eden entered into a secret agreement with the governments of France and Israel to take back control of the waterway by military means, with the additional possibility of removing President Nasser as head of state. As a result of this secret agreement Israeli troops entered the Egyptian Sinai Peninsula in late October 1956 (Briggs, 1995b: 94). Meanwhile British and French forces worked in partnership to bomb Egyptian airfields – without a prior declaration of war – and British and French troops were landed at Port Said on Monday 5 November, with the pretext of making peace between Israel and Egypt and with the intention of taking over the Canal. However, as a result of intervention by the US and the United Nations a ceasefire was agreed on 6 November (Gorst and Johnman, 1997; National Collection of Aerial Photography; Necky, 1991; Hansard, 1958).

The chairman of the BBC Governors at the time, Sir Alexander Cadogan, was a former senior civil servant at the Foreign Office where he had worked closely with Eden before the latter became Prime Minister. Cadogan was also a Director of the Suez Canal Company but acted in a professional manner in authorizing Hugh Gaitskell, Leader of the Labour Party, to speak on the BBC against Eden's policy on Suez in a televised address on 4 November 1956 (Briggs, 1995b: 81; 98). The chairman of the Independent Television Authority – the regulatory body for the new commercial TV network – was the art historian, Sir Kenneth Clark. A memoir later written by the head of Independent Television News (ITN) records that Clark was called in for a private meeting with Eden at which he was asked if he could 'slant the news about Suez'. Clark's response was that the law would not allow him to do this since ITV was required to work 'under an Act of Parliament, which called for impartiality' (Briggs, 1995b: 108–109).[2]

ITN had engaged strongly with the lead up to the military action and an ITN reporter, Ludovic Kennedy, made it clear later that he had refused to follow Foreign Office advice on describing the British landings in Egypt as an 'intervention' and not an 'invasion', noting in a subsequent autobiography that sending in the troops was 'one of the most crassly stupid political acts of modern times' (1989: 244). ITN had also shown its respect for the views of Egypt by interviewing Nasser himself at his home in Cairo the following year when diplomatic relations between Britain and Egypt were still severed (Bell and van Leeuwen, 1994: 131). And the BBC, in their own way, had greatly annoyed the British government by broadcasting an interview with one of Nasser's representatives in London in August 1956, with Eden asking angrily if the BBC staff who had arranged this were 'enemies or just socialists?' (Briggs, 1995b: 87).

There had been a ferociously divided debate on the issue of Suez at a specially arranged sitting of Parliament on Saturday 3 November 1956, with feelings running high both for and against military intervention. The government enjoyed a significant majority of Conservative Members of Parliament but the minority Labour Party, and its leader Hugh Gaitskell, were now emerging as strongly opposed to war. The 'state of uproar' in the House of Commons reflected a high level of disagreement in the country; and various public opinion polls had indicated that although support for Eden ran at around 48% between 39% and 46% of those surveyed were opposed to military intervention (Briggs, 1995b: 96; 100).

During this weekend of political turmoil the BBC broadcast live televised speeches by the leaders of both main parties. On the Saturday night, the 3 November, Eden argued that he was acting only in the interests of peace, sending troops into Egypt with the intention of separating Israeli and Egyptian forces. In the absence of any rapid response by the United Nations his intention, he said, was to 'prevent the forest fire from spreading' and to 'take police action at once'. Since 'three quarters of our oil comes from that part of the world' he argued 'we cannot allow a conflict'. There was no mention of the recent nationalization of the Suez Canal or of what was subsequently discovered to be the prior agreement of the three invading parties – Israel, Britain and France – to act together (Eden, 1956 – for the complete televised speech).

Gaitskell's speech on the following night, the 4 November, also delivered live by the BBC, had an air of desperation about it. His party held only a minority of votes in Parliament. But he clearly rejected 'the idea of trying to solve the Suez Canal problem by force'. The Prime Minister, he believed, was 'utterly discredited' and should accept the resolution of the UN General Assembly demanding an immediate ceasefire. He called for support from 'all those who care for the rule of law ... today we stand as the aggressor, India, Pakistan and Ceylon are all against us ... we have betrayed all that Britain has stood for' and spoke of 'criminal folly ... in defiance of the world we have taken the law into our own hands'. (Gaitskell, 1956 – complete televised speech; Briggs, 1995b: 96).

The timing of the televised speeches is extraordinary. One day after Gaitskell's speech British and French troops landed, battle ready, on Egyptian territory; a day later, on 6 November, the British government executed a complete U-turn and accepted the ceasefire demand from the UN General Assembly, having previously used its veto at the UN Security Council in a vain attempt at preventing UN involvement (Briggs, 1995b).

A greater power had intervened and there were other less visible actors at work. Evidence of military intervention on 5 November had caused a run on the pound, British Treasury reserves were greatly depleted and President Eisenhower refused to allow a rescue by the International Monetary Fund until the British gave a guaranteed date of departure for their troops. The writing had already been on the wall for a couple of months. In early September President Eisenhower had commented, in a confidential letter to Eden, that 'American public opinion flatly rejects the thought of using force' and added 'I do not see how the economy of Western Europe can long survive the burden of *prolonged* military operations, as well as the denial of Near East oil' (Dooley, 1989: 516; 504).

British broadcasters in the mid-twentieth century had been cautious about giving a platform to those opposing the policies of an elected government though they had made some space for the voices of opposition as the rubric of impartiality required them to do. By May of 1958 the British Parliament was noting, pragmatically, the compensation arrangements for the shareholders of the Suez Canal Company and the news story was over (Hansard, 1958). As regards the crisis itself – taken as a way-marker in the history of broadcasting impartiality – a note should perhaps be made that a combination of political secrets held at the heart of government, along with the challenge faced by broadcasters in attempting an explanation of the role of markets and 'big money' in public affairs, made it difficult for viewers and listeners to understand what was happening and why. Though the space accorded to dissent in this case demonstrates at least some 'regard for the opinions of others'.

The US 'fairness doctrine'

When a former member of the US Federal Communications Commission (FCC), Nicholas Johnson, spoke up in support of the idea that broadcasters should respect the principle of 'due regard for the opinions of others' he was defending a long-standing principle in the US – that of the 'Fairness Doctrine'. This concept was upheld by the US courts and the FCC until 1987.

In the pre-Internet world, broadcasting – though regarded as one of the great technologies of the twentieth century – operated largely as a one-way form of communication. It was also seen to be immensely influential. Writing in America in 1969 Johnson saw the 'broadcasting establishment' as 'without question the single most economically and politically powerful industry in our nation's history'. And he captured the sense of marginalization felt by those not accepted into the worlds of television and publishing, citing Martin Luther King on the black experience of exclusion. In King's words their only available option was to 'write their most persuasive essays with the blunt pen of marching ranks' (Johnson, 1970: 6; 12).

Attachment to the goal of fairness in communication placed special duties on the broadcaster, particularly in the 1930s and 40s, reflecting some aspects of the 'new deal' principles of the Roosevelt administration. The underlying philosophy here was arguably consistent with the principles of the already mentioned *Atlantic Charter*; clauses five and six had the aim of 'securing for all improved labor standards, economic advancement and social security' along with the opportunity for all to 'live out their lives in freedom from fear and want' (1941). In the sphere of broadcasting a 1941 ruling from the FCC in the 'Mayflower' case asserted: 'the public interest can never be served by a dedication of any broadcast facility to the support of his own partisan ends'. And it followed from this that: 'the broadcaster cannot be an advocate'. Rather it was the duty of the radio station: 'to provide full and equal opportunity for the presentation to the public of all sides of public issues' (Kahn, 1973: 368).

This public interest approach to licensing obligations continued into the 1960s with a Supreme Court ruling in the Red Lion case (1969). Here the Court noted that ten years earlier Congress itself, as the law-making body, had required broadcasters to:

> operate in the public interest and to offer reasonable opportunity for the discussion of conflicting views on issues of public importance.

The Supreme Court therefore adjudicated that: 'It is the right of the viewers and listeners, not the right of the broadcasters, which is paramount' (Kahn, 1973: 420; 426).

Even in 1983 the Federal Communications Commission still required broadcasters to 'present controversial issues that are of importance to the public' with 'contrasting points of view' (Corner and Harvey, 1996: 260–262). However, quite soon after this – and under pressure from industry voices supported by President Reagan – what had come to be known as the Fairness Doctrine was declared by the FCC to be 'unconstitutional' and abolished in 1987. As a result of this change much greater control over content was passed to the owners of television stations, thus, arguably, prioritizing the corporate free speech rights of broadcasters over the 'need to know' of the viewers and listeners. Opponents of the doctrine continued to argue that it had 'the potential to chill free speech and the free flow of ideas'. Thus, in the summer of 2011, the FCC Chairman, Julius Genachowski, was able to announce that the Doctrine had been 'properly abandoned over two decades ago' and would finally be removed from the FCC rule book (Nagesh, 2011). Others sought to keep alive the regulatory principle of 'fairness' (Pickard, 2018; Harvey, 1998).

The significance of these twentieth-century rulings and arguments is clearly changed by the advent of the Internet where access to various kinds of information is made much easier for individual users of the net. However, being able to afford a broadband subscription along with a computer or mobile as well as being able to access secondary and possibly tertiary education will or might limit the levels of public knowledge and understanding that could derive from Internet access. Just finding the appropriate information to identify and understand the 'conflicting views on issues of public importance' may be difficult. In addition, the advent of social media and the penetration of these media by powerful vested interests may 'tip the scales' in unexpected ways (Moore and Tambini, 2018). It is also worth remembering in this context a pre-Internet comment from communications scholar George Gerbner: 'publics are created and maintained through publications' (cited in Corner, 1995: 7). Thus the choice of publications or of information sources matters greatly.

Impartiality in the UK

The same decade that saw the abolition of the Fairness Doctrine in the US, saw a close ally of President Reagan – Prime Minister Margaret Thatcher – passing UK legislation that confirmed some of the same principles that were to be jettisoned in the US. Thus, Section 90 of the 1990 *Broadcasting Act* required national broad-casting services (in addition to taste and decency requirements) to ensure that:

> ... due impartiality is preserved on the part of the person providing the service as respects matters of political or industrial controversy or relating to current public policy.

It was also expected that 'all expressions of the views and opinions of the person providing the service' should be excluded, in so far as these opinions might relate to the specified 'public policy' matters (1990: 90.2b; 90.3a). Fortunately, this legal suppression of the views of the owners did not prevent vigorous investigation and debate (Finch, 2003). The 1990 Act also introduced a new concept that 'a series of programmes may be considered as a whole' (1990: 90.4). This proved to be espe-cially important for the still new Channel 4 Television, established in 1982 with a remit for 'innovation and experiment in the form and content of ... programmes', and a direction to produce programmes 'calculated to appeal to tastes and interests not generally catered for by Channel 3' (1990: 25.1). The then Chief Executive of Channel 4, Jeremy Isaacs, was keen to commission strongly opinionated pro-grammes that might be allowed to balance each other out over time (Isaacs, 1989:53). And this approach – with an emphasis on avoiding the bland aspects of 'balance' – was also advocated in a 1977 parliamentary report: 'due impartiality should not be a shield behind which the broadcasters shelter but a pass-key to open up public affairs' (Annan, 1977: 269).

The 1990 Act in several respects continued a tradition established by Britain's first piece of broadcasting legislation – the 1954 *Television Act*. This law ush-ered into existence the first privately-owned and advertising-funded institution, Independent Television (ITV) intended to compete, head-on, with the BBC. The 1954 Act outlined what were to be four enduring principles:

- programmes should 'maintain a proper balance in their subject matter and a high general standard of quality';
- 'any news given in the programmes ... is presented with due accuracy and impartiality';
- 'due impartiality is preserved on the part of the persons providing the programmes as respects matters of political or industrial controversy or relating to current public policy';
- 'no matter designed to serve the interests of any political party is included in the programmes' (Television Act, 1954).

When the BBC's new Charter was agreed in 2016 its long-standing Editorial Guidelines continued with a Section 4 dealing specifically with 'due impartiality' (BBC, 2020). This paper is not the place to explore detailed examples of pro-blem cases. But a helpful and sobering account of one high level accusation of lack of impartiality can be found in John Corner's analysis of a BBC news item from 1986. The item deals with a strike by American bombers, based in Britain and targeting particular locations in Libya including the city of Tripoli, with civilian casualties including members of Colonel Gaddafi's family. The Conservative party (in government at the time) argued that the emphasis on 'world-wide condemnation' along with the focus on civilian casualties evidenced a lack of impartiality (Corner, 1995: 68–74).

There have been many examples over the years of other accusations of a lack of impartiality in British television, coming from a variety of political directions. One especially powerful instance is offered in the debate about the BBC and other broadcasters having journalists embedded with their troops, for example during the period of the invasion of Iraq in 2003. BBC journalist Caroline Wyatt reflects on this process:

> In 2003 we had to sign up to embed as official 'war correspondents', sign the Green Book with the MoD [Ministry of Defence] ... and agree that all our copy and images would be screened by our military media minders ... an uncomfortable position for any journalist to be in ... It also meant that we had chosen a side to report from, albeit as part of a wider BBC team that also had journalists and crews inside Saddam Hussein's Baghdad, giving a different perspective and the other side to the war. (BBC, 2013)

By contrast, on occasion, unembedded Al Jazeera journalists had found themselves under attack – deliberately or otherwise – from invading US forces in Baghdad:

> On April 8, 2003, during the US-led invasion of Iraq, Al Jazeera correspondent Tareq Ayoub was killed when a US warplane bombed Al Jazeera's headquarters in Baghdad. (Jamail, 2013)

This was in a situation where the US military had been given the co-ordinates of the local Al Jazeera HQ (Al Jazeera, 2004).

This chapter has suggested that the principle of broadcasting impartiality continues to be an important one in the online and satellite era. However, it also notes that in particular instances of news coverage impartiality may be constrained by the interests of nation states and their governments. Examples are given of the extent to which the 'bias of empire' might undermine the principle of impartiality in British broadcasting with contrasting incidents cited from 1938 and from the Suez Crisis of 1956. Thus, while powerful similarities may be found in contrasting the US advocacy of giving 'due regard to the opinions of others' and the Al Jazeera emphasis on 'the opinion and the other opinion', unresolved issues remain in practice including those of agenda setting, state power and a judgement as to whose concerns matter most.

Notes

1   A European observer, Hugh Miles, noted 'In Arab countries Al-Jazeera is free and all that is needed to receive it is a satellite dish costing about $100. Dishes are now so

commonplace that when impoverished desert Bedouin get married they are no longer given jewellery but a satellite dish instead' (Miles, 2005).
2 The BBC's broadcasting monopoly ended in 1955 with the launch of the first commercial, privately-owned television broadcaster called 'ITV' (short for 'Independent Television'). ITV was established as a network model consisting of several regionally based companies each making their own programmes but increasingly co-operating in the provision of UK-wide services. The network was funded by advertising. A strong regulatory body, the Independent Television Authority was created at the same time by the 1954 Television Act. The ITA had the authority to ensure the provision of a wide range of programmes of high quality, with the legislation requiring impartiality in the provision of news. ITN or Independent Television News was a separate company set up by a consortium of ITV companies to supply news to the network (Sendall, 1982).

References

Abu Jaber, K. (1993), 'Back to the Future', in H. Mowlana*et al.* (eds.) *Triumph of the Image: The Media's War in the Persian Gulf – A Global Perspective.* Boulder: Westview Press, pp. 213–215.

Agar, H. (1973), *The Darkest Year: Britain Alone, June 1940 – June 1941.* London: Bodley Head.

Albaih, K. (2016), 'I remember …', in *Al-Jazeera* (2016b), *Vision: Forward Looking. Mission: Steadfast.* Doha: Al Jazeera.

Al-Jazeera (2004), 'Media and authority: Timeline'. Retrieved from https://www.aljazeera.com/news/2004/3/16/media-and-authority-timeline. Accessed: 24 May 2021.

Al-Jazeera (2006), 'The opinion … and the other opinion'. Retrieved from: https://www.aljazeera.com/archive/2006/10/200841010922766666.html. Accessed: 15 January 2020.

Al-Jazeera (2016a), 'Sykes-Picot: Lines in the sand'. Retrieved from: https://www.aljazeera.com/programmes/aljazeeraworld/2016/05/sykes-picot-lines-sand-160518114434646.html. Accessed: 15 January 2020.

Al-Jazeera (2016b), 'Vision: Forward looking. Mission: steadfast'. Retrieved from: https://network.aljazeera.net/sites/aj_corporate/files/aj_20th_book_-_final_-_english.pdf Accessed: 30 December 2019.

Al-Jazeera (2018), 'Our story'. Retrieved from: https://network.aljazeera.net/about-us/timeline Accessed: 10 February 2020.

Al Jazeera Media Network (2011), *This is Aljazeera 1996–2011.* Doha: Al Jazeera.

Annan Committee (1977), *Report of the Committee on the Future of Broadcasting.* London: HMSO, Cmnd. 6753.

Atlantic Charter (1941). Retrieved from: https://avalon.law.yale.edu/wwii/atlantic.asp. Accessed: 20 January 2020.

Barnett, S. (2011), *The Rise and Fall of Television Journalism: Just Wires and Lights in a Box?*London: Bloomsbury Academic.

BBC (2013), 'Embedded in Iraq: 'A tool in the military tool box, willingly or not'. Retrieved from: https://www.bbc.co.uk/blogs/collegeofjournalism/entries/6d495b61-c8f3-302f-857c-8e95d6838327. Accessed: 24 May 2021.

BBC (2020), 'Editorial guidelines. Section 4: Impartiality and "due impartiality"'. Retrieved from: https://www.bbc.co.uk/editorialguidelines/guidelines/impartiality. Accessed: 15 February 2020.

Bell, P. and van Leeuwen, T. (1994), *The Media Interview: Confession, Contest, Conversation.* Kensington, NSW: University of New South Wales Press.

Briggs, A. (1995a), *The History of Broadcasting in the United Kingdom, Volume 2: The Golden Age of Wireless*. Oxford: Oxford University Press.

Briggs, A. (1995b), *The History of Broadcasting in the United Kingdom, Volume 5: Competition*. Oxford: Oxford University Press.

Broadcasting Act (1990). Retrieved from: www.legislation.gov.uk/ukpga/1990/42. Accessed: 30 January 2020.

Corner, J. (1995), *Television Form and Public Address*. London and New York: Edward Arnold.

Corner, J. and Harvey, S. (eds) (1996), *Television Times: A Reader*. London: Edward Arnold.

Crawford, N. C. (2018), *Costs of War: A Report Published by the Watson Institute of Brown University*. Retrieved from: https://watson.brown.edu/costsofwar/files/cow/imce/papers/2018/Human%20Costs,%20Nov%208%202018%20CoW.pdf ... Accessed: 10 November, 2020.

Decree (1956), *Decree of Gamal Abdul Nasser on the Nationalization of the Suez Canal Company (Cairo, July 26, 1956)*. Retrieved from: https://www.cvce.eu/en/collections/unit-content/-/unit/02bb76df-d066-4c08-a58a-d4686a3e68ff/178e0373-75b1-4c85-bf6b-81c444b33c26/Resources#50e44f1f-78d5-4aab-a0ae-8689874d12e6_en&overlay Accessed: 10 February 2020.

Dooley, H. J. (1989), 'Great Britain's "Last Battle" in the Middle East: Notes on Cabinet Planning during the Suez Crisis of 1956'. *The International History Review*, 11(3) 486–517.

Eden, A. (1956), *BBC History*: 'Anthony Eden, Prime Minister, 3 November 1956' [Televised speech]. Retrieved from: https://www.bbc.co.uk/programmes/p07t36gr. Accessed: 15 February 2020.

Falk, R. (1992), 'Twisting the U.N. Charter to U. S. Ends', in H. Mowlana et al. (eds.), *Triumph of the Image: The Media's War in the Persian Gulf – A Global Perspective*. Boulder: Westview Press, pp. 175–180.

Federal Radio Commission (FRC) (1928), *Second Annual Report of the Federal Radio Commission to Congress*. Retrieved from: https://www.fcc.gov/document/second-annual-report-federal-radio-commission-congress-1928. Accessed: on 15 February 2020.

Finch, J. (ed.) (2003), *Granada Television: The First Generation*. Manchester: Manchester University Press.

Gaitskell, H. (1956), *BBC History*: 'Hugh Gaitskell, Leader of the Labour Party, 4 November 1956' [Televised speech]. Retrieved from: https://www.bbc.co.uk/programmes/p07t37px. Accessed: 14 February 2020

Gorst, A. and Johnman, L. (1997), *The Suez Crisis*. Abingdon and New York: Routledge.

Hansard (1902), Joseph Walton, House of Commons Debates, 22 January. Retrieved from: https://api.parliament.uk/historic-hansard/commons/1902/jan/22/british-interests-in-persia. Accessed: 20 January 2020.

Hansard (1958), Suez Canal Compensation Agreement. *HL Deb*. 14 May, Vol. 29, cc. 299–304. Retrieved from: https://api.parliament.uk/historic-hansard/lords/1958/may/14/suez-canal-compensation-agreement. Accessed: 15 February 2020.

Harvey, S. (1998), 'Doing It My Way – broadcasting regulation in capitalist cultures: The case of "fairness" and "impartiality"', *Media, Culture and Society*, 20, 535–556.

Hobsbawm, E. (1987), *The Age of Empire: 1875–1914*. London: Weidenfeld and Nicolson.

Holland, P. (2006), *The Angry Buzz: This Week and Current Affairs Television*. London and New York: I.B.Tauris.

Isaacs, J. (1989), *Storm Over 4: A Personal Account*. London: Weidenfeld and Nicolson.

Jamail, D. (2013), 'Iraq: The deadliest war for journalists'. Retrieved from: https://www.alja zeera.com/news/2013/4/11/iraq-the-deadliest-war-for-journalists. Accessed: 24 May 2021.

Johnson, N. (1970), *How to Talk Back to Your Television Set*. New York: Bantam Books.

Johnson, N. (1988), 'With due regard for the opinions of others'. *California Lawyer*, 8, August, 52–55. Retrieved from: https://ir.lawnet.fordham.edu/cgi/viewcontent.cgi?arti cle=1748&context=faculty_scholarship Accessed: 15 February 2020.

Kahn, F. J. (ed.) (1973), *Documents of American Broadcasting*, 2nd edition. Englewood Cliffs, NJ: Prentice Hall.

Kennedy, L. (1989), *On My Way to the Club*. London: Harper Collins.

Lahlali, M. (2011), *Contemporary Arab Broadcast Media*. Edinburgh: Edinburgh University Press.

Lynch, D. J. (2017), 'Britain pressed US to join Iran coup against Mossadegh'. *Financial Times*, 8 August. Retrieved from: https://www.ft.com/content/9ea5c5e0-7c50-11e7-9108-edda 0bcbc928. Accessed: 10 November 2020.

Lynch, M. (2006), *Voices of the New Arab Public: Iraq, Al Jazeera and Middle East Politics*. New York: Columbia University Press.

Malek, M. (2020), 'Oil in Iran between the Two World Wars'. Retrieved from: www.ira nchamber.com/history/articles/oil_iran_between_world_wars.php. Accessed: 10 January 2020.

Mangeri, L. (2006), *The Age of Oil: The Mythology, History and Future of the World's Most Controversial Resource*. Westport, CT: Praeger.

Mansfield, P. (2019), *A History of the Middle East*, 5th edition. London: Penguin.

Miles, H. (2005), 'Al-Jazeera: How Arab TV News Challenged the World'. *Hachette Digital*. Retrieved from: https://books.google.co.uk/books?id=EFt3RiYWcA4C. Accessed: 10 January 2020.

Mills, T. (2016), *The BBC: Myth of a Public Service*. London: Verso.

Moore, M. and Tambini, D. (2018), *Digital Dominance: The Power of Google, Amazon, Facebook and Apple*. New York: Oxford University Press.

Nagesh, G. (2011), 'FCC officially kills Fairness Doctrine, wiping it from rules', *The Hill*, 22 August. Retrieved from: https://thehill.com/policy/technology/177775-fcc-stri kes-83-outdated-rules-including-fairness-doctrine. Accessed: 19 February 2020.

National Collection of Aerial Photography (no date) 'Suez Crisis or Operation Musketeer'. Retrieved from: https://ncap.org.uk/feature/suez-crisis. Accessed: 14 February 2020.

Necky, P. L. (1991), 'Operation Musketeer – the end of empire. A study of organisational failure in combined operations'. Retrieved from: https://apps.dtic.mil/docs/cita tions/ADA240214. Accessed: 10 February 2020.

Pickard, V. (2018), 'The strange life and death of the Fairness Doctrine. Tracing the decline of positive freedoms in American policy discourse'. *International Journal of Communication* 12, 3434–3453. Retrieved from: https://repository.upenn.edu/cgi/view content.cgi?article=1770&context=asc_papers. Accessed: 18 February 2020.

Sakr, N. (2001), *Satellite Realms: Transnational Television, Globalization and the Middle East*. London and New York: I.B.Tauris.

Sands, P. (2005), *Lawless World: America and the Making and Breaking of Global Rules*. London: Allen Lane/Penguin Books.

Schayegh, C. and Arsan, A., eds. (2015), *The Routledge Handbook of the History of the Middle East Mandates*. Abingdon and New York: Routledge.

Sendall, B. (1982), *Independent Television in Britain, Vol. 1: Origin and Foundation, 1946–62*. London and Basingstoke: Macmillan Press.

Stanley Foundation (2006), 'Interview with Jamil Azar, Al Jazeera senior anchor'. Retrieved from: http://vps.stanleyfoundation.org/articles/2006memr_azar.php. Accessed: 10 January 2020.

Television Act, 1954. Current Law Statutes Annotated for 1954.

Yale University Library (2009), 'Early Arabic printing'. Retrieved from: https://www.library.yale.edu/neareast/exhibitions/earlyprinting1.html. Accessed: 10 February 2020.

3   Freedom of expression and social responsibility

Contested worldviews on media ethics

Noureddine Miladi

Introduction

The French newspaper Charlie Hebdo and Danish cartoons controversies ignited global and cross-culture differences regarding the boundaries of free speech. The publication of blasphemous cartoons about Prophet Muhammad have had inevitably global impact and the concerns they raised have not remained local anymore. Although the proponents of absolute free speech may argue that both cases are local in nature and they reflect the fundamental universal value of free speech, their impact has proven global in its outreach and extremely controversial. The repercussions of such media content have been dramatic in light of the outbreak of dissent from affected communities and the snowball effect it generated both in France and beyond.

However, the condemnation which such controversies caused should be put in context. Firstly, the war on Iraq, rise of Islamophobia across Europe, continuous Israeli occupation of the Palestinian land and Western support to Israel, all consolidated the overwhelming sense of resentment and despair. Secondly, Muslim minorities in the West feel targeted, largely by the tabloid media. Thirdly, the power of social media nowadays in disseminating information has turned the local into global. What concerns a small community in a remote place may become an issue internationally debated. Understandably then, the global resonance of the cartoons saga is a case in point, as it echoed not only among diasporic communities in the West but also in various Muslim countries in Asia and Africa.

This example begs the question of where should the media draw the line between the universal value of free speech and respect of sacred religious symbols. Should freedom of expression have limits? Which value comes first, social responsibility or individual freedoms? Does freedom of the individual supersede all other rights especially in relation to the collective common good?

This chapter attempts to unpack this debate and analyse the roots as well as divergent views on the debate. I discuss the development and politicization of the issue. I also argue that political cartoons as a form of satire should not be different from any other journalistic genre when it comes to raising ethical considerations. In the midst of the controversial responses on the cartoons, this

DOI: 10.4324/9781003203551-5

chapter proposes that the key contentious issue seems not between those who believe in free speech and those who do not as the French president Macron seems to imply. The problem lies in fact with those who unreservedly employ insult and blasphemy as normative modes in their discursive speech and not considering what impact that may have on society. It also lies between those who believe in responsible free speech across the board in relation to race, faith or colour and those who have double standards in terms of applying free speech (Miladi, 2021). Moreover, in this chapter, free speech is not regarded as absolute but a right that should be regulated in the public sphere. I argue that freedom of expression as a cornerstone of a democracy should aim to nurture a society based on tolerance, social peace, non-discrimination and open-mindedness.

Background to the Danish cartoons and Charlie Hebdo controversies

The Danish cartoons controversy has been considered a catalyst for what can be called a series of cultural misunderstandings and later deliberate blasphemy targeting the Muslim faith and its sacred symbols. The publishing of mocking cartoons regarding Prophet Muhammad by Danish newspaper '*Jyllands-Posten*' On 30 September 2005 resulted in thousands of complaints against the newspaper along with anger and grief by phone, email and fax messages. From Asia to Europe and the Arab World, Muslims took to the streets in protest condemning what they considered a direct attack on their Prophet.

As for Charlie Hebdo magazine, it was launched in 1970 after the French government shut down its predecessor *Hara-Kiri*. The same artists moved to the new company since then doing the same job (Waxman, 2018). The publication's history reveals a profound scepticism and incessant hostility towards figures of authority both in France and beyond. It is also notorious for its controversial content, described by many as distasteful and sometimes racist (Cohen-Almagor, 2015; Keck, 2016; Perolini, 2020). It also received criticism from religious groups since its satire amounts to hate speech. Critics find its content too derogatory and insulting to sacred symbols of various faiths (Lawless, 2015; Guyer, 2015; Hanafi, 2009; Amnesty International, 2020; Kabir, 2021). The newspaper became top news in 2015 when it published blasphemous cartoons of Prophet Muhammad, one of them depicting an image of him, named, and wearing a turban in the shape of a bomb. It was not the first time the magazine published mocking cartoons about Islam and Muslims, but it was the first instance associating the Prophet Muhammad with terrorism. Muslims found such cartoons very insulting and uncorroborated. It also helped provoke an extreme reaction from two gunmen, who stormed the Paris headquarters of the magazine on 7 January the same year and killed 12 journalists. Soon after this terrorist attack, a few newspapers across Europe published the cartoons as a form of solidarity with Charlie Hebdo and in support of uninhibited free speech while hundreds of others abstained. Various reputable newspapers and other media outlets in the West considered the reprinting and dissemination of such cartoons irresponsible journalism.

The above catastrophic event left the world in shock and in spite of the criticism erupting on the newspaper, no Muslim countries nor mainstream Muslim groups condoned the killings or the use of force to silence free speech. However, in order to understand the complexity of what led to this tragic incident and for the sake of deciphering the French approach to Islam and its culture, it is worthwhile briefly digging into the history of the French colonization era and its ramifications. It is also important to unveil the impact of France's problematic assimilation strategies of its immigrant communities over the last few decades.

The problematic assimilation agenda in France

To make sense of the continuous tension between France and its Muslim minority community, it is incumbent to fathom France's legacy of its colonial history and how it perceives its immigrant community. The origins go back to World War I, which had marked the arrival of tens of thousands of Algerians, Moroccans and Tunisians brought as soldiers to fight along the French army in French Imperial wars. The French government at the time brought 173,000 Algerian men, about 25,000 of whom died in the war. It also brought 56,000 from Tunisia, of whom 120,00 lost their lives. As for Morocco, it also sent tens of thousands of its troops to defend Paris at the time; hundreds of them died and many others settled in France since then (Seljuq, 1997). Moreover, in 1919 a further 119,000 Algerian youth were taken to Paris to work in French factories and help meet the demand of the war time industry (Laroui, 1970: 351). It was after WWII that immigrants from the North African countries started arriving in large numbers. The need for manpower to assist in rebuilding the French industry, and the low French birth rates made it possible for hundreds of thousands of immigrants to settle in France in a non-organized immigration. They were employed in factories, agriculture and mines.

However, in spite of their sacrifices and their contributions to rebuilding post-War France, both Arab and African immigrants were systematically marginalized. French historian Ralph Schor described the xenophobic attitudes of the French public to immigrants as early as between the Wars when he wrote: 'To everyone, the existence of foreigners in France is one of the biggest political, social and economic problems' (quoted in Bockel, 1991: 47). As a result of this general atmosphere of the time, the National Office for Immigration was launched during the same period in an attempt to organize the arrival and assimilation of immigrants following particular marginalization agenda.

This in fact reflected the same spirit since the late eighteenth-century France, when the well-known Judge Domat expressed the official stance of the French state. A peculiar look at the non-French, echoed in the official policies of the successive French governments towards Arabs in France, when he wrote:

> We exclude foreigners from public responsibilities, because they are not part
> of the core in the society that forms the nation-state. These responsibilities

require loyalty and affection to king and the law, which we do not presume in a foreigner. (cited in Bockel, 1991: 220)

Therefore, even until recently, the participation of immigrants in public life has provoked many debates. The official understanding of integration of immigrants in French society means assimilation; i.e. foreigners asked to completely denounce their religious and cultural baggage and fully adopt the French laicism identity in order to qualify for a full recognition. If they wish to integrate in the national community, Domat argues:

> We, therefore, request them to assimilate, i.e. to engage in a personal endeavour that leads them to denounce their foreign identity in order to gradually assume the French one: Hence, the access to the French nationality will be at the end of the road. (Bockel, 1991: 220)

In addition to rejection of their cultural heritage, other causes have stood as further impediments to the positive integration of the North African Arabs, for instance the systematic discrimination against them in terms of job opportunities, education and public office. Although this minority shares the same problems with the black community, Arabs have the highest unemployment rates in France (Chignier-Ribonlon, 1999: 149). The highest percentage of those employed are found in construction jobs.

Ethnic segregation as official and systematic preference

Discrimination in terms of space and geographical distribution formed a systematic plan enforced by the policies of successive French governments during the second half of the 20th century. Arab immigrants are confined to certain quarters in Paris as well as in other cities in France, from which they cannot depart. Renting and buying properties (far from the poorer areas) is hardly possible for a high percentage of families among this community. This has resulted in negative repercussions about access to jobs, good education and other social privileges. To mention one's address as '*Vaulx-en-Velin*', for instance, or any other Arab quarter, means the immediate elimination of a candidate from any potential recruitment for a job. Young people know it very well, argues Frank Chignier-Ribonlon, 'when you are Arab, add to that from the Vaulx, you will have no chances' (1999: 154).

Dress and other cultural symbols have also attracted much debate during the last few years. The *hijab* (veil or Muslim women's headscarf) issue has sparked yet again a turmoil that has been simmering on both sides: both among French Muslims and mainstream French society, especially the right-wing groups and educational establishments. The French political and educational system seeks the complete assimilation of the non-French into French culture and way of life. To be a true French citizen, 'foreigners' must denounce any form of 'cultural baggage' and conform to the rules of laicism. Therefore, the wearing of religious dress like headscarf for Muslim students has been banned in educational establishments.

The French government's decision to introduce a new law in 2003 banning conspicuous religious symbols in state schools and other state institutions divided public opinion in France and further brought the issue of integration of the second and third generation immigrants in French society to the forefront. Although this legislation, which took effect in 2004, included other religious signs apart from the *hijab* like the *kippas* and large crucifixes, it has been seen to be implicitly against the existence of the *hijab* in public schools. As a consequence, large demonstrations broke out in Paris and other larger cities in response to it to defend the rights of Muslim girls to wear the veil.

These developments increased the mistrust of younger immigrants towards French social justice, as it called to question their sense of identity and belonging. The double standards and feeling of insecurity and marginalization the younger generations are facing has increased their frustration and negative attitude towards the French system as a whole. France, the land of human rights? When it comes to Muslims, there are no rights, argue many of the disappointed youths (Cesari, 1998: 11). The denial of these rights includes personal choices for dress and fashion. 'In the name of secularism, or laïcité, Muslims in France cannot wear religious symbols or dress in schools or in public sector jobs' (Amnesty International, 2020).

Critiquing the French approach to individual freedoms

Scholars who have challenged the French approach to freedom of speech agree that nowadays we cannot use the notion of freedom as a vehicle for social exclusion. Personal freedom cannot be fragmented or made to fit. French historian François Burgat argues that:

> The problem is not adopting the French understanding of secularism, and not only the issue of respect for religions, or 'French values.' The problem is precisely the inability of France to respect the values and slogans it preaches. There is no doubt that freedom of expression is one of the most important universal values. However, France's practice in this topic differs from one freedom of expression to another, according to the person practicing that freedom. (Ayman, 2020)

In February 2021, French President, Emanuel Macron, stepped on the bandwagon in support of the blasphemous cartoons about Prophet Muhammad. He expressed a rather controversial official stance in that the cartoons are part of the right to speech. However, it is evident that not everyone in France upholds his views on the cartoons saga. The arbitrariness of this view was widely condemned. Also, while he condoned the notorious cartoons as a form of free speech, French President Emmanuel Macron sued French billboard owner, Michel-Ange Flori, who depicted him as Adolf Hitler. 'Flori, who owns about

400 billboards in the southern region of the Var, wrote that "I have just learnt that I will be heard at the Toulon police station following a complaint by the president of the Republic... So in Macronia you can make fun of the prophet's..., that's satire, but to make the president look like a dictator is blasphemy"' (van der Made, 2021).

Ségolène Royal (former French Minister and presidential candidate) expressed his disagreement and criticized Macron's bold insult of Islam and Muslims. He argued that 'The head of state should continue with freedom of speech not with cartoons that insult millions of Muslims around the world. All freedom of speech in the French law is limited by the prohibition of public insult and putting the others in danger' (Al-Jazeera, 2020).

Fine line between free speech and hate speech

In his study on the Danish cartoons about Prophet Muhammad, back in January and March 2006, Hervik (2008) contends that newspapers mainly employed negative frames to report the story about the cartoons saga. The key frame relates to picturing those opposing the cartoons as anti-free speech and that Danish newspapers such as *Jyllands-Posten, B.T.* and *Ekstra Bladet* were fighting a battle of values. By contrast, predominantly *Politiken* newspaper was against the cartoons where it disparaged the emphasis on free speech and argued that 'Demonization of Muslims is the issue, not free speech' (Hervik, 2008: 60). Although *Politiken* represented a rare voice in Denmark, it dared criticize *Jyllands-Posten* as 'drumming up nationalism and anti-Islamic attitudes'. The government too was accused of further escalating the events and the Prime Minister was described as a 'stubborn, arrogant manipulator' of the discourse on free speech (Hervik, 2008: 60).

It is worth noting that the resentment felt by Muslims around the world was not a new sentiment but preceded by various cases and incidents such as Salman Rushdi's *Satanic Verses* published in 1988, or the film *Innocence of Muslims*, which appeared in two versions in 2012: *The Real Life of Muhammad* and *Muhammad Movie Trailer*. But as much as this caused uproar in Muslim countries, it raised questions in the West about why the fuss? Among other issues, Prince Charles argues that these issues have signalled the death of morality. He contends that '... we have lost a sense of the sacred in our public life ... in each one of us there is a distant echo of this sense of the sacred'. This moral compass is what some argue needs to be reclaimed, as the loss of morality in human action has meant losing meaning and purpose.

However, the audacious responses from such newspaper as *Politiken* seem a rare occurrence in France when the Charli Hebdo affair broke out back in 2015. The case study analysis of the newspaper's cartoons on Prophet Muhammad brought to the fore debates concerning the thin line that exists between humour and offensive speech, freedom of expression and respect of sacred symbols revered by others. But, what was missed out in the French media discourse was the contention that editors of Charlie Hebdo seem to value free speech more than human dignity. They also seem to appreciate freedom of expression at the expense of cementing the social fabric of French society. For instance, it is evident that the cartoons publication was supported by many on the basis of free speech. Various examples can be cited from Europe and beyond. Whether from politicians or influential media outlets, the stance was that free speech vis-à-vis this case should be condoned. However, supporting free expression in this case is in contrast with other examples related to media freedom. To borrow from Hanafi (2009: 146) 'To present the Prophet Mohammad as a symbol of terrorism, as is done in one of the cartoons, is no different from presenting Prophet Moses as the symbol of right-wing Israelis' actions against Palestinians, an association that would be rightly condemned as anti-Semitic and is prohibited by the laws of many European countries'.

Therefore, one could argue that the ill-conceived cartoon drawings have not in fact consolidated any sense of the right to express oneself freely. On the contrary, it should be considered a form of hate speech that has led to hatred towards Muslims, alienation and violence. This is not to mention negatively affecting international relations between various countries and the Arab and Muslim world. Numerous occurrences can be quoted here which highlight the thin line between ethical journalism and illegal piracy, or free speech and hate speech. WikiLeaks for instance, since its appearance, has disclosed hundreds of thousands of official documents about USA foreign policy in addition to the activities of various other governments from around the world, which is a noteworthy case in point. By all standards, the released cables were sensitive and shocking but considered by some as precious material evidence about state corruption. Journalists, political activists and human rights organizations applauded the daring stance of Julian Assange and his investigative journalism project. Some even nominated him for a Nobel Prize, while the American government labelled him as a terrorist and called for his arrest for criminal offences.

Another example related to the Catholic Church in France, which on 11 March 2005 won a case against the clothing designers Marithe et François Girbaud. The controversial advertisement released at the time by the company based on Leonardo da Vinci's Christ Last Supper (BBC News, 2005). The image portraying 'female version of the fresco, which includes a female Christ' was considered 'a gratuitous and aggressive act of intrusion on people's innermost beliefs', by the court judge (BBC News, 2005). A similar ad previously challenged in Italy by the advertising watchdog, which argued that the ad's use of Christian symbols 'would offend the sensitivity of part of the population'. The Catholic Church used a similar argument against the advert, which also showed two of the apostles embracing a bare-chested man in jeans. A warning put by Italian Lawyer Thierry Massis that 'When you trivialise the founding acts of a religion, when you touch on sacred things, you create an unbearable moral violence which is a danger to our children'. 'Tomorrow, Christ on the cross will be selling socks' he further argued (BBC News, 2005).

Free speech and social responsibility

Based on the above discussion, one may wonder to what end do advertising companies trivialize the image of Jesus? We may also ask a similar legitimate question: what is beneficial to society in the portrayal of Prophet Muhammad, or in fact any prophet or religious symbol, as a terrorist or sexual pervert? Does insulting such figures serve freedom of speech any good? Or does it in fact have the very opposite effect? Surely, the answer to those questions brings us back to the aim of human speech. Because the acceptance of the 'right to blaspheme' discourse, I would argue, goes in line with the populist reductionism approach, which merely seek demonization of the other. In the words of Emmanuel Todd:

> Yes, of course, there's a right to blaspheme, but one must also have the right to say that blasphemy is not a priority and that it's idiotic … I was demanding the right to counter-blasphemy: to say that the caricatures of Muhammad were obscene, rubbish, totally historically out of sync and the expression of rampant Islamophobia. And, for saying that, I was accused of complicity with the terrorists. (Quoted in Hanafi, 2020)

Going back to the ethics of journalism practice, its basic ethos say not to cause harm to others, in this case to audiences/ readers who are at the receiving end. What is at stake here is that harm can be interpreted differently in different contexts. Yet one basic understanding of harm is what Feinberg (1984) calls the action that causes a 'set back' to others. What he meant by this is every spoken word, act or attitude that may negatively affect other people's interests. Riddle (2014) further explains this by arguing that a 'set back' includes any action that may impede people's health or career or endanger their prospects for personal development. The media are key according to Riddle, especially when violent content is seen to cause harm. If for instance 'a television programme prevents a child from being able to sleep for weeks on end, the interests of that child have clearly been set back' (2014: 70). The same goes when it comes to violent action, which leads to direct imitation.

The Islamic tradition attributes significant importance to human speech. The Qur'an reads that 'not a word does a person utter without having a "vigilant" observer ready "to write it down"' (Qur'an 50:18). 'Speak kindly to people' (Qur'an 2:83), 'and do not repel them but speak to them a noble word' (Qur'an 17:23), 'then give them a kind word' (Qur'an 17:28), 'speak to him with gentle speech' (Qur'an 20:44), 'be with the truthful' (Qur'an 9:119), 'if an evildoer brings you any news, verify ⬛it⬛ so you do not harm people unknowingly, becoming regretful for what you have done' (Qur'an 49: 6).

Therefore, in order to understand why Muslims cherish the figure of Prophet Muhammad, we may borrow the 'value theory' as a sociological framework to understand Muslims and Islamic cultural values. Value theory provides a detailed insight into the meaning of values among different groups and the significance of those values in their everydayness. As a moral philosophy, it encompasses various approaches that examine human values determining the practices of any given community. Hanafi (2009: 138) analysed the case of the Danish cartoons, which reflect what he calls 'the cultural hegemony and power structure deployed against undesirable groups' in France. He argues that 'Different groups of people may hold or prioritize different kinds of values (such as social justice) influencing social behavior' (Hanafi, 2009: 137). People's values do determine their actions and inclination. 'Values, culture, and social identities are determinative of behaviour, just as they are simultaneously shaped by the actions of their 'carriers' and members' he further argues (Hanafi, 2009: 138).

As a culmination to the debate on the Prophet Muhammad's cartoons controversy, the European Court of Human Rights (ECHR) ruled on 25 October 2020 that freedom of speech does not extend to 'defaming' prophet Muhammad. The court also ruled that the language used 'goes beyond the permissible limits of an objective debate' and 'could stir up prejudice and put at risk religious peace'. So, what makes Charlie Hebdo, along with its supporters such as the French government, insist that portraying Prophet Muhammad as a terrorist is a legitimate work of journalism and part of the value of free of speech?

But, as discussed above, there obviously exists a dichotomy between those who believe in free speech without limits and those who think there should be limits to what we write and utter. Between those who uphold the universal value of free speech with responsibility towards others, and those who maintain that freedom of expression should not come with accountability. In other words, the key contentious issue seems not between those who believe in free speech and those who do not as the French president seems to imply. The problem lies in fact with those who unreservedly employ insult and blasphemy as normative modes in their discursive speech and do not consider what impact that may have on society. It is also between those who believe in responsible free speech across the board in relation to race, faith or colour and those who have double standards in terms of applying free speech (Mildai, 2021).

In order to move the discussion forward, one may argue that responsible free speech entails an attempt at balancing citizens' right to freedom of expression with the rights to have religious feelings of various faith groups protected, in the meantime social peace and stability preserved in society. The right to freedom of expression is a qualified right: it allows expression that might 'offend, shock or disturb' but prohibits 'insults', 'abusive attacks' and 'hate speech' (Shah, 2017). Few argue that '... failure to prosecute Jyllands-Posten and Charlie Hebdo violates Articles 9(1) of the European Convention, the Danish Criminal Code and the French Freedom of Press Act 1881. Relying on ECHR's jurisprudence, I argue that the values of the Convention and democracy aim to nurture a society based on tolerance, social peace, non-discrimination and broad-mindedness. Public spaces in any society are shared areas and no single group – religious and non-religious – can monopolize nor intimidate it (Shah, 2017).

The Ethical Journalism Network (2020) aptly stated that:

> It's a tricky task to judge exactly what constitutes hate-speech. There is no accepted international definition and the tolerance levels of speech vary dramatically from country to country ... Freedom of speech is a right for everyone, including politicians and public figures and it is the job of the journalist to ensure that everyone has their say, but that does not mean granting a license to lie, or spread malicious gossip or to encourage hostility and violence against any particular group.

Is freedom of expression arbitrary?

The tragic murder in October 2020 of French teacher, Samuel Paty, ignited again debates about not only the boundaries of free speech but also who has the right to it. Paty had used cartoons defaming Prophet Mohammad as an example about freedom of speech in front of children in class. His decision to use such cartoons with young children also raised concerns regarding the arbitrariness of respect for freedom of expression in France. In what follows, I analyse the official French stance on this matter based primarily on President Macron's statements. Many have expressed the arbitrariness of how the value of free speech has been upheld. According to Perolini (2020), free speech does not seem to apply to everyone. He argues that 'The French government is not the champion of free speech that it likes to think it is. In 2019 a court convicted two men for 'contempt' after they burnt an effigy depicting President Macron in a peaceful protest'. Upholding ethical standards vis-à-vis free speech seems inconsistent when we refer to Macron's views on the Prophet. According to him, the cartoons fall into what freedom of speech encompasses. However, mocking political figures or symbols of the French republic is to him profane and an offence accountable for before the law.

In March 2015 the BBC reported that street preacher Michael Overd was cleared by a court of a charge by the Muslim community in Taunton, Summerset who accuse him of causing 'racially-aggravated' sentiment (BBC News, 2015). In an open street preaching gathering, Overd described Prophet Muhammad as a paedophile. Although shortly before this acquitting he was charged under the Public Order Act of condemning homosexuality as a sinful act. Giving the impression that 'some harms to some groups are worthy of legal redress, while others are not' (Keck, 2016: 8). The national demonstration of 11 January 2015 in response to the Charlie Hebdo massacre of 7 January signals that the pains of some people are more worthy than other people's traumas.

> Meanwhile, most European states have banned some forms of Islamophobic speech, but not the ones to which European Muslims themselves most object. The failure of these bans to cover published caricatures of the Prophet Muhammad (PBUH) has been a chief source of the double-standard complaint ... As a result, for European Muslims, existing law sends a clear signal of unequal citizenship. (Keck, 2016: 11)

Moreover, Keck (2016: 8) refers to a court case by the European Court of Human Rights (ECtHR) which interpreted the European Convention on Human Rights (ECHR) as protecting 'the religious feelings of believers' from 'provocative portrayals of objects of religious veneration'.

> In contemporary Europe, national legislatures could choose to extend the same sort of bans to Islamophobic and homophobic speech that they have extended to racist and anti-Semitic speech or they could choose to relax their existing bans on racist and anti-Semitic speech … the ECtHR could, in theory, try to nudge member states in either direction. In other words, ECtHR judges could find in ECHR Article 10's free expression provision a mandate that states provide greater freedom to express hateful ideas than they currently do. (Keck, 2016: 9)

Further examples can be listed by going back in history when in 1970 the French government shut down Hara-Kiri cartoons newspaper (which preceded Charlie Hebdo) for insulting one of the symbols of the French republic, President Charles de Gaul. Hara-Kiri's issue of 16 November 1970, 'announced the death of French President Charles de Gaulle via a cover line riff that conflated his death with a tragic nightclub fire that was also in the news at the time. The story deemed "too soon," … as well as a bad influence on youthful readers and not in line with the nation's values' (Waxman, 2018). 'Freedom of speech has never been absolute anywhere ever. In realistic terms, it is always measured against existing circumstances' (Fuller, 2020).

Another example is the Charlie Hebdo's cartoonist known as 'Sini' who was fired for being accused of sarcasm and labelled anti-Semitic (Ayman, 2020). Also, in November 2020, 'French police interviewed four 10-year-old children for hours on suspicion of "apology of terrorism" they apparently questioned Samuel Paty's choice to show the cartoons' (Amnesty International, 2020). 'But those who do not agree with publishing the cartoons also have the right to voice their concerns. The right to freedom of expression also protects the ability to criticize the choice to depict religions in ways that may be perceived as stereotypical or offensive. Being opposed to the cartoons does not make one a 'separatist', a bigot or an 'Islamist' (Amnesty International, 2020). Moreover, 'While the right to express opinion or views that may be perceived as offending religious beliefs is strenuously defended, Muslims' freedom of expression and religion usually receive scant attention in France under the disguise of Republican universalism' (Amnesty International 2020).

> In 2001, French cartoonist Denis Leroy was convicted of complicity in condoning terrorism for publishing, two days after the 9/11 attacks, a rendering of the planes hitting the World Trade Center in New York City, with a caption appearing to praise the attackers: 'WE HAVE ALL DREAMT OF IT … HAMAS DID IT.' (The caption was a parody of a well-known advertising slogan in France: 'You have dreamt of it … Sony did it'. (Keck, 2016: 15)

Should free speech have limits?

A constructive way of understanding political cartoons as a form of expression is to consider them subject of discussion, ways of educating the public about politics or exposing political corruption. Guyer (2015: 41) contends that '... the most effective political cartoons may initially provoke outrage and condemnation but ultimately promote dialogue, an exchange—in comment strands, on letters pages, at kitchen tables ... The cartoon isn't the end. The cartoon is almost the beginning'.

Discussing freedom of expression is always a delicate exercise and generates heated discussions. When we speak about exercising one's rights of freedom of expression, we should also think about the potential harm that may impact others, which leads us to consider social responsibility for what we say, draw and publish.

The central concern, then, is whether there are limits to freedom of expression: is there anything that cannot be said, or circumstances under which things cannot be said? Following on from these questions there is a cluster of other queries: If freedom of expression does have limits, just how can these limits be defined? Is the causing of offence one of the possible limits to freedom of expression? How can we identify the boundaries of what might legitimately be considered offensive? Is there any kind of right to take offence? Cartoons, like any other media content, should be weighed for its news value.

Going back to the cartoons controversy, it is a legitimate question to ask what service to society do the Muhammad cartoons have if they create an atmosphere of resentment? Or in the words of Akhlaq (2017: 9) 'How much do such cartoons inspire its audiences toward acquiring further rationality, improve humanity, or further progress'?

It is worth noting that the response of the French government was fully supportive of the schoolteacher who showed a blasphemous caricature of the prophet Mohammad, whereas in Belgium the authorities arrested a teacher after he showed similar images to his students around the same period (DW, 2020). In the UK, religious education (RE) is embedded in the National Curriculum, where pupils may learn about the fundamentals of other faiths. Educators may teach, among other religious subjects, Islam, Muslim celebrations, the Prophet Mohammad's life and Islamic culture.

That is why, as within France, the responses to the catastrophic killing of the Charlie Hebdo journalists varied between other European countries and across the world. Slogans such as *Je suis Charlie, Ahmed, or Juif*, reflected compassion with the victims but also others, and through the slogan *Je ne suis pas Charlie* people showed disapproval of the offensive line the publication had been taking. The essence of the debate is a clash between two opposing views on freedom of expression. One, put forward by *Jyllands-Posten* and its supporters, is that what occurred was simply an exercise of a right of freedom of expression that is central to the effective working of democratic society. The other, as expressed by Muslims opposing the publication of the cartoons, is that there are limits to freedom of expression, and that one of these is the denigration of religious symbols and through that insulting the community of religious people.

Philosopher Régis Debray is not an exception when he argues that one's freedom 'ends where the rights of others begin' (cited in Hanafi, 2009: 148). This was also the point of Amnesty International: Freedom of speech 'carries responsibilities and it may, therefore, be subject to restrictions in the name of safeguarding the rights of others' (2006).

While exercising its right under French law to mock all faiths and religious symbols, Charlie Hebdo is not right to exercise it at all times. Is it correct to insist on incessant mockery while it is evident that this has become upsetting to millions of Muslims in France and around the world? Does the condition of multiculturalism in France for instance call for certain respect?

Cohen-Almagor (2015) argues that 'Most of us can remember words that cut deeper than wounds. The parent who says you are a failure. The lover who admits betrayal. The women who laugh at you. The men who humiliate you. The employers who dismiss your dearest ambitions with a snort. They leave scars that may never heal. Likewise, religious belief can be so much a part of your identity that an assault on it is an assault on everything that makes you who you are'.

Grounds for universal freedom of speech

The most widely accepted formulation of the right of free expression is enshrined in the United Nation's (1947) Universal Declaration of Human Rights. Article 19 states that: 'Everyone has the right to freedom of opinion and expression; this right includes freedom to hold opinions without interference and to seek, receive and impart information and ideas through any media and regardless of frontiers'.

The revised codes of ethics of the Society of Professional Journalists (SPJ) emphasize the accountability of journalists to 'their readers, listeners, viewers and each other'. 'Ethical journalism treats sources, subjects, colleagues and members of the public as human beings deserving of respect. Journalists should: Balance the public's need for information against potential harm or discomfort. Pursuit of the news is not a license for arrogance or undue intrusiveness'. 'Show compassion for those who may be affected by news coverage … Consider cultural differences in approach and treatment' (Society of Professional Journalists, 2014).

It is important to note here that many news organizations abide by the above principles. Various critics in the West have also been outspoken regarding Islamophobia in the media and the cartoons controversy. Few consider it part of a constructive discourse. For instance James Taranto, from the Wall Street Journal, commented on the campaign 'Everybody Draw Mohammed Day' that

> The problem with the 'in-your-face message' is not just that it is inconsiderate of the sensibilities of others, but that it defines those others – Muslims – as

being outside of our culture, unworthy of the courtesy we readily accord to insiders. (Peter, 2011)

Tom Kent, Standards Editor for the Associated Press (AP) and a leading figure in the Ethical Journalism Network, explained

> AP tries hard not to be a conveyor belt for images and actions aimed at mocking or provoking people on the basis of religion, race or sexual orientation ... While we run many photos that are politically or socially provocative, there are areas verging on hate speech and actions where we feel it is right to be cautious. (Lawless, 2015)

In sum and in order to reconcile the notion of universalism with the postmodern notion of pluralism we need to consider the presence of limits for our freedom when it comes to freedom of others. Media coverage in France of the cartoons saga did not help to reach an agreement on the limits of free speech. On the contrary, scores of tabloid newspapers, radio and television channels demanded Muslims' full acceptance of blasphemy as part of what makes a French citizen, even if it regarded the Prophet Mohammad. The 'I am Charlie' slogan paraded by media outlets has come to signify 'I am French', insinuating that to disapprove of Charlie Hebdo's cartoons is not to belong to the French community and its values. The relaunch of Charlie Hebdo after the massacre was inaugurated with an even more insulting sexual image related to Prophet Muhammad. The newspaper was also subsidized from a government fund to cover its losses.

> ... repetitive and systematic blasphemy against Muhammad, the central character in the religion of a group that is weak and discriminated against, should – whatever the law courts have to say – be treated as an incitement to religious, ethnic or racial hatred. (Todd, 2015: 14)

Social problems in France seem reduced to the rise of terrorism among immigrants in the suburbs. 'The focus on Islam actually reveals a pathological need among the middle and upper strata to hate something or someone, and not just the fear of a threat arising from the lower depths of society ... Xenophobia used to be confined to the poorer sections of society, but these days it is moving up to the top of the social structure. The middle and upper classes are seeking their scapegoat' (Todd, 2015: 15).

In many ways, the general spirit of supporting unlimited free speech in France is a product of Western modernity, which has its roots in the Enlightenment. The Enlightenment project was a revolution of the authority of kings and queens and rejection of the hegemonic power of the church both morally and intellectually.

> The Enlightenment's spirit is the spirit of dialogue rather than monologue. It is a call to association instead of domination. In other worlds, although

cosmopolitanism is central for the Enlightenment, its respect for other cultures as well as its realism teach that freedom of expression is different from freedom of insulting. (Akhlaq, 2017: 78)

A fundamental Islamic value that continually resurfaces in the teachings of the Qur'an and Prophet Muhammad's tradition is freedom of conscience and tolerance of diversity of opinion even if it is about rejecting the faith. Since acceptance of faith is based on free will, none should be forced into accepting the Islamic creed, or follow a certain way of life. The Qur'an clearly established that '[t]*here is no compulsion in religion*' (2: 256). The second Kaliph, Omar bin Al-Kattab warned against any form of control of people's free will: 'How dare you enslave people while their mothers brought them to this world as free spirits' (Islamweb, 2021).

At the same time there is a call in the Qur'an to be respectful to others when you critique them. 'let not a people ridicule [another] people; perhaps they may be better than them; nor let women ridicule [other] women; perhaps they may be better than them. And do not insult one another and do not call each other by [offensive] nicknames' (Qur'an, 49: 11).

The world is more interconnected now than during any other time in the history of humanity. The French rejection of cultural diversity goes against the spirit of the modern era, in which every cultural/ faith group attempts to justify its *raison d'être* based on who really they are. Forcing straight-jacket cultural norms on minorities living in France is a form of totalitarianism that violates the UN declaration of human rights. Furthermore, compelling a minority faith group to accept blasphemy of their religious symbols as if it is a basic rule of freedom of expression is against the spirit of the Enlightenment.

Conclusion

In the case of the cartoon controversy there has been persistent refusal to consider it a case of blasphemy and defamation against Muslims. Both the Danish and French Law makers ignored calls made by Muslims for the inclusion of Islam in their laws on blasphemy and hate speech and the legal regulation of persistent mockery of their faith. The Muhammad cartoons specifically have been considered deeply hurtful to Muslims, in much the same way that Holocaust denial is hurtful to Jews and a manifestation of anti-Semitism. The ignorance towards Muslims' calls to protect their faith from abusive media sends a signal that as a minority they should tolerate 'free speech' of the majority even if it is hurtful and discriminatory. As suggested by Keck (2016: 22) 'To date, the ECtHR ... has echoed and amplified the signal sent by European states that their Muslim minorities are due less than fully equal protection of the laws'.

The critiques levelled in various works on the Charlie Hebdo saga and which oppose the official French double standards in dealing with freedom of speech are too manifest to ignore. The inevitable polarization of opinion has resulted in the media becoming a crucial political actor. Various news outlets chose their side by supporting Macron's stance. The government's 'spin doctors' have largely influenced the agenda of various TV and radio channels in addition to national newspapers. Unfortunately, 'Charlie Hebdo became a symbol of the freedom of expression, a value threatened by an intransigent and increasingly aggressive Islam and the European Muslims who practice it' (Tsagarousianou, 2016).

Unlike how the media or certain politicians portray the debate, the cartoon controversy should not be understood as a choice between liberal democracy and religious fundamentalism. It should be seen as an attempt to strike a balance between freedom of expression and respect to others. Between the right to free speech and social responsibility. For the sake of co-existence and mutual understanding there should be a prioritization of respect for others and recognition of their rights and feelings, which goes above freedom of expression.

Freedom of expression is not an absolute right. Journalists Under article 10 of the ECHR, and indeed under governing laws of every country in the world, should act responsibly and expected to serve the public interest. This is normally voluntary and self-driven given the autonomy under which the media function. This function should be in tune with a fine balance of the right to free speech and sense of social responsibility. As public bodies with potentially vast influence, both good and harmful, they are morally obligated to act with the prudence and respect that promotes peace and tolerance, not division and hatred.

References

Akhlaq, H. S. (2017), 'The source of the problem: Both Islam and the West have forgotten their roots (A philosophical study of the Charlie Hebdo Shooting). *Journal of South Asian and Middle Eastern Studies*, 40(3), 74–84.

Al Jazeera (2020), 'Beyond authority' (TV documentary), 20 November. Retrieved from: https://www.youtube.com/watch?v=lsho2IkNA9w. Accessed: 22 November 2020.

Alouane, Y. (1979), *L'Emigration Maghrebine en France*. Tunis: Cérès Production.

Amnesty International (2006), 'Freedom of speech carries responsibilities for all'. 7 February 2006.   https://www.amnesty.eu/news/freedom-of-speech-carries-responsibilities-for-all-0250/. Accessed: 2 March 2021.

Amnesty International (2020), 'France is not the free-speech champion it says it is'. 12 November. Retrieved from: https://www.amnesty.org/en/latest/news/2020/11/france-is-not-the-free-speech-champion-it-says-it-is/. Accessed: 22 November 2020.

Ayman, S. (2020), 'The French academic, Bourgat: Racist discourse against Muslims is a common international industry with Arab despotic regimes'. *Al-Jazeera.Net*. Retrieved from: https://www.aljazeera.net/news/cultureandart/2020/11/16 Accessed: 20 November 2020.

BBC News (2005), 'French court bans Christ advert'. Retrieved from: http://news.bbc.co.uk/2/hi/europe/4337031.stm. Accessed: 3 November 2020.

BBC News (2015), 'Taunton street preacher convicted for homophobic sermon'. Retrieved from: https://www.bbc.com/news/uk-england-somerset-32017649. Accessed: 19 March 2021.

Bockel, A. (1991), *L'Immigration au pays des Droits de l'homme*. Paris: Pblisud.

Cesari, J. (1998), *Musulmans et Republicains: Les Jeunes, L'islam et la France*. Paris: Editions Complex.

Chignier-Ribonlon, F. (1999), *L'integration de Franco-Magrebins. L'exemple de l'est Lyonnaise*. Paris: L'Harmattan.

Cohen-Almagor, R. (2001), *Speech, Media and Ethics: The Limits of Free Expression*. Basingstoke: Palgrave.

DW (2020), 'Belgian teacher suspended over Prophet Muhammad cartoon'. 30 October 2020. https://www.dw.com/en/belgian-teacher-suspended-over-prophet-muhammad-cartoon/a-55454081. Accessed: 2 March 2021.

Feinberg, J. (1984), *Harm to Others: The Moral Limits of the Criminal Law*. New York: Oxford University Press.

Fuller, E. G. (2020), 'Islam, cartoons of the Prophet, and murder'. Retrieved from: https://grahamefuller.com/islam-cartoons-of-the-prophet-and-murder/. Accessed: 10 November 2020.

Guyer, J. (2015), 'Political cartooning after the Charlie Hebdo attacks'. *Nieman Reports*, Winter 2015 2015.

Hanafi, S. (2009), 'Cultural difference or cultural hegemony? Contextualizing the Danish cartoon controversy within migration spaces'. *Middle East Journal of Culture and Communication*, 2(2009), 136–152.

Hanafi, S. (2020), 'Macron's populism and Islam. The election strategy that forges a new populism through its conceptualization of freedom of expression and "political Islam"'. Open Democracy, 2 November 2020. Retrieved from: https://www.opendemocracy.net/en/openmovements/macrons-populism-and-islam/. Accessed: 3 November 2020.

Hervik, P. (2008), 'Original Spin and it Side Effects. Freedom of Speech as Danish News Management', in E. Eide, *et al.* (eds), *Transnational Media Events: The Mohammed Cartoons and the Imagined Clash of Civilisations*. Goteborg: Nordicom, pp. 59–80.

Islamweb (2021), 'The story of how dare you enslave people ...'. Retrieved from: https://www.islamweb.net/ar/fatwa. Accessed: 19 May 2021.

Kabir, S. N. (2021), 'The Muhammad cartoon controversy in New Zealand newspapers'. *Journal of Arab & Muslim Media Research*, 14(1), 143–156, doi:10.1386/jammr_00028_1.

Keck, T. (2016), 'Hate speech and double standards'. *Constitutional Studies*, 1(1), 95–121. Retrieved from: https://uwpress.wisc.edu/journals/journals/cs.html. Accessed: 19 March 2021.

Laroui, A. (1970), *History of the Maghreb*. Princeton: Princeton University Press.

Lawless, J. (2015), 'Je suis Charlie? Attack sparks debate on free speech limits'. *Associated Press*, 10 January. Accessed: https://apnews.com/article/d627a6d81bce40ccbe59033808cfce27. Retrieved: 27 November 2020.

Miladi, N. (2021), 'The discursive representation of Islam and Muslims in the British tabloid press'. *Journal of Applied Journalism and Media Studies*, 10(1), 117–138.

Perolini, M. (2020), 'In Macron's France, free speech is only for some'. *Newsweek*, 13 November, retrieved from: https://www.newsweek.com/france-freedom-expression-1547310. Accessed: 22 November 2020.

Peter, T. (2011), '100 lashes if you don't die laughing' and 3 other Muhammad controversies'. *Christian Science Monitor*, 2 November. Retrieved from: https://www.csmonitor.com/World/Global-Issues/2011/1102/100-lashes-if-you-don-t-die-laughing-and-3-other-Muhammad-controversies/Everybody-draw-Muhammad-day. Accessed: 27 November 2020.

Pickard, V. (2010), 'Reopening the postwar settlement of US Media: The origin and Implications of the social contract between media, the state and polity'. *Communication, Culture and Society*, 33(2), 170–189.

Riddle, K. (2014). 'The Case of Media Violence: Who is Responsible for Protecting Children from Harm?', in M. Drumwright (ed.), *Ethical Issues in Communication Professions: New Agencies in Communication*. Abingdom: Routledge, pp. 65–84.

Seljuq, A. (1997), 'Cultural conflicts: North African immigrants in France'. *The Journal of Peace Studies*, 2(2).

Shah, N. A. (2017), 'Charlie Hebdo: Testing the limits of freedom of expression'. *Muslim World Journal of Human Rights*, 14(1), 83–111.

Society of Professional Journalists (2014), SPJ code of ethics (revised 6 September 2014). Retrieved from: https://www.spj.org/ethicscode.asp. Accessed: 27 November 2020.

Todd, E. (2015), *Who is Charlie? Xenophobia and the New Middle Class*. Cambridge: Polity.

Tsagarousianou, R. (2016), 'Muslims in Public and Media Discourse in Western Europe: The Reproduction of Aporia and Exclusion', in S. Mertens, and H. de Smaele (eds), *Representations of Islam in the News: A Cross-Cultural Analysis*. Lanham: Lexington Books, pp. 3–20.

Waxman, O. (2018), 'They didn't change at all': The persistence of Charlie Hebdo'. *Time*, 5 January. Retrieved from: https://time.com/5071192/charlie-hebdo-anniversary-history/. Accessed: 25 November 2020.

4   Global media ethics: Ideology, politics and eurocentrism

Mazhar Al-Zo'by

Introduction

The advent of capitalist modernity in its transnational mass-mediated digital forms has clearly inspired a critical discussion about the universal ethical virtues of media in modern history. At the heart of this discussion is the emergence of an ideological and epistemological formation of a hegemonic Western account of universal media ethics which is predominantly enshrined in Eurocentric liberal philosophical discourse. Such universal ethical project continues to assume the function of a process that was 'begun and finished in Europe, from where it has been exported across ever-expanding regions of the non-West. The destiny of those [non-Western] regions has been to [simply] mimic, never quite successfully, the history already performed by the West' (Mitchell, 2000: 1). While Eurocentric liberal ethical discourse is often complex and contradictory, as Shohat and Stamp (2014: 2) maintain, 'Eurocentrism as a mode of thought might be seen as engaging in a number of mutually reinforcing intellectual tendencies or operations'. In this regard,

> Eurocentric discourse projects a linear historical trajectory leading from classical Greece (constructed as 'pure,' 'Western,' and 'democratic') to imperial Rome and then to the metropolitan capitals of Europe and the US. It renders history as a sequence of empires: *Pax* Romana, *Pax* Hispanica, *Pax* Britannica, *Pax* Americana. In all cases, Europe, alone and unaided, is seen as the 'motor' for progressive historical change ... Eurocentrism attributes to the 'West' an inherent progress toward democratic institutions ... while elides non-European democratic traditions. (ibid.)

Conversely, and afflicted by the doctrinal complicities of colonial and orientalist representations, the non-Western is always presumed to be constrained by the cultural imperatives of irrationality, tradition, and localism, and therefore unable to symbolize in reason and universal moral principles. Unfit to construct abstract critical imagination, the non-Western mind was believed to be confined in the 'mimetic faculty, the prisoner of images from which it could not obtain a spectatorial distance' (Mitchell, 2000: 21), and thus prove itself as a rational

DOI: 10.4324/9781003203551-6

and universal subject of timeless truths and ethics. In contrast, in the European intellectual tradition, as Chakrabarty reminds us, the modern Western subject

> Came to be defined as the one who could occupy such a position of disembodied observer of the world. Freed in this way from the traditional constraints of habit or belief and transcending their localism, it was said, modern [Western] subjects could discover a universal faculty of reason and employ it to represent to themselves the experiences and feelings of others and to submit their own interior life to its pedagogy. (quoted in Mitchell, 2000: 20)

In this context, Western universal ethics represent a rhetorical strategy of civilizational difference that produce and reinforce the superiority of the European brand of intellectual production versus the moral and cultural inferiority of the non-West. Correspondingly, the framework of universal ethics is often extoled as the exclusive and normative domain of European liberal tradition. Thus, its epistemic narratives of ethical principles postulate a vision of a global geography in which the West inhabits its singular core.

The deployment of the notion of a singular monopoly of cultural and historical universal principles further finds its clear expression in Huntington's thesis on the clash of civilization. The fundamental premise on which Huntington's assumption is made is the uniqueness of Western universal values and beliefs as expressed in the cultural project of modernity and its civilizational (rationality, reason, democracy, and freedom) ethos. Culture (and therefore civilization) is a fault line between 'moderns' and 'premoderns'. However, and given the superiority and exclusivity of Western values, Huntington suggested that the West should abandon its effort to export such ideals as universal values because these values have little significance for other cultures given their inabilities to apply them to their own traditions, which are plagued with internal stagnation and flaws (Al-Zo'by, 2015a).

Whether the use of culture and civilization is deployed to articulate radical difference with the non-Western as in the case of Huntingtin, or as an ideological strategy to subsume and homogenize the other within the domain of the Eurocentric worldview, the discourse of universal ethics remains largely dismissive of the complex heterogonous forms and genealogies of its own history. In this respect, 'little theoretical work from non-Western perspectives has entered the epistemological discussion of universal ethical principles for media and journalism' (Rao and Wasserman, 2007, 29–30). While there has been some recognition of cultural differences within some European dominant paradigms, it remains too insignificant to constitute a serious transformative and critical scholarship on media ethics. This, it has been argued necessitates, an 'intervention in the development of universal ethical principles for media worldwide' (Ibid, 29), in which the non-Western indigenous historical conditions and cultural epistemologies should 'influence how media professionals and journalists make ethical decisions' (ibid). As Christians and Traber (1997) contend,

Can theoretical models be developed that are explicitly cross-cultural? Can moral principles be identified that are universal within the splendid variety of human life? Will a multicultural comparative ethics replace the dominant canons, most of them North Atlantic and patriarchal? (viii)

These more diverse alternative accounts, presumably, make possible a less Eurocentric framework in the formation of universal media ethics. However, simply expanding the history of such global media ethics to represent it as a global experience inescapably 'tends to homogenize other histories as aspects of the emergence of the West' (Mitchell 2000: xii). In other words, the simple epistemic inclusion of the 'non-Western' within the existing dominant Western framework risks the uncritical normalization of Western liberal narratives on media ethics, and paradoxically, re-affirms its globalization. Likewise, the discourse of alternative indigenous ethical frameworks should not be seen as ideologically neutral, and beyond the constitutive domain of power and domination. In fact, like their Eurocentric counterpart, the so-called 'indigenous' models are always imbued in networked power relations, and dynamically shaped by the currents and counter currents that animate most human societies. Thus the discourse of alternative media ethics runs the risk of the uncritical appropriation of some form of facile indigenization, and yet never generating a viable alternative ethical framework.

In order to analyse this intrinsic and complex interplay between homogenization and heterogenization, and between universalization and localization in global media ethical discourse, this chapter seeks to critically and broadly examine the emergence and formation of liberal global ethical principles as predominantly Eurocentric discourse. It will first chronicle the general rise of Western moral paradigm from Greek philosophy to the Enlightenment, and then it will assess its transplantation into modern media ethical discourse. Therefore, to disrupt and transform this prevailing narrative of media ethical ideologies, this chapter argues it is insufficient to simply investigate its polemical site of production; one must also seek its fundamental deconstruction and reproduction. To transform Western universal narratives on media ethics, its presence and influence, this chapter asserts that universal ethics must be shaped across geographical and cultural differences yet never disavow its universality. This is not intended as a categorical rejection of the very possibility of universal objective media ethics, but rather as a critique of the historical and cultural claims underling its Eurocentric singularity.

It should be stated form the outset that the critique levelled against Western liberal ethical practices is not grounded in the conventional viewpoint that these practices represent a deviation from the ideal conceptions of moral virtues. The chapter recognizes rather well the prevailing critique of some media's vested complicity with capitalist ideological strategies, marketing manipulations, fabrication of consent, and their crucial role in the promotion of an ethno-nationalist discourse in the form of disinformation or misinformation. However, the critique advanced here is primarily focused on Western media's professed claim for universal truth and objectivity. The chapter does not categorically imply that Western media ethics do not perform a vital function in political life and public ethics. Nevertheless, it contends that such ethical values are shaped by what Derrida (1976) calls '*logocentrism*'. This according to this formulation, 'means the reliance on fixed a priori transcendental meanings, that is, universal meanings, concepts and forms of logic that exist within human reason before any other kinds of thinking occur' (Barker, 1999: 73). Similarly, such logocentric logic relies on the notion of binary divisional structure of meaning in which a conceptual oppositional hierarchy of social and cultural values is maintained by a process of privileging, excluding and devaluating. Thus such binary forms of representations ultimately render and guarantee the claim for universal objectivity, transcendental rationality and timeless truth by appropriating and devaluing its presumed opposite, namely, 'parochial subjectivity', 'irrationality', and 'local traditions and practices'.

The philosophical foundations of Western liberal media ethics

The critical epistemological as well as the ontological debates regarding universal media ethics have been profoundly shaped by the broader discussion on general moral ethics. In the contemporary European context, and as stated above, Western liberal traditions have projected the legacy of this ethical discourse as a tanshistorical, linear, and singular trajectory travelling from ancient Athens to *Pax Americana*. Hence, the entire domain of liberal ethical philosophy has emerged as a distinct mode of Western scholarship, yet advanced and promoted as a timeless universal project. While rules of justice and codes of ethical injunctions have existed throughout time and in diverse traditions, from The Code of Hammurabi to the Ten Commandants, and the Vedas to the Dao; nonetheless, the genealogical foundations of universal ethical precepts are presented as the unfolding of the history of the West, and traced to classical Greek philosophy. Perceived as the first systemic endeavour to elaborate the underlying principles of moral conduct, the fundamental mode of ethical inquiry in the classical Greek tradition focused primarily on human actions and activities as articulated and manifested in notions of truth, justice, happiness (*eudaimonia*), and the virtue (*aretê*) of moral conduct and ethical judgement. Purportedly transcending the mythical explanations that characterized the ancient mode of moral contemplations, classical Greek philosophy sought to refocus the role of logic, science and reason as the foundation of universal truths (hence the assertion that it gave rise to global normative and metaethics). In other words, Greek ethical deliberations were seen as a search for truth, through rationality and reason. Correspondingly, the Socratic philosophical maxims and its ensuing intellectual legacy sought to overcome the traditions of scepticism and relativism that shaped many existing traditions, including that of the Sophists who were decried for their philosophical commitment to moral uncertainty and scepticism.

Mainly employing the didactic *maieutic* logic as a rhetorical strategy, the central feature of the Greek ethical doctrine is the moral capacity of the subject as an agent of moral judgement (often defined as virtue ethics). This was in contrast to most modern philosophical traditions where the ethical imperative is located in the human action itself and not in the agent's moral disposition for moral conduct (normative ethics).[1] For example, for Socrates and Plato to certain extent, the moral virtue of any conduct is qualified based on the character, attitude and values expressed by the moral agent. This is 'usually expressed in the claim that virtue is knowledge, implying that if one knows what is good one will do what is good'. (Parry and Thorsrud, 2021: no page).Thus the fundamental presupposition advanced in this dictum is that moral virtues are the outcome of moral instruction: teaching right from wrong and good from vice will unquestionably lead to a moral judgement, and therefore a moral conduct. By contrast, action-centred ethical virtues (normative ethics), as discussed blew, primarily focus on human actions and activities, their consequences and values, laws and the order to which they adhere. Characterizing principally most contemporary expressions of ethical theories, this philosophical thought can be represented in two different approaches

> Those who judge the morality of an action on the basis of its known or expected consequences are *consequentialist*; those who judge the morality of an action on the basis of its conformity to certain kinds of laws, prohibitions, or positive commandments are *deontologists*. The former include, e.g., those *utilitarians* who say an action is moral if it provides the greatest good for the greatest number. *Deontologists* say an action is moral if it conforms to a moral principle, e.g., the obligation to tell the truth. (ibid. – my emphasis)

My point here, however, is not to claim that classical Greek moral ethics (at least in its Socratic and Platonic expressions) were entirely dismissive of action-centred morality. Rather, my point is to illustrate how being a just and ethical person, in this case, comprises values of character intrinsic to the moral person, 'in the light of which they decide what actions justice requires of them and are inclined or disposed to act accordingly' (ibid.).

Socrates and Plato always grounded ethical and moral dispositions in the theory of ideal universal forms and knowledge, however, Aristotle rejected the notion of idealism and linked ethical virtues to 'practical wisdom'. More specifically, for Aristotle to know what was good and what is evil, or what is right and what is wrong is not sufficient to exhort moral conduct. A moral agent, he contended, has to also choose to act morally. In this regard,

> In the *Nicomachean Ethics*, Aristotle limits the heavy rationalism of Socrates and Plato in his description of virtuous action. *Hermeneia* belongs to the higher and purer operations of the mind but is not just theoretical knowledge (*episteme*); nor is it technical skill (*techne*) since it concerns more than utility. *Hermeneia. Practical wisdom. Phronesis.* Making a moral decision entails doing the right thing in a particular situation and the concrete needs interpretation. (Christians et al, 2008: 144)

In essence, this approach positioned Aristotelian ethics in the domain of practical reason where habits, customs along with social construction would converge on moral and ethical choices, which crucially expand the scope of human capacity in ethical reasoning. Aristotle's ethical and moral philosophy would thus provide the foundation for Middle Ages Christian moral theology. This was especially true for Thomas Aquinas doctrines in his *Summa Theologiae* on the role of free will and the ethics of virtue. Analogously, Aristotle's ethics, especially in the area of common good and moderation, had forged the tenth-century Muslim philosopher, al-Fārābī, and his notions of moral and rational virtues.

The central debates which animated the philosophical dialogues on ethics in classical Greek culture would endure as the pervasive feature of subsequent Western thought until the age of the Enlightenment. These pressing ethical investigations were fundamentally related to whether knowledge is a universal and objective principle as Plato maintained; or whether truth and virtues can be discerned deductively through reason and observation as Aristotle confirms. Moreover, is justice an expression of subjective and relative virtues mediated by social and cultural perspectives as the Sophists strongly suggested, or is justice a transcendental value irreducible to traditions and customs as Socrates argued? Thus, for virtue ethical theories (from the Greeks to St Augustine), God was the prime mover of ethical values. However, for European Reformation and Renaissance ethical philosophers God was replaced by 'man' in philosophical deliberations, but not as the inspiration for ethical thrust. Nevertheless, the philosophical and ethical objectivity in the Reformation era 'drew ideas from three aspects of early Greek thought: rational explanations, collections of fact, and an attitude of impartiality' (Ward 2004: 40). The revival of Greek thought in the age of European humanism, therefore, shifted the attention from theology (religion) to humanity (mainly European). It accorded notions of human freedom, choice, rationality, reason, and judgement primacy and 'universal' status in ethical reflections. Accordingly, the complexity and diffusion of a variety of ideas and ideals associated with moral principles, their nature and their application gave rise to an array of ethical philosophical approaches. The most prominent of these were 'normative ethics', 'metaethics', and 'applied ethics'. In all of these approaches, and as indicated above, the ethical concern is with moral action and conduct itself and not the ethics of virtue as was the case with Greek philosophy.

As one of the foundational moral theories, normative ethics is an expansive field of ethical inquiry concerned with the 'articulation and the justification of the fundamental principles that govern the issues of how we should live and what we morally ought to do' (Driver, 2007: 32). In this respect, normative ethics provides an evaluative matrix that is intended to both compel as well as guide moral action. As alluded to above, normative ethical theories are represented by two distinct approaches: the 'deontologists' approach (derived from the Greek term *deon*, which means 'duty') and the 'consequentialist' approach, which observes that the 'rightness' or 'wrongness' of a moral conduct is contingent chiefly on their outcome and consequences. The deontologist ethical doctrine is rooted in the presumed rational principles of obligation, duty, impartiality, fairness and justice. What makes a choice or an action ethical, in this case, is its observance and correspondence with moral standards, laws and positive injunctions. If confronted with a moral dilemma, 'right' will always precede and supersede the maximization of the good or its teleological or consequential benefit. That is, the expected consequence of an action, for the deontologists, is less privileged morally than the conformity to the truth and principles that express ethical values.

While Kantian ethics (after the German Philosopher Immanuel Kant, 1724–1804) is espoused by many philosophers and numerous ethical ideals from religious commandments to universal rights declarations, it unreservedly represents the central paradigm as well as the most systematic instantiation of deontologist form of ethical codes. Kant's central concept of 'The Categorical Imperative' elaborates this maxim and advances the twin pillars of universality and the principle of humanity that underlie this ethical dictum. According to Kant (1969), acting morally is to 'act only according to that maxim by which you can at the same time will that it should become a universal law' (44). Additionally, a moral judgement is that which is qualified as an end in itself and never as a means or a utility for further ends. Therefore, a moral agent, as Kant contends, should 'act so that you treat humanity, whether in your own person or in that of another, always as an end and never as a means only' (ibid., 54). The compelling drive of the Categorical Imperative mode of ethics, then, is never the consequentialism of the moral action itself, but in the universal rules, obligations and logical consistency in the practice of these moral actions. Ethical objectivity, it follows, is not the correspondence between judgement and its external factual object, but rather of a particular judgement and its consistency with the law and code of practical reason.

The contrast to the deontologist moral principal outlined above is the consequentialist and utilitarian form of normative ethics. The central doctrine in this philosophy is that moral judgement should be instructed and determined solely by the benefits generated by an action's outcome and therefore its instumentalization and maximization of the collective good of that action. This ethical approach was espoused and embraced by many Western philosophers, from the Greek Sophists to Machiavelli (1469–1527), and from Jeremy Bentham (1747–1832) to John Stuart Mill (1806–1873) to John Rawls (1921–2002). Its core analytic feature is 'utilitarianism', which holds that 'the moral quality of a person's actions, or character, is solely determined by the effects of the action or character trait in question' (Driver, 2012: 6). In formulating utilitarianism's essential character as a form of moral evaluation, the Enlightenment moral philosopher, Francis Hutcheson observed in 1746 that in judging the moral virtues of actions among many,

> ... or to find which of them has the greatest moral Excellency, we are led by our moral Sense of Virtue to judge thus; that in equal Degrees of

Happiness, expected to proceed from the Action, the Virtue is in proportion to the Number of Persons to whom the Happiness shall extend; (and
here the Dignity, or moral Importance of Persons, may compensate Numbers) and in equal Numbers, the Virtue is as the Quantity of the Happiness,
or natural Good; or that the Virtue is in a compound Ratio of the Quantity
of Good, and Number of Enjoyers. In the same manner, the moral Evil, or
Vice, is as the Degree of Misery, and Number of Sufferers; so that, that
Action is best, which procures⊠ the greatest Happiness for the greatest
Numbers; and that, worst, which, in like manner, occasions Misery.
(Hutcheson, 2004: 125)

For Hutcheson, like many proponents of the utilitarian moral philosophy,
including Hutcheson's own student, Adam Smith, when confronted with the
competing ethical choices, one is guided to perform a moral calculation
according to which one discerns the highest and maximum benefits regardless of
duties and responsibilities. In fact, Hutcheson's approach implores a moral
obligation to violate the law 'if in some very important Instances, the Violation
of the Law would be of less evil Consequence than Obedience to it' (ibid., 126).

An emergent dilemma, therefore, is whether some utilitarian ethical theories
uphold, or can fully account for, the notion of inalienable rights (individual or
collective) if the moral calculus is entirely grounded in consequential utility.
This, in turn, has led to the rise of two variations of utilitarian ethical models:
act-utilitarianism and rule-utilitarianism. Both models attempt to address and
redress the question of alienability within moral actions and ethical conclusions.
In this regard,

Act-utilitarianism holds that act X is right if and only if doing X will have
consequences at least as good for all affected parties as the consequences of
any alternative act open to the agent. Rule-utilitarianism holds that act X is
right if and only if doing X is in accord with a set of moral rules the general acceptance of which will have consequences at least as good for all
affected parties as the general acceptance of any alternative set of rules.
(McConnell, 2000: 33)

While normative ethics is fundamentally concerned with the epistemic and
analytic examination of moral judgement, metaethics, differently, is concerned
mainly with the origin, nature, scope and character of moral values. The commitment to moral categories such as absolute truth, universal reason, objective
realism has been a persistent and pervasive feature in Western metaethical discourse. In this regard, Western metaethics seeks to pursue an axiomatic paradigm of ethical principles based on universal and timeless values. Within this
ethical philosophical tradition, 'moral realism' occupies a prominent status,
which is often imported into applied and practical moral concerns and practices
such as media ethics. Adhering to the conviction that ethics should be grounded
in universal moral truths, Western moral realists envision that ethical values

must transcend individual and particular beliefs, as they are objective and not subjective values. Like classical Greek moral philosophy, moral realism anchors the precepts of moral objectivity in the scientific view of human nature and its inalienable needs.

However, unlike that of classical moral tradition, the foundation of moral property evolves from biological and social needs to the practices of universal rational human agency. Whether based on a naturalistic or idealistic view of moral norms, Western liberal metaethics, like its normative counterpart, has largely affirmed its moral codes and ethical judgement. These are both constituted and expressed by truth, objectivity, reason, and more importantly, independent of cultural norms and practices. The quest for transcendental 'moral certainty' in Western ethical paradigms has generated a discourse of 'epistemic objectivity', thus inspiring forms of ethical science, which has shaped modern media and information moral codes and virtues.

Western media ethics and public ethics

The transplantation of Western normative and metaethical moral ideals into codes, standards and practices of applied ethics finds its manifest expressions in the field of media and information ethics. At the centre of media ethics is the convergence of the purported metaethical values such as 'universal truth' and human dignity, as well as normative ethical principles such as duty, rules, objectivity and impartiality. The label 'journalist' initially appeared in the seventeenth century to designate a practice that was intended to differentiate it from the profession of 'men of letters who wrote in learned journals' (Ward, 2004: 89). However, the modern liberal evolution of media ethical practices as a moral creed coincided with rise of journalism as a general profession. Prior to that, the term 'journalist' was used infrequently but sporadically in the context of the nascent public communication industry (with the advent of print technology and print culture). The first article to use the word 'ethics' in its title was 'The Ethics of Journalism' by the Catholic writer William Samuel Lilly, whose 1889 article in The Forum became a chapter in his book On Right and Wrong' (Ferré, 2009: 16). In this regard, the author emphasized a combination of public interest (as a form of consequentialist ethics) as well as commitment to truth (as a form of deontologist ethics). Journalism as a profession, accordingly, conferred some 'freedom of the press' in essence 'to state facts, to argue upon them, to denounce abuses, to advocate reforms' (Lilly, quoted in Ferré, 2009: 16).

Closely related to the ascendance of journalism as a profession was the rise of liberal political institutions in the West, where questions concerning public political life were inextricably linked to the emergence of public criticism, citizenship, constitutional liberties and economic choice. As such, journalism and the press at large were accorded the label and status of the 'Fourth Estate' in order to illustrate the critical role they assume in public life and public ethics in so-called 'democratic societies'. Although with uncertainty, the phrase 'Fourth Estate' is generally attributed to the Irish philosopher, Edmund Burke, who is believed to have announced it in Parliament:

... there were Three Estates in Parliament; but in the Reporter' Gallery yonder, there sat a Fourth Estate more important than they all. It is not a figure of speech, or a witty saying; it is a literal fact – very momentous to us in these times. Literature is our Parliament too. Printing, which comes necessarily out of Writing, I say often, is equivalent to Democracy; invent Writing, Democracy is inevitable ... Whoever can speak, speaking now to the whole nation, becomes a power, a branch of government, with inalienable weight in lawmaking, in all acts of authority. (quoted in Ward, 2004: 170)

The fundamental assumption underlying the association of free media as the guardian of public ethics, freedom, and truth is the notion that it represents free societies and is ultimately the force that maintains freedom itself. Therefore, democracy, public ethics, and freedom are deemed to be both cultural values and political virtues which constitute the essence of the Western liberal project. So widespread was the discourse about 'press' in public life by the end of the eighteenth century that it was enshrined in the First Amendment in the US Constitution, thereby endowing it equal protection with religious rights. According to the First Amendment, 'Congress shall make no law respecting an establishment of religion or prohibiting the free exercise thereof; or abridging the freedom of speech, or of the press' (U.S. Const. amend. I). Similarly, and albeit its checks and balances, the French Declaration of the Rights of Man and of the Citizen (1789) paid similar homage to the press and its sacred public role. According to it, the 'free communication of ideas and opinions is one of the most precious of the rights of man. Every citizen may, accordingly, speak, write, and *print with freedom*, but shall be responsible for such abuses of this freedom as shall be defined by law'.

Despite the embryonic rise of public communication ethical discourse during that period, no explicit or systematic code of ethics was fully articulated as an ethical model. Such discourse remained largely a set of broad ideals about codes of conduct, 'ethics of factuality' or practical principles within the print culture industry. However, the evolution of public sphere politics in the West gave rise to a shifting ethical discourse relating to media (mainly press and popular print culture) concerns in public life. This also coincided with the emergence of media as a decisive instrument in the mass commercialization of societies, and the emergence of the 'yellow press'. This concern re-inspired the ideas and ideals of a liberal social contract grounded in 'an objective news press, with codes of ethics and other professional features'. (Ward, 2011: 63). As a result, the conception of media ethics as a full model and an explicit designation emerged at the end of the nineteenth century with the rise of journalism as an industry (Ferré, 2009: 16). This period was designated as the 'professionalism' era in media discourse (ibid.). Its dominant character of media ethics focused mainly on moral virtues such as objectivity, accuracy, decency, impartiality, duty, honesty and truth, all of which are central features in deontologist ethical codes. For example, in the United States (and perhaps the West at large),

William E. Miller, a member of the Kansas Editorial Association (KEA) crafted the first full code of ethical principles in journalism, emphasizing duty, responsibility and integrity. Many rules and guidelines for professional conduct in journalism were advocated and developed prior[2] to this. However, the KEA represents the first fully articulated professional journalist code of ethics that addressed the commercial and editorial aspects of the industry. Following the KEA code of media ethics, and the widespread intensification of media sensationalism, the 'Canons of Journalism' were endorsed at the inaugural annual meeting of the American Society of Newspaper Editors in 1923. These were the consummation of numerous public debates on the role, function and apprehensions about journalism in public life. The seven principles of the 'Canons of Journalism' reinforced the professional character of media ethics, with emphasis on values such as 'accuracy', 'impartiality','decency', freedom', 'honesty', 'responsibility', and 'fair play'. The ethical codes advocated by the Canons of Journalism 'summarized the ideals of journalism so well that the Society of Professional Journalists[3] adopted the Canons in 1926, and other newspapers and press associations used the Canons as a model for the code they would write' (ibid., 20).

However, by the 1940s and 1950s, the efforts to articulate a theoretical account of media ethical codes based primarily on professional objectivity abated in favour of new ethical principles grounded in the Hutchins Commission of 1947. The Hutchins Commission's proposed ethical mandate sought to emphasize the principles of social responsibility in media practices, including the obligations to the rights of citizens, commitment to public interest, and the duty to function as a forum of public ideas and ideals. While resisted by the industry itself, the moral commitments advanced by the Hutchins Commission's social responsibility approach were championed and espoused by many universities, and were instrumental in shaping journalism academic curricula throughout the USA and beyond to inspire journalists for many generations. However, with the dramatic rise and expansion of global communications in the 1980s and 1990s, many have appealed for new cosmopolitan and globally representative standards of media ethics. While not abandoning the ethical features of social responsibility, these appeals focused principally on cross-cultural values and asymmetrical power structure between north and south in hegemonic media practices. For instance, in 1980, the UNESCO's International Commission for the Study of Communication Problems proposed a New World Information and Communication Order (NWICO). This sought to vitiate the colonial legacy by promoting equitable global media representations, ending the imbalance of information flow between the north and the south, and committing to the diversity in cultural identities. Nevertheless, this fundamental concern about the colonial legacy didn't produce an epistemological alternative to Western ethical norms. Instead, a combination of normative ethics such as democracy, freedom, rational universal values, along with some virtue ethics such as moral responsibilities, accuracy, sincerity, and accountably would be reinscribed as universal media ethics (ibid, 25). Although assuming a global character, the nature and status of these codes of ethics remained fundamentally Western inspired. As Christians et al. (2008) conclude, this Eurocentric 'rational processes create basic rules of [media] ethics that everyone is obliged to follow and against which all failures in moral duty can be measured' (148). Furthermore,

> In mainstream professional ethics, an apparatus of neutral standards is con-structed in terms of the major issues practitioners face in their everyday routines. The influential theory—utilitarianism, for example—presumes one set of considerations that is applied consistently and self-consciously to every choice ... neutrality [therefore] is seen as necessary to guarantee individual autonomy, and through autonomous reason, principles and prescriptions are established as the arbiters of moral disputes. This commitment to neutrality made [such] ethics attractive for its compatibility with the canons of rational calculation. (Ibid.)

Universal ethics, politics and ideology

Western liberal ethical doctrine, in spite of its multiple expressions, is funda-mentally marked by the convergence of three foundational ideologies: meta-physical binary oppositionality, moral universality and ethical objectivity. In this case, the binary structure which characterized Enlightenment metaphysical liberal ethics must be situated within the logic and ideology of 'self' and 'other'. Through this process, ethical principles emerge as the universal norm and con-sciousness, and against which the 'other' is conceived as a natural and cultural deviation. Accordingly, the formation of the Enlightenment universal moral doctrine is predicated upon the cultural and intellectual distinction between the West and non-West, 'for, in order to be able to proclaim its [universal] humanity, the West needed to create its others as slaves and monsters' (Yegen-oglu, 2005: 95). Thus, to construct its frontier as civilized, rational, and uni-versal, and to affirm its radical difference from the cultural other, Western moral superiority perceived and confined its other as its binary opposition: irrational, backward and parochial. Furthermore, 'the intersection of [Enlight-enment] liberal humanism with the necessities of imperial polity' (Lloyd, 1991: 69), captures the affinity between Western moral attitudes with its colonial projects. Edward Said's (1978) insightful analysis illustrate how, 'the West's motivation to 'know' and 'represent' the [other] is fundamentally linked to its desire to master and control it by rendering it epistemologically and ontologi-cally distinct and different from itself' (Al-Zo'by, 2015b: 222).

In this will to dominate, Western universal moral doctrine characterizes the non-European as rationally resistant or lacking in the capacity for universal reason. At the same time, what makes Western universal moral doctrine so paradoxical is that it has emerged in the context of proclaimed universal human dignity, autonomy and human equality. Instead, the liberal discourse of uni-versal human ideals has advanced the development of racial science theory, 'for the belief in human equality required a belief in biological unfitness for [moral judgment]' (Fredrickson, quoted in Allais, 2016: 2). For instance, in paving the way for the coupling of race and ideology, Aristotle famously decreed 'some should rule, and others be ruled is a thing not only necessary, but expedient; from the hour of their birth, some are marked out for subjection, others for rule' (Aristotle, 2008: 32). Similarly, and espousing a moral racial hierarchy, Kant emphatically and joyously affirmed that 'humanity is at its greatest perfection in the race of the whites. The yellow Indians do have a meagre talent. The Negroes are far below them' (Kant, 2012: 576). Attributing the difference to mental and rational capacities, he further asserted that

> If we compare the character of the Oriental nations with the character of the Europeans, we here thus find an essential difference ... [:] All Oriental nations are completely incapable of judgment in accordance with concepts. It is a big difference to judge a matter according to shape, appearance, and intuition, and to judge [it] according to concepts. All Oriental nations are not in the position to explain a single property of morality or of justice through concepts; rather all their morals are based on appearance ... hence they are capable neither of a philosophy nor of [reason]. (Wood & Louden, 2012: 197–198)

Thus, for Kant and many Enlightenment philosophers like him, the non-European is not only unable to produce rational and universal judgements, but they are equally unfit to generate the capacity to act according to them. This was further expressed in Hegel's rendition of world history as the manifestation of dialectical opposition between the rational sovereignty of Western universal consciousness and its civilizational inferior other. Thus, the absence of historical consciousness among the non-European, for Hegel, provides a tacit justification for their enslavement. As he asserts, 'no absolute injustice is done to those who remain servants, for whoever lacks the courage to risk his life in order to obtain [universal] freedom deserves to remain a slave' (Hegel, quoted in Petry 1979: 69). For Hegel, then, freedom and elevated morality are the exclusive domain of European universal ethos.

The critique of Western universal ethical virtues has been largely limited to the exploration of alternative frameworks of media ethics. However, the appeal to alternative ethical models doesn't call into question the ideological assumptions that underlie and thus privilege Western liberal notions of universal objectivity, reason and truth. While endowing the West with such transcendental values, alternative ethics ascribe the non-western to the domain of the socio-historical margins of such virtues. This is not to argue that objectivity, reason and truth don't exist, but rather to argue that they are not the exclusive domain of the West. Furthermore, Western notions of universal and objective values must be deconstructed within the broader project of power relations seeking to disqualify and exclude alternative ways of thinking, to assert itself as the sole foundation of truth. As illustrated in his seminal work, *Genealogy of Morals*, Friedrich Nietzsche strongly repudiates the claim that Western ethical virtues are grounded in the foundations of universal ideals and timeless truths.

The Enlightenment proclaims that moral rational sovereignty is the privilege of universal reason and liberation. However, for Nietzsche, the project of Western Enlightenment ethics must not be understood as an outcome of human liberation and rational emancipation, but as the historical expression of power struggles and the will to dominate otherness and difference. Elaborating Nietzsche's notion of power, Michelle Foucault (1980) further explicates how Western Enlightenment conceptions of reason and morality are nothing but the residual features of power practices that rest on the structural interplay of authority, legitimacy and knowledge. For Foucault, then

> Truth isn't the reward of free spirit nor the privilege of those who have succeeded in liberating themselves. Truth is a thing of this world: It is produced only by virtue of multiple forms of constraint. And it induces regular effects of power ... that is, the type of discourse which it accepts and makes function as true. (Foucault, 1980: 131)

Accordingly, truth is always produced and realized through power relations, and conversely, can only be utilized and practiced through the production of truth. Moreover, in his critique of the power/truth nexus, Foucault (1980) explored the conditions under which discursive conventions about truth are unified and regulated. Such conditions devise and define a distinct domain of knowledge/objects (like that of that the Enlightenment) which demand a precise set of concepts that constitute what counts as truth.

Manifested primarily in media ethical codes, this 'regime of truth' described above construes what Hall (1979: 76) calls a 'dominant representational paradigm' rather than objective and universal norms. In this regard, the ideology of the Enlightenment moral principles inscribed in media ethical norms as objectivity, accuracy, impartiality, honesty, fairness and truth are actually the process of constructing, sustaining and reproducing definitive sets of meanings, conventions and practices. These in turn furnish the framework to naturalize, normalize and reinforce those practices and attitudes as universal features of common sense. As Hall so insightfully elaborates,

> [Dominant discourses] are not deliberately selected by encoders to 'reproduce events within the horizon of the dominant ideology' but constitute the field of meanings within which they must choose. Precisely because they have become 'universalized and naturalized', they appear to be the only forms of intelligibility available; they have become sedimented as the 'only rational, universally valid ones'. (Ibid., 343)

Consequently, far from constituting universal ethics of impartiality, liberal Enlightenment media conventions, norms, and rules unconsciously provide a framework for 'worthy' or 'unworthy' victimization; 'acceptable' or 'unacceptable' demonization; and 'friend' or 'foe' of civilization. So rather than objective ethical truths, what media constructs and construes in essence are 'preferred meanings', ascendant norms and dominant ideological interpretations. In this case what media disseminates is neither unmediated nor completely objective. Like all modes of communication narratives, 'media observe certain rules and conventions to get things across intelligibly. It is these, often more than the reality being conveyed, that shape the material delivered by the media' (Said, 1981: 44).

Beyond these metaethical fallacies underpinning the notion of 'truth' and 'objectivity' described above, the explicit assumption about the deliberative and democratic function of media in the public sphere has also come under serious criticism. The decline of the political possibilities under what Habermas (1972) termed as 'instrumental rationality' has manifested in the rise of the ideological subordination of civic subjectivities to mass commercialization and administrative power. Thus, instead of mediating and facilitating the field of public life through 'critical reasoning', mass media, inversely, has assumed the function of its uncritical mass-pacification. As Curran, Freedman and Fenton (2012) confirm,

> … media are more often about individual than collective emancipation, about presenting self (frequently in consumerist … terms) rather than changing society, about entertainment and leisure rather than political communication … and about social agendas shaped by elites and corporate power rather than a radical alternative. (180)

Hence, the professed democratic communicative deliberation in contemporary liberal societies fails to materialize into a transformative collective action. This depoliticization of public life through the ethics of mass media commercialization, mechanization and control marks what Habermas (1989) labels as 'the structural transformation of the public sphere' under the prevailing global neoliberal conditions. As the ideal domain of public debate and reflection, the public sphere, for Habermas, has degenerated into a 'forum of communication which privileges powerful and institutionalized actors while excluding smaller institutions and civil society– effectively undermining the public sphere' (Schäfer 2015).

Conclusion

To disrupt and provincialize the totalizing hegemony of Western monopoly on universal ethical principles, it is simply insufficient to promote alternative moral ideals based on local traditions and values. The conceptual and strategic circulations of alternative ethics presuppose the logical coherence of the West's originality and uniqueness, from which one seeks divergence with infinite possibilities. This, paradoxically, still affirms the singularity and universality of the West, and only provides the non-Western a relative expression of local morality modified by local circumstances. Instead, one should seek to dismantle the conditions of ideological assumptions, which disguise the structures of cultural domination, exclusion and superiority underlying the claims for singular universal certainty, objectivity, rationality and neutrality. Accordingly, to offer a more global framework, the universal project of media ethics must not be assigned a singular narrative in which the West occupies a unique and central status.

However, the defence of a universal mode of ethics outside the metaphysical foundations of Enlightenment ideology should be grounded in plural cultural human rights, but with universal values of justice, dignity, solidarity and equality. These values are not expressions of universal certainties and timeless truths as declared in Western liberal ethics, but rather forms of discursive ethics where competing and contested ethical values are subject to equal and critical debate and argumentation. In some ways, this is not unlike what Habermas (1989) has identified as the 'ideal speech situation', expressed in the 'domain of democratic debate where truth claims are subject to rational arbitration rather than determination by the power of vested interests' (Barker, 1999: 451). As stated above, this chapter is not intended as a categorical rejection of the very possibility of universal objective media ethics, but rather as a critique of the historical and cultural claims that underlie its Eurocentric singularity.

Notes

1 There are a few exceptions in modern philosophy – see Alasdair MacIntyre b. 1929, Elisabeth Anscombe 1929, Bernard Williams b. 1929.
2 See for example the *Philadelphia Public Ledger's* '24 Rules', and *The Journalist* (1907), the *Editor& Publisher* (1901), to name just a few.
3 Established in 1901, the Society of Professional Journalists is the oldest and most prestigious organization representing media professionals in the USA.

References

Allais, L. (2016), 'Kant's racism'. *Philosophical Papers*, 45(1–2), 1–36.

Al-Zo'by, M. (2015a), 'Die USA in der arabischen Welt – Moderne Kreuzzüge?', in F. Hinz (ed.), *Kreuzzüge des Mittelalters und der Neuzeit: Realhistorie –. Geschichtskultur* ['The USA and the Arab World – A Modern Crusade'?, in Crusades of the Middle Ages and Modern Times: Real History]. Didaktik, Zurich: Olms-Weidmann, pp. 87–117.

Al-Zo'by, M. (2015b), 'Representing Islam in the age of neo-orientalism: Media, politics and identity'. *Journal of Arab & Muslim Media Research*, 8(3), 217–238.

Aristotle, (2008), *Politics*. New York: Cosimo Inc.

Barker, C. (1999), *Cultural Studies: Theory and Practice*. London: Sage Publications.

Christians, C. and Traber, M. (eds) (1997), *Communication Ethics and Universal Values*. Thousand Oaks, CA: Sage.

Christians, G. C., Shakuntala R., Ward, J. A. S. and Wasserman, H. (2008), 'Toward a global media ethics: Theoretical perspectives'. *ECQUID NOVI: African Journalism Studies*, 29(2), 135–172.

Curran, J.Fenton, N. and Freedman, D. (2012), *Misunderstanding the Internet*. London: Routledge.

'Declaration of the Rights of Man and Citizen. (789) Liberty, equality, fraternity: Exploring the French Revolution'. Retrieved from: https://revolution.chnm.org/d/295. Accessed: 23 April 2021.

Derrida, J. (1976), *Of Grammatology*. Baltimore: Johns Hopkins University Press.

Driver, J. (2007), 'Normative Ethics', in F. Jackson and M. Smith (eds), *The Oxford Handbook of Contemporary Philosophy*. Oxford: Oxford University Press.

Driver, J. (2012), *Consequentialism*. London: Routledge.

Ferré, P. J. (2009), 'Short History of Media Ethics in the United States', in L. Wilkins and C. Christians (eds), *The Routledge Handbook of Mass Media Ethics*. New York: Routledge, pp. 16–27.

Foucault, M. (1980), *Power/Knowledge*. New York: Pantheon.

Habermas, J. (1972), *Knowledge and Human Interests*. London: Heinemann.

Habermas, J. (1989), *The Structural Transformation of the Public Sphere*. Cambridge, MA: MIT Press.

Hall, S. (1979), 'Culture, the Media and the Ideological Effect', in J. Curran and J. Woollacott (eds), *Mass Communication and Society*, London: Edward Arnold, pp. 315–348.

Hutcheson, F. (2004), *An Inquiry into the Original of Our Ideas of Beauty and Virtue in Two Treatises*, ed. W. Leidhold. Indianapolis: Liberty Fund.

Kant, I. (1969), *Foundations of the Metaphysics of Morals*, trans. L. W. Beck, with critical essays, ed. R. P. Wolff. New York: Macmillan.

Kant, I. (2012), Contents. In E. Watkins (ed.), *Kant: Natural Science* (The Cambridge Edition of the Works of Immanuel Kant). Cambridge: Cambridge University Press.

Lloyd, D. (1991), 'Race under representation', *Oxford Literary Review*, 13(1), 62–94.

McConnell, T. (2000), *Inalienable Rights: The Limits of Consent in Medicine and the Law*, Oxford: Oxford University Press.

Mitchell, T. (2000), 'The Stage of Modernity', in T. Mitchell (ed.), *Questions of Modernity*. University of Minnesota Press: Minneapolis.

Parry, R. and Thorsrud, H. (2021), 'Ancient Ethical Theory', in E. N. Zalta (ed.), *The Stanford Encyclopedia of Philosophy* (Spring Edition), forthcoming. https://plato.stanford.edu/archives/spr2021/entries/ethics-ancient/

Petry, E. (1979), *Hegel's Philosophy of Subjective Spirit, Volume 3: Phenomenology and Psychology*. Boston: Dordrecht.

Rao S. and Wasserman H. (2007), 'Global media ethics revisited: A postcolonial critique'. *Global Media and Communication*, 3(1), 29–50.

Said, E. (1978), *Orientalism*. New York: Pantheon Books.

Said, E., (1981), *Covering Islam*. New York: Pantheon Books.

Schäfer, M. S. (2015), 'Digital Public Sphere', in G. Mazzoleni, K. Barnhurst, K. Ikeda, M. Rousiley and H. Wessler (eds), *The International Encyclopedia of Political Communication*. London: Wiley-Blackwell.

Shohat, E. and Stamp, R. (2014), *Unthinking Eurocentrism*. London: Routledge.

Ward, S. J. A. (2004), *Invention of Journalism Ethics: The Path to Objectivity and Beyond*. Montreal: McGill-Queen's University Press.

Ward, S. J. A. (2011), *Ethics and the Media: An Introduction*. Cambridge: Cambridge University Press.

Wood, A. & Louden R. (2012), *Immanuel Kant: Lectures on Anthropology*. Cambridge: Cambridge University Press.

Yegenoglu, M. (2005), *Colonial Fantasies: Towards a Feminist Reading of Orientalism*. Cambridge: Cambridge University Press.

5   Rethinking global media ethics for a 'post-American' world

Daya Thussu

Introduction

The explosion of transnational information flows, accelerated by new digital technologies and institutional changes (political, economic, and legal), has profoundly affected the study of global media and communication. In our media-saturated world, we are influenced – cognitively, behaviourally and emotionally – by what we consume in a 24/7 communication ecology. 'It is because the media are central to our everyday lives that we must study them', wrote Roger Silverstone in his 1999 book *Why Study the Media?*, '... study them as social and cultural as well as economic and political dimensions of the modern world. Study them in their ubiquity and complexity. Study them as contributors to our variable capacity to make sense of the world, to make and share its meanings' (Silverstone, 1999: 2). The media world has profoundly changed since Silverstone wrote these words: the globalization and digitization of media and communication has opened up new frontiers for exploring ethical aspects of the mass media, including the primacy of a technocentric, data-driven journalism with its myriad socio-cultural and geopolitical implications.

In this chapter, the aim is to examine how media ethics has evolved in the digital space. I start with a review of the epistemology of ethics more broadly before going on to discuss media ethics. The chapter then moves on to examine non-Western notions of ethics, drawing on examples from India and China. A more internationalized version of ethics, it could be argued, is essential at a time when power equations are changing, with the pivot of power shifting back to Asia. Such change encourages researchers in our rapidly evolving field of study to approach issues of media ethics in a 'post-American' world. The globalization of media and the globalization of higher education should contribute to the research and teaching of media ethics, making it more cosmopolitan in its outlook and approaches and looking beyond the Western narratives and frameworks to re-evaluate what constitutes media ethics.

Epistemology of ethics

The philosophical basis of ethics arguably has its roots in religious literature. Every major religion practised in the world has a profound moral and ethical

DOI: 10.4324/9781003203551-7

dimension in its teachings and rituals. As Hamelink notes: 'The motive to avoid avoidable harm to others and to diminish people's suffering is a key concern in Confucianism, Taoism, Hinduism, Judaism, Christianity, and Islam' (Hamelink, 2015: 254). In the European philosophical tradition, the roots of the notion of ethics can be traced to ancient Greece, notably in the works of Socrates and Aristotle. The prominence of the dynamic between duty and the morality of human actions is at the heart of what is described as 'deontological' ethics (the term 'deontology' derived from the Greek *deon*, 'duty', and *logos*, 'reason or principle'), which has remained for millennia as the paradigm for discourses on virtue and ethics in public life.

Within the Western philosophical tradition, modern deontological ethics is closely associated with the work of German philosopher Immanuel Kant (1724–1804), who saw ethics as a universal principle based on respect for humanity, arguing that in a rational world where reason reigns supreme one should act in accordance with ethical and moral rules that are applicable to all (Kant, 1991 [1784]). This approach, embedded in Enlightenment thought, emphasized individual moral and ethical conduct. In other cultures, though the focus may be on the community rather than on the individual, such as in the Confucian tradition, where cultivation of socio-political harmony is of paramount importance. The value of societal ethics and morality is also emphasized in the Indian tradition, although there is a distinct element of individual moral accountability in the concept of 'dharma' (righteousness).

Media ethics

The ethical aspects of media are well delineated in the academic literature of media and communication (Ward, 2013; Ward, 2015; Rao and Wasserman, 2015). Journalism as a profession across the world includes an ethical dimension: as the 'fourth estate' in a democracy, journalists are supposed to play a crucial role as the 'watchdog' of those in power. Professional ethics – pursuance of truth, avoidance of personal bias and subjective interpretations of reality – are considered integral to good journalism. The role of the public service media – protecting the public interest and not being hostage to market forces – is the expression of a media ethics that champions the notion of the media as a public sphere, a third space not colonized by government or corporate interests and where public opinion is shaped in a democratic system (Tracey, 1998). A more radical approach – normatively radical at least, is advanced by Stephen Ward who argues that the ultimate aim is 'global human flourishing, a comprehensive and composite good that includes but goes beyond' the national 'principles of egalitarian liberalism, dialogic democracy and principled pluralism' (Ward, 2015: 200). In *Radical Media Ethics: A Global Approach*, he writes that 'the ethics of a global integrated media should be based on the principle that all humans are equally valuable moral agents of a single humanity, and all deserve a full and flourishing life' (ibid.: 200). However, as discussed below, this kind of argument emanating from a certain type of Western democratic model that presupposes universalist liberal values and is based on economic, social and political contexts not necessarily applicable to the rest of the world, is also being increasingly challenged.

Media ethics of a different kind have been practised in authoritarian political systems where journalism, and media more broadly, have traditionally been deployed as part of the propaganda that develops and sustains revolutionary consciousness and creates loyalty to the leadership and the party in power. In this version of ethics, the rights of the majority, the workers and peasants are considered more important than those of the individualistic bourgeois elite (the ruling classes), although it is the same elite which creates the narratives on ethics and political morality in authoritarian systems.

Ethical issues also informed the anti-colonial journalism which developed, particularly in India in the nineteenth century during the early decades of British colonization of South Asia (Sonwalkar, 2015). The initial approach was defensive and aimed at countering the negative portrayal of India's religious and cultural attributes. The writings of Rammohun Roy (1772–1833), who straddled the language cultures of Bengali, Persian, Sanskrit and English, used the printed word to defend Hinduism from attacks by colonial writers and officials and, in particular, in publications of the Baptist missionaries. For example, he launched three journals (the *Brahminical Magazine* (in English), *Sambad Kaumidi* (a Bengali weekly) and the weekly magazine in Persian, *Mirat-ul-Akhbar* (Mirror of News) to present the Indian case (Sonwalkar, 2019: 19). Roy started a trend which had its effect across the sub-continent as dozens of 'nationalist' newspapers and magazines sprung up. By 1860, there were more than 100 newspapers operating in India in Indian languages, in addition to many more in English (primarily aimed at the ruling colonial elite as well as aspirational and Anglicized Indians).

In the twentieth century, an ethicist par excellence was Mohandas Karamchand Gandhi (1869–1948), who led the world's biggest anti-colonial movement against the most powerful empire of modern times, earning him the title of the 'father of the nation' in India. For all his political life, Gandhi edited four periodicals notably *Young India* (later renamed as *Harijan*). As a new study of Gandhi and the media notes, Gandhi 'both made the news and was the news'. Often referring himself as a 'newspaperman,' he wrote in English, in Gujarati (his mother tongue) and in Hindi (the most widely used language in India) (Kaul, 2020: 2). His words were read very widely in South Asia and beyond, acting as rallying cry for anti-colonial sentiments. A deeply ethical and moral attitude, earning him the title of the Mahatma (Sanskrit for 'great soul'), was visible in his writings and, even more strikingly, in his public persona and politics.

Media ethics also was an important component to the emerging anti-colonial journalism in other parts of Asia as well as in the Arab world and in many parts of Africa. In the post-war world, as European colonialism retreated, a different imagining of news media was suggested by the newly independent nations. It is relevant to recall here that in the post-independence phase, India played a crucial role in articulating demands for a fairer and more balanced flow of information (championing what was then called the 'Third World'), leading to the 1970s debates within UNESCO about the creation of a New World Information and Communication Order (NWICO), which brought the global South, albeit briefly, into the global communication discourse. Ethical issues were central to the NWICO debates, which broadened the definition of media ethics within a larger framework of national development and demanded a fairer media representation of the developing world within a Western-dominated international media system (MacBride, 1980; Thussu, 2019). Since such communication discourses had an unambiguous campaigning frame, the professional ethics – including notions of objectivity – that we associate with modern-day journalism were largely absent. In addition, many developing countries clamouring for a free and democratic global media system, were exercising censorship and control of information in their own domestic media spaces.

Ethics and excessive marketization

Professional media ethics have evolved in the Western world over centuries: a certain code of conduct, editorial autonomy and professionalism has characterized elite media in Europe and the United States, though commercial imperatives and political influence have sometimes compromised the ethical aspects of journalism. Certain professional dos and don'ts deployed by the news organizations and professional bodies to establish journalistic norms and values – including notably seeking and reporting truth and speaking truth to power – are generally practised (Ward, 2013; Rao and Wasserman, 2015). At the same time, there is widely recognized and accepted political bias in the media, as well as such practices in the popular press as deception, invasion of privacy, libellous or malicious content, leading to public enquiries and court trials, notably the 2012 Leveson Report in the UK, published under the aegis of the British government in the wake of a phone hacking scandal involving the *News of the World*, a British tabloid (UK Government, 2012).

From its very inception, modern journalism has also been a business and therefore making news as a commodity remains an integral aspect of the media world. As the most commercialized culture, journalism in US was arguably the harbinger of entertainment-oriented journalism, starting with 'the penny press' in the 1830s, the pioneering popular newspapers providing diversions for working people. Noted one commentator: 'For a constituency being conditioned by trashy crime pamphlets, gory novels and overwrought melodramas, news was simply the most exciting, most entertaining content a paper could offer, especially when it was skewed, as it invariably was in the penny press, to the most sensational stories. In fact, one might even say that the masters of the penny press *invented* the concept of news because it was the best way to sell their papers in an entertainment environment' (cited in Gitlin, 2002: 51, italics in original). In later years, the penny press morphed into what was called 'yellow journalism', characterized by sensationalist reporting, including covering 'staged' and invented events.

In such a market-driven media ecosystem, commercial imperatives often compromise ethical standards as news has become more infotainment-oriented, often lacking context and driven by a celebrity-saturated content, raising questions about what was called 'dumbing down'. In Britain during the 1990s, where the phrase was coined, following the US experience, television programming was increasingly affected by the trend to entertainment-oriented content or what was then referred to as 'Newszak', characterized by 'insensitive conjoining of the sentimental and the sensational, the prurient and the populist' (Franklin, 1997: 3). This 'tabloidization' was defined by one commentator as 'the progressive displacement of citizen-enhancing material with material which has *no other purpose* than to shock, provoke, entertain or retain viewers; and the progressive erosion of professional journalistic values in favour of televisual techniques involving sensationalism, distortion, misrepresentation and dramatization of the trivial' (Barnett, 2011: 169, italics in original).

Such criticism can be understood in its structural context: in an advertisement-driven media ecology, the journalists and their managers are more susceptible to commercial imperatives, as Tracey suggests in his study of the decline of public service broadcasting: 'In a public system, television producers acquire money to make programmes. In a commercial system they make programmes to acquire money' (Tracey, 1998: 18). This, Tracey argues can lead to 'the trivialization of public discourse, an evangelism of the ephemeral, the celebration of the insignificant, and the marginalization of the important' (ibid., p. 264). Although the above-mentioned commentators mostly focus on the British case, the trend they highlighted is observable in many other countries. India, home to a strong anti-colonial media tradition where the deployment of media for 'nation-building' was constantly emphasized, has emerged in the past few decades as one of the most competitive media markets. A country which until 1991 had a highly regulated state broadcasting monopoly, today boasts of more than 400 dedicated news networks—unrivalled by any other country. However, as these networks have proliferated, the audience has fragmented, forcing journalists to compromise ethical standards, for example by sensationalizing the coverage, employing dubious practices to gather and manipulate information to maximize the audience, and thus lowering the threshold of taste and decorum. Such a trend is discernible in other parts of the world, too, even in China, where the state control of news media remains unchallenged and the party-managed media allows 'soft', entertaining and apolitical news.

I have previously defined such 'global infotainment' as 'the globalization of a US-style ratings-driven television journalism which privileges privatized soft news—about celebrities, crime, corruption and violence—and presents it as a form of spectacle, at the expense of news about political, civic and public affairs' (Thussu, 2007: 8). In the era of globalized multimedia conglomerates, deregulated and privatized communication systems (hard and software) and massive technological advances the commercial imperative appears to have been strengthened (Thussu, 2019). In the increasingly integrated digitized global space, media technologies and industries have created a culture in which people all over the world can share experiences of media events, from sports and entertainment to military conflicts and humanitarian disasters, and, through advertisements, become consumers of a free-market capitalism. In the process, the old structures of media – the gatekeeping role of professional editors of converting raw information into news – have been gradually eroding and are being replaced by an unfettered information overload, compromising ethical norms and conventions.

Media ethics in the age of digital surveillance

A transformational change in media ecology, triggered by the digital revolution has raised a new set of ethical and moral questions (Heider and Massanari, 2012). One of the most important is about privacy and surveillance (Zuboff, 2019). Mass surveillance, often associated with authoritarian governments, is also practised within a democratic and free Internet, the 2013 Snowden affair being a prime example (Greenwald, 2014). The *Washington Post* revealed, in a series of investigative reports, the extensive surveillance programme and worldwide mobile phone tracking of the National Security Agency (NSA) (an intelligence wing within the US Department of Defense). Edward Snowden, a contractor for the NSA accused the government of 'abusing [it] in secret to extend their powers beyond what is necessary and appropriate' (Washington Post, 2014). In particular, the NSA's PRISM programme allowed US intelligence agencies access to information from major global companies including Google, Facebook and Apple. In addition, it was also revealed that, under its Foreign Intelligence Surveillance Act, the US government collected 'the contents of electronic communications, including telephone calls and emails' of 'non-US persons located outside the US', according to a US government report (The NSA Report, 2013).

Another kind of surveillance is embedded in the digital platforms as more and more power is concentrated into fewer and fewer private entities: just two US-based conglomerates –Facebook and Google – overwhelmingly dominate the digital advertising revenue to the exclusion of other media organizations (Moore and Tambini, 2018; Boyd-Barrett and Mirrlees, 2019). The 'free' service and content that such platforms provide works as an efficient quid pro quo between the consumer and the producer. Two leading figures in Google justified it thus: 'as in a social contract, users will voluntarily relinquish things they value in the physical world – privacy, security, personal data – in order to gain the benefits that come with being connected to the virtual world' (Schmidt and Cohen, 2013: 257). Google and Facebook have a vast reservoir of real-time data on billions of individuals, and millions of institutions across the globe. Such data can be personalized, helping these companies to take control of user attention, making their lucrative platforms extremely attractive to advertisers as well as governments and politicians to control and commodify communication.

The globalization of the phenomenon of 'fake news', too, is a major concern in terms of ethics of journalism. The ubiquitous social media have created easy and free platforms for the creation, consumption and delivery of such content. As the largest social media platform in the world, Facebook has been particularly blamed for spreading fake news. The most prominent example of this was the company's dealings with Cambridge Analytica, a data analytics firm, after an investigation by the *New York Times* and the *Observer* of London showed that the firm had 'harvested' millions of Facebook profiles of US voters (as well as in countries such as India, Kenya, Malaysia and Nigeria) and used the data to build a software programme to 'predict and influence choices at the ballot box' (Rosenberg, Confessore and Cadwalladr, 2018; Cadwalladr and Graham-Harrison, 2018).

Such malpractices in the digital environment have prompted researchers to speak of a global 'information disorder', with dangers of 'information pollution' on a global scale, identifying three types of disorder: 'mis-information, when false information is shared but no harm is meant; dis-information, when false information is knowingly shared to cause harm, and mal-information, when genuine information is shared to cause harm, often by moving information designed to stay private into the public sphere' (Wardle and Derakhshan, 2017: 5). However, it the latter type of manipulation of information which can be most problematic from a media ethics perspective. A study by MIT researchers, which analysed 126,000 verified true and false news stories tweeted by more than 3 million people in the period 2006 to 2017, found that falsehood 'diffused significantly farther, faster, deeper, and more broadly than the truth' (Vosoughi, Roy and Aral, 2018: 1146).

From the perspective of media ethics among professional media organizations and journalists a higher level of vigilance has become necessary to ensure their credibility is not eroded under digital media pressures (Singer and Brooking, 2018). Already a number of professional fact-checking groups have emerged in the US, the European Union and elsewhere in the world, the majority working as not-for-profit organizations. Partly as a reaction to the global outcry against unethical informational behaviour, Facebook and Google and many other global digital organizations have started or funded journalism projects across the globe to ensure that the menace of fake news is under control.

At the same time, media organizations – even reputable ones – have been relying on 'paid' or 'native' advertisements and 'sponsored' content, where the line between editorial and advertising content is constantly and even deliberately being blurred. As media organizations deploy machine learning and Artificial Intelligence (AI) for curating and editing news stories, new concerns and issues about what is being termed as 'AI ethics' have been raised, and not just in the context of authoritarian political systems (see essays in Dubber, Pasquale and Das, 2020). If AI is deciding what information should be prioritized and how news agendas should be shaped, the ethical aspects of news media might become subservient to the tyranny of the algorithm since machines cannot 'feel' and our social-political reality, as reflected in good journalism, is often informed by subjective or intuitive judgements and values.

Media ethics for a post-American media world?

As we enter the third decade of the twenty-first century there is a growing realization of the changing power equations in the world, affecting the efficacy of the Western-centric global order, led by the US government and the Bretton Woods institutions (the World Bank, the International Monetary Fund and the World Trade Organization). This system is increasingly being challenged at a time when the role of the West as the main engine of global growth appears to be diminishing at the expense of the rise of such powers as China onto the global stage (Stuenkel, 2016; Cooley and Nexon, 2020). Some scholars see this as offering possibilities of a 'post-Western', 'sustainable modernity', based on Asian histories and cultures (Duara, 2014). Others are concerned about 'deepening disorder', with the implicit suggestion that disorder will rule in a post-Western world led by authoritarian governments (Tharoor and Saran, 2020). As Zakaria notes: 'On every dimension other than military power—industrial, financial, social, cultural—the distribution of power is shifting, moving away from US dominance. That does not mean we are entering an anti-American world. But we are moving into a post-American world, one defined and directed from many places and by many people' (Zakaria, 2008: 4–5).

The media ethics debates have not remained unaffected by the transformation of the global media and communication landscape, including the rise of Asian countries, complementing if not challenging the analytical frameworks of a journalistic ethics deeply embedded within a Eurocentric discourse. For example, ethical issues associated with the 'authoritarian' versus 'liberal' media theory debate which shaped the academic and policy discourse during the Cold War years, failed to notice that large civilizational powers such as China (the Sino–Soviet rift had taken place in 1950s) and India (a founding member of the Non-Aligned Movement) did not fit into such a neat bipolar division of the world. Such nations could contribute towards building a more inclusive theory of global ethics that takes on board the extraordinary changes in large countries with long histories and rising economic and cultural power (Hobson, 2012, Bell, 2015; Khanna, 2019; Hobson, 2020).

The relative neglect of non-European modernities, philosophies, history and culture has remained a major shortcoming of much of mainstream media research. It is not surprising then that few international scholars give full appreciation to the fact that the oldest systematic grammar in any language was developed in Sanskrit in the 6th century BC, that the Chinese were producing books a millennia before Europeans and the world's oldest surviving university is in Egypt – to pick a few examples representing the three great non-Western traditions: Indian, Chinese and Islamic. Such epistemological absences are not just confined to media and communication field but glaringly present in many other academic fields, including International Relations, as observed by two leading IR scholars: 'IR has been largely built on the assumptions that Western history or Western political theory *are* world history and world political theory' (Acharya and Buzan, (2019: 3), emphasis in the original).

The study of media and its ethics has evolved within Western academia and within that a US-UK core has dominated much of the theorizing. Broadly speaking, the media have been central to courses in communication studies in the US, with its various variants – health, development, intercultural, political and international – to the more 'culturalist' or critical approaches, associated with the European tradition. The dominant paradigm, emanating from the elite US media and communication studies departments, has been adopted in much of the rest of the world, without taking on board the local cultural and historical specificities and complexities or recognizing communication models beyond the Western framework, especially South-South cultural and communication exchanges.

One possible and partial explanation for such imbalance in scholarship could be that the intellectual markers – in terms of research agendas, publications, grants and projects – continue to be influenced by Western, or more specifically, US elite universities, as well as US-based professional organizations such as the International Communication Association (Wiedemann and Meyen, 2016). However, this situation is changing with the rapidly expanding and internationalizing media and communication studies, necessitated by the transformation of media and communication, especially in Asia. The need to internationalize the study of media and communication to take it beyond a Western-centric epistemology has been emphasized by many scholars (Thussu, 2009; Lee, 2015; Mano and milton, 2020).

In the realm of media ethics, issues surrounding digital ethics are becoming paramount in countries which have the potential to transform the Internet such as China (which has the world's largest Internet population – nearly a billion) and India (with more than 700 million users). India is home to the world's largest 'open' Internet (since the Chinese one is not open) and the country also has the highest number of registered users of both Facebook and WhatsApp, and unlike China, India has a huge demographic dividend: 70% of Indians are below the age of 35, increasingly digitally savvy and globalized (Agrawal, 2018; Arora, 2019).

However, unlike India and most of the rest of the world, China's Internet platforms are all Chinese and this has had a profound impact on using digital connectivity for developmental purposes, with impressive results, for example in eliminating extreme poverty – a key ethical consideration (Hong, 2017). In China, the growing use of mobile finance systems has expanded digital communication with a developmental dimension. This has become a successful model, being replicated in several developing countries where China has growing involvement and investment in the communication sector, part of what is sometimes described as a 'digital Silk Road', with fibre-optic cables, mobile networks, satellite relay stations and data centres (Xing, 2019). India's 'Digital India' programme, supported by $75 billion from public and private investment in a phased manner, and in operation since 2015, has helped millions of small farmers and entrepreneurs to improve their education, health, and livelihoods (Nilekani, 2018; McKinsey Global Institute, 2019).

Developmental journalism is generally not the focus of the dominant discourses on media ethics. The ethical aspects of media for development deserve more attention and countries such as China and India can offer interesting alternative models to do that. Indian scholars have had a significant impact on such thinking: for example, the work of the Nobel Laureate, Amartya Sen, especially his notion of 'development as freedom' has a strong ethical and moral dimension (Sen, 1999). Other scholars have raised ethical issues in relation to causes of extreme poverty and the contribution of social movements and community communication in dealing with it (Dutta, 2011; Thomas, 2019). Among Chinese scholars, the emphasis has been on the need for 'South-South development cooperation from China and other emerging market economies', which, it is suggested, 'is more likely to bring "quick wins" in poverty reduction and inclusive, sustainable growth' (Lin and Wang, 2017: 6).

Such calls for 'democratization in development thinking' (ibid., p. 14), are likely to grow in a post-American world. A 2019 United Nations report has proposed 'digital cooperation' to 'create a platform for sharing digital public goods, engaging talent and pooling data sets, in a manner that respects privacy, in areas related to attaining the Sustainable Development Goals' (UN, 2019: 8). Questions of media ethics will become increasingly important as digital communication deepens and the need for such 'digital cooperation' will further increase. In such a scenario, the notions of ethics based on Confucian ideas of 'harmony' and an ancient Indian concept of *Vasudhaiva Kutumbakam* ('the world is one family') may help provide potential alternatives to the Western definition of media ethics in the digital space.

In terms of epistemology, it is important to emphasize the problem of what historian Dipesh Chakrabarty has called 'asymmetric ignorance', in his provocative book *Provincializing Europe*. He argued that the Western academy has never been required to read non-Western histories, unlike scholars in the non-Western world, who have had to have an understanding of or at least familiarity with the European knowledge tradition. Long 'dead and gone' European intellectuals are routinely invoked', writes Chakrabarty, as 'though they were our own contemporaries' (Chakrabarty, 2007: 5). Others, notably Jack Goody, have also pointed out the existence of a pervasive Occidental bias in the Western narratives, even in the age of globalization. Goody notes that although 'most historians aim to avoid ethnocentricity (like teleology), they rarely succeed in doing so because of their limited knowledge of the other (including their own beginnings). That limitation often leads them to make unsustainable claims, implicitly or explicitly, about the uniqueness of the West' (Goody, 2006: 4).

As the above discussion has argued, in the new digital world the need to adopt a more cosmopolitan view of ethics, drawing on a range of approaches and perspectives, is an imperative, also reflective of the changing geopolitical and media power equation in a 'post-American' world.

References

Acharya, Amitav and Buzan, Barry (2019), *The Making of Global International Relations*. Cambridge: Cambridge University Press.

Agrawal, Ravi (2018), *India Connected: How the Smartphone is Transforming the World's Largest Democracy*. New York: Oxford University Press.

Arora, Payal (2019), *The Next Billion Users: Digital Life beyond the West*. Cambridge MA: Harvard University Press.

Barnett, Steven (2011), *The Rise and Fall of Television Journalism*. London: Bloomsbury Academic.

Bell, Daniel (2015), *The China Model: Political Meritocracy and the Limits of Democracy*. Princeton, NJ: Princeton University Press.

Boyd-Barrett, Oliver and Mirrlees, Tanner (eds.) (2019), *Media Imperialism: Continuity and Change*. Cambridge: Polity.

Cadwalladr, Carole and Graham-Harrison, Emma (2018), 'Revealed: 50 million Facebook profiles harvested for Cambridge Analytica in major data breach'. *The Observer*, 18 March.

Chakrabarty, Dipesh (2007), *Provincializing Europe: Postcolonial Thought and Historical Difference*, 2nd edition. Princeton, NJ: Princeton University Press.

Cooley, Alexander and Nexon, Daniel (2020), *Exit from Hegemony: The Unraveling of the American Global Order*. New York: Oxford University Press.

Duara, Prasenjit (2014), *The Crisis of Global Modernity: Asian Traditions and a Sustainable Future*. Cambridge: Cambridge University Press.

Dubber, Markus; Pasquale, Frank and Das, Sunit (eds) (2020), *The Oxford Handbook of Ethics of AI*. Oxford: Oxford University Press.

Dutta, Mohan (2011), *Communicating Social Change: Structure, Culture and Agency*. New York: Routledge.

Franklin, Bob (1997), *Newszak and News Media*. London: Arnold.

Gitlin, Tod (2002), *Media Unlimited: How the Torrent of Images and Sounds Overwhelms Our Lives*: New York: Metropolitan Books.

Goody, Jack (2006), *The Theft of History*. Cambridge: Cambridge University Press.

Greenwald, Glenn (2014), *No Place to Hide: Edward Snowden, the NSA, and the US Surveillance State*. New York: Metropolitan Books.

Hamelink, Cees (2015), *Global Communication*. London: Sage.

Heider, Don and Massanari, Adrienne (eds) (2012), *Digital Ethics: Research and Practice*. Oxford: Peter Lang.

Hobson, John (2012), *The Eurocentric Conception of World Politics*. Cambridge: Cambridge University Press.

Hobson, John (2020), *Multicultural Origins of the Global Economy: Beyond the Western-Centric Frontier*. Cambridge: Cambridge University Press.

Hong, Yu (2017), Pivot to Internet Plus: Molding China's Digital Economy for Economic Restructuring?*International Journal of Communication* 11: 1486–1506.

Kant, Immanuel ([1784] 1991) 'What is Enlightenment?', in Hans Reiss (ed.), *Kant: Political Writings*, 2nd edition. Cambridge: Cambridge University Press, pp. 54–60,

Kaul, Chandrika (ed.) (2020), *M. K. Gandhi, Media, Politics and Society New Perspectives*. London: Palgrave Macmillan.

Khanna, Parag (2019), *The Future is Asian: Commerce, Conflict, and Culture in the 21st Century*. New York: Simon & Schuster.

Lee, Chin-Chuan (ed.) (2015), *Internationalizing 'International Communications': A Critical Intervention*. Ann Arbor: University of Michigan Press.

Lin, Justin and Wang, Yan (2017), *Going beyond Aid: Development Cooperation for Structural Transformation*. Cambridge: Cambridge University Press.

MacBride, Seán et al. (1980), *Many Voices, One World: Communication and Society Today and Tomorrow*. International Commission for the Study of Communication Problems. Paris: UNESCO.

Mano, Winston and milton, viola (2020), 'Afrokology of Media and Communication Studies: Theorising from the Margins', in W. Mano and v. c. milton (eds.) *Routledge Handbook of African Media and Communication Studies*. London: Routledge.

McKinsey Global Institute (2019), *Digital India: Technology to Transform a Connected Nation*. New York: McKinsey Global Institute.

Moore, Martin and Tambini, Damien (eds) (2018), *Digital Dominance: The Power of Google, Amazon, Facebook, and Apple*. Oxford: Oxford University Press.

Nilekani, Nandan (2018), 'Data to the people: India's inclusive Internet'. *Foreign Affairs*, 97 (5), 19–26.

Rao, Shakuntala and Wasserman, Herman (eds) (2015), *Media Ethics and Justice in the Age of Globalization*. London: Palgrave Macmillan.

Rosenberg, Matthew; Confessore, Nicholas and Cadwalladr, Carole (2018), 'How Trump consultants exploited the Facebook data of millions'. *The New York Times*, 17 March.

Schmidt, Eric and Cohen, Jared (2013), *The New Digital Age: Reshaping the Future of People, Nations and Business*. London: John Murray.

Sen, Amartya (1999), *Development as Freedom*. Oxford: Oxford University Press.

Silverstone, Roger (1999), *Why Study the Media?* London: Sage.

Singer, Peter and Brooking, Emerson (2018), *LikeWar: The Weaponization of Social Media*. New York: Houghton Mifflin Harcourt.

Sonwalkar, Prasun (2015), For the Public Good: Rammohun Roy and His Tryst with Journalism Ethics', in Shakuntala Rao and Herman Wasserman (eds), *Media Ethics and Justice in the Age of Globalization*. London: Palgrave Macmillan, pp. 155–173.

Sonwalkar, Prasun (2019), 'From Akhbarat to Print: The Hybridity of News Culture in Early Indian Journalism', in Shakuntala Rao (ed.) *Indian Journalism in a New Era: Changes, Challenges, and Perspectives*. New Delhi: Oxford University Press, pp. 17–34.

Stuenkel, Oliver (2016), *Post-Western World*. Cambridge: Polity.

Tharoor, Shashi and Saran, Samir (2020), *The New World Disorder and the Indian Imperative*. New Delhi: Aleph.

The NSA Report (2013), *The NSA Report: Liberty and Security in a Changing World by the President's Review Group on Intelligence and Communications Technologies: Richard Clarke, Michael Morell, Geoffrey Stone, Cass Sunstein, and Peter Swire*. Princeton: Princeton University Press.

Thomas, Pradip (2019), *Communication for Social Change: Context, Social Movements and the Digital*. New Delhi: Sage.

Thussu, Daya Kishan (2007), *News as Entertainment: The Rise of Global Infotainment*. London: Sage.

Thussu, Daya Kishan (2009), 'Why Internationalize Media Studies and How', in D. K. Thussu (ed.) *Internationalizing Media Studies*. London: Routledge, pp. 13–31.

Thussu, Daya Kishan (2019), *International Communication: Continuity and Change*, 3rd edition. New York: Bloomsbury Academic.

Tracey, Michael (1998), *The Decline and Fall of Public Service Broadcasting*. Oxford: Oxford University Press.

UK Government (2012), *Leveson Inquiry – Report into the Culture, Practices and Ethics of the Press*. London: Department of Digital Media, Culture and Sports. Available at: https://www.gov.uk/government/publications/leveson-inquiry-report-into-the-culture-practices-and-ethics-of-the-press.

United Nations (2019), *The Age of Digital Interdependence: Report of the UN Secretary-General's High-level Panel on Digital Cooperation*. New York: United Nations.

Vosoughi, Soroush; Roy, Deb and Aral, Sinan (2018), 'The spread of true and false news online'. *Science*, March, 1146–1151.

Ward, Stephen (ed.) (2013), *Global Media Ethics*. Malden, MA: Wiley-Blackwell.

Ward, Stephen (2015), *Radical Media Ethics: A Global Approach*. Cambridge: Wiley-Blackwell.

Wardle, Claire and Derakhshan, Hossein (2017), *Information Disorder: Toward an Interdisciplinary Framework for Research and Policy Making*. Strasbourg: Council of Europe.

Washington Post (2014), *NSA Secrets: Government Spying in the Internet Age*. *Washington Post* E-book, published in partnership with Diversion Books.

Wiedemann, Thomas and Meyen, Michael (2016), 'Internationalization through Americanization: The expansion of the International Communication Association's leadership to the world'. *International Journal of Communication*, 10, 1489–1509.

Woolley, Samuel and Howard, Philip (eds.) (2018), *Computational Propaganda: Political Parties, Politicians, and Political Manipulation on Social Media*. Oxford: Oxford University Press.

Xing, Li (2019), 'China's Pursuit for the "One Belt One Road" Initiative: A New World Order with Chinese Characteristics?', in L. Xing (ed.) *Mapping China's 'One Belt One Road' Initiative*. London: Palgrave Macmillan, pp. 1–27.

Zakaria, Fareed (2008), *The Post-American World*. London: Allen Lane.

Zuboff, Shoshana (2019), *The Age of Surveillance Capitalism*. New York: Profile Books.

Part 2
Media ethics in practice

6   Freedom of speech, responsibility and human rights in Islam

Fethi B. J. Ahmed

Introduction

During the last few years, the concept of 'new media' has come to mean modern methods of communications and information in the digital era. Traditional methods of communications have declined in popularity and use among institutions, groups, and individuals, and in some contexts have been symbolically dethroned. In the communication and information industry, new media outlets increasingly rely on digital technology to reach a large community at the local and global levels in the fastest and most cost-effective manner. Many scholars maintain that in this era of globalization, modern digital technology has compressed human time and space and made the world a global village. Moreover, it has enabled the users to reply, comment and share the broadcast media content. Besides, people can now initiate communications and transmit information via their computers, smart phones, tablets, and use new channels via the Internet and social media to engage with online services through which they can create and share a variety of materials (Eid, 2014: 192–195).

Numerous moral issues can be discussed concerning the usage of new media, including unethical practices such as the fabrication and propagation of false news, breach of privacy, the spread of hatred and racism, and defamation. Many social media platforms have become platforms for ideological dissemination, backed by money and political power, to serve certain agendas. The practice of freedom of speech has in some contexts been taken to be absolute, without limitations, while in other it has been applied selectively, sometimes to persecute marginalized groups or to serve political power.

Responsibility, as a moral and legal principle, is obviously tied to freedom of speech and to any positions of trust. It exists in all actions and intersects with all human affairs and basic rights. It has most often been lacking or even totally absent in new media practices. These ethical problems have become very complicated due to many factors, particularly globalization, which has had profound impacts on the ways in which people interpret themselves, interact with others, deal with their surroundings, and see their place in the universe. Social media communication has sliced across different cultures and jurisdictions, creating a zone of massively extended freedom for the real-time, instant

DOI: 10.4324/9781003203551-9

publication of user thoughts, without any intermediation of traditional editorial restraints. The high speed and frequency of digital technology communication and a lack of professionalism, quality control, effective legislation, awareness of the harm of unethical acts, and commitment to global citizenship and social responsibility are all contributory factors to the problems of modern freedom of speech, responsibility and human rights issues. These are analysed in the current chapter from an Islamic perspective, within the context of new global media ethics. This is a multidisciplinary approach that integrates media studies, sociology, ethics, human rights, Islamic legal maxims and higher objectives of Sharia. It uses the analytical method of the content analysis process.

Discussion on freedom of speech in Islam is derived from the Qur'an, the supreme source of Islamic jurisprudence and ethics, and the fundamental source of the Islamic worldview. In this chapter special reference made to verses 8:27, 49:6, 2:256, 2:283, and 22:30. Also, discussion will explore the Prophet's tradition (known as *Sunnah* in Arabic) and investigates significant narrations (*hadiths*) such as Al-Bukhari 67:134, Muslim 45:136, and Ibn Majeh, 13:34. Besides, the study examines the application of the higher objectives of Sharia (*Maqasid al-Shariah*), especially the protection of the intellect and progeny/honour, and the major legal maxims (*Al-Qawai'd Al-Fiqhiyyah Al-Kulliyyah*), particularly exploring the principle of '*al-dharar yuzal*' (harm must be eliminated). This work also analyses relevant reports from the Universal Declaration of Human Rights (UDHR), the European Convention on Human Rights (ECHR), and the Universal Islamic Declaration of Human Rights (UIDHR) with regard to the fundamental right of freedom of speech and social responsibility.

The significance of this study stems from developing a systematic understanding of freedom of speech as guaranteed by international human rights law and charters, as well as the Islamic tradition. Moreover, it offers a view on responsibility as fundamental ethical principle. It also shows the correlation between freedom of speech and responsibility within the context of the different segments of new and old media practices. It argues that freedom of speech is a crucial value in Islam, guaranteed for all creatures, and imbued with commensurate responsibility and liability. Other than foundational principles based on the early Islamic community, this study is not concerned with the practical implementation of Islamic law in various historical settings – which include abuses of *de jure* Islamic principles – rather the scope of analysis is restricted to Islamic ethical doctrines. Ultimately, this study aims to elicit further discussions on the subject, and to attract research interest in this important but relatively overlooked area.

Conceptualizing freedom of speech

Definition and scope

Understanding what freedom of speech means is essential for our analysis; in some contexts, it is defined as freedom of expression or action. The term 'speech' is not fundamentally important, since the most vigorous debate is about the meaning of freedom. Digging into the historical roots and different theories of the idea of freedom is not the aim of this study. However, it is instructive to consider a concise summary of the views of ancient and contemporary philosophers. The primordial conception of freedom is that one may do what one wishes, which is conventionally circumscribed by the addenda that one may not harm others in doing so, by using force and misrepresentation (Epstein, 1987: 55–56). Human rights conventions affirm that humans are born free, have rights to freedom in all forms, and are entitled to struggle by all available means against any infringement or abrogation of this right (UN, 2015: 1–3; IC, 1981: II/a & b).

Exploring the idea of 'freedom of speech' in the major human rights conventions enhances our understanding of the subject. According to the UDHR and the ECHR, everyone has the right to freedom of opinion and expression (UN, 2015: 19; ECHR, 2013: 10/1). The Universal Islamic Declaration of Human Rights states that 'Every person has the right to express his thoughts and beliefs so long as he remains within the limits prescribed by the Law' (IC, 1981: XII/a). However, as explained in the following paragraphs, the exercise of this freedom may be subject to certain formalities, conditions, and restrictions as defined by law, in the interests of national security and public well-being. Human rights conventions and laws basically focus on the rights of humans and obviously use the term 'everyone', placing these rights into different categories such as political, economic, cultural and life rights. In recent decades new laws have been legislated to preserve the rights of other creatures, namely animals, as well as the environment in general. However, the extent of freedom of speech in the Islamic tradition is very broad, commensurate with its metaphysical ontology, and such freedom is guaranteed not only for humans, but for all creatures, including angels, jinn, animals, birds, insects and inanimate objects.

There are numerous verses, incidents, and stories recorded in the Qur'an that testify to the scope and scale of freedom of speech that Allah grants to His creatures. For instance, the Angels expressed their opinion and spoke to Allah about the creation of Adam, foreboding that he (i.e. humanity) would spread corruption and bloodshed on earth, to which Allah responded with explanation of His decision and the purposes of the creation (Qur'an, 2012: 2/30). Besides, the Qur'an recorded that Iblis (Satan) disobeyed Allah, and refused to bow down to Adam, displaying his sin of pride and arrogance. Furthermore, he expressed his intention and willingness to use all possible means to misguide human beings (Qur'an, 2012: 2/34; 38/82–83; 7/12, 17).

The Qur'an declared free speech a universal right, and it actively engages with critiques of itself and of Abrahamic monotheism. This includes the Qur'an's record of the theological debate that occurred between Nimrod and the Prophet Abraham. Nimrod argued with Prophet Abraham about his Lord and openly claimed god-ship. Prophet Abraham challenged him, arguing that his Lord gives life, causes death and brings the sun from the East, thus Nimrod would have to exhibit similar power to prove his divine authority, changing the laws of the universe and making the sun rise from the West (Qur'an, 2012: 2/258).

Another relevant example is the story of Pharaoh and Prophet Moses in the Qur'an. This story is extensively reiterated and described from various angles, and it shows the scope of freedom of speech that the Pharaoh enjoyed to the extent that he openly questioned God and spoke freely about serious religious issues, including the existence of God and the legitimacy of the Prophet Moses and the authenticity his message/religion. Moreover, it is worth mentioning that Pharaoh also gave freedom of speech to Moses in their audience, but denied freedom of speech and belief to his subjects/ employees and the sorcerers. Allah's giving Pharaoh freedom of speech and belief includes letting him testify to his monotheism before his death (Qur'an, 2012: 20/49–71; 79/24; 28/38–40; 10/75–93). These examples reflect the extent of freedom of speech preserved for everyone, including the opponents who are empowered to express their views on God, the Prophets, religion and any other issues.

A brief reading of the history of Islam and the biography of the Prophet Muhammad (pbuh) reveals numerous examples that practically demonstrate how freedom of speech and the practice of consultancy were deeply rooted and broad in scope in the application of Sharia in Islamic tradition. For example, during the expedition of *Badr* (2 AH/ 623 AD) one of the Prophet's companions, Al-Hubab bin Munthir, spoke with total freedom directly to the Prophet Muhammad to express his opinions regarding the military base that the Prophet took for his troops. He thought that the location of the base was not good, and he suggested changing it, to encamp at the nearest water well and make a basin or reservoir full of water, and then destroy all the other wells so that the enemy invaders would not have access to water. The Prophet approved his plan and carried it out in order to improve the capability of Muslim troops to defeat the tribe Quraish (Al-Mubarakpuri 1996: 135). In a similar context, in 5 AH/ AD 628 during the expedition of *Al-Khandaq/* the Trench (also named *Al-Ahzab /* the Confederates), the war situation was extremely dangerous as Quraish managed to form a large confederation of allies seeking to exterminate the Muslim community and city-state in Medina, including external Arab tribes and internal collaborators (Qur'an, 2012: 33/10–12). In the midst of this severe situation, Prophet Muhammad summoned his advisory committee to discuss a plan to defend Medina. Salman Al-Farisi (one of the companions) expressed his opinion and proposed the digging a deep trench around Medina as a defensive line to prevent the enemies from invading the city. The Prophet (pbuh) accepted Salman's opinion because it was very effective, as the Arab fighters at the time were not used to such tactics (Al-Mubarakpuri, 1996: 195).

During the rule of the Rashidun Caliphs (11AH/ 622 AD to 41AH/ 661AD), freedom of speech continued to be preserved, and people were empowered to exercise their rights. For instance, both Abu Bakr Al-Siddiq and Omar Ibn Al-Khattab recognized the people's right to freedom of speech, particularly to criticize the actions and policies of the Caliph (i.e. in terms of government, and the Caliph personally). This was clearly stated in their inauguration speeches, in which they enjoined people to support them if they did right, and to correct them if they did wrong. Moreover, they encouraged people to comment on government policies, decisions, and held the ruler accountable for his actions. They also granted the scholars much freedom to think, criticize and develop new rulings to address emerging social, economic and political issues. Moreover, in many incidents the people could speak their minds openly even in the mosque, and express their disagreement with the Caliph's opinion (Ibn Kathir, 1988: 6/301; Al-Tabari, 1967: 4/215).

Significance of freedom of speech

Islam as well as the international human rights laws and conventions lay great importance on the centrality and universalism of freedom of speech, considering it to be a fundamental right, not a gift; the foundation of faith, a pillar of democracy, and the underpinning of development, innovation, and stability for individuals and communities. In human rights discourse, fundamental freedoms such as general freedom, freedom of speech, conscience, and belief for the individual and communities concur with several articles of the Universal Declaration of Human Rights (UDHR). For example, the Declaration states that all human beings are born free and are entitled to all rights and freedoms, without distinction of any kind. Moreover, it emphasizes freedom of speech by stating 'Everyone has the right to freedom of opinion and expression; this right includes freedom to hold opinions without interference and to seek, receive and impart information and ideas through any media and regardless of frontiers' (UN, 2015: 1–4, 19).

Islam has made freedom paramount, and practically liberated people from all sorts of oppressions and slavery in their belief, society, politics and economy. One of the noteworthy examples is freedom of belief and conscience, even if this belief leads the person to embrace a religion or an ideology other than Islam. The Qur'an states that there should not be any compulsions in religion, and people should respect each other's freedom of religious choice (Qur'an, 2/256; 10/99).

However, religious scholars, social scientists and advocates of democracy differ on the scope, scale and limitations of freedom of speech. These remain controversial, as no uniformity can be expected over almost any aspect of the subject because of cultural, religious and ideological differences. Perhaps ethical norms reduce some differences because they are shared among people of different religious traditions across the globe.

Islam and international human rights law promote large-scale freedoms in general and freedom of belief and speech in particular. Hence, it is intrinsically cause for enthusiasm that there is more freedom of speech nowadays, especially with the digital revolution, whereby people from around the globe can share their opinions and channel their comments on any news and information via social media such as Facebook and Twitter. It is noteworthy that freedom of speech is one of the most important success criteria to assess the commitment of media professionals and agencies to ethics, because it is unfair to hold them accountable if they are not free, although sometimes the media becomes part of the story and event, and not a mere honest transmitter.

Nevertheless, as far as freedom of speech is concerned, it is important to note that there is always a gap between the ideals and the reality in all societies, and there are overt curtailments of such freedoms in many countries, particularly in Africa and Asia. Although freedom has a great impact on the media and is inseparable from democracy, many dictators and political regimes worldwide ban or restrict freedoms, especially freedom of speech, seeking to silence journalists under the principle that 'whoever is not with us is against us'. This means that people who go against the regime or ruler will face all sorts of punishment, including assassination, imprisonment, dismissal from their jobs, harassment, deprivation of rights of travel, and being blacklisted etc. Reports on freedom of journalism show that hundreds of journalists are being killed each year; many others have been abducted or jailed, and numerous others have been sacked from their job. The Committee to Protect Journalists (CPJ, 2021) confirmed that between 1992 and 2021 about 1,397 journalists and media workers were killed, and about 892 (approximately 64%) of them were deliberately murdered. Most of them were assassinated in Muslim countries, including the savage murder of Jamal Khashoggi by Saudi agents in the Saudi Consulate in Istanbul in October 2018. Moreover, more than 1,865 journalists are imprisoned worldwide.

Limits on freedom of speech

Within this systematic approach, one of the critical questions that arises is whether freedom of speech is unconditional and uncontestable, or whether it is subject to limitations that apply to other rights and liberties. In other words, does freedom of speech give people the right to say anything they want, and anywhere they want? It is vital to stress the necessity of the ethical and legal limitations on freedom of speech to ensure the sustainability of the environment of freedom, and to avoid any harm to the rights and dignity of individuals and communities. Islam as well as international human rights law imposes some limitations on freedom of speech. For instance, the Universal Declaration of Human Rights states that

> in the exercise of his rights and freedoms, everyone shall be subject only to such limitations as are determined by law solely for the purpose of securing due recognition and respect for the rights and freedoms of others, and of meeting the just requirements of morality, public order and the general welfare in a democratic society. (UN, 2015: 29)

Similarly, the UIDHR states that everyone has the right to express thoughts and beliefs as long as they remain within the limits prescribed by applicable laws. However, no one is entitled to disseminate falsehood or to circulate reports which may outrage public decency, or to indulge in slander, innuendo or to cast defamatory aspersions on other people. Furthermore, it affirms that there is no bar on the dissemination of information provided it does not endanger the security of the society or the state, and is confined within the limits imposed by the Law (IC, 1981: XII/a & d). This essentially rational and measured approach was a finely crafted legal doctrine 40 years ago, but contemporary human rights discourse faces new challenges that were not foreseen by the drafters of historical law on freedom of speech at the national and international levels. Rasool (2016) commented that the acceptance of freedom of speech is critical to the self-image and dignity of individuals and communities and a pillar of democracy, but such acceptance is neither unconditional nor uncontested. Kamali (2016) recognized that in an era of instant worldwide publication via social media, it is impossible to feel calm in a society that only demands freedom of expression, but is unmindful of its limitations.

It is understood from the Islamic sources, particularly the Qur'an and *Sunnah*, that the chief reason behind the limitation on freedom of speech is the potential of causing harm (*dharar*) to other creatures. Islam prohibits all sorts of harms on all creatures and emphasizes on the avoidance of harm based on the Islamic principle/maxim 'harm must be eliminated' (*al Dhararu uzal*), analogous to the 'offence principle' in the Western tradition, whereby any harm inflicted on an individual or a group has to be removed and remedied. This Islamic legal maxim was derived from the prophetic *hadith* 'There should be neither harming nor reciprocating harm' (Ibn Majah, 2021: 13/34; Ibn Anas, 2021: 36/1435).

Dharar to humans means inflicting physical, moral, mental, social and/or psychological damage on an individual or the community at large. Harm that can obviously be caused by freedom of speech channelled through traditional and new media. These broadly include intrinsic attacks on the dignity and honour of individuals and their freedom of belief etc., and the promotion of chaos in society, incitement to crime and violence, hurtful speech and physical harm. For this reason, Islam strictly bans telling lies, backbiting, slander, obscenity, insults, sedition, blasphemy (i.e. pugnacious attacks on Islamic and non-Islamic religious beliefs and systems outside the context of formal, respectful debates and discourse), fake news, espionage, hurtful speech, subversive and unlawful conduct, defamation, disclosures of confidential information etc. For example, Allah says, 'O you who believe! no people shall ridicule other people ... nor shall you slender one another, nor shall you insult one another with names ... O you who believe avoid most suspicion ... and do not spy on one another, nor backbite one another ...' (Qur'an, 2012: 49/11–12, cf. 4/148). It is worth mentioning the prohibition of insulting idols. Literally nothing is as antithetical to Islam as idol worship, yet Allah forbade Muslims from insulting idols due to the *dharar* it would bring upon idolaters in their reciprocal attacks on Allah (Qur'an, 2012: 6/108). Besides, the Prophet Muhammad (pbuh) took these teachings further in the prominent saying: 'A Muslim is one from whose tongue and hand other people are safe' (Al-Nasai', 2021: 47/11).

Conceptions of responsibility

Meaning and aspects of responsibility

The term 'responsibility' is derived from 'response', and a review of its lexical usage in some dictionaries suggests that it is 'The opportunity or ability to act independently and take decisions without authorization ... a thing which one is required to do as part of a job, role, or legal obligation' (Oxford, 2021), and 'Something that it is your job or duty to deal with' (Cambridge, 2021). It also means 'The state or position of being responsible' (Collins, 2021), 'A duty that you have to do because it is part of your job or position' (Macmillan, 2021), 'A particular burden of obligation upon someone who is responsible: to feel the responsibilities of one's position' (Macquarie, 2021), and 'The state or fact of being responsible, answerable or accountable for something within one's power, control or management' (Dictionary.com.). However, a concise and operational definition of responsibility could be 'obligation to satisfactorily perform a task' (McGrath and Whitty, 2018: 695).

Personal responsibility means 'an obligation to oneself; it is an individual duty for a person to ensure his/her good character and behaviour irrespective of how that individual was brought up and what kind of conditioning he/she had received' (Ekanem, 2014: 2). The concept of individual responsibility means

> the accountability of an individual or collective actor for actions that have already been performed or are going to be performed in the future ... responsibility points to actions and also to plans of actions. In other words, responsibility can be retrospective and prospective. (Maier, 2019: 27)

The different aspects of responsibility are best summarized as: 'causal responsibility', 'liability responsibility', 'role responsibility', and 'capacity responsibility'. *Causal* responsibility means holding someone responsible for an event or an outcome according to a causal connection between what that person has done and the event. *Liability* responsibility is connected to praise or blame (i.e. someone is held liable for a certain event that he or she caused). *Role* responsibility refers to a certain task or role that one is assigned or occupies, and the specific responsibilities this task or role involves. *Capacity* responsibility means that a person can only be held responsible or be assigned responsibility for something or someone if he or she possesses fully the faculties of understanding and reasoning, and is in control of his or her conduct (Hart, 2008: 212–222).

Voegtlin (2016) reviewed a wide range of literature on other dimensions of responsibility and offered some interesting ideas in relation to blame and virtue. Blame usually occurs when there is violation of a moral norm, when someone's behaviour is morally blameworthy. This means that the agent has capacity-responsibility, has done something wrong, and is causally responsible for the harmful incident. In the context of virtue, responsibility is used in the sense of moral responsibility, which refers to moral deficiency, such as the absence of care for or concern about the welfare of others, which in other words means an absence of virtue-responsibility. Responsibility is here a question of relationship that describes how things are and how things should be or should have been. Thus, responsibility is both descriptive and normative, and both prospective and retrospective.

Islam and responsibility

Islam emphasizes responsibility, and holds people responsible for their actions, whether big or small. The Qur'an teaches that 'Whoever has done an atom's weight of good will see it. And whoever has done an atom's weight of evil will see it' (99/6–8; also 31/16), and in the *hadith* 'all of you are guardians and are responsible for your wards …' (Al-Bukhari, 2021: 67/134). It is understood from the Islamic sources that responsibility is a trust that should be maintained at all times: 'O you who believe do not betray Allah and the Messenger, nor betray your trusts, while you know' (Qur'an, 2012: 8/27).

Draz (2008), as one of the most prominent contemporary Muslim scholars in moral philosophy, in his chief work *The Moral World of the Qur'an* offered a thorough analysis of the concept of responsibility (*al-Mas'uliya*) from ethical, religious and social perspectives. He distinguished responsibility from the two main moral concepts of 'obligation' (*al-Ilzam*) and 'sanction' (*al-Jaza'*). He emphasized that these three notions are interdependent and inseparable. Draz devoted his second chapter to a deep discussion of the idea of responsibility, focusing on its meaning, scope and conditions, with illustrative examples. He adopted the etymological meaning that to be responsible is to be obliged to answer for something, or to be accountable to someone.

However, Draz (2008) defined responsibility as a natural disposition, which is the capacity to take something upon oneself, and then the power to discharge one's undertaking through one's own endeavours. He pointed out that necessity and contingence are the two characteristics that comprise the respective spheres of responsibility. He maintained that some degree of responsibility is attached to human life at every moment, citing examples such as a father being is responsible for the material and moral well-being of his children; a teacher being responsible for the moral and intellectual education of young people; a magistrate being responsible for the application of justice; and a policeman being responsible for public security.

Based on his careful understanding of the Qur'an, Draz (2008) categorized responsibility into three types: religious, social and moral responsibility. He clarified that the Qur'an mentions all three of them together in one verse 'Believers, do not betray Allah and the Messenger, or knowingly betray others' (8/27). He stressed that any type of responsibility, as soon as it has been accepted, is a purely moral responsibility. While considering the universal character of the principle of responsibility, Draz developed the following key conditions for moral and religious responsibility:

- **Personal/individual:** This means that there can be no transfer, extension, participation or confusion, even between father and son. The Qur'an teaches 'He who commits a blameworthy act only commits it against his own soul' (4/111), '… no soul will bear another's burden …' (17/15), and 'Fear a day when no father will be able to atone for his son, or son for his father, in anyway' (31/33).

- **Knowledge and consciousness:** This applies to individual or collective knowledge, and means that no one will have to account for his actions without having been informed and made aware of their rules and duties beforehand. For instance, Allah says, 'Allah would never misguide a people after guiding them until He had made it clear to them what they should avoid' (Qur'an: 9/115) and '… We never punish until We have sent a Messenger' (17/15).

- **Will:** This means that an involuntary action must be excluded from the realm of responsibility. Therefore, it is important to take into account the way in which actions were produced and performed, as well as their relationship with the person. However, an innocent deviation of the will does not make one guilty under the law. Generally, the human will appears throughout the Qur'an as free and autonomous. Thus, it is clear that only the voluntary and the intentional act incurs responsibility. It is mentioned in the Qur'an that 'you are not to blame for any honest mistake you make, but only for what your hearts premeditate' (33/5, cf. 2/223, 5/89, and 17/25). Furthermore, the Prophet (pbuh) said: 'There are three whose actions are not recorded [not responsible for their actions]: a lunatic whose mind is deranged till he is restored to consciousness, a sleeper till he awakes, and a boy till he reaches puberty' (Abu Dawud, 2021: 40/51).

- **Freedom and independence:** Responsibility and freedom are strongly connected because it is unjust to hold people responsible/accountable for their actions and sayings if they are not free. For example, there will be no blame on a believer for abjuring his faith when compelled to do so under torture, in order to escape their violence: 'Whoso disbelieves in Allah after his belief – except for him who is forced to do so and whose heart is still content with faith – but whoso finds ease in disbelief, on them is the wrath of Allah' (Qur'an: 16/106). The same is true of the person who has to eat forbidden food because of the necessities of hunger, as well as the sin of a woman forced into prostitution by a despotic master (Qur'an: 2/173; 24/33).

To recap the above-mentioned conditions of responsibility, only normal adults (whether individuals or groups of individuals), aware of their obligations, autonomous, and having free will at the moment of acting are held responsible and answerable for their actions, including in terms of criminal responsibility under Islamic Sharia as well as spiritual accountability before their Creator (Draz, 2008: 67–116).

Responsibility of media professionals

It is evident nowadays that the role of media practitioners is significant because of their ability to influence a large number of people and penetrate to their minds, souls and hearts. Eid (2014: 191) argues that 'media practitioners have the ability to seriously impact how audiences perceive experiences and events'. They can easily influence the national security of countries and the international community using the different means of mass media. Moreover, in various countries around the world, money is used to incite media professionals to attack political opponents, rather than bringing abstract informational benefits to people. Hence, it is very important to introduce the key values that are related to responsibility from an Islamic ethical perspective that apply to media professionals, particularly in relation to their character, the source of their material, the content they transmit and the means they use. Adopting the following values is essential for a global media ethics understanding.

- Trustworthiness: Working in media or in any other profession is a trust, and media professionals should be worthy of such trust. Allah says, 'O you who believe do not betray Allah and the Messenger, nor betray your trusts, while you know' (Qur'an: 8/27), and 'Who are faithful to their trusts and avoid breaking their pledges' (Qur'an: 23/8; cf. 17/34).
- Truthfulness: Media codes of ethics indicate that media professionals should always be truthful in their work, including the transmission of correct and accurate information without falsification, tarnishing or inflation of events or stories. This has clearly been highlighted in the Qur'an ('... stay away from perjury' (22/30; cf. 33/35)), and in the *hadith* 'It is obligatory for you to tell the truth, for truth leads to virtue and virtue leads to Paradise ... and beware of telling of a lie for telling of a lie leads to obscenity and obscenity leads to Hell-Fire ...' (Muslim, 2021: 45/136). Avoiding verbal hypocrisy is also essential in being truthful, '... They say with their mouths what is not in their hearts; but God knows what they hide' (Qur'an: 3/167). Today, many media professionals and agencies have deviated from the two principles mentioned above.
- Witnessing with the truth: Media professionals are witnesses in society and they should not bear witness with deceit, or cover-up the truth. The Qur'an teaches: '... not conceal testimony. Whoever conceals it is a sinner at heart ...' (2/282–283; cf. 22/30; 65/2).
- Commanding good and forbidding evil/corruption: One of the important roles of media professionals is to command good and forbid evil in all areas of their work; to seek the truth and provide guidance toward good practice are ethical values. Allah says, 'You are the best community that ever emerged for humanity: you advocate what is moral/right, and forbid what is immoral/wrong ...' (Qur'an: 3/110, cf. 31/17; 5/79; 11/97–98; 22/41).
- Checking the content and verification of the source and authenticity of news: One of the fundamental duties of a media professional is to verify

the content and authenticity of news, as Allah commands: 'O you who believe if a *fasiq* [rebellious evil person] brings you any news, investigate, lest you harm people out of ignorance, and you become regretful for what you have done' (Qur'an: 49/6, 12). The Prophet (pbuh) said: 'It is enough falsehood for a man to relate everything he hears' (Abu Dawud, 2021: 43/220).

- Contribution to the preservation of life, religion, intellect, honour/family and wealth in society and the world. In the Islamic tradition, these 'Higher Objectives of Sharia' (*Maqasid al-Shariah*) are the supreme objectives of the religion in terms of the organization of human affairs, and they have to be preserved at all times by individuals, groups, and states. For instance, Allah says, 'O you who believe! Protect yourselves and your families from a Fire, whose fuel is people and stones ...' (Qur'an, 2012: 66/6). A *hadith* states "all of you are guardians and are responsible for your wards ..." (Al-Bukhari, 2021: 67/134), and the UDHR declares that 'The family is the natural and fundamental group unit of society and is entitled to protection by society and the State' (UN, 2015: 16/3).

- Giving advice to rulers and the general public: One of the most influential roles of media professionals is offering advice, guidance and education for the leaders as well as the public on any sector of life. They have an educational responsibility towards their viewers. The Qur'an instructs, '... and recommend one another to the truth ...' (103/3) and '[Prophet] give good news to My servants who listen to what is said and follow what is best ...' (39/17–18).

- Sticking to principles and professionalism, and resisting subversive influences that undermine independence, trustworthiness and truthfulness. Many media personnel and agencies have media codes of ethics and professional ethical guidelines and protocols, but they do not observe them, or commit themselves to do so in any serious way. This is perhaps because of the powerful influences of politics, money and ideological affiliations. Media experts are potentially exposed to political and material influences. Therefore, it is incumbent upon media professionals to stay safe from all kind of influences, as understood from the Qur'anic teachings: 'And do not exchange God's covenant for a small price. What is with God is better for you, if you only knew' (16/95); 'And do not consume one another's wealth by unjust means, nor offer it as bribes to the officials in order to consume part of other people's wealth illicitly, while you know' (2/188). Besides, a *hadith* states: 'The Messenger of Allah cursed the one who bribes and the one who takes a bribe for a judgment' (Al-Tirmidhi, 2021: 15/16).

Sketch of new media practices and the higher objectives of Sharia

Muslim jurists derived the 'Higher Objectives of Sharia' from the principles of the Qur'an and Sunnah, agreeing that Islam institutes five major objectives, namely the protection of freedom in terms of: (1) faith/religion, (2) life/soul, (3) mind/intellect, (4) wealth/property, and (5) lineage/honour. Looking at the activities of the new media and many of its users in relation to freedom of speech, one could easily conclude that they fail in one or more of these areas, especially in terms of the mind, religion and honour. Although social media platforms such as Facebook and Twitter have many advantages, their inappropriate use has led to ethical violations, including posting negative comments and insulting or offensive opinions about each other, breaching confidentiality and defamation. These violations may cause drastic effects on people's physical and mental well-being, identity, belonging, formal and informal learning, civil and political engagement, risk and safety, family and intergenerational relationships, consumer practices, and so on. Eid (2014) highlighted that if journalists choose to engage in unethical behaviour they fail not only their own ethical standards, but also the societies they serve. Hence, the following paragraphs highlight the significance of Islamic ethical values and the Higher Objectives of Sharia for modern media practice. It is important to showcase how some events, incidents, experiences and media cases could be addressed with the framework of the Higher Objectives of Sharia.

Preservation of faith/religion

This originally referred more simply and comprehensively to 'protection of religion', but it has been reinterpreted in modern legal contexts to mean 'freedom of faith/belief'. This is understood from some verses in the Qur'an, including 'There shall be no compulsion in the religion' (2/256, cf. 10/99; 109/6). Besides, religious topics are among the hot issues discussed on social media. In many instances, media users go beyond the limits and publish material that could be considered anti-religious, blasphemous and mockery, although where this is criticized at all it is usually on the grounds of ethnic discrimination (e.g. against Muslims), while generally being defended as inviolable freedom of speech. This usually instigates sensitivities, tensions, hatred, violence, and even provokes terrorist attacks against and among religious groups.

This issue mainly (but not exclusively) concerns egregious attacks against Muslims and Islam, in the general milieu of vitriolic Islamophobia that has surged in the West and worldwide since 9/11. Building on primordial hatred of the Muslim other and European colonial ideologies, the identification of Muslims and Islam as the enemy of the West since 2001 has provided fertile ground for media exploitation of anti-immigrant racism and Western foreign policy tropes demonizing 'others' (Zempi and Awan, 2021). For instance, in 2005 the Danish newspaper *Jyllands-Posten* published 12 editorial cartoons depicting the Prophet Muhammad (pbuh) with a bomb in his turban. As calculated, this act enraged Muslims around the world, who viewed it as highly blasphemous and inciting hatred against them. Therefore, millions of Muslims in many countries around the world protested and boycotted Danish products (Reuters, 2020). The French magazine *Charlie Hebdo* capitalized on this notoriety by republishing the Danish cartoons in 2006, and flagging sales were boosted after publishing new cartoons insulting the Prophet Muhammad (pbuh) and Islam in 2015, which were subsequently republished in 2020. Violent, criminal reactions by outraged Muslims were denounced by global leaders, who staunchly defended the right to insult the Prophet Muhammad (pbuh), Islam and Muslims. Muslims considered these insults and provocations to comprise blasphemy, mockery and hatred, masked by dogmas of freedom of speech. As a result, many Muslims protested and there were deadly riots in many Muslim countries and a fatal attack on *Charlie Hebdo*'s office, leaving 12 dead, including 11 people inside, among them the top editor and some of its leading cartoonists, and a police officer on the street in addition to several wounded (Onishi, 2020).

Preservation of the soul/life

This refers to the right to life and the prohibition of any threats to the life of a human being. The Qur'an clearly prohibits killing, including suicide. Allah says, '... whoever kills a person—unless it is for murder or corruption on earth—it is as if he killed the whole of mankind; and whoever saves it, it is as if he saved the whole of mankind ...' (5/32, cf. 6/151; 4/92–93; 4/29). It has been reported that Prophet Muhammad (pbuh) said:

> Verily! Your blood, property and honor are sacred to one another like the sanctity of this day of yours, in this month of yours and in this city of yours. It is incumbent upon those who are present to inform those who are absent. (Al-Bukhari, 2021: 3/9, 47; 78/73)

The UIDHR states that human life is sacred and inviolable; every effort must be made to protect it, and no one shall be exposed to death, except under the authority of the Law (IC, 1981: I/a). The ECHR reiterates the same principles (ECtHR, 2013: 1/2–3). Therefore, media platforms ban all kinds of material that incite violence and/or promote killing or suicide, and if such material has been posted, it will obviously be removed by the editor.

Preservation of mind/intellect

Islam promotes the preservation of mind or the intellect in at least two important ways: (a) the prohibition of intoxicants: For instance Allah says, 'O you who believe! Intoxicants ... are abominations of Satan's doing. Avoid them, so that you may prosper' (Qur'an, 2012: 5/90, cf. 2/219); and (b) the injunction to seek knowledge and avoid superstition, fanaticism and unthinking stupidity, while it promotes rational analysis. For example Allah says, 'And when it is said to them, "Follow what God has revealed", they say, "We will follow what we found our ancestors following?" Even if their ancestors understood nothing, and were not guided?' (Qur'an, 2012: 2/170); 'In the creation of the heavens and the earth, and in the alternation of night and day, are signs for people of understanding' (3/190); 'Say, "Roam the earth, and observe how He originated the creation"' (29/20); 'And do not occupy yourself with what you have no knowledge of. The hearing, and the sight and the brains—all these will be questioned' (17/36). Social media and the Internet are means of knowledge that could be used constructively to preserve the intellect by seeking and disseminating knowledge and information. They also could be used distractively in promoting rumours, false news, racism, hatred, humiliation, indoctrination and intellectual shallowness. A study conducted by Chandra et al. (2017: 48) found that 15% of respondents had seen vulgar language, and 15% defamation or humiliation.

Preservation of progeny/honor/dignity

To maintain this objective, Islam encourages people to marry and establish a family. Allah says, 'And of His signs is that He created for you mates from among yourselves, so that you may find tranquility in them; and He planted love and compassion between you ...' (Qur'an, 2012: 30/21); 'And wed the singles among you, and those who are fit among your servants and maids. If they are poor, God will enrich them from His bounty. God is All-Encompassing, All-Knowing' (24/32, cf. 4/1; 16/72; 49/13). Besides, Allah commands people to care for their families, children, and kinsfolk: 'O you who believe! Protect yourselves and your families from a Fire ...' (Qur'an, 2012: 66/6). Moreover, Islam prohibits the spreading of wickedness and immorality. Allah says, 'Those who love to see immorality spread among the believers, for them is a painful punishment, in this life and in the Hereafter ...' (24/19, cf. 4/25; 23/5–7; 25/68–69).

Besides, Islam enjoins people to respect one another's privacy and preserve everyone's dignity in life or after death. Breach of privacy is not limited to what is inside people's house, but also their wallets, files/documents, computers, mobile phones, social media accounts, projects, and anything they have acquired or developed and wanted to keep confidential and private. Allah says, 'O you who believe! No people shall ridicule other people ... Nor shall any women ridicule other women ... Nor shall you slander one another, nor shall you insult one another with names ... O you who believe! Avoid most suspicion—some suspicion is sinful. And do not spy on one another, nor backbite one another ...' (Qur'an, 2012: 49/11–12, cf. 24/ 27–29; Al-Bukhari, 2021: 3/9, 47, 78/73). Moreover, the UIDHR states that every person has the right to their honour and reputation, including protection against calumnies, groundless charges, or deliberate attempts at defamation and blackmail, and every person is entitled to the protection of privacy (IC, 1981: XXII, VIII). Chandra et al. (2017: 48) found that 15% of respondents had seen vulgar language, 15% defamation or humiliation, 14% sharing of personal problems, 3% other (including cyber bullying, harassment, stalking and gender inequality, human rights and fake death news). The study concluded that defamation, humiliation and vulgar language are the most prolific unethical practices seen on social media.

Preservation of wealth/property

Islam encourages people to work and follow legitimate means to acquire and develop their wealth, and protect their properties. Allah says, 'It is He who made the earth manageable for you, so travel its regions, and eat of His provisions ...' (Qur'an, 2012: 67/15), and the Prophet Muhammad (pbuh) said: 'Nobody has ever eaten a better meal than that which one has earned by working with one's own hands. The Prophet of Allah, David, used to eat from the earnings of his manual labor' (Al-Bukhari, 2021: 34/25). Moreover, Islam prohibits eating *suh*, which includes all kinds of illegal earnings, such as those from theft, gambling, usury and bribery etc. There are numerous verses in the Qur'an that prove this, including 'And do not consume one another's wealth by unjust means, nor offer it as bribes to the officials in order to consume part of other people's wealth illicitly, while you know' (2/188, cf. 5/33, 38, 42, 62–63; 2/275; 4:10). The UIDHR affirms that no property may be expropriated except in the public interest and on payment of fair and adequate compensation (IC, 1981: XVI).

In sum, social media and the Internet have nowadays become major tools of commerce and business transactions. Online shopping and electronic payment for goods and services have become widespread practice among new media users. Besides their huge benefits, people as well as governments in many countries around the globe have been attacked in their properties and wealth, and they have been cheated and blackmailed, with their wealth hijacked through illegal and unethical cyber activities. Other examples of unethical practice by social media users include misrepresenting their level of expertise or the services they provide to the public and the products they sell or promote. Chandra et al. (2017: 48) found that 11% of respondents had been exposed to fraudulent services, 8% to insulting advertisements, 7% to scams, and 3% to other threats.

Conclusions

Freedom in general and freedom of speech in particular, is a fundamental value in Islam. It has been established that freedom of speech is an essential right for all humans (regardless of their religious or ideological affiliation). Moreover, its scope has been broadened up to cover any issues including the most sensitive topics, such as questioning the oneness of God, the truthfulness of Prophets, and the authenticity of the religious teachings. However, it is important to note that real life experience shows that Muslim-majority countries vary greatly in respect of scope and scale of freedom of speech granted to their peoples.

It has been established that freedom of speech does entail that people may say anything they want and anywhere they want. Moreover, individual freedom does not expand to the right to violate the rights of other people, including their privacy and personal dignity. Furthermore, it does not permit people to promote chaos in society or incite to crime, violence and racism. It is vital for media professionals to avoid harm (*dharar*) to others while exercising freedom of speech and information. In order to regulate freedom of speech and ensure a sustainable freedom environment, Islam invokes the essential principle known as the 'elimination of harm', known as the 'offense principle' in the Western tradition. This simply means that a person or a group of people and agencies must eliminate harm while exercising their rights to freedom of speech using any media platforms.

Furthermore, it has been argued that media professionals and social media users have to be committed to the key values, including truthfulness, trustworthiness and commanding good and shunning evil. Moreover, they should endeavour to contribute to the preservation of universal principles, particularly the sacred inviolability of the intellect and honour. It is important to stress that media professionals should not deviate from the above discussed values and principles. Eventually, freedom of speech is the success criteria for media ethics, because media professionals and social media users can only be held accountable for their actions and sayings if they are free, to the extent that free will and freedom of speech are practically synonymous.

Responsibility is an important ethical value which is strongly tied to freedom of speech. They are two inseparable principles, and fundamental concepts in ethics and human rights. Responsibility depends on the condition of the individual, because only a normal adult, aware of obligations, and *compos mentis* at the moment of acting can undertake responsibility for actions of free speech. Once defined in such terms, agents become answerable for their actions. It should be emphasized that the conditions of responsibility, principally consciousness and free will, at least as set by Draz (2008), guarantee freedom of speech for media professionals and social media users without any liability. Therefore, only a normal adult/individual or a group of individuals who are aware of their obligations, who are autonomous, and who have free will at the moment of acting are responsible and answerable for their actions.

By way of conclusion, media practitioners, media networks and agencies, and social media users have a great responsibility for the well-being and development of individuals and communities by their commitment to work with integrity and professionalism within the framework explained as the 'Higher Objectives of Sharia and the Islamic Legal Maxims'. It is worth stressing that abuse of freedom of speech and irresponsible acts, whether by traditional or new media users and practitioners, are considered unethical and intrinsically harmful for all sectors of life. However, people's misconceptions and misuse of freedom of speech, together with a lack of commitment to responsibility, could be changed not only by legislation and punishment, but most importantly by creating awareness that media ethics is paramount, hence it is important to foster related education, training, incentives and exposure to excellent examples. Furthermore, codes of ethics should be developed to provide principles and guidelines to individuals and organizations that are engaged in the media industry, to equip them with knowledge and skills to distinguish between what is right and what is wrong as well as to make ethical decisions.

References

Abu Dawud, S. Ibn (2021), *Sunan Abi Dawud*. Retrieved from https://sunnah.com/abuda wud. Accessed: 15 February 2021.

Al-Bukhari, M. Ibn I. (2021), *Sahih Al-Bukhari*. Retrieved from: https://sunnah.com/ bukhari. Accessed: 15 February 2021.

Al-Mubarakpuri, S. (1996), *The Sealed Nectar-Biography of the Noble Prophet*. Riyadh: Dar-us-Salam Publications.

Al-Nasa'i, Abu A.A. Ibn S. (2021), *Sunan Al-Nasa'i*. Retrieved from: https://sunnah.com/nasai. Accessed: 15 February 2021.

Al-Tabari, M. Ibn J. (1967), *Tarikh Al-Tabari* (in Arabic). Cairo: Dar al- Ma'arif.

Al-Tirmidhi, A. (2021), *Jami' Al-Tirmidhi*. Retrieved from: https://sunnah.com/tirmidhi. Accessed: 15 February 2021.

Cambridge Online Dictionary. Retrieved from: http://dictionary.cambridge.org/dictionary/british. Accessed: 15 February 2021.

Chandra, K., Singh, N. K., Gounder, S., Verma, R. and Mudaliar, S. (2017), 'The unethical practices on social media'. *IOSR. Journal of Humanities and Social Sciences*, 22(7), 46–54.

Collins English Dictionary. Retrieved from: www.collinsdictionary.com/dictionary/english. Accessed: 15 February 2021.

Committee to Protect Journalists (CPJ) (2021), 'Data: "Journalists killed" & "Journalists imprisoned"'. Retrieved from: https://cpj.org/data. Accessed: 15 February 2021.

Dictionary.com (2021), *Online Dictionary*. Retrieved from: http://dictionary.reference.com. Accessed: 15 February 2021.

Draz, M. A. (2008), *The Moral World of the Qur'an*, trans. Danielle Robinson and Rebecca Masterton. London: I.B.Tauris.

Eid, M. (2014), 'Ethics, Media, and Reasoning: Systems and Applications', in Rocci Luppicini (ed.), *Evolving Issues Surrounding Technoethics and Society in the Digital Age*. IGI Global, pp. 188–198.

Ekanem, S. A. (2014), 'Personal responsibility and social development: Implication for global ethics'. *Academic Journal of Interdisciplinary Studies*, 3(4), 479–485.

Epstein, R. A. (1987), 'The fundamentals of freedom of speech'. *Harvard Journal of Law and Public Policy*, 10(53), 53–60.

European Court of Human Rights (2013), *European Convention on Human Rights*. Retrieved from: www.echr.coe.int. Accessed: 15 February 2021.

Hart, H. A. (2008), *Punishment and Responsibility: Essays in the Philosophy of Law*. Oxford: Oxford University Press.

Ibn Anas, M. (2021), *Al-Muwatta'*. Retrieved from: https://sunnah.com/malik. Accessed: 15 February 2021.

Ibn Kathir, M. bin I. (1988), *Al-Bidaya wa Al-Nihaya* (in Arabic). Beirut: Maktabat al-Ma'arif.

Ibn Majah, Y. (2021), *Sahih Ibn Majah*. Retrieved from: https://sunnah.com/ibnmajah. Accessed: 15 February 2021.

Islamic Council (1981), *Universal Islamic Declaration of Human Rights*. London: Islamic Council.

Kamali, M. H. (2016), *Ethical Limits on Freedom of Expression with Special Reference to Islam*. Islam and Applied Ethics Book Series. Doha: Research Center for Islamic Legislation and Ethics.

Macmillan Dictionary. Retrieved from: www.macmillandictionary.com. Accessed: 15 February 2021.

Macquarie Dictionary Online. Retrieved from: www.macquarieonline.com.au. Accessed: 15 February 2021.

Maier, R. (2019), 'Self-responsibility: Transformation'. *American Behavioral Scientist*, 63 (1), 27–42.

McGrath, K. and Whitty, J. (2018), 'Accountability and responsibility defined'. *International Journal of Managing Projects in Business*, 11(3), 687–707.

Onishi, N. (1 September2020). 'Charlie Hebdo republishes cartoons that prompted deadly 2015 attack'. *The New York Times*. Retrieved from: https://www.nytimes.com/2020/09/01/world/europe/charlie-hebdo-cartoons-trial-france.html. Accessed: 15 February 2021.

Oxford Dictionaries Online. Retrieved from: http://oxforddictionaries.com. Accessed: 15 February 2021.

Quran. (2012), Translated by Talal Itani. Retrieved from: https://www.clearquran.com/. Accessed: 15 February 2021.

Rasool, I. (2016), *Freedom and Its Limitations: Ensuring Dignity, Avoiding Authoritarianism*. Islam and Applied Ethics Book Series. Doha: Research Center for Islamic Legislation and Ethics.

Reuters Staff (2 November2020), 'Timeline: Violence marks 15-year furore over cartoons of Prophet Mohammad'. *Reuters*. Retrieved from: https://www.reuters.com/article/us-france-security-cartoons-timeline/timeline-violence-marks-15-year-furore-over-cartoons-of-prophet-mohammad-idUSKBN27I1U3. Accessed: 15 February 2021.

United Nations (2015), *Universal Declaration of Human Rights*. Retrieved from: https://www.un.org/en/udhrbook/pdf/udhr_booklet_en_web.pdf. Accessed: 15 February 2021.

Voegtlin, C. (2016), 'What does it mean to be responsible? Addressing the missing responsibility dimension in the ethical leadership research'. *Leadership*, 12(5), 581–608.

Zempi, I, and Awan, I. (eds) (2021), *The Routledge International Handbook of Islamophobia*. Abingdon: Routledge.

7 Philosophical roots of media ethics in the Islamic tradition

Noureddine Khadmi

Introduction

Media ethics has become a fundamental issue in today's world, given its current two-dimensional strands: abundance of media outlets and multiplicity of origins. The media glut can be seen through the magnitude of multimodal media, mainly digital communication that has pervaded the world and led to what is known as digital globalization. The multiplicity of media terms of reference consists of its diverse philosophical, political, social and legal backgrounds. This multiplicity has affected the media landscape and the variation of its normative and moral viewpoints depending on the context.

Thus, morality has also become a central concern for media practice. The search for a shared global ethical foundation is urgent. This shared foundation constitutes a consensual frame of reference, in absence of a common basis whose constituents are agreed upon. To embody the ethics of human co-existence and to distance the world from the moral decline that it may slide into, a degree of philosophical and legal dialogue and a level of moral decency in digital media is needed. Codes of ethics should consider people's vital and strategic challenges, distinctiveness, sacraments and sanctities. They should also hark back to what humans have in common, Adam and Eve. These ethics spring from the origins of creation, nature, dignity, and the need to secure peaceful co-existence. The Qur'an (55: 10) stresses the shared meaning of co-existence on earth '*He laid out the earth for all beings*'.

The holistic Islamic vision represents a guiding theoretical and practical framework to ensure media ethics through global cooperation. The Qur'an states: '*Cooperate with one another in goodness and righteousness, and do not cooperate in sin and transgression*' (5: 2). The Islamic vision also refers to the Islamic philosophy concerning media and media ethics. Islam's vision of media ethics is anchored in its texts, involving fundamentals and practical approaches to applying media ethics to modern contexts. Media ethics refers to the human values that should be observed by the media according to the Islamic vision, the common human ground and objectives of media standards.

The research problem in this chapter revolves around the extent to which an Islamic vision of media ethics should be interpreted and applied to real life. It

DOI: 10.4324/9781003203551-10

also investigates what is required to develop joint media approaches based on common moral principles, despite a multiplicity of worldviews. It is expected that this research will contribute to filling a gap in academia regarding scientifically deep-rooted ethics of communication and media in the Islamic approach.

This chapter therefore aims to achieve the following:

1 Present a scientific, methodological, and realistic approach regarding Islam's view on media ethics which ensures the media have a common moral foundation that bypasses ideological influences and bias. The Islamic approach advocates for collective action and free will to achieve a humane, pluralist and civilized developmental system that respects privacy and personal identity. It also recommends managing dialogue and events efficiently and deservedly, without dominance, obstruction or distortion and without undermining the humanity and values of those in discussion.

2 Adopt a holistic approach to frame the issue with a general philosophical underpinning Therefore, a desired model should be extrapolated from religious scriptures and goals and should call on Islam's theoretical and practical requirements when developing approaches according to context and purpose.

In order to analyse the above issues, this chapter will embark on presenting the general Islamic fundamental beliefs about media ethics. Then it will discuss more specific fundamentals, namely the legislative, functional and expressionist principles. Finally, it will focus on the operational and instrumental frameworks that can be applied to the course of social changes taking place in few Arab countries.

General Islamic fundamental belief about media ethics

This general fundamental belief represents the holistic framework for Islam's view about the divine, the cosmic and human existence, for existence refers to the existence of the Creator of the entire universe. It also refers to the existence of the creatures from all races, species, functions, locations and namely the existence of humankind and the environment in which they live. The Islamic worldview assumes that Allah (God) is the Creator of existence. He created it for humankind to inhabit and conquer the universe that He has tamed for them.

Two facts are attributed to the aforementioned fundamental belief:

Firstly, the uniqueness of Allah as opposed to the diversity of creation: The Creator is characterized by His uniqueness that no one would dare claim. The Qur'an reads: *'There is nothing like Him, for He "alone" is the All-Hearing, All-Seeing'* (42: 11). However, creatures are characterized by diversity and multiplicity. One aspect of diversity is gender i.e. male or female. Almighty Allah stated: *'And that He created the two mates - the male and female -'* (53: 45). He also stated: *'And We created pairs of all things so perhaps you would be mindful'* (51: 49). Other aspects of diversity are family, tribe, ethnicity and geographical location as reflected in functions, sectors, groupings and classifications.

Scientific specialization, political jurisdiction and cultural specificity are but a few examples of diversity.

Secondly, honouring human beings and harnessing existence for them. Islam honours human beings and states that God made all other creatures subservient to them, subject to certain requirements: freedom, responsibility and reckoning. These requirements were illustrated to them by sending messengers to reveal laws, explain the rulings and purpose of religious practices. Achieving all that requires a fruitful approach, a relevant context, an advanced cumulative process, evidence of validity and compatibility with era and location. Communication activities can be purposeful and beneficial if the above-mentioned guidelines are observed.

When observing the general Islamic fundamental belief about media ethics, journalists are expected to act according to their belief in the Creator and their knowledge of His decrees. Doing so indicates that media practice emanates from a message of not only deep belief in existence, values, morals and purposes but also of knowledge and actions relevant for any give situation. Knowledge, in this respect, refers to the great responsibility that Allah has delegated to human beings during their life. It also refers to the job of investigation and news tracking in its historical, human and natural context as well as in its modern international, geographical and technological contexts.

In fact, sending messengers each with a mission was at the origin of a greater purpose of God's revelation to human beings. He informed them about the purpose of existence and their agency in this existence. *We surely sent a messenger to every community, saying, 'Worship Allah and shun false gods'* (16: 36). Sending Prophet Muhammad and revealing the Holy Qur'an was the ultimate informational message regarding revelation and religious guidance. This informational message contained thorough contents on the issues of existence, its laws and its conditions.

The story of the creation of Adam represents a divine piece of information for angels about Adam's creation, honouring and assignment, as indicated in various verses: '"Remember" when your Lord said to the angels, 'I am going to place a successive ⊠human⊠ authority on earth.' They asked "Allah", 'Will You place in it someone who will spread corruption there and shed blood while we glorify Your praises and proclaim Your holiness?' Allah responded, 'I know what you do not know' (01: 30).

The stories of earlier times also included examples of objective and reliable recollections about what had happened and a request to learn lessons, to contemplate and to gain better insight so that error and misconduct would not be repeated. The purpose of such accounts was also for the sake of transcendence, liberation and civility. Almighty Allah stated: 'So narrate "to them" stories "of the past", so perhaps they will reflect' (07: 176). This indicates that thoughtful consideration of such stories is required to move from one state to another.

The benefit of applying fundamental Islamic belief to the reality of existence in general lies in two foundations. The first foundation concerns the uniqueness of the Creator and diversity of creation. Also noteworthy is the awareness and immense capacity required to maintain harmony across creation through unifying formative and mandatory laws which dictate phenomena such as behavioural instinct. The aim of establishing such regularity is for humanity to be aware of these rules and adhere to them, since there is no contradiction between them. Humanity should revise these when they fail to observe them.

In sum, media ethics emanate from the holistic view about the media's informative and deliberative mission. This mission aims at establishing mandatory regularity over formative orderliness by matching the formative rules to the mandatory rules in a way that reflects current events, their concomitant circumstances and challenges. It should also reflect the disparity between actors in terms of talents, positions and gains. The mission also aims at achieving the purposes of the regularity assuring a safely populated existence with fruitful potential assets.

In Islam, natural instinct is both formative and legislative because it is originally a congenital condition inherently prepared for a fit mandatory condition. Instinct is embedded in the human being and it is characterized by the ability to be mandated to do good or evil. At the same time, instinct is subject to evaluation and rehabilitation in case of deviation. Instinct is required to strike a balance between its original innate condition and its changing phases. In this way, it will swing between stability and change or progress and regression.

Saying that, it can be argued that media ethics are innate, and that natural instinct is a moral value for media and is part and parcel of the media's deliberative mission to create the news, to negotiate thought, to combat the jostling backgrounds and the crumbling doctrines over instinct. The role of media ethics is to determine the suitability of the news, to proofread it and to classify it. It is also to deny or reduce what may violate the origin of creation and the value of instinct. Deviations from natural instinct can be observed in calls for ethnic cleansing, human torture, sexual tampering, environmental corruption, and political and international oppression.

The Islamic legislative fundamentals for media ethics

These fundamentals refer to a set of provisions and *Sharia* rules that frame media ethics and all the related issues in Islamic legislation, as explained below.

1 Islamic law (Sharia) provisions for media ethics

Sharia provisions refer to the Islamic view about media and media ethics. In principle, media practice is considered a permissible matter but it becomes forbidden when it leads to false accusations, when it instigates unrest or diverts people's attention away from the values of right, freedom, responsibility and justice. However, the media's role becomes necessary when it aims at building a balanced human being, strengthening the developmental, democratic and educational capabilities of a nation, and resisting tyranny, occupation and corruption.

Therefore, Islamic legislation stipulates truth and honesty when reporting news. It also stipulates strict objectivity and professionalism when exchanging ideas or announcing news. It forbids mendacity, disinformation, slander and offending people for cultural, religious or racial affiliation. Among *Sharia* provisions for media ethics, are individual duties and collective duties. An individual duty refers to what every single Muslim is required to do like fasting Ramadan, performing prayers. In media ethics, Muslim journalists are required, religiously, and individually to opt for honesty and refrain from deception and immorality. The collective duty, however, refers to what is required of a group of Muslims who are competent in a given field, like medicine or engineering. The same applies to media ethics for Muslims specializing in media and journalism. This indicates that the media is of great importance for society and for the state, just as medicine, engineering, education and administration are. One of the aspects of the legislative approach to media ethics is human actions, such as a person's words, deeds, intent and insinuation. That action is subject to legislation in terms of religious precepts. For instance, fasting for the whole day is an act performed by the fasting person, even if it is actually abstinence from food, drink and sexual intercourse. This abstinence is considered a performed act by the doer, like prayer and Hajj (pilgrimage). The same applies to media ethics, as it is an act carried out by the journalist; they either comply with the correct ethics or foster corruption. Hence, this act is permissible or forbidden according to its nature and circumstances. It also includes editing, analysing information and any investigative work. By definition, it is a human act that is duty-bound or prohibited depending on its benefit or harm according to Islam's view of what is lawful or unlawful and according to common sense and established custom.

Religious legislation approves of human behaviour that is in accordance with *Sharia* and legal judgement. Broadly speaking, the law covers human actions, prevents forbidden acts like crime, and hold the doers to account through punishment. This precision is important to understand the Islamic vision of media ethics, a comprehensive perspective that considers all aspects of media ethics, namely being duty-bound or prohibited. This vision also considers the distinction between individual duty and collective duty and the fact that the human act must be a common topic, shared by religion, law and psychology.

2 Universal legal provisions for media ethics.

These are the universal legal principles of media ethics. The term 'legal maxims' covers the different aspects of media ethics that are related to its meaning and nature. The maxim 'acting according to benefit', for example, it is expressed in several formulas and rules, as in the following: 'sentencing is dependent on benefit', 'securing benefit and warding off evil', 'harm must be eliminated', and 'Islam promotes freedom'. These maxims, along with many others, apply to media and communication. 'Islam promotes freedom' is a maxim that applies to freedom of information and press and the right of people and organizations to responsible free media. The purpose is to resist tyranny, occupation and corruption and disclose facts, expose crimes, compensate for injury and empower people for the sake of competition, governance and efficiency.

The meaning of 'acting according to benefit' with respect to media ethics is manifested in countless forms as in commercial, environmental, cultural, nutritional and sports media. This meaning is reflected in the journalists' adherence to honesty, objectivity and transparency. Thus, every citizen can obtain information that is assured to be ethical, deliberative and encouraging dialogue, which upholds their rights as people in a balanced society. Media ethics in this case involves not only spreading but multiplying the values of good health, comfort and hope.

Islamic legislative basis for media ethics

A- Intention

Intention is the heart-felt purpose and the intrinsic orientation that guides the work we do. A good example of this is a person's determination to fast, which is guided by his/her heart and their inner self, seeking reward from God. The Islamic legislation has attached great importance to intention in performing actions requiring predetermination. The Prophet's tradition puts emphasis on fitting action to good intent: 'The value of an action depends on the intention behind it'.[1]

This *hadith* (Prophet's saying) lends itself to two interpretations:

1   Action is valid from the legal point of view. The act is not valid unless it is based on intent and determination.
2   Action is rewarded and gratified by Almighty Allah on the Day of Resurrection.

These two matters are important in bringing about the benefit of completing any action in compliance with what is required, taking into account the state of the doer, their capabilities and circumstances and in reaping bounty and reward. They have a great impact on establishing, improving and perfecting the act, since intention provides impetus to our motivation.

As for media ethics, intent is very significant. In order to have his/her reward from God, a Muslim working in the media field is expected to do their work efficiently and to the benefit of society. A Muslim's intention and compliance with the religious guidance to truth, trust and verification is a good deed to be gratified and rewarded.

One of the legislative features is the management of the diverse intentions and purposes among media actors with different religious, intellectual and political backgrounds. Islamic legislation points out this difference and confirms the principle of peaceful interaction and non-interference in people's intentions. It instead calls for good management of the multiplicity of backgrounds and purposes, and for maximizing objectivity, minimizing personal whims and ideological interference. In other words, when journalists commit themselves to working objectively to ensure the validity of their work in compliance with requirements and norms, despite their different inner motives, intent and purposes, they heed the principles underlying media ethics. What is important is preserving objectivity and credibility to achieve people's best and ward off injustice. For instance a meeting of media professionals including Muslims, Christians, Jews, Buddhists, atheists and others, for a humanitarian, developmental, health and environmental media cause. All of them meet for a just cause regardless of their backgrounds and intent. What is important for them is serving the cause objectively and observing professional standards to achieve the targeted benefits for the people it concerns.

From this Islamic legislative viewpoint, we may deduce the principle of impetus related to intention and purpose to accomplish a task according to its highest standards. In this example, diverse arrays of media professionals meet for a humanitarian cause, despite differing in their motives and intentions, whether these are religious, humane, juristic or customary. These motives overlap in governance, transparency, reputation and relevance.

B – *Islamic jurisprudence and innovation in media ethics*

The Islamic jurisprudence represents a theoretical and practical background, which helps empower media ethics in changing circumstances. Jurisprudence helps mobilize all the necessary means, procedures and systems to develop the media mission, and bring about benefits to people. In this regard, Islamic legislation encourages innovation and considers it part of its fundamentals, purposes and requirements to keep pace with developments in all aspects of life.

The Islamic higher objectives (*maqasid*) for media ethics

This fundamental refers to Islamic higher objectives when considering media ethics. One of these objectives aims at securing benefit and warding off evil. This is evidenced in media's bringing about benefits in relation to its issues, fields and contexts. Consider the example of the collegiate or vocational sectors. They bring about their benefits in an ethical and professional journalistic way, with a participatory and interactive dynamic between sector actors and governmental, administrative, legal or civil actors.

The above-mentioned fundamental is dealt with through three different levels according to the following discretionary and legal notes.

Firstly, the higher purpose of creation according to the Islamic worldview. This relates to the fundamental belief in the oneness of God and the ultimate goal of human existence, which consists of worshipping the Creator and bringing about benefit to humanity. Media performance and media ethics may be based on this higher teleological foundation with respect to asserting the oneness of the Creator, and to reclaiming and benefiting humankind.

Secondly, the aims of *Sharia* (Islamic law) which are known in Islamic theology to be preserving religion, soul, offspring, wealth and reason. *Al-Shatibi* (1997) considers these universal principles observed in every religion. They constitute the focal point of the benefits man has in his lifetime, his identity and dignity. Therefore, preserving one's religion is maintaining one's faith based on his/her choice. Islam adopts freedom of thinking and freedom of belief. But it has asserted clear guidance about the oneness of the Creator (Allah) and clear guidance of Prophet Muhammad's message as the seal of the prophets.

As for preserving one's soul, it is about safeguarding one's livelihood and safety. The same goes with preserving the mind, which is preserving the centre of thinking, the faculty of understanding, and the workplace of sense, experience, expression, deduction and induction. Preserving the offspring is the preservation of human reproduction – quantitatively and qualitatively – for the sake of continuity of life on earth. Finally, preserving wealth means not to waste it, but invest it to increase, and use it with moderation. Work is the legitimate way to earn money, and need is the inability to earn money and satisfy needs due to old age or illness.

These five universal principles constitute an essential basis for media ethics, in terms of preserving the human being and protecting his religious, psychological, mental, domestic and financial rights, through the media's prudence. The same principles also guide Islam's approach to education, arts, organization, law and constitution.

However, it should be noted that these universal guiding principles remain open to expansion by enriching their lexis according to previous observations and contexts, for instance by adding values such as freedom, human rights and protection of the environment.

Based on the above, in the Islamic tradition the media are expected to broadly operate within the following objectives:

- Evoke discussion, disentangle facts from falsehood, promote critical thinking, facilitate access to information, and ensure developmental and knowledge–building opportunities.

- Guarantee the preservation of privacy and dignity, address relevant themes and phenomena, whilst not compromising people's reputations or violating their rights.
- Publicize truth and disprove falsehoods, allow nations to enjoy their national, liberal, developmental and sovereign rights, and enable people to benefit from their various rights such as access to food, sports, healthcare, a safe environment and good governance.
- Serve society and benefit humankind; strengthen the meaning, regular functioning and competence of the state; fight corruption by setting anti-corruption standards and establishing tools to dismantle fraudulent systems and reinforce development, reform and public will.
- Ensure the safety of individuals, placate the despair and panic caused by fake news, which intentionally intimidates and disseminates fear.

Media ethics as being deeply rooted in Islamic expressions

Etymology is linked to the communicative dimension of humankind based on monotheism and plurality. Human beings express God's oneness in a shared sense, while showing plurality through the diversity of creatures' origins and status. Plurality is denoted by people's various socio-cultural backgrounds, nationalities and languages. The Qur'an reads:

> O *humanity! Indeed, We created you from a male and a female, and made you into peoples and tribes so that you may 'get to' know one another. Surely the most noble of you in the sight of Allah is the most righteous among you.* (49: 13)

Human beings are considered free thinkers as they relate expressing to thinking. They are also described as creative artists, since expression is linked to creative fine arts in the traditional and contemporary sense. The traditional sense refers to the expressive role of art in theatre, calligraphy, image and cinema, while the contemporary sense depicts art through new mediums, such as digitally and through street art. The latter (the modern sense) is now known as the information revolution that conveys the will of liberated peoples, supports their dignity, defends human rights, protects the sovereignty of nations, and highlights changes within a country. The Islamic Expressionist origin of media ethics reveals how Islam acknowledges 'expression' in a broader existential sense. Human 'Expression' is the revelation of thought using speech, signs or symbols.

One of the essential characteristics of human beings is that they voice their thoughts and emotions through technological tools, knowledge-management devices, and media platforms. Other means of expression may include signs or body language, which are considered by scholars as equally important as words. To justify this point, two arguments are provided. The first argument supports the idea of 'dumb signs when used as utterances'. The second argument is in favour of 'reference signs employed by speakers'. Sheikh Mohammed Al-Tahir ibn Ashour states:

> Voicing implicit intents and purposes through speech makes humans unique, i.e., distinct from other animal species. Therefore, verbal communication is one of the greatest blessings. Non-verbal elucidation is indeed another major human attribute even if it is devoid of words such as insinuation, signs, nodding and hinting. (Ibn Ashour 1984a: 233)

The possession of such characteristics and the intellectual capacity this requires, ennobles humankind through delivering speech and expressing what human beings reason and think. It also holds them accountable vis-a-vis their rights, freedom, values and regulations.

Media ethics draws on Islamic ethos in terms of thinking freely, exercising freedom of expression, yet also exercising social responsibility so as not to offend anyone or be offended. The Qur'an stresses personal liability over the spoken word. We read in chapter Al-Isra (17)

'Do not follow what you have no "sure" knowledge of. Indeed, all will be called to account for "their" hearing, sight, and intellect' (17: 36). Other verses stress the importance of providing proof to allegations, opinions, or decrees in order to ensure credibility and honesty. For instance: 'Produce your proof if you should be truthful.' (2: 111)

One should also ascertain truth before making judgements: 'O you who have believed, if there comes to you a disobedient one with information, investigate, lest you harm a people out of ignorance and become, over what you have done, regretful' (49: 6). It also delimits one's stance in order to avoid prejudice and achieve justice. With all its various forms, 'expression' can be related to words, signs or written texts.

The previously mentioned verses have two significant benefits: The first benefit has to do with connotations on the authenticity of 'expression' in revealing the true nature of human beings, a key criterion which is meant to elevate human beings and distinguish them from other creatures. The meaning implied by connotations is further backed by other verses from the Qur'an, such as:

1   'The Most Merciful (1) Taught the Qur'an (2) Created man (3) [And] taught him eloquence' (55: 1–4). Ibn Ashour (1984) states: 'and taught him clear expression' is the third condition through which humans glorify God with thankfulness and gratitude for their existence and for the countless blessings of expressing their desires, wants or needs. In other words, it is God who has taught human beings to enunciate and express themselves to benefit others as well as receive benefits in return. Qurtobi (2006) argues 'it is the art of eloquence that has made humans superior to animals'.

2   'Have We not made for him two eyes? And a tongue and two lips?' (90: 8–9). This verse is explained by Ibn Katheer (1999) as 'having eyes for the visualization of the world, a tongue for the articulation of speech and self-expression, and lips for sustaining talk'. The tongue and the lips have a major role in the pronunciation of speech, a fact proven by The Quran and determined as an innate human characteristic.

3   'And untie the knot from my tongue that they may understand my speech, and appoint for me a minister from my family, Aaron, my brother, increase through him my strength' (20: 27–31). Ibn Abbas asserts that 'To God, Moses poured his complaints fearing murder by the Pharaoh's people, he lost his tongue. Becoming tongue-tied, Moses was unable to speak and asked God to grant him the assistance of his eloquent brother Aaron. The Lord assured Moses not to have any fear and granted his wish, as such, unleashed Moses' tongue' (Ibn Katheer, 1999: 5/282). In this case, Moses asked God to loosen his tongue, which is a means of self-expression.

The second benefit related to the impact of 'expression' on media ethics: Media upholds the fundamental right of freedom of expression, particularly free speech, through following a set of principles, morals and ethics. The Qur'an emphasizes attaining knowledge, being honest and assuming individual responsibility for information dissemination, communication transfer, and idea propagation.

The origin of self-expression in Islam can be proven in various ways:

1   Legal texts, some of which were previously mentioned, while others comprise the Sunnah of the Prophet. For instance, the Messenger of Allah was reported saying: 'He who believes in Allah and the Day of Judgement shall speak good or keep silent' (Sunnah.com 2021a). Good speech revolves around words that are productive and beneficial. It should be free from offence along any lines, such as religious, ethnic and so on. Another Hadith argues that 'Indeed a man may utter a statement that he does not see any harm in, but for which he will fall seventy autumns in Hell' (Sunnah.com, 2021b). Therefore, those who spread disinformation receive severe punishment, since it can be very damaging. Consequently, in Islam, the media should be held responsible for any fake information, deceptive news, or distortion of reality it promotes, rely on carefully selected information, and distance itself from censure and condemnation of all kinds.
2   The Islamic interpretations of 'expression' are deeply rooted in religion, the universe, and humankind: the need to teach eloquence to people is clearly stated in the Quran '[And] taught him eloquence' (55: 4).

Based on the principles of Islamic jurisprudence, particularly in semantics, classic scholars argue for the value of lucidity. In his book Mustasfa, Al-Ghazali (1993: 187) argues that 'to your knowledge, deciphering the semantic dimension of a given word relies on the word itself. A word may designate a unique explicit meaning. It can also convey multiple meanings based on its contextual interpretations or imply implicit connotations that are congruent with its pragmatic communicative functions'.

The Sunnah (Prophet's tradition) explains the previous Qur'anic versers. It aids understanding of their meaning and clarifies how acts of worship need to be carried out. Sheikh Abdelwaheb Khallef stresses that the Qur'an is the word of God. It mentions several acts of worship whose provisions or procedures are not detailed. For instance God states the need for worship 'And establish prayer' (2: 43), fasting 'O you who have believed, decreed upon you is fasting' (2: 183), and conducting the pilgrimage 'And [due] to Allah from the people is a pilgrimage to the House' (3: 97). Yet details needed to conduct prayers, fasting or pilgrimage are conveyed through the Prophet's sayings and deeds, since God endowed him with this privilege. Allah says 'And We have sent down to you "O Prophet" the Reminder, so that you may explain to people what has been revealed for them, and perhaps they will reflect' (16: 44).

Accordingly, the clearly established *Sunnah* stands as proof for Muslims and depicts religious Laws (*Sharia*) that need to be followed. *Sharia* sets several legislations, basic duties and provisions. These rulings issued by Prophet Muhammad and Muslim abide by them.

The Qur'an states: '*And We have sent down to you the Book as clarification for all things*' (16: 89). Ibn Ashour reminds that

> everything implies the inclusiveness of all created things within a customary setting. Divine religions and legislations are recognized to purify souls, provide advice on ethics, rectify any imbalances in civil society, indicate rights, stress God's oneness and uniqueness, and highlight the honesty of Prophet Mohamed (peace be upon him). They also deal with scientific facts and all cosmic matters, describe the conditions of nations, reveal the reasons that lay behind peoples' success or failure, and get sagacity and exhortation from the previous historical records, laws, civilizations, and deeds. (Ibn Ashour, 1984b: 253)

Then, He adds, 'As such, all the secrets and stories derived from science and knowledge can stand as evidence for everything on earth. Humans learn from particularization. They can be enlightened by what Prophet Muhammad, his companions, or former scholars wrote. They can also be informed of 'carrot-and-stick' measures to be aware of the rewards offered to the rightful people and the punishment meted to sinners, and be cognizant of the World Hereafter, life and doomsday' (Ibn Ashour 1984a: 23). He further argues that the major purpose for stating everything clearly is for deep contemplation and insight of the reader.

The Islamic operational vision of media ethics

Media ethics operate within a functional framework that includes institutions and experts. The Islamic operational vision refers to any work linked to the Islamic view as a whole in real life. It has two dimensions: the first one concerns the theoretical view of Islam, which relies on giving much importance to employability and work, while the second one deals with the implications, directions, challenges, and benefits of employability.

Linking the theoretical vision to work is considered part of the very nature of this vision and its requirements. It contributes to the establishment of the Islamic vision of media ethics. It rests on the principle that reflection is at the heart of work, and that work is the fruitful result of reflection. As such, these two concepts are intertwined as stated in the exegetics of the Quran, deductive inference, rhetoric, semantics studies of various approaches, logical reasoning, and the sent-down revelation. All this information is perfectly applicable to media. Media reflects humanitarian work that adheres to rules and decency. It is also controlled by Islamic visions and the sent-down revelations, which help its work practices to be carried out accordingly. Justifications derived from religion and reality can be presented, such as verses on linking speech and work. In the Qur'an we read:

> *Do as you will. Your deeds will be observed by Allah, His Messenger, and the believers. And you will be returned to the Knower of the seen and unseen, then He will inform you of what you used to do.* (9: 105)

Other verses stress the association of faith to work '*By time (1) Indeed, humankind is in loss (2) except those who have faith, do good, and urge each other to the truth, and urge each other to perseverance (3)*' (103: 1–3).

An operational vision has pre-requisites. The functioning of media ethics in real life is contingent on various circumstances, challenges and capabilities. It necessitates a functional framework which includes institutions, experts, laws and regulations. It deals with a diverse array of contexts, and should broadcast widely even topics of controversy and hot debate. The Islamic vision regarding work demonstrates its broad approach to media freedoms, suggesting it should raise diverse topics on people's conditions, issues and interests. Such freedom incentives hard work and progression in such a career.

Humanitarian aspect of the media

The media have a humanitarian dimension that aligns with its ethics and values. It mirrors humanism, which advocates human values such as dignity, liberty, accountability, achievement and fair rewards based on equity and benevolence. It also reflects the ethics embedded within human beings, their nature and their instincts. Addressing the humanism of humankind uncovers the truth about Islamic foundations of media ethics, such as the fundamental belief in the humanity of humankind. This demonstrates the centrality of humanity in media because God bestowed His Honour on human beings and endowed them with upright conduct. This allows them to peacefully coexist with the universe and its natural and cosmic laws. This builds a moral foundation for the media, which can act as a guide for any deviations, such as environmental abuse or ethnic cleansing.

Among the numerous humanitarian dimensions of media, there are two essential features that concern human diversity:

1   Human diversity can be seen in gender identification within a family, known as feminine and masculine. God says: '*And that He creates the two mates - the male and female*' (53: 45). He also says: '*O humanity! Indeed, We created you from a male and a female, and made you into peoples and tribes so that you may "get to" know one another*' (49: 13).
2   Diversity in social identities may be along many lines, such as ethnic, sectarian, political, religious and so on. This exemplifies the principle of God's oneness, as opposed to the diversity of the rest of the world's creatures, including multitudes of human beings, animals and universes.

The diversity of human beings at a biological level and an ethnic and cultural level has a significant effect on the provisions of Islamic legislation and philosophy. It has a crucial impact on the succession of human beings in this life, on the passing of generations on earth, and the management of public and private affairs. Moreover, it influences the media's humanitarian dimension, which corresponds with Islam's overarching themes of cosmic and human existence. For this reason, the media has a moral duty to conduct its work whilst acknowledging God's oneness and serving the diversity of humankind. It should carry out its job according to *Sharia*, where it is reasonable and beneficial to others.

Verse (49:13) mentioned above highlights the diversity of humankind, as previously explained. It shows different gender identities, including male and female. To illustrate this point, the expression 'We have created you' denotes that creation is an attribute given to the Creator- God. But the expression 'And made you' evokes social diversity by referring to many peoples, tribes and various forms of social groupings that differ greatly. The last expression can also reveal the flexibility of these social groups; they may change over time depending on their obligations and interests. One may further elaborate on the reference above and say that the diversity rule has two distinct forms:

- Diversity within the family: It is based on heterosexuality, complementary roles, equality, shared responsibility and fair reward. God says: 'And their Lord responded to them, *"Never will I allow to be lost the work of [any] worker among you, whether male or female; you are of one another"'* (3: 195). This condition is characterized by consistency in gender identification that is innate and intuitive. Accordingly, it aligns with the obligations and responsibilities needed for setting a family, reconstructing communities and populating the earth. Diversity within the family is known as the principle of current matrimony within the universe of human beings, animals and others. It is a constant feature of the history of humanity over the centuries, despite differences in religion and norms.
- Diversity in other domains, such as political, social and economic: Such diversity is based on ethnic, linguistic, geographical and cultural specificities, each with their own vital interests and circumstances. All are addressed by the Quranic expressions which are abundant with miraculous evidence of their regeneration, change and development. On the contrary, diversity within a family is based on inherited biological characteristics that may help determine its continuity.

Media and democratic transition in the Arab Spring countries

On a final note, it is worth reminding that before the Arab spring revolutions, media outlets in most of the Arab countries were, a mouthpiece for Arab regimes (Miladi and Mellor, 2021). This role led to the obstruction of truth. In such conditions, tyranny was presented as firmness, and imprisoning the innocent became no more than a strict application of the law. Those regimes developed an array of tools and mechanisms to serve among the media circles: intellectuals, Muftis, journalists, academics, powerful lobbies and charlatans. One of the phenomena that emerged was coopting media entities, confronting free voices, systematically disseminating misinformation, glorifying the ruler and sanctifying the party in political power. An extremist type of media emerged under the guise of globalization. It neglected to uphold good values such as human diversity, dignity and rights. It commodified women, human beings and whole nations. It also debased religious and cultural symbols and the elites and perpetuated sectarianism. For all these reasons, the media landscape during the Arab revolutions turned into platforms to help restore peoples' freedom, dignity, diversity and rights to organize. It advocated freedom of expression, access to information, the practice of religious rituals, and freedom of belief. This era of collective struggle in which the public capitalized on technological developments, including social media and virtual spaces has its promises and challenges.

Note

1 Sahih Bukhari Book 1: Revelation, chapter 1 "How was the beginning of the revelation to the Messenger of Allah (pbuh) & sequel 54, 2029, 3898, 5070, 6689, 6953.

References

Al-Gazali, A. H. (1993), *Al-Mustafa*. Beirut: Dar Al-Kotob Al-'ilmiyah.

Al-Qurtobi (2006), *Compilation of the Provisions of the Qur'an. 20/113*. Beirut: Al-Rissaala Foundation.

Al-Shatibi, I. (1997), *Almuwafaqat (2/9)*. Ryadh: Dar Ibn Affan for Publishing and Distribution.

Ibn Ashour, M. T. (1984), *Al-Tahrir Watanweer (Commentary on the Qur'an), 27/233*. Tunis: Dar Al-Nashr Al-Tunisiyah.

Ibn Ashour, M. T. (1984b), *Al-Tahrir Watanweer (Commentary on the Qur'an), 14/ 253*, Tunis: Dar Al-Nashr Al-Tunisiyah.

Ibn Katheer, A. (1999), *Interpretation of the Meanings of the Noble Qur'an*. Riyadh: Taiba Publishing and Distribution House.

Khalef, A. (n.d.), 'Science of Jurisprudence Principles', Al-Da'wah Islamic Library, Chabaab Al-Azhar, 8, pp. 38–39.

Miladi, N. and Mellor, N. (2021) (Eds.), *Routledge Handbook on Arab Media*. London: Routledge.

Sunnah.com (2021a), 'Riyad as-Salihin', vol. 1, p. 705, Hadith 26. Retrieved from: https://sunnah.com/riyadussalihin:705. Accessed: 11 May 2021.

Sunnah.com (2021b), 'Jami` at-Tirmidhi', vol. 4, Vol. 10, Hadith 2314. Retrieved from: https://sunnah.com/riyadussalihin:705. Accessed: 11 May 2021.

8 Ethics of investigative journalism

Jamel Zran

Introduction

Investigative journalism: From a consensual 'why' to a controversial 'how'

At the end of 2020, in the local and international context of Corona pandemic effects, Tunisia regained hope in the future of the democratic transition, which started in 2011. For the first time in the history of the country, a senior official, a minister, was sent to prison. This was after an investigative TV programme broadcasted a report about a toxic waste deal. The report revealed that tons of hazardous waste imported from Italy to Tunisia as household waste to be recycled and sent back to Italy.[1] Despite attempts at cover-up, the affair touched many high-ranking political and administrative officials. For the first time, Tunisian people and elites discovered the contribution that the press and investigative journalism can make to public interest protection.

Indeed, despite the professional transgressions, and the buzz programmes dominating the media landscape after 2011, investigative journalism has become an executive and societal monitoring mechanism to confront corruption and secure the democratic transition. Revealing such a corruption scandal was a dose of hope for the public and media. It means that, by providing a context of freedom, constitutional and legal guarantees, and appropriate financial conditions, the press can be of a great benefit to society and democracy. Many journalists and opinion leaders in Tunisia bemoan the money and the time wasted since independence in the absence of a monitoring fourth power with an investigation spirit.

This shows the importance of the correlation between investigation and freedom of speech with democracy. Sharing freedom of speech is the true gate for sharing social justice and wealth. A 'free press can contribute, through investigation, to countering executive authorities' abuse (Qamoua, 2015). There is consensus that investigative journalism is important in consolidating traditional democracies and driving modern democracies or democratic transition countries, like Tunisia, forward to maturity (Charfi and El-Bour, 2014). Investigations reveal to the public and its representatives acts of injustice, law transgression or tampering with public interests. Many investigations have prompted officials to introduce reforms and exclude influential people.

DOI: 10.4324/9781003203551-11

This is not specific to Tunisia. Investigation appears in press outputs in many Arab countries like Morocco, Lebanon, Jordan and Iraq. Originally, this outcome was not expected of investigative reports, aimed most of the time at mere publication or buzz. Adherence to the power and effectiveness of investigative journalism requires adherence to and defence of a set of ideals, including access to a better and just world, as aspired to by average citizens and professional journalists (Bourdieu, 1996).

After the Watergate scandal in 1974, specialists, analysts, academics and journalists differed over the definition of investigation. The most common definition was suggested by Investigative Reporters and Editors, the most important organization of investigative journalists in USA. The organization affirms that an investigative journalist is a journalist who draws attention, through his/her personal initiative work, to important social issues that some people or entities want to keep under wraps. The basic goal of investigation is to disclose information and data covered-up by some parties and kept concealed from public. The primary purpose of an investigative journalist is to reveal secrets related to the public interest, wherever they are (Charon, 2003). Another trend considers that obtaining and analysing important official information using conventional journalistic methods can be considered an investigative report.

In both definitions the main target is to demonstrate and explain complex and intertwined social facts, without necessarily accessing unknown worlds to spread a secret (Hunter, 1997), but, in practice, the two trends adopt different methodologies. Few think that, the reporter must be aware of the underlying relationships between people and events to reveal their symbols and their connotations. The investigation, thus, depends in the first place on the ability of the journalist to collect and analyse a huge amount of interconnected data using modern communication technologies such as Internet and digital publication to reach an exclusive and unprecedented result in the press landscape (OCDE, 2018).

Journalism professionals believe that nearly 90% of the information found in the corridors of public and official institutions (ministries, establishments and embassies). The job of an investigative reporter is not to search for confidential and exclusive information. It is, rather, to bring to light the objective significance of what is confidential and kept hidden. This view highlights the old and lasting controversy within the press concerning objectivity, ethics and investigative reporting methods.

An investigative journalist relies on data that usually appears to be an objective and impartial report of a social or political event. But the selection of such very data for publication, and the choice of the publication timing, may not escape subjectivity. The most objective journalists end up turning into journalist-activists for a cause, even if they do not have any self-interest (Hunter, 1997). To this end, few journalists may pretend to be someone else, like a doctor, a policeman or a beggar to reach their source. This, however, raises an ethical issue. Should a journalist be undercover to illuminate public opinion? Could a journalist's concealment contribute to the concealment of the profession of journalism, its prestige and its history? One of the basic features in journalism is appearing as a journalist, a visible person, i.e. in an uncovered status. To conceal one's identity from another may suggest dishonest purposes. The problem is that some officials may count the journalist persona non grata, an informant, therefore they withhold information, avoid talking to him/her, and prevent them from access to data. This leads few journalists to take on the challenge of disclosing information or practices that harm the public.

Research problem and methodology

If the answer to 'why investigate?' becomes almost consensual in media and communication literature, the answer to 'how to investigate?' is still controversial and furnishes many intellectual, professional and ethical debates. This chapter aims to discuss the ethical ethos of investigative journalism, and the specific methodology required for such journalism compared to conventional journalism work.

In response to officials' opacity and information blackouts, journalists may resort to twisted methods to access information. Officials may argue that their manipulative methods to conceal information serve public interests. But such ways of concealing information serve lobbies, corrupt legislation, and manipulation of public interests, under the pretext of national security, private life and higher interests. This argumentation raises the following question: To what extent can we consider the investigative unconventional methods a violation of journalism ethics and codes of honour?

To provide an answer to this crucial question, I will analyse few investigative reports as a sample. The aim is to study how journalists reach their sources, the approved methods they adopt, and whether the journalist is entitled to adopt concealment, deception and infiltration. Has a journalist the right to tamper with the sources and disguise himself to obtain information? Does Machiavelli's famous principle of 'the end justifies the means' apply to investigative journalism? Or is the journalist required to be transparent and should reveal his identity at all times?

Most of the discussions on investigative journalism ethics have focused on methodology. Is there an ideal method which is effective in exposing officials' wrongful behaviour? Is resorting to deception legitimate when the journalist's goal is to unveil the truth? Can we justify specific methods in case of an information blackout? Are TV reporters allowed to use hidden cameras to gain access to a news story details? Can journalists use false identities, lie, or steal and/or buy secret documents to obtain concealed information?

In his book on journalism ethics, the American journalist Ron F. Smith devotes his tenth chapter to what he calls 'deception' phenomenon in journalism. He distinguishes two categories of deception. The first is the passive deception. 'Reporters using this approach simply do not identify themselves as reporters. They let others assume they are just members of the public' (Smith, 2011). An elaborate example of passive deception was provided by Washington Post reporter, Neil Henry, in 1983, who was investigating the exploitation of jobless and homeless people. The second category is positive deception, where the journalist impersonates another person. Harry Romanoff, a journalist for the Chicago American newspaper, used to impersonate a doctor or a police officer to obtain a specific type of news. Ron F. Smith asserts that 'For nearly 100 years journalists used variations of these two kinds of deception and rarely gave ethics a second thought'. 'Undercover reporting goes back to the 1890s when Nelly Bly pretended to be insane to find out how patients were treated in Blackwell's Island Insane Asylum. Her three articles for the old *New York World* were headlined "Ten Days in a Mad-House"'. According to Smith, despite the success of undercover reporting in uncovering many cases, most studies confirm that 70% of journalists and mass media believe that journalist's impersonation cannot be justified. The American Poynter Institute website confirmed that an investigation of an Indian camp published by Poonam Agarwal, an Indian journalist, in 2017, resulted in the suicide of the soldier who was secretly filmed using a hidden camera, although his name and photo were not revealed in the video. This incident raised anew the question of ethics in investigative journalism (Bernier, 1994).

This unconventional way of dealing with press sources and backgrounds of conflict remains controversial. Despite the buzz created by deceptive investigative reports, they usually raise ethical questions. In 1979, The Pulitzer Prize Board decided not to award the Sun-Times the prize, because The Mirage Tavern was based on deception. On the other hand, few journalists describe lying and bypassing the law as the art of yellow journalism, like the journalist Jack Schaefer of the American Politico website, who believes that almost all journalists practice simple deception at least, which is not like lying.

List of journalistic investigations: Research sample table

In Table 8.1, I present few investigative reports distributed historically and geographically. Few published in France and Britain, others in America, and few examples from the Arab region. The sample taken from various media outlets, the written press, television, and Internet websites.

Table 8.1 List of Few Investigative Journalism Reports which Employ Unconventional Methods

Investigative report	Journalist	Newspaper	Country and date	Notes
Ten Days in a Mad-House	Nellie Bly	The New York World of Joseph Pulitzer	The United States 1887	Pretending to be insane to spend 10 days in a notorious mental hospital[2]
Panorama Princess Diana Interview	Martin Bashir	The BBC	Britain November 1995 Watched by 22.8million people	Lying to be able to interview Princess Diana

Investigative report	Journalist	Newspaper	Country and date	Notes
United Kingdom Parliamentary Expenses Scandal	Jon Ungoed-Thomas	The Daily Telegraph	Britain 2009	Paying for documents to reveal UK MPs misuse of allowances and expenses and embezzling of public money
Physical and verbal assaults on disabled people in private care centres	Hanan Khandaqji	*Arij* website	Jordan 2014	Training and impersonation to investigate physical and verbal assaults on disabled people in private care centres
The most famous meat factory in Egypt producing carcinogenic luncheon meet	Marwa, Yassine And Maha Bahansawi[3]	Egyptian Today	Egypt, October 2011	Impersonating factory employees to investigate a factory producing carcinogenic luncheon meat in Egypt[4]
Leaking and disclosure, undermining exam fairness	Musab Al-Shawabkah	Jordan journals *El-Balad* Radio	Jordan August 1, 2012	Impersonating a student to investigate, after he enrolled to sit for the high school graduation exam
Flick (The Policeman)	Valentin Gendrot	Book	France 2020	Impersonating a police officer: employed as assistant policeman

Research theoretical and historical framework

Investigative journalism has an intellectual reference base that intersects with sociology, and a professional reference base related to journalism and honour codes.

Sociological reference

Journalism investigation, as a chronicle of events, cannot be isolated, intellectually, and historically, from social investigation. The journalist is the sociologist of the moment (Neveu, 2013). It is worth noting that the press has gained benefit and developed through openness to social sciences, which depends, in many contexts, on social investigation techniques. Equally, social sciences, through their empirical and micro- sociological boom, embodied in the Chicago School, have benefited from the explosion of information and communication technologies, especially the widespread availability of the cinema, radio and written press, and the emergence of television. Since the first decade of the last century, communication and media in the United States of America have been associated with the project of social sciences based on empirical foundations. The starting point for this project was the Chicago School. The school's micro-sociological approach to the study of human group organization is in harmony with their consideration of the role of cognitive scientific tools in resolving major social imbalances (Mattelart, 2004).

Robert Ezra Park (1864–1944) was one of the School's most influential figures. He applied his findings to the suburbs of the United States, which he considered advanced models for the investigative press. In contrast to the European School tending towards theoretical sociology in search of large interpretive systems, Park introduced to the Americans concepts close to 'objective situations'. These practical concepts can help them to create cognitive tools to analyse 'attitudes' and 'behaviours'. These are the very tools aimed at by the press, away from the intellectual abstraction based on epistemological backgrounds.

To put its experimental research into practice, the Chicago School chose the city as a 'social laboratory'. The city, as a stage for 'social mobility', embodies disorganization, marginalization, acculturation and integration. As a modern frame, it is also the preferred place for media action in that period. It offered the target audience, and the most covered topics, especially the investigations of crime, money and sexuality cases. These were the preferred topics of popular journalism at the end of the nineteenth century and the beginning of the twentieth century, and they were more available in the city than in the countryside.

To illustrate the intersections between functional sociology and journalism, we refer to how the Chicago School, between 1915 and 1935, focused on the issue of immigration and the integration of immigrants into the American society. In his study of ethnic groups, Park's central question revolved around the integrative role of newspapers, especially the numerous foreign language publications. He studied the nature of news and information, the journalism professionalism, and the differences that distinguish journalistic publications from advertising and marketing (Park, 1922).

This intersection between the empirical background of social sciences and the journalism investigative method serves us to show that investigation, as a sociological and journalistic concept, is a response to a societal need. Investigation is the basic method in experimental sociological research. It is carried out through oral and written interviews and data collection and analysis. It may refer to all forms of experimental sociological research and quantitative and qualitative analysis. Investigations' analysis requires classification systems based on measurement and evidence units (Charon, 2003). These very investigative techniques are used by investigative journalism. The oral interview is the press talk. The documented data essential for a credible investigation, are the journalist's sources including reports and secret documents. In journalism, too, data is documented and referenced, like the Watergate book and movie, Nelly Play's book and Valentin Gendrot's *Flic*.

The mutually nourishing relationship between sociological investigation and investigative journalism continues throughout history. Still, one is understood in terms of the other. Journalism provides the investigator with rapid coverage and documentation at the time of the event. Sociology provides him with methods to investigate this event away from the pressure of the moment. Sociology provides accurate research techniques, including the use of figures, data, testimonies, graphs, footnotes, references and sources-tools crucial for any journalistic investigation. Such techniques are not the product of classic press coverage. They are, rather, invoked from empirical functional sociology. What is most important are the implications of this contractual relationship on the ethical level. The morals we evaluate investigative journalism through derive their rigour from that of the investigative techniques and approaches in functional sociology. Therefore, investigative journalism is known as in-depth-journalism, digging deeply into topics, and showing ethical identification with sociological research. A common basis for both domains is respect for information sources, objectivity and self-denial. The investigative journalist starts to footnote his references, evidence his findings with frameworks, figures, tables, and statistics, and rely on interviews and documents, all of which are sociological research tools. The same tools are adopted by the sociologist for an empirical investigation, and by the journalist for an objective investigation (Erik Neveu, 2013).

Professional references: codes of honour and codes of conduct

There are many professional reference texts framing journalism ethics in general. All these texts refer, directly or indirectly, to the situations a journalist may encounter in dealing with his information source. Before talking about codes of honour and ethics in journalism, it is worth mentioning the intellectual and historical contexts in which these ethics emerged. The most important reference is item 19 of the Universal Declaration of Human Rights, which affirms the right of everyone to obtain information, an affirmation adopted by the International Federation of Journalists in the preamble of its Universal Declaration of Ethics for Journalists. No journalistic moral reference can be embodied in the absence of freedom of speech, the right of communication and access to information, and the right of the audience to know public issues news without any guardianship or influence by the state or the financial and political lobbies (Hunter, 1997).

Literature on journalism ethics goes back to the Charter of the National Syndicate of French Journalists (1918), and, later, to the Code of Conduct for American Journalists 1926, the Code of Conduct for British Journalists 1938, and then the Declaration of Principles issued by the International Federation of Journalists on the Conduct of Journalists, known as the 'Bordeaux Declaration' (1954). Equally important is the Declaration on the Rights and Duties of Journalists known as the 'Munich Declaration' (1971). Mention can also be made of the UNESCO Declaration on Media (1983) and the European Council decision on journalistic ethics (1993). Moreover, many other editorial charters and codes of conduct specified the journalist's relationship with his source. This survey of the above declarations and codes of ethics sheds light on some exceptions where undercover reporting is allowed:

- With reference to the Charter of the International Federation of Journalists, updated at its Tunis 2020 conference, article 4 stipulates that:The journalist shall use only fair methods to obtain information, images, documents and data and he/she will always report his/her status as a journalist and will refrain from using hidden recordings of images and sounds, except where it is impossible for him/her to collect information that is overwhelmingly in the public interest. He/she will demand free access to all sources of information and the right to freely investigate all facts of public interest.[5]

-In a comparative context, with reference to the editorial charter of the French News Agency (AFP), the section on 'Introducing ourselves as a journalist' states that 'French Press journalists must report their status as such, and cannot conceal their identity or disguise unless there is an obligation, like assuring their personal safety'.[6] The honour charter notes the problem of access to sources and discerns some exceptions for impersonation and under-covering, namely in case of danger or of important data inaccessible by classical methods.

Unconventional methods or 'how' to access information in investigative journalism

Professionally, an investigative journalist is committed to honestly transmitting information, but he/she may find himself/herself in a complex situation where officials hide information for fear of being condemned, their interests being harmed, or their truth being revealed. A journalist then may find himself/herself compelled to use 'unconventional', or 'twisted' methods, and to investigate undercover.

In his investigative report, Musab al-Shawabkeh, a Jordanian journalist, pretended to be a student sitting for a high school graduation exam in order to reveal the fraudulence of a network trading exams.[7] The Daily Telegraph gave bribes when investigating the UK MPs expenses. Some journalists may infiltrate personal data, record people, or film them secretly, transgressing ethics codes, for the sake of a stunning revelation or corruption prevention, which may have an impact on opinion trends.

On the one hand, press ethical charters stipulate the principle of honesty and direct methods to obtain information. All professional structures disapprove twisted methods, undercover and secret or manipulative manners of whatever kind. On the other hand, the first principle of the International Federation of Journalists states that the journalist is bound to satisfy the right of his audience to know the truth. This may lead to contradiction and confusion between the right to access information and the inability to do so through conventional methods. Some investigative reporters adopt 'the end justifies the means' principle and take it as a slogan. They prioritize the right of public to know the truth over the principle of using direct methods, especially when this truth regards daily reality and public concerns.

To understand this overlapping and complex problematic situation, we will cite and analyse a set of investigations carried out through unconventional methods. These samples vary chronologically and geographically. They are from different periods and countries, and diverse media outlets. Due to the recency of investigative reports in the Arab region media, I have limited the sample to investigations supported by Arab Reporters for Investigative Journalism (ARIJ), an Arab international non-governmental organization.[8]

Below is a summary of each sample, indicating the subject of the investigation, the reason for undercover or impersonation, and the impact of the investigation on public opinion.

Nelly Bly's impersonation of an insane journalist

Nellie Bly was known for her statement, 'We have to live in pain to write about it', which may hint at her experience of many situations which led her to investigate them, including the situation at the Women's Lunatic Asylum on Blackwell's Island. Her resulting exposé, entitled *Ten Days in a Mad-House*, is the first and most famous investigation. Nellie Bly, whose real name is Elizabeth Jane Cochran, investigated undercover to bring public attention to the brutality and neglect to which patients were subjected in New York. She also made a trip around the world in 72 days, which is a challenge and a record. Nellie focused in her early years on writing about working women, and especially on publishing investigative articles about female factory workers. Before working for the New York World, she worked for the Pittsburgh Dispatch.[9] She collected her articles published in the New York World and published them in a book in which she narrates her experience in this hospital, where she embedded herself 10 days at the Women's Lunatic Asylum on Blackwell's Island, New York in 1887. To enter the hospital, Nellie arranged with her newspaper to spend a whole day in front of the mirror mimicking insanity. After these exercises, her strategy was to impersonate an insane patient to investigate the harsh treatment of patients and the methods of management at the Asylum. She witnessed spoiled meals, cold baths and forced starvation. (Albessard, 2013).

What is important, as advocates of this stealth approach argue, is the success of the investigation in triggering the hospital's reform through the Supreme Court. Also, many charities and correctional institutions have donated money and aid to better run the hospital. Bly's book was then translated into a movie in 2015.[10] Defenders of Nelly Bly's method argue that she would not have published all these facts if she had not impersonated a mad person, and the hospital would not have been reformed if she had not published all those terrifying facts, which had been kept secret.

Interviewing Princess Diana on the BBC

More than 25 years ago, BBC reporter Martin Bashir interviewed Princess Diana. The interview was broadcast in November 1995 and watched by 22.8 million people. Princess Diana revealed many facts and secrets about her private life, and the interview has become widely known. It was discovered later, according to the allegations of the princess's brother, that the Panorama reporter used devious means to obtain information from the princess. He showed false documents and was weaving lies about her employees, claiming that they had received money to spy on her. Diana talked about the collapse of her marriage and said her famous phrase that 'there were three of us in this marriage',[11] herself, Charles and Camilla Parker Bowles, whom the prince Charles later married got with. Diana also revealed her extramarital relations. Diana and Prince Charles officially separated in 1996. The following year, she died in a car accident in Paris with Dodi Al-Fayed.[12]

Princess Diana's brother, Charles Spencer, confirmed that the 'Panorama' reporter, Martin Bashir, who conducted this historic TV interview, showed him forged documents to gain his trust and that of his sister Diana. The journalist was an obscure journalist. After this interview he became a widely known journalist and a religious issues reporter at the BBC. The problem is that the journalist turned out to have used unethical methods to gain fame by revealing details of a celebrity's private life.

With reference to journalism ethics, in particular the public's right to know the truth and the journalist's obligation to avoid twisted methods unless the news is of great importance to public interest, one should wonder how important Princess Diana's personal life secrets were to the public interest. Considerations should have been- 'How will this interview impact the audience?'; 'Does the audience need to know what is happening behind the princess's room walls?', and 'Were these enough justifications for the journalist to use twisted methods?' Few are of the opinion that this television interview violated all ethics, and that the only beneficiary of such an interview was the journalist who became famous.

The United Kingdom MPs expenses scandal

In 2009, the Daily Telegraph (a UK tabloid newspaper) disclosed widespread misuse of allowances and expenses by 50 UK Members of Parliament (MPs). This aroused widespread anger among the British public and resulted in the resignation of Prime Minister Gordon Brown. Several Members of the Parliament were prosecuted and sentenced, and three were imprisoned. The newspaper paid a sum of money estimated at 110,000 pounds in exchange for the collected information and concealed its source for their safety. Four years before, journalists Ben Leapman of the Sunday Telegraph and Jon Ungoed-Thomas of the Sunday Times had been plugging away at the story, fighting in court to force MPs to allow access to the information under the Freedom of

Information Act, and reaching a decision related to British MPs' corruption expenditures (Winnett and Rayner, 2019). Yet the Daily Telegraph managed to get ahead and buy the scandal's data and documents,[13] eventually publish a story that shook Westminster, which boosted the Telegraph newspaper sales by tens of thousands. In an interview, Andrew Pearce, a journalist, and assistant editor for the Daily Telegraph, said that the newspaper paid 110,000 pounds in exchange for the information, 'money well spent for the public benefit' according to him (Winnett and Rayner, 2019).

However, few think that the tabloid infringed people's privacy by revealing their personal data. Ostensibly, the way through which the newspaper obtained information appears twisted and harmful to journalism ethics, but thereby, the public was able to discover the details of the government's corrupt expenditure and embezzlement of public money, which led to the re-election of the British Parliament. Some of these expenses were spent on MPs' home and second home improvements, travelling, unjustified vacations and other privileges.

Undeniably, although revealed through seemingly underhand methods, the truth had an impact on public opinion. Sums of money were recovered into the state's coffers from more than 18 MPs[14] in the midst of the crisis Britain was going through at the time. Thus, transgressing ethical boundaries seems to have become justified, although still these techniques were rejected by many journalism experts. For some journalism officials, disclosing the private data of a corrupt parliamentarian abusing public funds is legitimate since it is for public welfare, unlike revealing details of celebrities' personal lives. Illegal ways of obtaining information such as through being undercover, via penetration of private data, by offering bribery, and lying encroach journalism ethics and violate all ethics charters of conventional journalism. They may, however, be allowed in investigative journalism for the sake of public interest and risk-worthy information.

In France: the policeman journalist

In September 2020, Valentin Gendrot, an investigative reporter, published a book about police working conditions in security departments, entitled *Flick*. The book was a best-seller. The journalist penetrated security centres undercover to investigate police experiences. The book sparked an unprecedented debate about the legitimacy of the information collection method. The French Attorney General issued an investigation into the published information about police work methods and corruption (de Rubercy, 2020).

He even assumed the status of a policeman for two years. He applied for a policeman post. Once accepted, he undertook a three-month-training course and worked as a contracted policeman. He talked about this in his book and said that it was an insufficiently long training course for a particularly important job. He mentioned that a topic as important as family disputes was allocated no more than three training hours. The investigative journalist spoke in detail about policemen work routine and private life. Many policemen in France commit suicide because of the pressure of the profession. They witness injustice and keep quiet. A policeman does not disclose the transgressions of his fellow policeman. He cannot report him if he makes a mistake. If it happens that a policeman uncovers his colleague's transgressions against a citizen, he/she is viewed as a whistle-blower, even if the citizen is harmed. The journalist also revealed police violations regarding human rights, racism, discrimination, and moral and material violence practiced against the detainees.

This was not the first time Valentin Gendrot investigated undercover. He posed as a day worker at a call centre, and a street vendor. He published an investigative book on the working conditions of low-income workers.

This method of data collection, like Nelly Bly's, is an infiltration of an unknown world surrounded by secrecy and corruption covering harm to people. The journalist's impersonation of someone else to illuminate public opinion is an answer to 'how' to investigate. According to Hunter (1997), the investigative journalist cannot, in some cases, reveal the truth of transgressions unless he impersonates someone pertaining to the context where those transgressions took place.

Journalists working in an Egyptian Luncheon meat factory

The investigation was triggered by a spontaneous question asked by Oum Hajer, the mother of one of the pupils in an Egyptian school: 'What is this luncheon meat made from?' The mother's question incited the journalists to investigate and get an answer. They reported:

> We just asked ourselves where to start. The answer was to apply for a job at one of the luncheon meat factories. But we asked ourselves, "How can we go into the factory?". The only way was to be undercover and work in the factory so that we could accurately monitor the manufacturing process step-by-step. The task was arduous, but the public interest target was worthy the challenge. Many questions came to our minds, such as, "What will happen if one of the employees discovers who we are?" Many answers, whispers, assumptions, and terrifying scenarios came into mind, all of which we tried to suppress while the factory security official was showing us our tasks.[15]

The journalists reported the working conditions and the luncheon meat manufacturing process. They recorded health standards transgressions. The expired luncheon is recycled, without consideration for customers' health. They decided to take samples to accredited laboratories for reliable results. Their findings were approved by two laboratories accredited by Cairo University, including the Regional Office for Food Safety and Quality.

Dr Muhammad Abbas, a senior micro-analysis specialist who accompanied the journalist during the sampling process and samples delivery, advised him to purchase three different samples of luncheon meet (beef, olive and basic), which they got from one of the well-known factory outlets in 'Ataba'.

After six weeks, microbiological analyses revealed that the three samples contained aflatoxin, a carcinogenic fungal toxin, resulting from 'Aspergillis' species, especially 'Aspergillis flavus'. The fungal portions in the samples were exceedingly high according to the Egyptian standard specification, reaching 120 colonies instead of 5 colonies maximum.

The results showed presence of nine bacterial colonies per gram in the 'beef and olives' luncheon meat. Forty colonies were found in the 'basic' luncheon meat, while according to standard specifications there should be no bacteria at all. It revealed different bacteria types: Coliform, caused by faecal matter- which is the most hazardous; E. Coli- which is a pathogen that causes food poisoning; and MRSA proving that the product contained bowels, which does not conform to the food health and safety standards.

The results also revealed an unpleasant and unacceptable odour in the three samples, and that the protein percentage was lower than specified. While the Egyptian luncheon manufacturing standards required a protein content of 15%, the protein found to be 8%, around half of the required proportion. The fat amount averaged 7%, while the standards specified that it should be no less than 35%. The ash (mineral/ fibre) component was 2.9% while the required fraction is 3.5%. Despite the results of the investigation, the people managing this factory have not been held accountable. No judicial investigation opened, and the factory has not closed.

A journalist volunteering at a care centre which hosts people with disabilities in Jordan for investigation purposes

The Jordanian journalist Hanan Khandaqji investigated the physical and verbal assaults on disabled people in private care centres. Using an unconventional method, she was able to publish details from inside the centres. She volunteered in a care centre to reveal the investigated facts to the public.[16] Adopting the participatory observation approach, the journalist volunteered twice at one of five special education centres in West Amman. She worked for two-week periods. During these periods she witnessed physical and verbal abuse of some disabled people. Her report reveals that people with simple and moderate disabilities were beaten, mistreated and neglected, amid the rare monitoring of relevant authorities. For her investigation purposes, the journalist sought the help of another volunteer, who managed to enter another centre in West Amman and record the assaults on children. This investigation unveiled the fragility of the systems protecting the rights of disabled people in the 'care' centres.

Wondering whether the journalist may, morally and professionally, impersonate a trainee at the centre, we should consider that even the family cannot visit these disabled people without the prior approval of the centre. One of the supervisors of a private centre, Samir (a pseudonym), confirmed to the journalist that there are conditions for family visits; 'Some centres specify one day for visits. The family cannot visit their relative without a prior coordination with the administration'. Mona, 30 years, talked about her 40-year-old brother, a mentally disabled man, unable to speak and communicate. She said that, 'The administration of the centre prevents us from going into my brother's room, under the pretext of his privacy not being violated. They make us wait in a room until they take him down'. Khaled, a father of a patient, did not know, when he left his son Yousef a few months ago in one of the largest private centres in Amman, that he would return to find him sitting in a government hospital, after he had suffered second and third-degree burns while he was at the centre. The investigation mentioned that this father did not believe the superintendent who claimed that Youssef poured hot water on himself. The official reports attached to this investigation, issued by the National Centre for Forensic Medicine, confirm that 'the child was burned with chemical incendiary substances, not water, and, given their distribution and nature, the burns cannot be accidental.'

This investigation received wide interest from public opinion in Jordan. The investigative journalist confirms that, although she monitored more than a dozen centres where physical violations have taken place, the media spokesman of the Ministry of Social Development, the government watchdog, has confirmed that only two centres have been closed in the last two years, due to several violations.

The student journalist revealing an exam fraud network in Jordan

The investigative journalist, Musab Al-Shawabkah, supported by *Arij* network, decided to carry out a survey entitled 'leaking and disclosure, undermining exams fairness'. After several months of work, Al-Shawabkah was able to reveal the secrets of networks trading with high school qualification exams. He managed to do so after having applied to re-sit the examinations of the public high school diploma as a free candidate, a procedure allowed under law.

Through the use of an advanced secret camera, a smartphone, documents, and participative observation, the journalist disclosed significant secret misconduct about examination rooms. A group of officials in the Ministry of Education colluded with security personnel, parents, students, professors, and invigilators, in the crime of cheating in the exam as part of a collective unimaginable fraud.

The investigation file contains concrete revelations of networks specialized in trading test answers in public secondary examinations in at least five Jordanian cities. The questions and answers sold in the black market. The networks designate one student, officially registered, to photograph the exams with a cell phone, and leaks them to the operation room. There, quick question-solving professors are waiting for the purpose. When ready, the answers are sent by the supporting logistics via a cellular or a high-tech earphone to the 'customer' sitting for the exam. In the exam room, the process is guaranteed by invigilators. Some of them would sometimes take the exam answers outside the exam halls.

The journalist filmed the collusion taking place. Invigilators of exams did not stop cheating and allowed smartphones to be used, contravening exam regulations, the law and their job. Some of them even dared to ask the invigilator for help. The cheating process also involved delivering the answers after the questions are leaked via tiny but well-connected telephone handsets. 'Client' students pay specific prices for the respective network exam rooms, ranging from \$30-\$150 per question and a similar price for the answer. Questions are sometimes leaked one day before the exam, for a higher price. They get leaked from within the Ministry of Education, which reveals the collapse of the control systems and the unprecedented education system corruption.

In the investigation, one of the education directors, Mohamed Kloub, admits that some of the answers are forced into the examination rooms by students' parents with the help of the network 'agents' supervising the exam. After the investigation, the journalist was summoned by the Minister of Education, who scolded him, threatened him, and accused him of negatively reporting about the image of Jordan and its national education system (Arab Reporters for Investigative Journalism, 2012).

Investigative journalism ethics: The problem is 'how' to investigate?

Dealing with sources in investigative journalism can be summarized as the struggle between the ends and means. The same old question is whether an investigative journalist must reveal his identity or can instead pose as a citizen journalist, a police journalist or a judge journalist. The release of an investigative book by the French journalist was not the first time a journalist investigated undercover. Before this book, the French public watched '*Les Infiltrés*', a programme adopting leaks and penetration as investigative journalism methods. This programme also raised debates about the legitimacy of using a hidden camera, secretly recording, disguising and infiltrating into places without permission, especially when the journalist investigates for entertainment rather than public service purposes.

The '*Cash Investment*' programme was also criticized for using unusual journalistic techniques. According to the French Press Code of Conduct, an Associated France Press (AFP) journalist must identify himself/herself as such, and not circumvent or resort to deception, except in exceptional cases and with the approval of the administration.[17] Some journalists advocating deception methods, including Aurore Gurius, justify penetration through the influence of the public relations offices, which monitor the dissemination of any information in public and private institutions. This prompts journalists to investigate undercover and break this information blockade. The author of *Flick* advocates the undercover and penetration approach. He advocates that it is a mission of public interest to research deeply to find out what is happening behind the walls. Patrick Eveno, believes that not only does the journalist have to penetrate, but also practise various methods and approaches to offer the audience accurate and source-confirmed information.[18]

The National Syndicate of Journalists in France denounced the methodology of concealment, penetration and anonymity adopted by few TV investigative programme. They particularly denounced *Les Infiltrés*, on Channel 2. The channel broadcast an investigative programme which looked into child sexual abuse in April 2010. The information was obtained without the sources' knowledge and consent. This invoked an ethical question. All ethical charters, including the 1971 Munich Declaration Charter, deny the legitimacy of resorting to twisted ways to obtain and transmit news.[19] In spite of the significance of what such programmes reveal, few believe that the use of devious methods can only undermine public issues by making them sensational. Transmitting the truth for the purpose of shock and surprise harms the privacy right. From this perspective, what underlies such investigations are leaks, marketing and advertising, under the pretext of illuminating the public.

However, ethical issues are not limited to data collection methods. Corruption is also an important ethical issue in investigative journalism. Bernier (1994) argues that corruption has many forms, including bribery, publishing specific reports, denying specific reports or paying money for collected information. The harm that a report may cause to citizens should also be considered. Therefore, issues related to privacy are the most debated, given the dilemma of journalists aiming to satisfy the rights of people to knowledge, and to privacy as well.

In sum, one may argue that the press in any country may investigate within the framework of its commitment to the democratic accountability of officials, but will the citizens benefit from such investigations? Whose interest does investigative journalism serve when publishing a news story? Does the press satisfy its social responsibility by uncovering transgressions for instance? Whose interests will be affected? Whose rights could be violated? Does investigation concern the public welfare? Was there a violation of the right to privacy without a serious public issue necessitating this violation? These questions are in the heart of the relationship between investigative journalism and ethics. An example of this relationship is the tragic end of Princess Diana whose pursuit by the paparazzi was arguably one of the causes of her death. After the accident, a massive wave of discontent emerged against journalists, denouncing the way that their assumed right to obtain some pictures could contribute to the destruction of people and institutions.[20]

In this respect, we should consider that the public does not seem to accept the journalist's right to use all methods in search for information. People consider privacy violations with suspicion, regardless of the importance of the news story. In some countries the press can become less credible if they employ these methods, while the symbolic capital of the press is trust and credibility. Some journalists may contribute to this loss of trust. Citizens generally believe that journalists are ready to obtain any news story at any cost. Questionable methods used to make reports may also undermine the credibility of news reports in general, thus reducing public sympathy with journalists and investigative journalism.

As stated above, there is no magic solution for the ethics question in journalism. Ethical rules, however perfect and positive, do not offer decisive solutions applicable for all cases. As suggested by Smith (2011), most professionals agree that journalists should not be lenient but rather enthusiastic and ardent regarding sensitive issues such as fairness, balance, accuracy and objectivity.

They should constantly keep ethical standards in mind in the various stages of investigation and be ready to justify their decisions to the editor-in-chief, to colleagues and to the public. Journalists should consider the interests that maybe harmed by their investigation. They should also do their job according to the professional standards and specifications built-upon the long-standing journalistic heritage that established journalism ethics.

Conclusion: Digital investigation and ethics

Journalistic investigations take place in different circumstances, deal with different sources, and invoke different standards and criteria. Therefore, it is difficult to develop ethical rules common for all aspects of investigative reporting, even though there are some agreed upon rules and values that have become standards in journalism. Meanwhile, journalists are also subject to statutory legislations that are more explicit and binding than the journalism ethical standards. Journalism ethics relate to the ability to balance the public interest, i. e. the right of people to know (and therefore the right of the journalist to access information), and the right to keep private. Judging decisions ethically depends on the moral framework referred to in the justification and the values adopted in the very context. Journalists and editors-in-chief need to decide who benefits from publishing the investigative report (OECD, 2018).

The hesitant and faltering performance of investigative journalism locally and internationally affects the performance and reputation of the press in general and the democratic experience in particular. Historically, the press had acquired through investigation the status of a Fourth Estate. Today, in the absence or withering away of this fourth power, it is difficult to monitor the three traditional powers independently. The instability of investigative journalism performance is due to historical, intellectual, political and economic reasons. The direct reason is the important, quick and sometimes significant influence of investigative journalism on public opinion trends. In addition, the investigative journalism industry is not an easy process. This serious and militant journalism is covered by an intellectual ambiguity hindering its anchoring in the daily journalistic culture. It remains, for many people, an intellectual luxury.

The anticipated imminent problem in the future of investigative journalism is the monopoly and polarization caused by the technological, economic and political globalization of media and communication in the world. The effects of globalization have begun to cast a shadow on journalism. A marketing and electoral aspect has become part and parcel of the media as a platform for freedom of speech and public interaction. The Internet, being a rapid, low-cost and universal way of spreading information, may be the last resort for investigation and journalism. It may be the magic wand for a new category of press, with new ethics and new processing methods. This press can produce a new methodology taking cyberspace and online interaction as references. Probably a good example of this type of journalism is Mediapart investigative website founded by Edwy Plenel (former editor-in-chief of French newspaper *Le Monde*).

Notes

1 On 21 December 2020, the Public Prosecutor of the First Instance Court of Sousse 1 issued 4 committal warrants against Mustafa Laroui, the dismissed Minister of Local Affairs and Environment, the director of the National Agency for Waste Recycling, the director of the National Agency for the Protection of Environment, and employees of the Regional Environment Administration in Sousse, in relation to the case of 'waste imported from Italy', as reported by the court's spokesman, Jaber Al-Ghunaimi, to Tunis Africa Press.
2 https://www.womenshistory.org/education-resources/biographies/nellie-bly
3 https://www.youtube.com/watch?v=1_VFOPSlecQ
4 https://www.youtube.com/watch?v=1_VFOPSlecQ
5 Global Charter of Ethics for Journalists, Article 4. Issued by the International Federation of Journalists.
6 https://www.afp.com/
7 https://www.wattan.net/ar/news/18393.html
8 https://arij.net
9 https://ar.wikipedia.org/wiki/%D9%86%D9%8A%D9%84%D9%84%D9%8A_%D8%A8%D9%84%D9%8A
10 *Escaping the Madhouse: The Nellie Bly Story* is a movie of Karen Moncrieff with Christina Ricci, Judith Light, and Joshua Bowman.
11 http://www.bbc.co.uk/news/special/politics97/diana/panorama.html
12 New allegations by Princess Diana's brother about her BBC interview, BBC website, 7 November 2020.
13 https://www.bbc.com/news/uk-politics-48187096
14 https://www.telegraph.co.uk/news/newstopics/mps-expenses/5310200/MPs-expenses-Paying-bills-for-Tory-grandees.html
15 https://arij.net/investigation/%D8%A3%D8%B4%D9%87%D8%B1-%D9%85%D8%B5%D9%86%D8%B9-%D9%84%D8%AD%D9%88%D9%85-%D9%81%D9%89-%D9%85%D8%B5%D8%B1-%D9%8A%D9%86%D8%AA%D8%AC-%D9%84%D8%A7%D9%86%D8%B4%D9%88%D9%86-%D9%8A%D8%AD%D8%AA%D9%88
16 This investigation was carried out with the support of the ARIJ Network (Reporters for Investigative Journalism in the Arab World) and Radio Al Balad, under the supervision of Saad Hattar and Majdoline Allan. The investigation was also published on the BBC and won the German Development Media Award for Human Rights Journalists.
17 https://www.afp.com/sites/default/files/paragraphrich/202010/charte_deontologique_afp_ar.pdf
18 https://www.franceculture.fr/emissions/le-temps-du-debat/le-temps-du-debat-emission-du-mardi-15-septembre-2020
19 https://www.revue-etudes.com/article/les-limites-du-journalisme-d-immersion-13055
20 https://www.franceinter.fr/societe/violences-racisme-formation-low-cost-un-journaliste-raconte-son-infiltration-dans-la-police

References

Albessard, J. (2013), '*Nellie Bly, première femme journaliste, Bulletin de la Société*', *Jules-Verne*, no. 182, Avril 2013, p. 57.
Arab Reporters for Investigative Journalism (2012), 'How Jordanian students cheat in high school exams'. Retrieved from: https://en.arij.net/investigation/how-jordanian-students-cheat-at-high-school-exams/. Accessed: 22 May 2021.

Bernier, M. (1994), *Éthique et déontologie du journalisme*. Sainte-Foy: Presses de l'Université Laval.

Bourdieu, P. (1996), 'Journalisme et éthique: Actes du colloque fondateur du centre de recherche de l'Ecole Supérieure de Journalisme'. (Lille), *Les cahiers du journalisme*, Juin 1996, n°1.

Bradshaw, M. (2008), *Investigative Journalism: Context and Practice*. London: Routledge.

Charfi, S. and El-Bour, H. (eds) (2014), *Journalisme d'investigation et pouvoir des médias Obstacles, enjeux et perspectives*, Le colloque international Journalisme, 24 et 25 April 2014, L'Institut de Presse et des Sciences de l'Information et Konrad Adenauer-Stiftung.

Charon, J. (2003), 'Le journalisme d'investigation et la recherche d'une nouvelle légitimité'. C.N.R.S. Editions, *Hermès*, 2003/1 n° 35. Retrieved from: https://www.cairn.info/revue-hermes-la-revue-2003-1-page-137.html. Accessed: 21 February 2021.

\o "Joséphine de Rubercy" de Rubercy, J. (2020), 'raconte son infiltration dans la police', *France Inter*, 5 September. Retrieved from: https://www.franceinter.fr/societe/violences-racisme-formation-low-cost-un-journaliste-raconte-son-infiltration-dans-la-police. Accessed: 8 August 2021.

Guerfali, R. (2014), 'De la crise du journalisme tunisien: Éthique, déontologie et listes noires'. 15 April 2014. Retrieved from: https://nawaat.org/2014/04/15/de-la-crise-du-journalisme-tunisien-ethique-deontologie-et-listes-noires/. Accessed 21 February 2021.

Hunter M. (1997), *Le Journalisme d'investigation, Que sais-je*. Paris: Poche.

Hunter, M. (1997), *Le Journalisme d'investigation en France et aux États-Unis*. Paris: PUF.

Labarthe Mener, G. (2020), *l'Enquête: arts de faire, stratégies et tactiques d'investigation*. Paris: Éditions Antipodes.

Mattelart, A. and Mattelart, M. (2004), *Histoire des théories de la communication*. Paris: LaDécouverte.

Neveu, E. (2013), *Sociologie du journalisme*. Paris: La Découverte.

OECD. (2018), 'Le role des medias et du journalism d'investigation dans la lute contre la corruption' [The role of the media and investigative journalism in fighting corruption]. Retrieved from: https://www.oecd.org/fr/corruption/anti-corruption/Le-role-des-medias-et-du-journalisme-d-investigation-dans-la-lutte-contre-la-corruption.pdf. Accessed: 25 June 2021.

Park, E. R. (1922), *The Immigrant Press and its Control*. Americanisation Studies. New York: Harper.

Patrick, A. (1997), *Le Journalisme d'investigation selon la Convention européenne des droits de l'homme*. Paris: Legipresse.

Qamoua, N. (2015), 'Investigative journalism or retaliatory journalism: Blackmail, dirty laundering, and corruption. Media reporters in the dock'. *Al-Sabah Weekly Newspaper*, 23 March 2015.

Robert, W. (2009), "MPs expenses: Paying Bills for Tory grandees". *Telegraph.co.uk*. Retrieved from: https://www.telegraph.co.uk/news/newstopics/mps-expenses/5310200/MPs-expenses-Paying-bills-for-Tory-grandees.html, Accessed: 21 February 2021.

Smith, R. (2011), *Ethics in Journalism*. New York: Wiley-Blackwell.

Thierry, M. (2002), *11 Septembre 2001: L'effroyable imposture*. Paris: Carnot.

Weinberg, S. (1996), *The Reporter's Handbook: An Investigator's Guide to Documents and Techniques*. London: St. Martin's Press.

Winnett, R. and Rayner, G. (2011), *No Expenses Spared*. London: Transworld Publishers.

9 Fake news as a challenge for media credibility

Suzana Žilič Fišer and Irena Lovrenčič Držanič

Introduction

The importance of online media has been significantly increasing throughout the past decade, and many of the most prominent news media are becoming predominantly online services. Research shows that consumers spend most of their online time on social media, which have also become their primary news sources (Shearer and Matsa, 2018). At the same time, media trust has been decreasing in recent years, both for traditional and social media. The Edelman trust barometer (Edelman Trust Barometer, 2020) has shown that globally, trust in traditional media decreased by five points in 2020 in comparison to the previous year. Meanwhile, trust in social media globally decreased by three points. In the European Union, this decrease was smaller for traditional media and larger for social media. Even though social media is often the leading news source, their news content is perceived as less trustworthy than traditional media.

Decreasing media trust could also be an issue for traditional media. Low media trust has been linked to the use of non-mainstream news sources, such as social media and blogs (Fletcher and Park, 2017). However, the content of these non-mainstream sources is not produced according to the professional standards that news organizations use. The value of journalism is not only in reporting but also in verification, contextualization and interpretation of information (Chen et al., 2015).

Trust in the media has further decreased as media production changed to suit the new media landscape. The research conducted by Allcott and Gentzkow (2017) showed that trust in news on social media is lower in comparison to traditional media, partially due to the different editorial requirements for its publishing. Critics most often observe a lack of time for more thorough research as the main culprit for the decline of media trust (Holiday in Cooke, 2018). The crisis in journalism is partially caused by other production changes, as well as transformed media consumption habits. Nevertheless, online media, especially social media, also have some obstacles, such as publishing misinformation or fake news. Social media enables news consumption at a low cost, with easy access and rapid dissemination. The widespread introduction of fake news has the potential of producing highly negative impacts on individuals and society (Shu et al., 2017).

DOI: 10.4324/9781003203551-12

Media credibility and trust are essential because they are the foundation of journalistic ethics. The fake news phenomenon has shown the consequences of disseminating unverified information to a large audience, such as confusion, doubt and a reliance on false information (Rapp and Salovich, 2018). Due to this, it is important to study the challenges regarding low media trust and credibility and the possible solutions to these problems. This chapter aims to detect the challenges of the current media landscape, focusing on changes in media production processes on one hand and media consumption and perception on the other. The survey results presented here pertain to fieldwork carried out in Slovenia, a Member State of the European Union. A recent study has shown that media trust in Slovenia is comparable to other EU States as traditional media have been perceived as the most trustworthy and social media the least trustworthy. According to the data, it may be argued that there exists a crisis of trust, as well as a crisis of European media (Speck, 2020).

The issue of challenges in media perception and media production is, above all, related to the basic principles of journalism. Trust and credibility are embedded in the mission of journalism from the perspective of media ethics. The production processes within journalism should be the safeguard of these principles. Accordingly, media users are aware of these basic principles that safeguard journalism and that trust in the media diminishes when certain principles are not adhered to.

Media credibility crisis

The leading role of the media in a democracy is to provide its citizens with the relevant information they need (Calvo-Porral et al., 2014). Previous studies have shown that people are less likely to rely on media outlets they do not perceive as credible (Johnson and Kaye, 1998). The Internet has increased the amount of incorrect information in news stories, which raised the issue of credibility and trustworthiness of the news and information available. According to Johnson and Kaye (1998), the key characteristic of the Internet is free access, meaning anyone can upload information. Experts have argued that this could affect the credibility of online news, which is frequently not fact-checked by media professionals when compared to other news platforms (newspapers, radio and television). Furthermore, not all news sources are bound by the same editorial and gatekeeping rules as the print and broadcast media (Flanagin and Metzger, 2000). The importance of media credibility has thus increased due to the quantity of incorrect information and fake news.

Additionally, the rapid spread of fake news is also seen as an indicator of a crisis in journalism and the media. Some see fake news as an attack that could undermine the credibility of professional journalism (Nielsen and Graves, 2017). The term news is indeed defined as content that is expected to be independent, reliable, accurate and comprehensive, whilst journalism is expected to report the truth (Kovach and Rosenstiel, 2007). Despite such assurances, the public has shown a growing scepticism regarding the fairness, accuracy and trustworthiness of the media (Calvo-Porral et al., 2014).

In researching media credibility, it is necessary to differentiate between mainstream online media, independent online media and index news sources, such as news.google.com (Chung et al., 2012). The most common online news sources are mainstream online media, which are very similar to offline media, as they employ journalists and have well-organized news production systems. On the contrary, independent online media do not have access to the same production standards (journalists and editors), and they produce news exclusively for a website. As a result, these news sources offer specialized news, which are produced by various contributors. This practice is commonly criticized for the risk of insufficient professionalism as a consequence of accepting contributions from biased contributors. The third type of online media are index news sources, which aggregate content from other news sources. News stories are then categorized and reviewed by software-driven algorithmic editorial teams instead of human editors. The authors of the aforementioned study (Chung et al., 2012) found that mainstream online media are perceived as more credible than other media, while independent media were perceived as the least credible. This might be the result of either offline brand image or professional news production processes.

Media consumption changes have also influenced the decrease of media credibility. These changes have occurred especially among young people, who increasingly access news on mobile devices (Mitchell et al., 2016). Social media platforms have become among the most common news sources; however, users are wary of their role as news source (Shearer and Grieco, 2019). One of the reasons users choose online sources is their evaluation that the traditional media are insufficient news sources and choose alternative news websites (Wilson et al., 2011). Students also tend to choose online news sources because of the easy access and convenience of obtaining information (Metzger et al., 2003).

Media production changes might further burden the decrease in media credibility. Over the years, small blogs became the entry point for news into the mainstream media. This means news is brought to the media's attention by initially being published on small blogs, and due to less rigorous editorial standards, this news is more likely to be fake or contain partially fake information (Holiday in Cooke, 2018). These websites lack any editorial review as there are low to no barriers for publishing citizen-produced content, and this news can further spread to traditional channels of dissemination and thus become part of mainstream media (De Saulles, 2015). The trend of empathetic journalism has three main characteristics: the rejection of gatekeeping and control, frustration with homogeneity, and personalization leading to the fragmentation of news media. Users can choose among an increasing number of different news sources, which may be ideologically more aligned with them. While fragmentation offers choice and multiple perspectives, it also increases unbalanced reporting (Holiday in Cooke, 2018). In *iterative* journalism, the stories are published online as they are in pieces or iterations. Stories are published with only a few facts that can be added, as the main goal is to be first and to attract emotion. Similarly, citizen journalism started with the intention of being a watchdog of the community. However, this type of journalism faces several challenges. First, citizen journalists often report about a limited number of topics and as Karlsson and Holt (2014) found, the majority of news covered business news, entertainment and sport. The reason might be easy access to press releases and reposting of marketing content about this news. Secondly, their resources are limited, similar to professional media resources. Thirdly, they struggle with professional work ethics and editorial policy (Karlsson and Holt, 2014).

Social media itself has even influenced production processes, for example, Twitter. This platform is also a micro-blogging site that is based on instant dissemination of information. The quality of news on this platform is lower than in traditional news organizations due to cheaper production and faster dissemination through the platforms, which require a large volume of news to be produced. The same rules apply to the production and dissemination of fake news (Shu et al., 2017). Nevertheless, a few studies, such as Shearer and Gottfried (2017), show that Twitter was used as a news source by 74% of users, while Facebook was used for that purpose by 68% of the users.

The online news environment also rewards spectacle in reporting, which is done at the expense of fact-checking and verification (Chen et al., 2015). Due to these changes, online news media either choose to reproduce the content from traditional news sources, create original content and add hyperlinks with additional information, or create original content designed specifically for the Internet by enabling the readers' comments and opinions (Pavlik in Chung et al., 2012). From Holiday (in Cooke, 2018), media producers also became less concerned if the information is later found to be incorrect, as it can be corrected or retracted. However, audiences are unlikely to observe the updated news content.

Moreover, a few other earlier studies related to the investigation of online users' perception of traditional media compared to online news platforms revealed that they expect traditional media to follow standards of fairness, balance and objectivity. At the same time, they do not have the same expectations for news blogs (Johnson and Kaye, 2010). Before the development of social media sites, online news platforms were praised for the opinionated analysis and points of view missing from mainstream media (Bruns, 2005). Online news media were seen as more critical, fair and objective. Additionally, these media presented different perspectives and their writers considered free from any pressures (Wilson et al., 2011). Despite the appreciation of the freedom of opinion associated with online platforms, news stories from traditional media organizations were perceived as more credible than user-generated news sources (Cassidy, 2007).

The perception of media and production processes in the media industry is closely related to content distributed on all media platforms. Accordingly, trust in media content is reduced when wrong or misleading content is on the increase. Therefore, the issue of fake news is highly connected to the overall perception of today's media.

Fake news

Multiple definitions of fake news have been produced in recent years. According to Wardle and Derakhshan (2018), it is defined on a scale between mis-information (unintentional sharing of false information) and disinformation (deliberate sharing of incorrect information). Others define fake news as news that is entirely false or contains intentionally misleading elements (Bakir and McStay, 2018). Lastly, Lazer et al. (2018) defined fake news as fabricated information that mimics news media content in form but lacks the editorial norms of accuracy and credibility of information. Fake news also negatively influences the audience's trust in other media organizations.

Internet platforms, such as social media, have been tools that have enabled the production and growth of fake news due to the way they operate (Lazer et al., 2018; Bakir and McStay, 2018). Bakir and McStay (2018) define five factors that have contributed to the spread of fake news. These are (a) the financial decline of traditional news media, (b) changes in the news cycle, (c) the rapid circulation of misinformation and disinformation in user-generated content, (d) the emotionalized nature of online discourse; and (e) the growing number of people capitalizing on social media and search engine algorithms. One of the transformations of the media industry is based on time and cost – time and cost to produce, distribute and consume. After the financial crisis in 2008, social media was the perfect substitute that enabled the media industry alternative access to the global market at a lower cost.

The cost of creating a website to act as a production and distribution channel is low, and their monetization enables financial gains from advertising and social media dissemination (Lazer et al., 2018). Additionally, the spreading of fake news is facilitated through algorithms, which are designed to display content matched to a user's previous behaviour. This reinforces pre-existing beliefs (Bakshy et al., 2015). The reasons for such algorithm designs are people's inclination to seek information congruent with existing knowledge, beliefs and opinions, in order to avoid information that contradicts it (Case, 2007). Additionally, fake news has the ability to draw audience views and engagement away from news produced by legitimate media, which could be a problem for traditional media organizations struggling to find online audiences. Struggling to find an audience is a common problem in the communication industry, where media plays the most prominent role. Therefore, the need to engage with audiences was followed by the need to arouse emotion. This gap between reality and the audience could be quickly filled with fake news.

Fake news does not influence all media users, but some exert confusion, miscommunication, doubt, and reliance on inaccurate content for problem-solving (Rapp and Salovich, 2018). According to Bakir and McStay (2018), fake news is driven by the economics of emotion, which means that users' emotions are leveraged to generate attention, which converts into advertising revenue.

Another cause of the rapid dissemination of fake news might be peer-to-peer propaganda. Social media is a tool for information-sharing between friends and family. This means users experience media content as something shared by their trusted friends, which shapes their opinions and assumptions (Haigh et al., 2018). Legitimacy and credibility of fake news are further increased by the publication of the same news on multiple websites, which makes fact-checking difficult (Shao et al., 2018). Apart from the negative consequences of fake news, this phenomenon has also influenced journalism positively as it could serve as an opportunity to reconsider the role of journalists and reinforce the boundaries of journalism. Additionally, media organizations and media scholars might develop new solutions regarding the issue of misinformation.

Changes in media consumption behaviour

Before discussing the results from our audience study regarding the perception of media content, it is worth highlighting the changing nature of media consumption behaviour across various countries. Media consumption habits of digital natives and other media audiences have undergone significant changes over the last few years. Several studies have pointed out that social media is becoming the primary source of news for an increasing number of users. For instance, Shu et al. (2017) observed two main reasons for this change. First, the use of social media to access news is more time-efficient and less expensive than traditional news media, such as newspapers or television. Secondly, users can engage with content, for example, share or comment on the news with friends or others on social media (Shu et al., 2017). Moreover, research shows that social media is used as a news source by 52% of users worldwide, and 23% trust that news (Reuters institute, 2019). In another study by Shearer and Matsa (2018), results show that 68% of adults in the USA get news from social media. Facebook is the most common news source for 43% of adults in the USA. Interestingly their study also reveals that 57% believe the content is mainly inaccurate, although they still choose social media as their news sources (Shearer and Matsa, 2018).

The previously described changes have led to a steady decrease of trust in news media, both in traditional, as well as online media. Nielsen and Graves (2017) see this issue as part of a wider discontent with the information landscape, one that is paired with scepticism, which is observed even in countries that exhibit high trust in public institutions, such as Finland. Scepticism and changed consumption habits have led to a so-called post-truth era.

European audiences perception of media content

Our study presents data from a European study the authors first conducted among young adults aged 18–31 during November and December 2018. The study was repeated in November and December 2019 for a comparison of results. An online survey questionnaire was used for this purpose, with a convenience sample among undergraduate and graduate students. Perceived media credibility was measured for five media types (television, radio, print, online media and social media). These media types were selected due to findings from previous studies that illustrated the increasing significance of social media platforms for news seeking (European Commission, 2017). Respondents were asked to evaluate a few traditional and online news sources according to the following categories: Neutrality, objectivity, independence from political and economic interests, in-depth reporting, representation of different perspectives and sensationalism. Additionally, they were asked to evaluate whether social media (Facebook, Twitter, Instagram, Snapchat and YouTube) might replace traditional and other online news sources. The results from recent studies of audience research in different countries were also compared with the results from our survey.

The following presents key findings from this study which will help form a picture of their media perception. 155 respondents completed the survey questionnaire in 2018 and 88 respondents in 2019. The majority of them were women (65% in 2018 and 56% in 2019), and the average age of respondents was 26 (SD=1.6, min=18, max=31) in 2018 and 21 (SD=1.8, min=18, max=31) in 2019. The majority of respondents in both studies were undergraduate students (79% vs. 92%).

Media usage

Respondents of this survey reported the highest media usage for social media and multimedia websites. In 2018, 43% of respondents used them for one to three hours per day, 27% used them for three to five hours, and 16% used them for more than five hours. In 2019, half of the people surveyed used these platforms for one to three hours per day, 26% used them three to five hours, and 9% used them for more than five hours. Other common news sources were online news media, the usage of which increased, as 3% of respondents used them for more than five hours per day (in comparison to 1% in the previous years). Traditional media were used less often, with the highest usage for radio and the lowest for print media. The percentage of users who listen to the radio for more than five hours per day has decreased from 2% to 1%, but more people listen to it for three to five hours (4% vs. 5%) and one to three hours (24% to 26%). The media usage data could indicate the habits of young adults. More accurate information could be gathered from a longitudinal study where respondents would report their daily media usage. These results indicate the perception of media usage of digital natives. It should be stressed that the usage of different platforms does not always develop on the conscious level. Digital natives are comfortable with technology and computers at an early age and consider technology an integral part of their lives. Their lives have been exposed to the influence of modern information technologies; thus, they think, learn and understand the world differently than the previous generations. They also differently perceive their actions and relations to the outside world. Additionally their perception of time spent with media is important data that helps us to understand their way of living.

Media trust and credibility

In addition to attempting to find out users' consumption habits, we asked our respondents to indicate their level of trust in the media outlets they use. Respondents were asked to evaluate the media outlets according to their selectivity of topics, selectivity of facts, the accuracy of depictions and journalistic assessment with a list of statements. Radio was rated the highest as the media that reports on important topics, while user-generated content on social media was rated the lowest. The editorial content on social media was evaluated as providing more important topics but significantly less than traditional media (radio, print, television) and online news media. In terms of providing relevant and diverse perspectives on topics, the highest-rated medium was print, followed by radio and television. Traditional media was followed by online news media, which surpassed editorial content on social media and user-generated content. Traditional media was also found to provide the most verifiable and factual information, while user-generated content on social media was rated the lowest. Similarly, expression of opinion and criticism was found to be the most appropriate on radio and other traditional media, followed by editorial content on social media, online news media, blogs and user-generated content on social media.

Overall, participants rated user-generated content on social media as the lowest in credibility, as they provide the least important topics and least diverse perspectives. This content was also perceived to be the least verifiable and factual. Respondents perceived the author's opinion and criticism to be the least appropriate in comparison to other news media. This shows that discontent with the information landscape is the main characteristic of social media users, as they value the content in traditional media more, especially print and radio.

Replacement of traditional media

Respondents were asked to evaluate whether social media platforms might replace traditional media and other online news media. Results from Figure 9.1

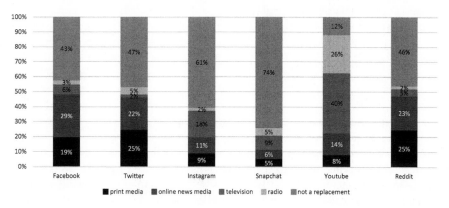

Figure 9.1 Social media as a replacement for other media

show that 43% of respondents did not see Facebook as a replacement for other media, while it was considered the most likely to replace online news media (29%) and print media (19%). The majority of respondents did not perceive Twitter to be a replacement (47%), but few said it could replace print media (25%) and online news media (22%). Other social media platforms (Instagram, Snapchat and Reddit) were even less often perceived as a replacement for traditional and online news media. Only YouTube was perceived to be a replacement for television (40%), radio (26%) and online media (15%).

Digital media and the post-truth era

The spreading of fake news on digital media has changed both the media landscape and media consumers. The latter respond to misinformation with lower trust in news on social media (Clayton et al., 2020). Fake news is known to utilize emotion to intentionally persuade consumers to accept biased or false beliefs (Shu et al., 2017). Over time, exposure to fake news has changed the way users interpret real news. They have become distrustful and confused, which hinders their ability to differentiate what is true from what is not (Rapp and Salovich, 2018).

Misinformation has many potentially adverse impacts on individuals and society and many dangerous consequences. The presence of misinformation can cause people to stop believing in facts altogether. Misinformation is not just about being misinformed, but it is also about the overall intellectual well-being of a society (Lewandowsky et al., 2017).

According to Valadier (2017), a society based on human relationships needs trust, one of the major ingredients, and cannot ignore the search for truth and truthfulness. How can we trust someone when we suspect the truth is distorted? It is hard to see how democracy and human communities could survive the institutionalization of lying or the domination of virtual space. The human communities are linked with invisible relations which are based on trust. This could be transferred to society as whole where democracy plays a role. Democracy is not just a procedural system nor just a matter of obeying arbitrary rules, but Valadier (2017) stressed that it needs truth and attempts to find the truth. Without trust, the basic principles of democracy are threatened and endangered. This crisis in journalism and media, in the form of decreased media trust, has led to a post-truth era, where an audience is more likely to believe information that appeals to their emotions as opposed to factual information. According to Cooke (2018), social media is ideal for sharing pieces of yellow journalism or click-bait content, which was observed long before the fake news phenomenon. Interestingly, participants in one study perceived the issue of fake and true news as a spectrum rather than a distinct difference, as they did not believe there was any entirely factual news (Nielsen and Graves, 2017).

According to Thussu (2009), 'real news' is in a state of crisis, faced with a range of challenges that include declining audience numbers, decreasing profits and a broad credibility loss. As for Thussu, fake news reminds us that entertainment is a doubly articulated concept. On one hand, 'to entertain' means to amuse and to give pleasure. On the other, it means to engage with and to consider. Fake news does both. It makes the news pleasurable, but more than that, it continuously calls on its viewer to consider. With the fake news era journalism is facing serious questioning. Is it still based on the demand for governmental accountability, a performance of democratic dialogue and a resource for citizen engagement? As Thussu stressed (2009), we are in an age when the 'real news' too often fails on all of those accounts, while fake news stands at the leading edge of an effort to reimagine the possibilities of journalism. Its increasing popularity and its growing significance in the serious world of news and politics supports the suggestion that it is not fake at all. Unfortunately, as suggested by Thussu, fake news may indeed be 'the way of the future'.

In the post-truth era, when we need entertainment and emotion, they should be a part of the media narrative as emotions are easy to engage with. Moreover, our emotions are authentic, and we do not need to question the facts and figures – we do not check if they are real. For the audience, only feelings and emotions matter. With emotional feedback, the publisher could catch the needed attention as emotions are an easy way to connect. Scholars of media and communications are well aware that propaganda historically worked by targeting and influencing emotions. Additionally, the rise of computational propaganda moves researchers into analysing how it targets emotions and affects users through social media. Computational propaganda reflects the affective online strategies used to target particular emotions to manipulate feelings (Boler and Davis, 2018, Grassegger and Krogerus, 2017).

Over the years, the role of emotions in media content has increased significantly. McStay (2016) first defined contemporary media as empathic media, which means they use personally and emotionally targeted news. This was specifically visible in media reports during the 2016 US elections. The role of emotion in fake news growth is part of the broader issue of the economics of emotions. Emotions are used to increase attention and generate profit in other media products, such as in advertisements (Bakir and McStay, 2018). The idea that news can be free of subjective bias is an illusion. However, in a time when the media is trying to salvage its mission to report the truth, the demands to put emotions aside are more reasonable than ever before.

Research on the effects of the post-truth era started after the 2016 US elections when the term fake news became popularized. The existence of post-truth caused by fake news had implications for journalism. Journalism is based on the principle of serving the public and public interest. However, journalism as presented today and also in the past needs an audience, the audience is the ultimate goal. Chomsky's theory, based on the propaganda model, suggested that media is interested in the sale of a product – the audience – rather than the pursuit of quality journalism in the public service. Herman and Chomsky (1988) stressed that the propaganda model focuses on wealth and power inequality and its multilevel effects on mass-media interests and choices. It traces the routes by which money and power can filter out the news fit to print, marginalize dissent, and allow the government and dominant private interests to get their messages across to the public.

Nowadays, the power lies with those who are the most vocal and influential on social media. These individuals can mobilize millions of followers or fake online personas through which a small group of operatives can create an illusion of a widespread opinion. Moreover, fake news and lost media trust has endangered the media industry and democracy.

The changes caused by journalism, misinformation and social media have influenced society and modern democracy. Truth has always been at the heart of democracy. As Farkas and Schou (2019) stressed, the crisis of society needs to be resolved by reinstating truth at the heart of democracy, even if this means curtailing civic participation and popular sovereignty. They argue that these solutions neglect the fact that democracy has never been about truth alone: it is equally about the voice of the democratic populace.

Proposed solutions

The media industry faces challenges to strengthen its role from the romantic past, when it was accountable to the public, serving the public interest and offering credible information. In a broader context, fake news detection is related to fact-checking issues in general. Detection of fake news is essential to prevent confusion, doubt and reliance on inaccurate material. Scholars have proposed instructional activities, technological tools and literacy practices for encouraging users to evaluate information sources (Rapp and Salovich, 2018). During the last few years, several fact-checking services have been established to analyse the accuracy and credibility of online content.

Fake news detection is additionally challenging due to users' inability to recognize fake from accurate information. Part of the reason can be found in the user's selection of sources of verification. Nielsen and Graves (2017) note that users either trust the brands/news media (source cues), people/friends and family (social cues) or do their own online research (Tandoc et al., 2018).

On the production side, media organizations are advised to invest in fake detection software. However, according to Shu et al. (2017), automatic detection is still challenging, as fake news is deliberately misleading, making it more difficult to detect. Fake news is mocking factual news by citing authentic sources in a different context to confirm their inaccurate information (Feng et al., 2012), making textual analysis insufficient in fake news detection. Additionally, most fake news covers events with recent events that have not been verified, and the high volume of social media activity causes data to be incomplete and difficult to fact-check in a short time (Tang et al., 2014).

Clayton et al. (2020), on the other hand, researched various detection systems proposed by Facebook. The company developed two types of warnings; the first were general warnings about fake news, and the second were warnings about individual articles. General warnings were found to reduce the perceived accuracy of false headlines, especially when tags 'Rated false' and 'Disputed' were added to the content. Another solution is stance detection, which was identified as the first step towards automatically detecting fake news. This method proposes a comparison of whether the news article content is related to the headline (Hanselowski et al., 2018). Facebook also decided to remove accounts, content and ads that violate their policies, reduce the distribution of false news and inauthentic content by penalizing spam and low-quality sites. Additionally, they utilized tools to inform people about the issue of fake news by displaying related articles from third-party fact-checkers and creating an educational tool for identifying false news (Lyons, 2018).

On the other side are measures to strengthen citizens' ability to recognize fake news. Apart from critical thinking, different literacy skills need to be trained, for example, critical information literacy, digital literacy and media literacy (Cooke, 2018). The need for the development of digital literacy has been shown in digital natives as well, even though they are part of the generations that are immersed in digital technologies and should, thus, be digitally literate (Ng, 2012). The media landscape with many platforms and enormous amounts of information pose a challenge for society and its citizens. Digital natives should be prepared for the media world, and, therefore, different literacy approaches are needed. They should have the relevant skills to digest information and place them in a particular context. It follows that media literacy, digital literacy and, mostly, critical thinking literacy are forming important competencies for the development of society.

Conclusion

The roles and popularity of different media outlets change over time due to technological and societal changes. Online media have grown in importance, and social media platforms now function as gatekeepers to news sources. Audiences now need less time to find news, but, at the same time, their engagement with news content is monitored by algorithms. A crisis of trust in journalism, rapid news production and dissemination have led to an era where audiences value their emotions and beliefs higher than fact and accuracy. Misinformation has long been observed in media. Today, in the age of social media, the issue is more concerning, as fake news can be instantly disseminated to large audiences. Platforms such as social media have become the news intermediaries and invisible gatekeepers.

Moreover, we have entered an era where the virtual has replaced the real, and a general mistrust has endangered human relations, human well-being and democracy as such. Living in a world where we cannot trust words, institutions, human beings is a society where nothing is real. Our lives become transferred to a virtual place where everyone can present themselves as they wish to be perceived. This also applies to the presentation of institutions who are presented as they want to be. The world is reported through the various platforms in ways the main actors want us to perceive it. However, media users do not believe these presentations, and this general distrust is damaging society at all levels.

As this chapter stressed, there are few possible solutions on both the production and audience sides to diminish the influence of fake news. The detection of fake news is in the media's best interest, as the publication of such content further damages its reputation and decreases the user's trust in media. To counter this, media audiences need to be trained in digital literacy to recognize fake news. This is of vital importance to preserve the media's role in society as media trust is constantly decreasing. Moreover, the value of journalism is also in verification, contextualization and interpretation of information. As a consequence, credibility is of vital importance for building trust from the consumers' point of view even though we are aware of changed consumption habits. Digital natives are inclined to substitute some traditional media with social media and other online services, but they appreciate reliable information. Discontent with the information landscape is the main characteristic of social media users, as they value the content in traditional media more. This perception of young users is promising as they know that digital literacy and a certain level of regulation are part of responsible and credible media systems.

According to Herman and Chomsky (1988), the news is shaped according to various factors, also called five filters. However, it is promising to understand that the audiences are the solution. Only audiences have the power to stop the fake news flow. In a society where we cannot trust elected officials because they have proven to be untrustworthy, the audience needs to become its own 'fact-checker'.

References

Allcott, H. and Gentzkow, M. (2017), 'Social media and fake news in the 2016 election'. *Journal of Economic Perspectives*, 31(2), 211–236.

Bakir, V. and McStay, A. (2018), 'Fake news and the economy of emotions: Problems, causes, solutions'. *Digital Journalism*, 6(2), 154–175.

Bakshy, E., Messing, S. and Adamic, L. A. (2015), 'Exposure to ideologically diverse news and opinion on Facebook'. *Science*, 348(6239), 1130–1132.

Banning, S. A. and Sweetser, K. D. (2007), 'How much do they think it affects them and whom do they believe? Comparing the third-person effect and credibility of blogs and traditional media'. *Communication Quarterly*, 55(4), 451–466.

Boler, M. and Davis, E. (2018), 'The affective politics of the "post-truth" era: Feeling rules and networked subjectivity'. *Emotion, Space and Society*, 27, 75–85.

Bruns, A. (2005), *Gatewatching: Collaborative Online News Production*. New York: Peter Lang.

Calvo-Porral, C., Martínez-Fernández, V. A. and Juanatey-Boga, O. (2014), 'Mass communication media credibility: An approach from the credible brand model'. *Intercom: Revista Brasileira de Ciências da Comunicação*, 37(2), 21–49.

Case, D. O. (2007), *Looking for Information: A Survey of Research on Information Seeking, Needs, and Behavior*. London: Academic Press.

Cassidy, W. P. (2007), 'Online news credibility: An examination of the perceptions of newspaper journalists'. *Journal of Computer Mediated Communication*, 12(2), 478–498.

Chen, Y., Conroy, N. J., and Rubin, V. L. (2015), 'News in an online world: The need for an "automatic crap detector"'. *Proceedings of the Association for Information Science and Technology*, 52:1, 1–4.

Chung, C. J., Nam, Y., and Stefanone, M. A. (2012), 'Exploring online news credibility: The relative influence of traditional and technological factors'. *Journal of Computer-Mediated Communication*, 17(2), 171–186.

Clayton, K., Blair, S., Busam, J. A., Forstner, S., Glance, J., Green, G., Kawata, A., Kovvuri, A., Martin, J., Morgan, E., Sandhu, M., Sang, R., Scholz-Bright, R., Welch, A. T., Wolff, A. G., Zhou, A. and Nyhan, B. (2020), 'Real solutions for fake news? Measuring the effectiveness of general warnings and fact-check tags in reducing belief in false stories on social media'. *Political Behavior*, 42, 1073–1095.

Cooke, N. A. (2018), *Fake News and Alternative Facts: Information Literacy in a Post-Truth Era*. Chicago: American Library Association.

De Saulles, M. (2015), *Information 2.0: New Models of Information Production, Distribution and Consumption*. London: Facet Publishing.

Edelman Trust Barometer (2020), 'Edelman Trust Barometer 2020'. *Global Report*. Retrieved from: https://www.edelman.com/sites/g/files/aatuss191/files/2020-01/2020%20Edelman%20Trust%20Barometer%20Global%20Report.pdf. Accessed: 10 November 2020.

European Commission (2017), 'Media use in the European Union'. Retrieved from Report. Available at: https://ec.europa.eu/commfrontoffice/publicopinion/index.cfm/ResultDoc/download/DocumentKy/82786. Accessed: 10 November 2020.

Farkas, J. and Schou, J. (2019), *Post-Truth, Fake News and Democracy: Mapping the Politics of Falsehood*. London: Routledge.

Feng, S., Banerjee, R. and Choi, Y. (2012), 'Syntactic stylometry for deception detection'. *Proceedings of the 50 Annual Meeting of the Association for Computational Linguistics*, 2, 171–175.

Flanagin, A. J. and Metzger, J. M. (2000), 'Perceptions of internet information credibility'. *Journalism and Mass Communication Quarterly*, 77(3), 515–540.

Fletcher, R. and Park, S. (2017), 'The impact of trust in the news media on online news consumption and participation'. *Digital Journalism*, 5(10), 1281–1299.

Grassegger, H. and Krogerus, M. (2017), 'The data that turned the world upside down'. *Vice Motherboard*. Available at: https://hartle.ca/wp-content/uploads/2017/01/The-Data-That-Turned-the-World-Upside-Down-_-Motherboard.pdf. Accessed: 25 April 2021.

Haigh, M., Haigh, T. and Kozak, N. I. (2018), 'Stopping fake news: The work practices of Peer-to-peer counter Propaganda'. *Journalism Studies*, 19(14), 2062–2087.

Hanselowski, A., Avinesh, P. V. S., Schiller, B., Caspelherr, F., Chaudhuri, D., Meyer, C. M. and Gurevych, I. (2018), 'A Retrospective Analysis of the Fake News Challenge Stance Detection Task'. *Proceedings of the 27th International Conference on Computational Linguistics*, pp. 1859–1874.

Herman, E. S. and Chomsky, N. (1988), *Manufacturing Consent: The Political Economy of the Mass Media*. New York: Pantheon.

Johnson, T. J. and Kaye, B. K. (1998), 'Cruising is believing? Comparing Internet and traditional sources on media credibility measures'. *Journalism and Mass Communication Quarterly*, 75(2), 325–340.

Johnson, T. and Kaye, B. (2010), 'Choosing is believing? How web gratifications and reliance affect Internet credibility among politically interested users'. *Atlantic Journal of Communication*, 18(1), 1–21.

Karlsson, M. and Holt, K. (2014), 'Is anyone out there? Assessing Swedish citizen-generated community journalism'. *Journalism Practice*, 8(2), 164–180.

Kovach, B. and Rosenstiel, T. (2007), *The Elements of Journalism: What Newspeople Should Know and the Public Should Expect*. New York: Three Rivers Press.

Lazer, D. M., Baum, M. A., Benkler, Y., Berinsky, A. J., Greenhill, K. M., Menczer, F., Metzger, M. J., Nyhan, B., Pennycook, G., Rothschild, D., Schudson, M., Sloman, S. A., Sunstein, C. R., Thorson, E. A., Watts, D. J. and Zittrain, J. L. (2018), 'The science of fake news'. *Science*, 359(6380), 1094–1096.

Lewandowsky, S., Ecker, U. K. and Cook, J. (2017), 'Beyond misinformation: Understanding and coping with the "post-truth" era'. *Journal of Applied Research in Memory and Cognition*, 6(4), 353–369.

Lyons, T. (2018), 'Hard questions: What's Facebook's strategy for stopping false news?'. *Facebook Newsroom*, 23 May. Retrieved from: https://about.fb.com/news/2018/05/hard-questions-false-news/. Accessed: 18 November 2020.

McStay, A. (2016), 'Empathic media and advertising: Industry, policy, legal and citizen perspectives (the case for intimacy)'. *Big Data and Society*, 3(2), 1–11.

Metzger, M. J., Flanagin, A. J., Eyal, K., Lemus, D. R. and McCann, R. (2003), 'Credibility for the 21st century: Integrating perspectives on source, message and media credibility in the contemporary media environment'. *Annals of the International Communication Association*, 27(1), 293–335.

Mis, M. (2016), 'More than half online users get news from Facebook'. *YouTube* and *Twitter*: study. Retrieved from: https://www.reuters.com/article/us-media-socialmedia-news-idUSKCN0Z02UB. Accessed: 22 August 2020.

Mitchell, A., Gottfried, J., Barthel, M. and Shearer, E. (2016), 'The modern news consumer'. *Pew Research Center*, 7 July. Retrieved from: https://www.journalism.org/2016/07/07/the-modern-news-consumer/. Accessed: 22 August 2020.

Ng, W. (2012), 'Can we teach digital natives digital literacy?'. *Computers and Education*, 59(3), 1065–1078.

Nielsen, R. K. and Graves, L. (2017), *"News You Don't Believe": Audience Perspectives On Fake News*. Oxford: Reuters Institute for the Study of Journalism.

Rapp, D. N. and Salovich, N. A. (2018), 'Can't we just disregard fake news? The consequences of exposure to inaccurate information'. *Policy Insights from the Behavioral and Brain Sciences*, 5(2), 232–239.

Reuters Institute (2020). 'Digital news report'. Retrieved from: http://www.digitalnewsreport.org/interactive/. Accessed: 10 February 2020.

Shao, C., Ciampaglia, G. L., Varol, O., Yang, K. C., Flammini, A. and Menczer, F. (2018), 'The spread of low-credibility content by social bots'. *Nature Communications*, 9(1), 1–9.

Shearer, E. and Gottfried, J. (2017), 'News use across social media platforms 2017'. *Pew Research Center*, 7 September.Retrieved from: https://www.journalism.org/2017/09/07/news-use-across-social-media-platforms-2017/. Accessed: 29 July 2021.

Shearer, E. and Grieco, E. (2019), 'Americans are wary of the role social media sites play in delivering the news'. *Pew Research Center*, 2 October. Retrieved from: https://www.journalism.org/2019/10/02/americans-are-wary-of-the-role-social-media-sites-play-in-delivering-the-news/. Accessed: 22 August 2020.

Shearer, E. and Matsa, K. E. (2018), 'News use across social media platforms'. *Pew Research Center*, 10 September. Retrieved from: https://www.journalism.org/2018/09/10/news-use-across-social-media-platforms-2018/. Accessed: 10 November 2020.

Shu, K., Sliva, A., Wang, S., Tang, J. and Liu, H. (2017), 'Fake news detection on social media: A data mining perspective'. *ACM SIGKDD Explorations Newsletter*, 19(1), 22–36.

Speck, D. (2020), 'Market insights'. *Trust in Media 2020*. EBU. Retrieved from: https://zukunft.orf.at/rte/upload/corona/ebu-mis-trust_in_media_2020_slide_deck.pdf. Accessed: 10 November.

Tandoc Jr, E. C., Lim, Z. W. and Ling, R. (2018), 'Defining "fake news."'. *Digital Journalism*, 6(2), 137–153.

Tang, J., Chang, Y. and Liu, H. (2014), 'Mining social media with social theories: A survey'. *ACM Sigkdd Explorations Newsletter*, 15(2), 20–29.

Thussu, D. K. (2009), 'The Era of Global Infotainment', in S. Allan (ed.), *The Routledge Companion to News and Journalism*. London: Routledge, pp. 362–373.

Valadier, P. (2017), 'Post-truth: A danger to democracy'. *Etudes*, 5, 55–64.

Wardle, C. and Derakhshan, H. (2018), 'Thinking about 'Information Disorder': Formats of Misinformation, Disinformation, and Mal-Information', in C. Ireton and J. Posetti (eds), *Handbook for Journalism Education and Training*. Paris: UNESCO, pp. 55–69.

Wilson, S., Leong, P., Nge, C. and Hong, N. M. (2011), 'Trust and credibility of urban youth on online news media'. *Jurnal Komunikasi: Malaysian Journal of Communication*, 27(2), 97–120.

10 Media ethics and the challenges of democratic transition in Tunisia

Moez Ben Messaoud

Introduction

As the Tunisian revolution enters its tenth year, Tunisians alive today are almost unanimous about the gains achieved in terms of media freedom, after years of being subject to the threat of interference by political power and the traditional centres of influence. However, despite the great strides that the battle for media freedom has made in Tunisia, many concerns are prevalent among the professional circles today in relation to the emergence of a new environment in which the political, economic and legal influences intertwine. Many of these institutions suffer from severe financial difficulties that have affected the quality of programme content and the social climate for journalists and the various workers in the sector. Moreover, the new mechanisms for distributing advertising revenues between the various media outlets, and their subjection to follow-up and viewing rates due the race to create a 'boom', necessitate a rethinking of the economic and commercial models adopted, within the framework of the system envisaged to organize the media scene in Tunisia.

The liberation of the media from the tight grip from the former regime of Tunisia does not necessarily mean that it will stay away from political disputes, and that it will stand at the same distance from all political parties. Perhaps the media's handling of the electoral issue during the last electoral period in the fall of 2019 is the best proof of this. The media dealings with the electoral issues during that period sparked widespread controversy and conflicts, which, in some cases, reached serious compromise in relation to the employment of some politicians by media outlets to serve their electoral goals. This created a crisis of confidence among the public, and forcefully have brought to the forefront the quest of media ethics.

This situation may be an indication that the Tunisian media has not yet moved beyond the stage of adjustment, as part of the period of democratic transition, and remains in need of further reforms. There is a need to accelerate the organization of the media scene and for the media to self-adjust according to the code of honour and the code of ethics for the journalistic profession, in accordance with international standards.

DOI: 10.4324/9781003203551-13

Media scene before and after the revolution

Tunisian media in the pre-2011 period was subject to strict control imposed on both independent and state-owned media alike. The media industry in Tunisia was also subject to the supervision and influence of a number of government agencies that had a monopoly on all stages of media production. By adopting the method of 'carrot and stick' with the various media outlets, the previous regime rewarded those who praised it, and punished those who dared to criticize it (Al-Issawi, 2012).

The obsession with controlling the media is not only characteristic of the previous regime – that is, the regime of Zine El Abidine Ben Ali – but also of the era of former President Habib Bourguiba, who ruled Tunisia between 1957 and 7 November 1987, the date of his removal from office by former President Zine El Abidine Ben Ali. Bourguiba used to call in many of his speeches to the media to 'educate the people', 'lead', 'educate' and 'direct' and 'spread the spirit of patriotism' (Bourguiba, 1982). The media was thus tools for leading and directing the public within the framework of a vertical relationship, in which the right to set its work programmes is reserved by the ruler, and these means and structures sought to polish the image of the Bourguiba regime and market it internationally 'in service of primarily developmental goals' (National Commission for the Reform of Information and Communication, 2012).

Bourguiba also used the media to demonize and humiliate political opponents and human rights defenders. Although this scene changed during the era of Prime Minister Mohamed Mazali (1980–1986), who was known for his relative openness to thought and the media, the margin of freedom did not change much. 'Due to the regime's complete control over the media scene, either by possessing media outlets and controlling their content or by intimidating violators, Bourguiba's opponents did not have any outlets to express their views' (Miladi, 2021a: 45). By the late 1980s, the regime of former President Zine El Abidine Ben Ali (7 November 1987 – 14 January 2011) had developed its methods of dealing with the means of communication to ensure they were tools to promote positive perceptions aimed at legitimizing his choices and policies.

The Tunisian Agency for External Communication played a pivotal role in this media landscape. After the establishment of the Tunisian Agency for External Communication on 7 August 1990, that is, the goal of it was to 'enhance the media presence of Tunisia abroad and to publicize the national policy in all fields'. As the agency focused its attention on the media material directed outside Tunisia or dealing with Tunisian affairs in the international press – the powers of the agency were expanded at the beginning of January 1991 to include monitoring the distribution of public advertisements in the written media, and then the audio-visual media beginning in 2005 (Circular of the First Ministry No. 23 dated 1 June 2005).

The Independent National Commission for Media Reform in Tunisia recognized in its final report the seriousness of the effects of the aggression that afflicted the Tunisian press and media institutions during the rule of Zine El

Abidine Ben Ali. It made a set of recommendations in order to erase the negative repercussions that afflicted the journalism profession, especially its ethical and professional standards. It also warned of the widespread manifestations of 'media chaos' and what it described as an 'overdose' of freedom of expression, after the dissolution of the Ministry of Communication. The commission also considered that one of the signs of this chaos is the transformation of television and radio spaces, newspaper pages, and news sites into arenas for settling personal and political accounts: throwing accusations without evidence, discrediting others, and spreading rumours without verifying them.

Democratic transition and the new challenges to media ethics

There is almost a consensus that freedom was the most prominent gain achieved during the revolution of 14 January 2011, in terms of lifting restrictions on political and civil society organizations. This new situation opened up freedom of expression and provided for a pluralistic media scene. It was accompanied by efforts to develop legislation related to the press and broadcasting media. However, 'despite the steps taken, the practice indicates the continuation of various deficiencies ... giving the image of a media sector that is still fragile' (Al-Haddad, 2019).

Despite granting licences to dozens of periodicals after the revolution and to more broadcasters, the media scene has not changed in depth. Conflict over the media in Tunisia, in relation to politics has been raging since January 2011. The decline in the decades-long media hegemony over the Tunisian public space is due to the dilemmas that the media sector itself suffers from, mainly related to the old legacy of despotism, but also to a number of factors arising from the general political situation in post-revolution Tunisia, the most important of which are summarized in the following (Al Jazeera Center For Studies, 2012).

1- Most media organizations do not rely on professional journalists. The owners of these institutions prefer to rely on the services of amateurs in journalistic work, or in the best cases, rely on a precarious employment, which makes the journalist subject to the directions of the owner of the media institution who personally determines the specifications of the media product. There exists also a decline in training of academics and professional journalist, weakness of the legislative framework, and lack of basic policies governing media institutions.

2- Facilitating licences to issue periodicals: In a short period, the number of periodicals reached about 300, in a process that few called 'media chaos'. Although this development was normal in the post-revolution period, it did not usually lead to an improvement in the media content, but on the contrary to a decline in its quality. Influence by a number of businessmen associated with the previous regime the newspaper sector was also recorded. For instance, two businessmen alone control about 20 titles.

In view of the lack of professionalism of most journalists and their old involvement in the media scene that preceded the revolution, the paradigm shift is witnessing some difficulties. Perhaps the first of these difficulties is 'the heavy moral legacy that this institution bears on its shoulders, which makes the transition from official media to public media extremely difficult, in light of the adoption of old laws, the same structure, and the media figures working in the sector' (Ben Messaoud, 2019: 306).

This situation was further complicated by the escalation of protests in public squares, after the issue of privatizing the public media was raised by some of the figureheads of the *Ennahda* movement, pushing the media towards a possible and protected pluralism, which has kept this an up-to-date topic in the public sphere, for a long period of time. Considering that the media sector is one of the biggest stakes in the eyes of various intervening parties, whether political or professional, it was evident for this issue to attract the attention of all Tunisians in the context of the democratic transition, and for it to become a matter of public debate. 'The square in front of the headquarters of the Tunisian Television Foundation has become a symbolic sign of the existing political struggle, and the race to absorb the media of the public service' (Ben Messaoud, 2019: 306). In this regard, civil society organizations have played an important role in bringing all interested groups to the table in this case the media, political opposition, the government, National Authority for Media and Communication Reform, and the Tunisian Journalists Syndicate, in order to discuss and manage how to distance the public media sector from all political disputes.

The search for excitement, bias and absence of ethical standards

Although the Tunisian media entered the phase of 'absolute freedom' in the period after 14 January 2011, as a normal move to 'restricted freedom', media institutions continued to face the difficulties resulting from the blurring of legal texts, the absence of adequate state support, clear mismanagement and restructuring, and mismanagement of resources. This made it easier for pressure groups and interest lobbies as suggested by (Al-Haddad, 2019) to penetrate the sector, with their skills and capability to finance and control trends and major media options.

It can be argued that the media sector has not witness a tangible improvement in the level of employment, wages, professional and social rights of journalists. It rather continued to be confused by definitions of professional practices, which have been translated into many slips in professionalism. In the period after 14 January 2011, many media outlets got into a chaotic situation, which distorted the professional standards of their journalism work. Media practice witnessed many dangerous phenomena that violated the ethics of the profession, such as the search for excitement, ideological influence and trade union alignment.

Moreover, what is prevalent about various media outlets after the revolution is profit-making. This situation has filtered excitement as the predominant tool and means to attract the audience and raise the ratings, whether in viewing, listening or reading. Entertainment programmes, gameshows, reality television and financial profit contests, usually prepare the ground for scandalous and exciting scenes that attract attention and reach the point of shock by exceeding all limits, including violations of professional ethics, as well as laws and regulations. 'This has touched on the Tunisian people's sense of the public space, such that the media would later be – after securing a high rate of public follow-up – the entrance by which to spread rumours and discord and serve narrow interests and agendas with ideological and political disputes' (Al-Haddad 2019).

It is a strange irony that the pre-revolution media, despite the reality of authoritarianism and tyranny, did not witness examples of this chaos and excitement, but on the contrary, it was more committed to respecting public taste and the specificities of society and its traditions and beliefs, which were mainly of a conservative character. According to some, this chaos is due to the vagueness of legislation and the weakness of control regulation, monitoring and oversight structures.

Among the most dangerous emerging phenomena, that are also seriously threatening media freedom and professional ethics, is the phenomenon of partisan and political alignment mainly related to the struggle for power and wars of positioning in the circles of government and political and financial influence. It is 'an alignment, mostly disguised, unannounced, targeting public opinion and trying to influence its daily choices as well as its electoral choices, using methods of guidance, carrots and intimidation, demonizing offenders, praising, slandering, distorting, obscuring and selecting false news and analyses' (Al-Haddad, 2019).

In the context of this conflict, some accuse professional unions and self-monitoring structures, chief among them the 'HAICA', of submitting to ideological influences, 'falling into favouritism, serving funders/investors, and pressure groups, and engaging in settling political scores' (Al-Haddad, 2019). Any time the legal status of the audio-visual communication authority – as a temporary body whose mandate expired since May 2, 2019 – is raised, records of 'HAICA' members with civil society parties and organizations still do not come to light. But its decisions are referred to without scrutiny. Being ink on paper, they inhibit people from making any real changes at the level of the broadcasting media.

The dependence of few media outlets on political parties, and the desire to play a political role, has contradicted the principle of its independence, and has created confusion in the identities of the various media outlets. The editorial line became dependent on centres of influence and the forces controlling the national decisions, and the economic and financial interests of the lobbies, which caused confusion in the media scene. So, positions, visions, and editorial trends could be transformed overnight from one extreme to the other and become inaccurate and distorted by political developments and developments, to the extent that a friend could turn into an enemy and vice versa without much logic and without reasonable justifications.

There is no doubt that a careful post-reading of the media's handling of issues such as political assassinations, terrorism, and the economic situation over the past years, and its impact on the political scene and major national events, will undoubtedly demonstrate how the spread of false news has grave consequences on the political atmosphere in the country. This is because it seems aimed at causing discord and societal division and disrupting the democratic transition in Tunisia. In this regard, a report on the reality of the Tunisian media, published by the Arab Group for Media Monitoring, in cooperation with two Tunisian associations: the National Council for Freedoms and the Coalition for Tunisian Women network, indicated that 90% of Arabic-speaking newspapers contain speech urging hatred, 10% of French-speaking newspapers contain speech urging hatred, 13% of media outlets contain an implicit or explicit call for violence, and 58% of media outlets comment on hate speech by political or religious parties (Al-Haddad, 2019).

In sum, although more than ten years have passed since the January 2011 revolution, the media in Tunisia are still entangled with politics to the point of sometimes being dependent on lobbies, interests and parties. This predicts that the conflict will continue until the authentic, fair and transparent democratic practice and peaceful transition of power is stabilized. Perhaps 'among the most prominent of these paradoxes is the issue how to organise media freedom, preventing any politically motivated authority from interfering again with the press and journalists, while maintaining professional ethics, possibly through a form of self-regulation' (Al-Youssefi, 2019).

Reform priorities and requirements

The near consensus about the success achieved, in relation to winning the battle for media freedom in Tunisia after 14 January 2011, should not cause us to underestimate the caveats and concerns that remain, in light of the interference by the politicians and traditional centres of influence. The political, economic, legal, and structural factors influencing the media overlap according to the status of media institutions themselves, and the impact of the follow-up rate measurement processes on the ability of the media outlets to obtain their share of the advertising revenues and ensure continuity. Therefore, it is imperative to acknowledge the importance of the need to enhance the future gains of media freedom, and to rethink the adopted economic and commercial models. This is especially the case with the private media companies, many of which have suffered from severe financial difficulties that affected the quality of their work.

This crisis of confidence was particularly evident during the 2019 general elections. The media dealing with the electoral issues caused widespread controversy and conflicts that have sometimes reached the point of sparking convulsive campaigns. This exposed the essence of the problem, which now cannot be circumvented or overlooked. The Independent High Authority for Audio-visual Communication (HAICA) recorded these concerns in the post-elections report 'the grave breaches recorded in the coverage of the legislative election campaign', as a 'serious problem' 'that affects the will of the voters, and thus changes the election results' (Independent High Authority for Audio-visual Communication, 2019).

The professional imbalances that affect the ethics of journalistic work in the Tunisian media go beyond the electoral period and have also become one of the most important causes of the crisis of trust within the public, or the cause for the transfer of large sectors of its trust. In fact, it is a complex, multifaceted crisis, that has an echo in credible opinion probes. In a study published by the 'Barr Al-Aman' association, in 2018 and which evaluated public policies, of those interviewed (1,841 persons), 65% expressed their confidence in 'the media'. The confidence range included confidence in a few media outlets (34%) to none of them (31%), compared to 19% whose confidence appeared to be moderate. Only 6% of the respondents registered had high confidence in the national press. This study also revealed that 45% of the respondents did not expect anything from the Tunisian media, while 35% of them expected it to provide reliable news. Also, only 12% were satisfied that media outlets included the expression of multiple positions, ideas and opinions (Barr al Aman, 2020).

These results, which seem shocking to some, are

> not much different from what was presented by the "Sigma Conseil" Foundation in relation to the rate of Tunisians' confidence in institutions and structures, in the latest opinion poll issued in April 2020, where the media ranked 12th, and it was preceded by the army, security forces and even Imams and religious scholars. (Al-Youssefi, 2020)

In this context, perhaps the biggest gain achieved by the media sector in Tunisia is the Joint Framework Agreement signed on Wednesday 9 January 2019. It is the first of its kind in the history of the press sector, and it serves as an example of how media policy can be formulated through partnership between various concerned parties such as professional unions, government, media institutions and independent amendment structures, especially taking into consideration the material and professional conditions of journalists. The resulting setting of a minimum wage in the range of 1,400 raw dinars, and the acceptance that the journalism sector can benefit from grants and privileges that supplement the basic wage, is very important.

This guarantees the dignity of the journalist and enables him/her or her to work in a more comfortable and independent manner, minimizing the capacity of the now obvious financial or political inducements to pressurize those with poor living conditions. The agreement also stipulates, among other important issues, that at least 50% of jobs in journalism allocated to candidates with a university degree in the fields of journalism, news and/or communication sciences, and that the signatory parties make a commitment not to contract out work that can be carried out by the journalists of their own institution.

The transparency of the financing of media institutions is one of the most important issues that must be dealt with seriously and with great efficiency.

Various manifestations of corrupt funding have penetrated the various media outlets. 'Indeed, doubts abound that some journalistic institutions are primarily based on suspicious money, serving factional or sectoral agendas and interests, or as a doorway for money laundering. Only five audio-visual institutions have published their financial budgets, as stipulated in chapter 30 of the book of conditions drafted for the purpose by the watchdog 'HAICA' (Al-Haddad, 2019). Noticing this, the Tunisian legislator made sure that journalists, media professionals and owners of media institutions are among the categories of organizations covered by the National Authority for Combating Corruption and Bribery, who must declare their income sources and interests.

The issue of funding transparency goes beyond fears of suspicious financing and the penetration of interest lobbies of the media sector, to the actual structure of media institutions themselves. Instead of obtaining funding from sound sources such as advertising, sales or legally permitted activities, dependence upon suspicious, emergency and shifting sources of finance, as well as financial and administrative corrupt practices, deprive institutions of professional stability.

The absence of an established professional economic culture is a prominent phenomenon in the Tunisian media, not only in the private sector, but also in the state-funded public media institutions themselves. These institutions have been experiencing financial and administrative management problems that have made them live in a state of financial deficit and indebtedness, while the media in the private sector infiltrated by interest lobbies and various centres of influence. In the context of organizing the profession, many professional bodies call for the need to approve the drafts into the Journalists Union, to block the way to the intruders who have distorted the sector, and to regulate the profession, in a similar way to how other professional sectors such as lawyers, doctors, engineers and pharmacists have been regulated. These structures that grant the professional status to those working in the sectors they represent remain the main reference for any accountability, or withdrawal of capacity in the event of violations or deviations. However, it seems that any depriving the press sector of a professional union has been mainly according to the desires of the political authority, and the various centres of influence, power and control, and so the financial, economic, political and ideological directions have continued to dominate various media.

Therefore, self-regulation of the media sector is one of the urgent priorities for organizing the sector in the written, electronic and audio-visual fields, because this amendment can provide possibilities for accountability, correction and refining the media performance from all negative aspects. It is also important to expedite the re-focusing of the High Authority for Audio-Visual Communication to be in accordance with its role as stipulated in the constitution. 'The current body that was established by virtue of Decree No. 116 of 2011 is temporary and has lost the ability to have useful influence. It no longer has a legal justification for existence as it lacks two vital elements: Integrity and independence', according to Al-Haddad (2019).

The regulation can be defined in its general outlines as 'an intervention aimed at correcting a system when necessary, in order to develop it and achieve its stability. As for the amendment in the field of audio-visual media, it is based on a basic principle, which is to guarantee freedom of expression and communi-cation through broadcasting media. Decree No. 116 of 2011 establishing the High Independent Authority for Audio Visual Communication (HAICA) affirms that this means that journalists' professional and ethical obligations should be respected to prevent the extreme and destructive use of this freedom. The same decree has also indicated the principles that define these obligations. It mentions in chapter 5 a basis for the exercise of rights and freedoms, which is: 'respect for international treaties and covenants related to human rights and public freedoms, that govern freedom of expression, equality and pluralism in the expression of ideas and opinions, that need to be objective and transparent'. The implementation of these principles should be governed by regulations related to respect for the rights and reputation of others, including, in particular respect for human dignity and private life, respect for freedom of belief, protection of children, and equality in this area.

HAICA is granted supervisory and reporting powers according to Article 15 of Decree No. 116 of 2011. The commission seeks to regulate and amend audio-visual communication in accordance with the principles of 'supporting democracy, human rights and the rule of law'. It supports and protects freedom of expression on the national, public, private and association audio-visual communication sector. Additionally, it supports the rights of the public to information and knowledge, by ensuring pluralism and diversity in programmes related to public affairs. The aim is to establish a pluralistic, and balanced audio-visual media scene that consecrates the values of freedom and justice and rejects discrimination on the basis of origin, gender or religion; ensures accurate and balanced media programming, and encourages high-quality educational programming. HAICA encourages the distribution of audio-visual communication services to cover the widest possible geographical area locally, regionally, nationally and internationally. It help the development of programming and broadcasting that expresses the national cultures. It promotes the employment of modern technologies, to enhance the financial and competitive capabilities of audio-visual communication facilities in Tunisia.

Despite all these powers granted to the High Independent Authority of Audio-visual Communication (HAICA), the criteria adopted by the authority, to filter programmes and advertising material, in order to stop them broadcasting, or to prevent members of political parties from owning audio-visual media has not been effective, and any attempt to regulate or to comment on these seems to have fallen upon deaf ears when it comes to many owners of radio or TV channels. For example the owner of Nessma TV, Nabil Karoui, who is the head of the Heart of Tunisia political party, and founder of the Zaitouna channel, Osama Bin Salem, who is a leader in the Renaissance movement. These are still today broadcasting outside the law that is supposed to regulate the audio-visual sector in Tunisia.

As for the regulation of the press sector, a Press Council was created in Tunisia on 16 September 2020 after a delay of nine years and as 'a culmination of cooperation efforts between various civil society organisations' (Miladi, 2021b: 275). According to the draft Basic Law, The Press Council monitors adherence to the ethics of journalistic practice, directs media institutions and journalists towards quality journalism and protects their independence, as well as expressing opinion on draft laws and regulations related to media.

With the existence of professional bodies and unions specialized in dealing with journalists' concerns and legal compliance of the media, the Council undertook two basic tasks, namely addressing citizens' complaints related to press production and establishing ethical charters for the media, thus improving the quality of journalism and meeting the needs of the public. The Press Council works through a set of mechanisms. The most important of which is to accompany and support the media in carrying out actions that adhere to professional and ethical principles. Also, it works to assist the media in developing a sense of honour and to make moral charters with the public so that the public is no longer a passive recipient and has a voice in defining programmes, especially with regard to the contents of public media.

The council functions like a 'court of honour' based on a professional code of ethics prepared for this purpose, like other monitoring organizations. The concept of self-regulation in democratic societies, for which freedom of expression and the right of the public to access information are fundamental pillars, is often based on accountability in relation to the media. What is meant by this term is the ability to demand an interpretation of media performance, that is, to assume responsibility, and then to demonstrate the ability to assume duties towards society and individuals. The self-amendment sought through this approach is the one that the actors in the media field decide freely and voluntarily, that is, they lay down for themselves a set of rules of conduct in the form of an ethical charter and regulations such as the Press Council, to work to ensure respect for ethics. Such voluntary structures aim to limit state interference, so that the media, accompanied by journalists working in them, assume their social responsibilities related to the rights and freedom of the press. 'Thus, the self-regulation mechanism represents a means of reducing the serious professional errors, deviations and slippages that may result from a combination of factors' (Al-Youssefi, 2019).

International Declaration of Ethics for Journalists stipulates that

> Whoever professes journalism professionally is required, within the framework of the honour of the profession and within the general context of national law in his/ her country, to recognize the competence of the self-regulating bodies of the profession of journalism, which are open to public complaints and protected from any form of interference, whether by governments or any other party. (IFJ, 2019)

Moreover, the Press Council has a further function, which is to enable citizens to submit their complaints without resorting to the judicial process, which is usually long and costly. It also works to settle disputes between the complainant and the media outlet or journalist that is the subject of the complaint. From this standpoint, this stage represents a mediation stage, and when this stage of initial mediation fails, a complaint is directed to the Ethics Committee.

In this context, Najat Zemmouri, a member of the governing body of the Tunisian League for Human Rights, considered that the establishment of the Press Council in Tunisia represents an important step towards building a mechanism for self-amendment and reforming the media system, and that this institution will not replace the judiciary, but rather it will oblige media professionals to respect the basic principles of respecting professional ethics through effective and pedagogical decisions (Al-Arab, 2020).

While the former head of the Journalists Syndicate, Naji Bghouri, affirms that

> the Press Council will work to monitor and follow up on journalistic practices and their conformity with professional standards and ethics in journalistic work, and to play the role of mediator between the media and the public, in addition to developing, informing and spreading the culture of quality journalism. (Al-Arab, 2020)

The Press Council also assumes the role of educating about the rights and duties of the media and the journalists working in it, as well as the definition of their freedoms and responsibilities. It can initiate a public dialogue about the media, journalism and democracy to secure citizens' rights regarding the media and educate them about these issues. The Press Council can also encourage the media and journalists to adopt best practices when tackling some of the challenging topics, such as suicide and terrorism, hate speech, individual freedoms, and more. The council is also qualified to 'address structural problems that affect the work of journalists, such as media ownership and sources of funding, lack of diversity, the impact of intense competition, the strategy of monopolizing information by a particular public authority, and other problems' (Al-Youssefi, 2019). Finally, this body assists media institutions to establish the right mechanisms to ensure respect for the ethics of the profession and to play the role of mediator between the profession and the public.

In addition to the above significant roles assigned the Press Council, it is worthwhile pointing out the need to develop educational curricula at graduate and post-graduate level. One key institution for instance that have a leading role is the Institute of Journalism and Information Sciences of the University of Manouba.

Conclusion

In sum, after more than ten years since the 14 January 14 2011 revolution, and the country's long march of democratic transition, the Tunisian media have not been freed from the dominance of the previously ruling political powers and ideological influences. The political class, the social and professional parties, and the various components of civil society have been so far unable to formulate strategic visions and plans to protect the country from its crises. There is no doubt that this is mainly due to political instability, and external interference.

The Tunisian media scene, which was supposed to be free and impartial now after the gains of the revolution of 14 January 2011, continue today to work with journalists without adequate resources and training, and in an environment with controversial professional standards, and a lack of ethics governing media work. On the pages of many printed and electronic newspapers, and on the pages of social media, exciting and sensational editorial guidelines properly outlines. However, journalism practice on the ground testify to a different facet characterizes sometimes by fabrication, plagiarism and defamation.

The current stage of democratic transition has at least proved that most Tunisian media institutions are not based on a clear funding model and a declared liberalizing policy. Some media outlets move from one source of funding to another, in a way that lacks the simplest rules of transparency. Perhaps, what complicates the situation argues Al-Haddad (2019) is the conflicting agendas of the various forces and centres of influence and the instability of the political situation, which distract every will to build a media policy that takes the media out of its crises and problems, and from destructive infringements of ethics.

Factors that seem to have contributed to the fall of some of the Tunisian media into the political alignment, ideological polarization and ethical problems include:

- The absence of professionalism in dealing with the various events that Tunisia has lived through, the most important of which are the recent municipal, legislative and presidential elections.
- The retreat of the Tunisian media from carrying out its watchdog role.
- Financial inducements affecting the media agenda.

Few television programmes on Tunisian television that claim to be of investigative nature instead have limited their efforts to just reporting events, or to conveying news or information as it comes to them. This has helped to transform some media outlets into tools of reflection for some controversial political and partisan faces and figures, as part of the search for 'buzz' (sensation) to catch viewers from other channels and quickly increase viewership. The criteria for objectivity, credibility and impartiality required by media work, must not only be based just on transmission of news or information, but should also involve interpretation, extrapolation and constructive criticism. Instead of this professional and ethically constrained discussion, the traditional public audience has become a content maker through the citizenship press and the blogging movement and has participated in the circulation of a lot of content by interacting with it, commenting on it and sharing it, often without much discernment or ethical control.

References

Al-Arab (2020), 'A Tunisian press council to establish an ethics in reconciling the public with the media' (in Arabic). Retrieved from: https://cutt.ly/yc9fSUR. Accessed: 3 January 2021.

Al-Haddad, K. (2019), 'Post-revolution Tunisian media: From the hegemony of the authority to the hegemony of ideology and the lobbies of interests' (in Arabic), Center for Strategic and Diplomatic Studies. Retrieved from: https://cutt.ly/Mc9iotS/. Accessed: 10 December 2020.

Al-Issawi, F. (2012), 'Tunisian media is in a transitional stage' (in Arabic), Retrieved from: https: //carnegie-,mec.org/2012/07/10/ar-pub-48923 Accessed: 10 October 2020.

Al Jazeera Center for Studies (2012), 'Tunisia, a political battle with media tools' (in Arabic). Retrieved from: http://studies.aljazeera.net/ar/positionestimate/2012/05/201256144046792645.html. Accessed: 12 April 2021.

Al-Youssefi, M. (2019), 'Why do Tunisian journalists need a "court of honor"?' (In Arabic). Retrieved from: https://institute.aljazeera.net/ar/ajr/article/1255. Accessed: 23 November 2020.

Barr al Aman (2020), 'Study about Media in Tunisia'. Bar al Aman, CFI and Media Scan in September 2018. Retrieved from: https://www.facebook.com/barralaman/ Accessed: 23 September 2020.

Ben Messaoud, M. (2019), 'Media, Communication, and Democratic Transition in Tunisia: The Stakes of Transitioning to Governmental Communication in the Service of the Citizen and a Public Sphere Practicing Political Action', in J. Zran and N. Miladi (eds), *Media and the Democratic Transition in the Arab World* (in Arabic). Tunis: Arab Media & Communication Network (AMCN) and Sotumedia Publication, pp. 283–316.

Bourguiba, H. (1982), *Sermons (1979, 1981 and 1982)*, (in Arabic). Publications of the Ministry of Information, Official Press. Tunisia: Ministry of Information.

Bredoux, L, and Magnaudeix, M. (2012), *Tunis Connections, Survey of Franco-Tunisian Networks under Ben Ali* (in French). Paris: Editions du Seuil.

Circular of the First Ministry No. 23 of 1 June 2005.

Facebook Tunisia (2020), 'International report: The speech of violence and hatred is the stubbornness of the Tunisian media'. Retrieved from: https://www.facebook.com/340080496007507/posts/2821120041236861/. Accessed: 13 November 2020.

IFJ (2019), 'International declaration of ethics for journalists'. Retrieved from: https://www.ifj- arabic.org/fileadmin/user_upload/IFJ_Declaration_of_Principles_on_the_Conduct_of_Journalists.pdf. Accessed: 13 August 2020.

Independent High Authority for Audiovisual Communication 2013–2014 (in Arabic). Retrieved from: https://cutt.ly/oc9d2Gw. Accessed: 8 September 2020.

Independent High Authority of Audiovisual Communication regarding the 2019 elections. Retrieved from: https://cutt.ly/Lc9UfN7. Accessed: 15 September 2020.

Miladi, N. (2021a), 'Broadcasting in Tunisia from Independence to post 2011 Revolution Era', in N. Miladi and N. Mellor (eds), *Routledge Handbook on Arab Media*. London: Routledge (pp. 450–460).

Miladi, N. (2021b), 'Tunisia: The transformative Media Landscape after the Revolution in Arab Media Systems', in Carola Richter and Claudia Kozman (eds), *Arab Media Systems*, pp. 267–284. Retrieved from: https://www.openbookpublishers.com/product/1281. Accessed: 21 April 2021.

National Authority for Media and Communication Reform (2012), 'General report'. Retrieved from: https://cutt.ly/Qc9j0jw. Accessed: January 2020.

National Fact-Finding Commission on Corruption and Bribery (2011), First Ministry, Republic of Tunisia.

11 Journalism ethics and conflict-sensitive reporting

The case of Al Jazeera network

Hala A. Guta

Introduction

Although conflict and wars are ancient as human history, the coverage of conflicts and violence has always been a contentious area in journalism and media studies. More specifically the literature presents different arguments in relevance to the ethical principles of media coverage of conflict and violence. On the one hand, objectivity, and detached journalism, within which journalists are perceived neutral fact reporters and conveyers of information, has been a long-held tenet of ethical journalism. As such opponents of peace journalism consider the notion 'at best meaningless, and at worst a uniquely unhelpful and misleading prescription for journalism' (Lyon, 2007: 2). On the other hand, proponents of peace journalism have continuously challenged the view of detached journalism and called for a more active role to be played by media professionals when covering violent conflicts. This latter view conceptualizes news as a process of knowledge production in contrast with news as merely a source of information (Christians, 2019). Moreover, advocates of peace journalism argue that the concept is not about ignoring the facts on the ground and engage in peace propaganda but rather a call for increased sensitivity in reporting conflicts. Hence, peace journalism is also referred to as conflict-sensitive reporting (Lukacovic, 2016).

One of the earliest scholarly contributions that laid the foundation for peace journalism was Galtung and Ruge's (1965) seminal work, *The Structure of Foreign News*. Their widely cited paper on news values presented 12 factors that determine newsworthiness or the factors that transforms events into news. Subsequently, Galtung (2014) updated the concept of news values to focus upon four factors. He stated that traditional media tends to focus upon elite nations, elite people, actors (in contrast with processes or structure) and negative events. Galtung (2014) argued that for events concerning ordinary people to be selected as news, they must satisfy the negativity and magnitude factors. In other words, the higher the number of the victims and the degree of negativity, the more likely the event will be newsworthy when it comes to ordinary people. The result of this standpoint, argued Galtung, is news that is elite-focused, violence-oriented and dominated by a polarizing win/lose mindset. Galtung problematized conventional violence-focused

DOI: 10.4324/9781003203551-14

reporting as 'war journalism' and proposed an alternative model. Galtung further developed the insights from the Galtung and Ruge (1965) news values into the theoretical framework of peace journalism.

Born in conflict-ridden region, throughout its history, conflict coverage was an integral part of Al Jazeera's coverage. The network has branded itself as a counterhegemonic source of news in a world dominated by Western media; a claim that is reflected in its motto, which positions it as 'the voice for the voiceless'. Al Jazeera's role as an important and alternative voice in the global media landscape has been highlighted on various occasions, including the 11 September 2001 attacks and the subsequent US invasion of Afghanistan, the 2003 invasion of Iraq, and the ongoing Palestinian–Israeli conflict. More recently, through the network's continuous coverage of the 2011 Arab Spring, Al Jazeera has become 'an integral part of the political fabric of the region, with a potential influence on public policy and public opinion in the Arab world' (Rinnawi, 2012: 119). Al Jazeera's 'daring news values' (Miladi, 2016: 71) and 'crude way of doing journalism' (Zayani, 2016: 92) is undoubtedly challenged Western mainstream norms.

Considering its importance as a global media player, and its claims of providing an alternative model of journalism, the question arises whether Aljazeera's claim to be the voice of the voiceless and the network that challenged established narratives is extended to providing an alternative model for conflict-sensitive reporting? Does Al Jazeera measure up to claim of providing alternative perspective, or does it follow the established mainstream Western media coverage of international news, just with a global South flavour? If Al Jazeera is offering a different perspective, what lessons can we learn that can contribute to peace journalism and global media ethics?

To answer these questions, this chapter is set to examine Al Jazeera coverage of the events in Syria as a case study. Examining the battle of Raqqa in 2017 as a case study, the chapter builds upon the seminal work of Galtung and Ruge (1965) concerning news values and the subsequent theoretical framework of peace journalism as its point of departure. Adopting a comparative approach to assess the similarities and differences between AJA and AJE's coverage of conflicts, this chapter attempt to investigate Al Jazeera's claim to being the voice of the voiceless and take a closer look into Al Jazeera's coverage of conflict. The goal of this chapter is investigating whether the network truly provides an alternative point of view when it comes to conflict-sensitive reporting; to establish the ethical standards that guide Al Jazeera in terms of its coverage and the lessons that can be learnt from Al Jazeera journalism ethics in contribution to global media ethics.

Peace journalism and journalism ethics

Peace journalism is a style of journalism that applies tools and insights of conflict transformation when reporting about violent conflicts. Galtung introduced the concept of peace journalism building on the arguments presented in Galtung and Ruge (1965). According to Galtung when mainstream media reports focus upon direct violence, they 'also serve to naturalize and legitimize various forms of social violence' (Lynch, 2013: 36). Any overview of peace journalism as introduced by Galtung must begin with an explanation his earlier work on positive peace and the violence triangle.

During the early period of peace and conflict studies, the dominant paradigm was that absence of war implies. Galtung referred to the state of absence of war as negative peace and introduced the concept of positive peace, in contrast (Galtung, 1964). Negative peace is only concerned with the manifestations of conflict and, thus, peace researchers who view peace as absence of war are involved in finding ways to control physical manifestations of violence (Beer, 2001). Positive peace, on the other hand, seeks to transcend dealing with the manifestations of violence by addressing the causes of violence (Galtung, 1964, 1990, 1996). To this end, Galtung sought to expand the focus of peace and conflict research with the aim of achieving harmony and integration rather than simply preventing violence.

In addition to the concept of positive peace, Johan Galtung also introduced the notion of the violence triangle. In this regard, Galtung (1990, 1996) distinguished between three levels of violence: direct violence, structural violence and cultural violence. Direct violence refers to physical acts of violence, while structural violence is the type of violence that is embedded in the social structure and generally results from social injustices. Cultural violence can be attributed to the 'aspects of culture, the symbolic sphere of our existence – exemplified by religion and ideology, language and art, empirical science and formal science (logic, mathematics) – that can be used to justify or legitimize direct or structural violence' (Galtung, 1990:1). Typically, the three levels of violence are interconnected and violence can begin in any corner of the triangle, but 'the underlying assumption is simple "violence breeds violence"' (Galtung, 1990: 295).

According to Galtung, changing this vicious triangle of violence can only be achieved by working with a virtuous triangle of peace (Galtung, 1990). While political arbitration and agreements deal with direct violence and policies deal with structural injustices, addressing cultural violence requires questioning the cultural positions implicated in dehumanizing the other. Addressing cultural violence calls for challenging cultural norms. Consequently, the concepts of positive peace and the violence triangle make discussing issues of social justice, social institutions and cultural norms equally important to political negotiations. In this regard, the role of social institutions, such as the media, and the ability they must perpetuate or mitigate violence has gained more importance in the field of peace and conflict research. Conflicts, especially those along ethnic and religious lines, can divide societies and be deeply embedded in the cultural norms creating vicious cycles of culturally directed violence. In conflict situations, media institutions can be manipulated to perpetuate this cultural violence; conversely, they can also be used to promote cultural peace. In this area, the role of peace journalism emerges.

If we return to *The Structure of Foreign News*, we can argue that the mainstream media focusing upon elites (nations and people), reporting more negative events and valuing actors over process have led to the prominence of news that is violence-oriented and which utilizes elites as its main sources. This reporting is episodic with insufficient exploration of a conflict's causes and consequences. This model is what Galtung calls war journalism. War journalism focuses on episodes of conflict and uses polarized frames of reference in which there are always two parties: 'their' point of view versus 'our' point of view. Once the mass media focuses on direct violence, issues of structural and cultural violence are often ignored. When a ceasefire or peace agreement is signed and a state of negative peace is achieved, the focus of the mainstream mass media shifts to another hot spot experiencing direct violence. The result is not only the masking of issues of structural and cultural violence but the way in which those issues are ignored serves to legitimize them (Lynch and McGoldrick, 2005).

Trying to find an answer to the pressing question of how the media can contribute positively to cultural peace, Galtung proposed peace journalism as an alternative model to the status quo of war journalism. Hence cultural violence often legitimizes or conceals direct and structural violence, the mass media can play an influential role in promoting cultural peace by addressing those cultural aspects that legitimize violence. Mass media can also shed light on issues of direct and structural violence that are normally buried beneath the surface because of the prejudices of the dominant group or the marginalization of the dominated group. Galtung called upon journalists to explore conflict formation and provide a thematic overview of the conflict's causes with all the parties involved rather than simply focusing upon episodic reporting. Accordingly, peace journalism gives a voice to all parties but mostly focuses upon parties that have often been ignored by the mainstream media. Unlike war journalism, which focuses on the direct and visible manifestations of a conflict, peace journalism focuses upon the invisible consequences of the conflict. These are the structural and cultural aspects of the struggle (Galtung, 1996).

Considering the intricate nature of violent conflict situations, adopting peace journalism can be complicated. However, Lynch and McGoldrick (2005) argue that peace journalism can be achieved 'when editors and reporters make choices – of what to report, and how to report it – that create opportunities for society at large to consider and value non-violent responses to conflict' (p. 5). Therefore, peace journalism is about making conscious choices by editors and journalists. Making choices inherently involves moral reasoning. The concept of peace journalism is rooted on the premise that reporting news is not a neutral endeavour and journalists are not objective and detached witness of reality as conventional journalism assumes. Indeed, as noted by Hanitzsch (2007) 'news is not a "mirror" of reality … and any serious inquiry into conflict coverage must acknowledge that news accounts are inevitably based on cognition and contingent (re)construction of reality' (p. 5). Acknowledging the fact that editors make choices everyday about what to report, whom to quote, which photos to use, one can argue that journalists and editors are inevitably intervening in promoting certain narrative and specific frames. If this is the case, McGoldrick and Lynch (2000) argue that journalist face an ethical choice, a choice 'about the ethics of that intervention—therefore the question becomes 'what can I do with my intervention to enhance the prospects for peace'?' (p. 22).

Peace journalism proposes that journalists consider peace as an ethical imperative that 'is not reduced to the politics of war, but, along with human dignity and truth, is a fundamental way to understand the sacredness of life intrinsic to our humanness' (Christians, 2007: 6). Hence engaging in conflict-sensitive reporting, promoting peace, or taking the 'high road', becomes an ethical and moral choice for journalists (Galtung, 1998). By highlighting peace initiatives, toning down ethnic and religious divisions and focusing upon people's suffering, the peace journalist works towards deescalating current conflicts and preventing further conflicts. The goal of peace journalism is to bring about peace and avoid recurrence of conflict. By doing so, peace journalism advocates are committed to universal ethical principles such as the sacredness of life as the one principle that transcends cultures, religions, and ethnicities (Christians, 2007). As such peace journalism is compatible with the calls for more inclusive and universal global communication 'ethical principles as human dignity, truth, and nonviolence' (Christians and Nordenstreng, 2004: 21).

However, the peace journalism model proposed by Galtung has faced criticism regarding its application even among the proponents of conflict-sensitive reporting. Galtung's peace journalism model has been criticized for placing considerable emphasis on the individual journalist's choices and paying less attention to the organizational and institutional culture and values under which most journalists operate. News production is often subject to organizational rules that journalists cannot simply ignore in favour of their own beliefs (Hanitzsch, 2007). This is, indeed, a legitimate concern as newsroom production practices often dictate the final version of a news story regardless of the individual journalist's ideals.

Tenenboim-Weinblatt, Hanitzsch and Nagar (2016) have argued that the Galtung's peace journalism model is characterized by a normative dualistic approach that pays insufficient attention to the nuances of news' narratives and frames. Tenenboim-Weinblatt et al. (2016) have appealed for a more contextual approach that considers different factors when analysing news narratives, such as the actors involved and the events and the context in which they are represented. In keeping with that claim, this chapter argues that a framing analysis is the most suitable approach to evaluating media reports.

Framing analysis is employed to gain a better understanding of the nuances and narratives employed in the stories and framing methodology is often used in empirical studies that investigation conflict coverage (Lukacovic, 2016). Framing researchers have argued that media discourse is presented as a 'set of interpretive packages' or frames that serve as the central organizing idea of any news story (D'Angelo, 2002; Gamson and Modigliani, 1989). In terms of media frames, these organizing ideas or frames can be thought of as themes that '[connect] different semantic elements of a story (e.g. descriptions of an action or an actor, quotes of sources and background information) into a coherent whole' (Pan and Kosicki, 1993: 59).

To investigate the framing processes utilized by AJA and AJE in covering the battle of Raqqa, this paper employed a multidimensional approach to the framing analysis. In this approach, various elements or dimensions of the story are recognized and included in the framing analysis. The multidimensional package included the following elements: The master frame or narrative, the frame sponsorship or selection of sources quoted within the story, the nature of the coverage (thematic or episodic), and the conflict effects (visible or invisible) (Guta, 2019). I recognized three criteria that frames should meet to be regarded as frames: (a) they possess identifiable conceptual and linguistic characteristics, (b) they are commonly observed and (c) they are reliably distinguishable from other frames (Capella and Jamieson, 1997: 47).

The 2017 battle of Raqqa

Raqqa was the first city to fall to Syrian opposition armed groups in 2013. However, its importance was highlighted when the Islamic States in Iraq and Sham (ISIS, also known as IS and ISIL) seized control of the city in January 2014, declaring it the Caliphate capital. Thenceforth, Raqqa became home to many foreign ISIS fighters, and the city 'played a central role in the IS narrative of reconstituting an Islamic state (*dawla Islamiyya*) across large swaths of Iraq and Syria' (Yacoubian, 2017).

The June 2017 battle of Raqqa was the fifth and final phase of a military operation, Operation Euphrates Wrath, that began in November 2016. The campaign to liberate Raqqa from ISIS's grip was launched by the Syrian Democratic Forces (SDF), a US-backed coalition of Kurdish and Arab fighters, who were supported by airstrikes from the US Air force (Hassan 2017). The battle of Raqqa began at dawn on 6 June 2017, when the SDF launched its offensive and ended on 20 October 2017, when the SDF and the coalition declared victory and the collapse of Raqqa as the ISIS de facto capital.

Al Jazeera's news values

This chapter employs a quantitative content analysis method to consider Al Jazeera's news values, and qualitative framing analysis to uncover indicators of peace and war journalism. Data were collected from Al Jazeera Arabic (AJA) and Al Jazeera English (AJE) websites for the first four weeks of the battle (6 June to 6 July 2017). Only stories reported by Al Jazeera were considered; no stories from other news sources were included even if they appeared on the Al Jazeera websites.

For AJE, the search yielded 25 stories. All the stories were relevant to the battle, reported by the channel and were not duplicated. For AJA, the search yielded 94 stories. After removing the duplicate or irrelevant stories and the stories by other media outlets, the total number of stories was reduced to 62.

Systematic sampling was employed by selecting every other story. Accordingly, the total number of stories analysed from AJA was 31. The total number of stories analysed from the two channels was 56 ($N = 56$).

All the stories were manually coded and analysed using the modified Galtung (2014) news values. Stories were coded to determine their focus (elite nations and people), whether the stories referenced actors (persons) or processes and whether the stories reported upon negative events. For the sake of the analysis, the notion of elite nations was modified from the original categorization by Galtung and Ruge (1965) to include nations relevant to the Middle East and countries of geopolitical relevance to the conflict under study such as Turkey. Table 11.1 summarizes the findings of the content analysis.

Table 11.1 News values in AJA and AJE coverage of Raqqa

	AJE	AJA
Elite nations	25 (100%)	31 (100%)
Elite people	23 (92%)	30 (98%)
Actors (not process)	23 (92%)	30 (98%)
Negative	24 (96%)	31 (100%)

Al Jazeera's Arabic frames

Analysis of AJA's coverage revealed three major frames: A humanitarian frame, a military frame and a geopolitical conflict frame. Here it is important to differentiate between the military and geopolitical conflict frames: The military frame refers to narratives of direct violence and often includes details of battles, military operations and troop movements and strategies. Geopolitical conflict refers to wider conflicts between international actors and includes the actors' competing geopolitical strategic interests. It is worth noting that the military conflict and geopolitical conflicts were often linked.

The humanitarian frame was the most prevalent standalone frame in the AJA coverage of the fight against ISIS. The humanitarian frame was identified in 12 of the 31 stories analysed (39%). As the battle of Raqqa unfolded, AJA made it clear that this battle would result in high humanitarian costs. On 7 June 2016, as the SDF began advancing towards Raqqa, AJA reported on the details of the advance but concluded its analysis with a description of what these operations would mean for the civilians in the city. When the international coalition was accused of using weaponry loaded with white phosphorus in Raqqa, the AJA reports discussed these events with a clear focus upon the consequences they would have upon the human lives inside the besieged towns. AJA also covered the reactions and effects on civilians when, on 9 June 2017, concerns were raised by the international community that white phosphorus had been used by the SDF and international coalition in populated areas of Raqqa.

Although peace journalism scholars advocate giving ordinary people a voice by focusing upon such people in the reporting of conflicts, AJA relied mostly upon official sources. However, AJA did demonstrate a focus upon the issues of ordinary people in its coverage on different occasions. For example, AJA's coverage of the online campaign #Save_People_In_Raqqa quoted activists instead official sources. Another example is 1 July 2016 story on the Syrian Network for Human Rights concerning the number of civilian casualties in the first half of 2016, which amounted to 5,300 victims. The report provided details of the casualties attributed to each party, including the Syrian government and army, the US-led coalition, Russia, the Kurdish self-rule administration and other armed Syrian opposition groups. Reports of the civilians suffering inside Raqqa were imbedded in most stories as a reminder of the high human cost of conflict. Occasionally, AJA also used the testimony of eyewitnesses and activists to illustrate the humanitarian frame.

Considering that the data were collected at the beginning of the battle for Raqqa, it is not surprising that reports detailing military operations, troop movements and captured war sites were ubiquitous. However, it is also worth noting that AJE did not highlight the details of the military operation to the same extent that AJA did. The military frame was present in 14 stories (43.75%) in the battle for Raqqa. The military conflict frame was often intertwined with a geopolitical conflict frame. This was predictable considering the complexity of the fight against ISIS and the diverse range of actors involved, along with their conflicting interests. Because the military conflict frame was linked to geopolitical conflict, I will also discuss this frame in the context of the geopolitical conflict frames in the following section.

The geopolitical conflict frame was the third frame identified in the AJA coverage (11 stories). The battle of Raqqa was led by a coalition of the SDF, of which the Kurdish militia's People's Protection Units (YPG) comprised the major part. However, the involvement of the YPG triggered a conflict with Turkey. Turkey considered the arming of the SDF, and the YPG in particular, a threat to its national security given the relationship between the YPG and the Kurdistan Workers' Party (PKK), an armed Turkish opposition group. AJA reports often alluded to the competing geopolitical interests within different military operations. For instance, a story entitled 'SDF advances to a strategic location in Raqqa' stated, 'it is worth mentioning that the SDF is trying to prevent the Syrian regime forces from cutting through the southern side of Raqqa' (AJA 21 June 2017). The story went on to report accusations by the SDF that the Syrian army had shelled its base southwest of Raqqa The YPG-Turkish conflict was also present. Turkey made several statements that were reported as, 'Turkey will take action against anyone who threatens its national security' (AJA, 25 June 2017). On 15 June 2017, the coalition forces downed a Syrian military jet. This led to tensions and an exchange of accusations between Russia and the United States. In this regard, the geopolitical conflict frame can be summarized as consisting of a series of conflicts between Russia and the United States, between the SDF and the Syrian regime, between the SDF and

Turkey, and, finally, between ISIS and all the warring parties. However, considering the battle of Raqqa to be, in the first place, a battle against ISIS, the AJA reports focused more upon the other competing parties. These parties included the United States and its international allies on one side, and Russia, Iran and Assad's regime on the other. Another prevalent feature in the AJA coverage that highlighted the geopolitical conflict frame was the use of ethnic labels. A qualifying statement that these were the forces 'of which the Kurdish People's Protection Units constitute the majority' followed most mentions of the SDF.

Al Jazeera's English frames

While AJA adopted three frames in its Raqqa coverage, the humanitarian frame was the most prevalent in AJE's reporting of Raqqa. There was an undeniable focus on human suffering from all sides of the conflict and the high human cost of the war. Almost every story included information and narratives concerning the cost to the town's civilians and fighters, with 12 stories (48%) showing the identifiable linguistic and conceptual salience of the frame.

Like AJA, when reporting on the advances made by the SDF and the coalitions, AJE did not ignore the human cost of liberating Raqqa from ISIS. While other media outlets celebrated the SDF and the coalition forces advances, AJE constantly reminded its audience that the battle for Raqqa 'has been marked by fears for the thousands of civilians [who are] still trapped in the city, particularly as the SDF begins what is expected to be an all-out battle for control of dense urban space'. The report went on to raise concerns about the 'estimated 40,000 children [who] were trapped inside the city and enduring extremely dangerous conditions' and cited UNICEF reports in this regard (Al Jazeera, 10 June 2017). As the battle intensified, AJE aired a story on the advances made by the SDF fighters and the allied coalition on 17 June 2017. Although the story had a central narrative of military operations against ISIS, the human suffering was not absent from the narrative. Footage of the elderly, women and children was presented amidst footage of the battle in the 2.5-minute report. As the report described the challenges that awaited the residents as they began evacuating the town of Raqqa, it was clear that there was a conscious choice on the part of the channel to focus not only on the military side of the battle but also its humanitarian aspects.

Using eyewitnesses and giving people a voice was another noticeable feature in many of the AJE stories, especially in the video reports. In a report about the thousands of civilians trapped inside Raqqa that aired on 1 July 2017, residents of Raqqa recounted the horrific experiences they were witnessing, the shelling, the food shortages and running for dear life. Footage of mothers and their children was a vivid reminder to the viewers of the human cost of this war (AJE 1 July 2017). AJE's reports on Raqqa were also characterized by reporting the human suffering on all sides and exposing transgressions from all sides. An illustrative example is a story that ran on 6 July 2017. While the headline of the story reads 'US-led airstrikes "killed 224" civilians in Raqqa', the body of the story reports upon the actions of ISIS fighters who had used civilians as human shields. Nevertheless, the death toll of both the SDF and ISIS fighters was also reported.

Although military operations and geopolitical conflict were present in the AJE news reports, they did not qualify as identifiable frames because they were often under-reported or minimized. AJE remarkably focused upon the humanitarian frame than military operations or competing geopolitical interests.

Both AJA and AJE employed a range of communicative techniques to reinforce the humanitarian frame. These included the use of metaphorical language such as 'bloodbath' (AJA 21 June 2017) and the statement that Raqqa had been 'silently slaughtered' (AJE 6 June 2017). Other communicative devices included visual representations consisting of either still photographs or film footage of civilians in dire situations (AJA 6 June 2017), vulnerable groups, such as mothers with children and the elderly, and the dead bodies of people in civilian attire.

Frame sponsorship

If we think of frames as a 'set of interpretive packages' that serve as the central organizing idea of any news story (D'Angelo, 2002), then the interpretation that is included becomes essential to identifying the frame sponsorship. In framing analysis, the sources used are important indicators of the frame sponsorship. In this case, the analysis revealed that both AJA and AJE used a diverse range of sources. As the conflict in Syria is complex and there are many actors involved, this diversity was also reflected in the sources. Despite the diversity, AJA relied mostly upon official sources for its information. These sources included military commanders, state authorities and international officials, among others. This reliance upon official sources, especially military commanders, may explain the prevalence of the military frame. While official sources represented the majority of the individuals quoted, AJA also used 'unidentified internal sources'. While AJA did not reveal the identities of those sources, the reports came from inside Raqqa, and these sources are more likely to have been eyewitnesses. Evidently, AJE interviewed a greater variety of civilian eyewitnesses than AJA. Other sources, such as the UN, Russia and Iran, were also quoted but with less prominence (see Table 11.2).

Table 11.2 Sources of Raqqa Coverage

Sources	AJE	AJA
Officials	19	32
Unidentified inside sources	-	13
Civilian eyewitness	6	-
Activists	2	7
NGOs	7	3
ISIS	0	2

Effects

By its nature of being a physical violent conflict, the battle of Raqqa was a direct violence event. Therefore, the visible effects and issues of direct violence were dominant. Although both Al Jazeera channels reported extensively upon humanitarian issues, issues of structural and cultural violence did not take centre stage. Out of the 61 news stories analysed, only one story focused upon peacebuilding and reconciliation efforts. However, it is worth noting that the sample analysed was reported during the peak of the fight to seize Raqqa from ISIS control, and it is not uncommon for journalists reporting from the battle-field to focus upon direct violence. The literature assessing reporting from war zones accentuates the tendency to emphasize the direct and visible manifesta-tions of conflict, a trend criticized by peace journalism advocates (Fahmy and Johnson, 2005).

Journalism ethics and Al Jazeera's conflict reporting

Although framing analysis of AJA and AJE coverage of Raqqa revealed clear differences in the way the two channels framed the conflict, both channels made human suffering their interpretive lenses of the conflict. AJE humanitarian frame was more prevalent and the channel focused more on the human cost of the conflict. Although human suffering and focus on people were present in AJA's reporting, there was an equal focus on military operations and geopoli-tical conflict. The focus on human suffering does not compromise journalism professional standards as all party were represented in the news reports aired by the two channels.

These findings demonstrate that Al Jazeera has introduced an alternative approach not only to conflict reporting but also to journalism ethics in relation to professional journalism and impartiality. AJE's focus on the humanitarian frame is consistent with peace journalism tenants and the recommendations of the Ethical Journalism Network. Ethical Journalism Network advocates that, when reporting conflicts, journalists should 'humanise the conflict process – putting names to faces; talking to the victims of war on all sides; allowing people to grieve and express their anger; focusing on the human tragedy that is being endured by all the communities involved' (White, 2016: 49). Previous studies confirm our findings, that Al Jazeera's focus on human suffering and its choice of airing footage of death and pain is a moral choice to authorize ordinary people voices and shed light on the ugly reality of war (Figenschou, 2011; Zayani, 2016).

Since its inception in 1996, Al Jazeera has branded itself as the network that provided a voice for the voiceless and offered alternative narratives to that of mainstream media. Al Jazeera's code of ethics stresses the adherence to jour-nalism professional code values such as truth, honesty and objectivity. The network code of ethics also emphasizes the importance of presenting the facts but also, 'giving full consideration to the feelings of victims of crime, war, persecution and disaster, their relatives and our viewers, and to individual privacies and public decorum' (Al Jazeera code of ethics 2020). Al Jazeera editorial standards advocate against presenting direct violence on the screen, 'unless they are important elements of a news story' (Editorial standards: 96). Despite the accusations of being sensationalist, over airing footage of war and violence, Al Jazeera's editorial standards advocate against using emotional appeals and instead focus 'on the mind of viewers not their hearts' (p. 39). However, the literature on Al Jazeera suggested that the network has chosen multiple times to air scenes of bloody conflicts. Waddah Khanfar (2005), the former Director General of Al Jazeera network, explained that broadcasting images of death and suffering is often a conscious moral choice, because if Al Jazeera 'cover these images, and use very remote and shy coverage ... [Al Jazeera is] also making it easy for the killer ... making it easy for the people who do the war, who run away without punishment'. Along the same lines Ahmed Al Sheikh, a senior manager in Al Jazeera explained that while Al Jazeera indeed adhere to professional journalism values and ethics such as truth-telling, impartiality and honesty, the network practices what he labelled as 'crude journalism'. A journalism version that makes a moral choice to show the ugly face of the war and human suffering,

> especially that this is an area filled with war, conflicts, and blood, therefore we can't use Picasso's brush every time to beautify it and war is ugly, we can't do like Picasso, we have to show things how they are, deliver them how they are; this is the difference [between Al Jazeera and mainstream western media]. (personal interview)

However, despite the focus on human suffering, elite sources dominated the voices represented in both channels. AJE reported ordinary people's voices slightly more than AJA. This has led to focus on direct violence while ignoring the invisible effects of this conflict. Moreover, little consideration was given to structural and cultural aspects of the conflict. This is particularly important in highlighting the power of frame sponsorship as those who have access to media are provided the opportunity to make their views legitimate and eventually decide on the master narrative of a given story. The reliance on official sources has clearly contributed to the dominance of military and geopolitics conflict frames in AJA coverage. In this case the concepts of 'frame sponsorship' and 'web of subsidies' become influential. Pan and Kosicki (2001) noted that resources available to journalists (including sources and access to information) greatly influence the framing process. The web of subsidies or the 'institutionally structured and strategically cultivated networks' represent a 'news net' for journalists from whom they can receive information, and in the process also influence frame building (Pan and Kosicki, 2001: 45). It is apparent that the difference in farming between AJA and AJE can be attributed to AJA's utilization of official sources which in turn made the geopolitical and military conflict frames more noticeable.

Analysis of Al Jazeera's coverage demonstrates the importance of news values that guide any media organization and the impact those values have on the way conflicts are covered. According to Galtung and Ruge (1965), mainstream media traditional values place more importance on negative events and elite people and nations. This has resulted in dominance of war oriented journalism where the focus is often on direct violence and elites as these news satisfies the conventional news values and more likely to find their way to the headlines. The call for peace journalism is a call to an alternative approach that does not only report on episodes of direct violence but rather explores the conflict formation and causes; include diverse voices, mostly exposes people sufferings, and focuses on the invisible consequences of the conflict (Galtung, 1998).

While Al Jazeera's focus on human suffering demonstrates ethical orientation that values the voice of ordinary people, the analysis of Al Jazeera's coverage of Syria reveals tendency towards reinforcing conventional journalism values. AJA and AJE coverage were characterized by focus on episodic reporting that centres direct violence with insufficient attention to the long-term structural and cultural violence.

However, it is important to note that peace journalism should be conceptualized as continuum rather than a descriptive normative set of checkboxes. Adopting a conflict-sensitive reporting is an ethical and moral orientation that is inclusive and approach conflict coverage with sensitivity that aims at exploring the conflict and ways of transforming it rather than oversimplifying it as two-party conflict. If we conceptualize peace journalism as an orientation rather than a set of rules, then we can argue that despite falling short in some areas, Al Jazeera's provides evidence that an alternative approach to conflict-sensitive reporting is indeed possible without falling into the tarp of sensationalism. The network's shortcoming discussed in this chapter could be attributed to two reasons: the genre of news analyzed in this case study and its focus on direct violence, and a more structural reason that is related to Al Jazeera's position in region plagued by many conflicts. Mohamed Krichen (2016), a senior anchor at AJA, pointed out in a personal interview that Al Jazeera's position had its influence on the way conflicts are covered, stating that 'We are part of the war machine in coverage ... maybe as reporters, as media, we are also victims of this situation because we have no other choice than covering the situation this way'.

Yet I argue that what Al Jazeera needs is an ethical point of departure at the individual and organizational level that challenges the traditional views of objectivity and detached journalism when it comes to conflict-sensitive reporting. The literature on Al Jazeera has ample examples to demonstrate how the network had adopted non-conventional journalistic style on many occasions. Peace journalism advocates argue that journalists and editors can make choices on the ways news is reported. Moreover, a focus on editorial policies that are more in line with Al Jazeera's mission as an alternative voice in the global media landscape, a voice that has an ethical responsibility towards more conflict-sensitive reporting, will indeed strengthen the network's contribution to conflict-sensitive reporting.

Conclusion

Mass media's role in inciting and escalating violence has been the subject of numerous studies in the field of mass communication (Allan and Seaton, 1999; Seib, 2005). It has been repeatedly argued in the literature that the mainstream media, through a focus upon direct violence and elite nations and people, undermines peacebuilding efforts and legitimizes structural and cultural violence. This chapter investigated AJA and AJE's coverage of conflict based on the 2017 battle for Raqqa as a case study. It aims to find out the extent to which Al Jazeera contributes to providing an alternative voice in peace journalism, conflict-sensitive reporting and a fresh perspective for a global media ethics practice.

The Syrian war has been one of the major conflicts in the Arab region during modern times. The conflict is complex and has involved multiple national and international players representing competing and conflicting interests. Covering such a conflict is undoubtedly challenging. Investigating Al Jazeera's coverage from the point of view of news values has revealed a focus on elites and negative events. This is not surprising considering the events under study.

Framing analysis of coverage revealed that AJA adopted three major frames: a humanitarian frame, a military frame and a geopolitical conflict frame. On the other hand, the humanitarian frame was the most prevalent in AJE's reporting. Both channels used a diverse range of sources. Yet, despite the diversity, both AJA and AJE relied mostly on official sources for information.

Applying the tenets of peace journalism to the Al Jazeera's coverage shas shown that the network demonstrated that conflict-sensitive reporting can indeed be achieved without falling into the trap of sensationalism and propaganda or compromising journalism ethics. Yet both AJE and AJA fell short on giving agency and voice to the victims as elite sources dominated the voices represented on both channels. Although Al Jazeera as a whole reported upon a wide range of actors, its reporting lacked context and little consideration was given to the structural and cultural aspects of the reported conflict.

It is important to note though that these findings can be attributed to the nature of hard political news and conventional professional practices that favour this type of reporting when covering violent conflicts. Extending the analysis into other genres might lead to a better understanding of Al Jazeera's nature of coverage when it comes to conflict-sensitive reporting. Moreover, the findings showed that Al Jazeera network might need an ethical point of departure on the side of journalists and editors and clear editorial policies that are more in line with its mission as an alternative voice in the global media scene.

References

Allen, T. and Seaton, J. (1999), *The Media of Conflict: War Reporting and Representations of Ethnic Violence*. London: Zed Books.

Beer, F. (2001), *Meanings of War & Peace*. College Station, TX: Texas A&M University Press.

200   *Hala A. Guta*

Capella, J. N. and Jamieson, K. H. (1997), *Spiral of Cynicism: The Press and the Public Good*. New York: Oxford University Press.

Christians, C. G. (2007), 'Non-Violence in Philosophical and Media Ethics', in R. Keeble, J. Tulloch and F. Zollmann (eds), *Peace Journalism: War Journalism, War and Conflict Resolution*. New York, Peter Lang, pp. 239–292.

Christians, C. G. (2019), 'Truth as an Ethical Principle', in H. Sadig (ed.), *Al Jazeera in the Gulf and in the World*. Contemporary Gulf Studies. Singapore: Palgrave Macmillan, pp. 35–65.

Christians, C. G. and Nordenstreng, K. (2004), 'Social responsibility worldwide'. *Journal of Mass Media Ethics*, 19(1), 3–28.

D'Angelo, P. (2002), 'News framing as a multiparadigmatic research program: A response to Entman', *Journal of Communication*, 52(4), 870–888.

Fahmy, S. and Johnson, T. J. (2005), '"How we performed": Embedded journalists' attitudes and perceptions towards covering the Iraq War'. *Journalism & Mass Communication Quarterly*, 82(2), 301–317.

Figenschou, T. (2011), 'Suffering up close: The strategic construction of mediated suffering on Al Jazeera English'. *International Journal of Communication*, 5(3): 233–253.

Galtung, J. (1964), 'An editorial'. *Journal of Peace Research*, 1(1), 1–4.

Galtung, J. (1990), 'Cultural violence', *Journal of Peace Research*, 27(3), 291–305.

Galtung, J. (1996), 'Cultural Peace: Some Characteristics', in UNESCO (ed.), *From a Culture of Violence to a Culture of Peace*. Paris: UNESCO, pp. 75–95.

Galtung, J. (2006), 'Peace journalism as an ethical challenge', *Global Media Journal, Mediterranean Edition*, 1(2), 1–5.

Galtung, J. (2014), 'Galtung and Ruge – News Values: An update by Prof. Galtung'. Retrieved from: https://www.galtung-institut.de/en/2015/galtung-and-ruge-news-values-an-update-by-prof-galtung-october-2014. Accessed: 20 January 2020.

Galtung, J. and Ruge, M. H. (1965), 'The structure of foreign news: The presentation of the Congo, Cuba and Cyprus crises in four Norwegian newspapers'. *Journal of Peace Research*, 2(1), 64–90.

Gamson, W. A., and Modigliani, A. (1989), 'Media discourse and public opinion: A constructionist approach', *American Journal of Sociology*, 95(1), 1–37.

Guta H. A. (2019), 'Al Jazeera: Non-Violence and Peace Journalism', in H. Sadig (ed.), *Al Jazeera in the Gulf and in the World*. Contemporary Gulf Studies. Singapore: Palgrave Macmillan, pp. 191–220.

Hanitzsch, T. (2007), 'Situating peace journalism in journalism studies: A critical appraisal', *Conflict & Communication Online*, 6(2), 1–9. Retrieved from: www.cco.regener-online.de/2007_2/pdf/hanitzsch.pdf. Accessed: 10 August 2017.

Khanfar, W. (2005), Personal interview with Leon Barkho, 19 March 2005.

Krichen, M. (2016), Personal Interview. Doha, Qatar.

Lyon, D. (2007), 'Good journalism or peace journalism?'. *Conflict and Communication Online*, 6(2), 1–10. Retrieved from: www.cco.regener-online.de/2007_2/pdf/loyn.pdf. Accessed: 10 August 2017.

Lukacovic, M. (2016), 'Peace journalism and radical media ethics'. *Conflict & Communication online*, 15(2), 1–9. Retrieved from: www.cco.regener-online.de/2016_2/pdf/lukacovic2016.pdf. Accessed: 24 December 2020.

Lynch, J. and McGoldrick, A. (2005), *Peace Journalism*. Stroud: Hawthorn Press.

Lynch, J. (2013), *A Global Standard for Reporting Conflict*. New York: Routledge.

Miladi, N. (2016), 'Reporting News in a Turbulent World: Is Al Jazeera Re-writing the Rules of Global Journalism?', in E. Abdelmoula and N. Miladi (eds), *Mapping the Al Jazeera Phenomenon Twenty Years On*. Doha: Al Jazeera Centre for Studies, pp. 71–90.

Pan, Z. and Kosicki, G. (1993), 'Framing analysis: An approach to news discourse', *Political Communication*, 10(1), 55–75.

Pan, Z. and Kosicki, G. (2001), 'Framing as a Strategic Action in Public Deliberation', in S. Reese, J. Gandy, and A. E. Grant (eds), *Framing Public Life: Perspectives on Media and Our Understanding of the Social World*. New York: Routledge, pp. 35–65.

Rinnawi, K. (2012), 'Cyber uprising: Al-Jazeera TV channel and the Egyptian uprising'. *Language and Intercultural Communication*, 12(2), pp. 118–132.

Seib, P. (2005). 'Hegemonic no more: Western media, the rise of Al-Jazeera, and the influence of diverse voices'. *International Studies Review*, 7(4), 601–615. Retrieved from: http://www.jstor.org/stable/3699677

Tenenboim-Weinblatt, K., Hanitzsch, T., and Nagar, R. (2016), 'Beyond peace journalism: Reclassifying conflict narratives in the Israeli news media'. *Journal of Peace Research*, 53(2), 151–165.

White, A. (2016), 'Ethical Choices when Journalists Go to War', in F. Darija, C. Spahr, and V. Zlatarsky (eds), *Conflict Reporting in the Smartphone Era – from Budget Constraints to Information Warfare*. Konrad-Adenauer-Stiftung, Media Program South East Europe.

Yacoubian, M. (2017), 'Governance challenges in Raqqa after the Islamic State'. United States Institute of Peace. Retrieved from: https://www.usip.org/sites/default/files/SR414-Governance-Challenges-in-Raqqa-after-the-Islamic-State.pdf. Accessed: 24 December 2020.

Zayani, M. (2016), 'News Reporting and the Politics of Representation: Al Jazeera's Culture of Journalism', in E. Abdelmoula and N. Miladi (eds), *Mapping the Al Jazeera Phenomenon Twenty Years On*. Doha: Al Jazeera Centre for Studies, pp. 91–98.

Part 3

Global media ethics global challenges

12 Journalistic deontology in news coverage of poverty in the digital age

Why objectivity is bad when reporting on inequality

Jairo Lugo-Ocando and Steven Harkins

Introduction

Since the inception of cyberspace, the potential of digital and interactive technologies for greater inclusions of voices and broader representations of society has been articulated through a powerful metaphor that promises not only the dissemination of knowledge, but also the opening of new spaces for public discussions and better representations of the 'other' (Lynch, 2016; Lugo-Ocando, 2019). Accordingly, this initial narrative argued that the digital era would unleash the necessary space for voices and actors that were in the past excluded from the public sphere (Arquilla and Ronfeldt, 1997; Norris, 2001). The aspiration was that this could be the beginning of a participatory era that was able to accommodate more diverse views and ideas into the public debate. All this was supposed to be achieved by linking audiences directly with the sources of information while allowing the true flow of information to happen.

It was thought that by connecting directly citizens and allowing them to exercise the ability to communicate with others, both locally and globally, one could foster a new era for journalism: one that was supposed to allow grassroots to reach the wider public and promote causes that so far had been marginalized from the mainstream media spaces. If media owners, powerful corporations and editors had to compete with other channels for the control of the news agenda in more equal terms, it was said, then the news made by the people and for the people could have a better footing in society's priorities. In this context, many commentators expected a news agenda that would talk about structural challenges of society, including the central issues of poverty and inequality in ways that were not referred to before. All this thanks to the collective pressure of 'participatory publishing' (Nguyen, 2006) in the face of promising civic initiatives such as OhmyNews in South Korea and other similar experiences, which highlighted the potential of citizen journalism in the digital age (Kim and Hamilton, 2006; Thurman, 2008).

To be sure, the new medium promised uncensored, unfiltered and uncompromised manners of doing journalism where many saw the potential for a new deontology when communicating news. It was by no means a new dream, as the idea of rendering the media space to the masses can be traced back to the

DOI: 10.4324/9781003203551-16

initial years of Lenin in power in the Soviet Union when he opened the pages of the newspaper Pravda to hundreds of thousands of letters from the people. Then, a new ethics for journalism was thought of, in which real 'scientific journalism' would look at 'structural causes' for society's malaise by providing a direct voice to the masses (Lenoe, 2004; Lugo-Ocando, 2019). These attempts, as we know, degenerated into propaganda to support the totalitarian state under Lenin himself, and later Stalin. However, the experiment did leave in the air an appetite for greater access to the media and for a journalistic deontology that could report beyond the manifestations of poverty and into its causes such as inequality and the ownership of the means of production.

This chapter looks at how and why these initial promises were not only never achieved but also why it was, from the start, an unrealistic set of goals. In so doing, we explore the British media coverage of poverty at home and abroad as a case study that allows us to illustrate our key argument: That the digital revolution has actually had very little impact upon Western journalists when it comes to the ethics surrounding the news coverage of poverty. In our view, the practices, aesthetics and overall approach to poverty in the newsroom remains unaltered by the technological change in the media landscape. We argue that this is because the deontology of journalism in relation to poverty remains linked to prevalent professional normative aspirations such as 'objectivity', which impede the incorporation of structuralist notions, concepts and world-views into the narrativation of poverty in the news.

The chapter draws on Ward's (2008) argument that scholars need to widen the conceptual base of journalism ethics by adopting a global perspective. Our analysis calls for a move away from the parochial and traditional ways of understanding journalism ethics and argues for a more comprehensive framework that challenges the values and goalposts set by the liberal and positive traditions of journalism in the West. In so doing, we aspire, that 'journalism as a political institution' (Schudson, 2002) could propose values and approaches that allowed for structuralist and critical coverage of poverty. In this sense, we believe that the promises made by the digital revolution only sound utopian because journalism deontology has remained the same and limits more critical approaches by reporters.

We can now see that the Internet promise was a return to that aspiration of unfiltered and open access to information and voices that could tell their own stories (envisaged in the brief Soviet enlightenment). The presence of the unfiltered voices of the people with little or no mediation in the media space, it was believed, would create the necessary pressure upon the legacy media to embrace other forms of reporting poverty. This promised to be a new era for journalists as facilitators for the people's voices rather than just being gatekeepers just being gatekeepers of news or information they receive. The expectation was a change of the journalistic culture in ways in which reporters could be pre-occupied more with social justice and less in just presenting 'verifiable' facts. It was a time in which many voiced their expectations for citizen journalism, flooding the media space and competing on equal terms with the traditional news providers while changing the overall media landscape.

However, contrary to these initial promises of the mid-1990s, we are still far from having a media ecology that is truly inclusive of the voices of those living in poverty. Their views, lives and ideas have often been bypassed or left behind in the mainstream news agenda (Harkins and Lugo-Ocando, 2017; Lugo-Ocando, 2015). In hindsight, perhaps techno-deterministic narratives that hype the possibilities of the cyberspace were too readily embraced. In actuality, these spaces remain rather closed to the many, particularly given the growing digital divide within society (Compaine, 2001; Warschauer, 2004). So, the question goes, why, in all these years has journalism in the times of the Internet, not fulfilled its multiple promises to offer adequate spaces of representation to the voices of excluded individuals and communities? What have been the determinants hindering the potential of these technologies to provide a proper voice to those living in poverty?

The answer is partially due to the way journalism is practiced by those who produce most of the mainstream news content. Added to this, reporters continue to be bound by a deontology for which the rules make it right to detach oneself from the suffering of others and focus instead only upon the manifestations of poverty. It is a deontology for which 'objectivity' means excluding structuralist and historical materialist analysis from the narratives presented to the public because of the fear of being 'ideologically' labelled, even when these analytical tools are the only ones capable of denouncing the consequences of inequality and the monopoly of the means of production. In other words, the fact that most journalists still follow a particular deontology has undermined the possibility of developing new ways of reporting poverty and inequality in the digital world.

Take for example, the news coverage of women's exploitation and suffering in rural India and how the Western media has focused on 'empowerment' as the solution. In this particular case, reporters often present the manifestation of gender poverty in terms of statistics and accounts of the lack of accessible basic services and goods. The consequent call is therefore to 'empower' them by incorporating women into the labour market despite the fact that most of them already work at home, both as housewives and farmers. As some researchers have shown, while the media centres upon the neoliberal narrative of 'incorporating them into the labor market' – in a way in which actually their workload would easily double – it nevertheless tends to obviate the fact that actually women already account for nearly 70% of all farmers in that country, despite owning less than 4% of the land (Lugo-Ocando and Nguyen, 2017: 94).

Hence, our contention is that despite the radical transformation of the media ecology across the globe, the aesthetics of news reporting of poverty and inequality are still determined by basic ethical norms, such as objectivity and impartiality, which impose limits on the way poverty and social exclusion are covered and reported by the news media. Hence, journalism – as a political institution – remains embedded in the ideal of detachment and balance and excludes from their narratives, structural issues such as economic inequality and ownership of means of production because they are considered to be too ideological. Consequently, inequality and poverty tend to remain invisible in the news coverage of poverty.

By examining the aesthetics and deontology of news gathering and production we want to understand better how particular forms, formats and practices survive and adapt to the new digital era. Particularly, in relation to how the news media in general, by means of the imposition of its organizational newsroom cultures upon individual journalists, managed to perpetuate approaches and practices that served to conserve traditional narratives and stereotypes of those living in poverty, while hindering the potential of technologies to change that. The chapter concludes by arguing that news coverage of poverty is dominated by parochial concerns and that the digital revolution has not disrupted these dynamics. The chapter supports the argument set out by Ward (2008) for whom the conceptual base for journalism ethics needs to be widened in order to incorporate other perspectives. In so doing, we aim to contribute to the de-Westernization debate around ethics set in this book and highlight the need for a new journalistic deontology, particularly among Western reporters, that demands structural change rather than just palliative measures when it comes to poverty.

New and old media

Let us start by examining the 'old' ways of reporting poverty. By this we refer to the manner in which the legacy – or traditional mainstream media – cover poverty as social and political issues and incorporate it into the news agenda and then go on to compare this to the way the new digital-native outlets do it. Using the Nexis UK database this study examined 272 news articles on economic inequality written between April 2017 and the end of December 2019, a period that covered two UK General Elections. The sample used, included articles from two tabloid newspapers from different ideological perspectives, the *Sun* (right) and the *Daily Mirror* (left). The sample also included *The Times*, the *Daily Telegraph* and the *Guardian* which were selected to represent the traditional broadsheet market with a range of institutional editorial perspectives. These titles were chosen as being broadly representative of the UK legacy news market although it should be noted at this stage that the tabloid newspapers in the selection are not known for high standards of ethical practice. For example, the *Daily Mirror* is well known for the period when it was edited by Piers Morgan who was sacked for publishing staged photographs of British soldiers in Iraq (Taylor, 2005: 41). The *Sun* is well known for creating controversy over its victim-blaming coverage of the Hillsborough disaster (Sanders 2003: 42). In spite of these ethical controversies these newspapers are amongst the biggest – selling UK newspapers and play a key role in shaping the national conversation.

The articles were coded in terms of their style or genre with a clear distinction made between 'objective' and 'non-objective' styles. This was an important distinction because selecting a specific genre allows journalists to introduce opinions in their work. For this study, 'hard news stories', 'reportage' and 'feature articles' were considered 'objective' genres. Whereas 'open-ed' (or opposite the editorial page), 'profiles' and 'editorials' were considered 'non-objective'. Our close reading of the sample suggested that UK newspapers were more likely to report economic inequality as a factor in hard news stories if they were external to the United Kingdom. For this reason, the articles were also coded in terms of geographical location. We also examined the articles in terms of news sources to assess whether the reports contained testimony from those living in poverty, with a particular focus on the inclusion/exclusion of voices from the Global South.

The press and poverty

Tabloid newspapers only accounted for 5% of the articles in our sample. This may be because the phrase 'economic inequality' was unlikely to be used in these publications because of their linguistic style and brevity of their articles. Nevertheless, some notable findings emerged from examining this sample in relation to global media ethics. Firstly, 'economic inequality' is only reported as a rationale for poverty in objective news stories if their focus is international. Indeed, 86% of the articles from the tabloid newspapers in our sample were from objective articles and all of these articles focused on international issues. Hard news items identified economic inequality as a factor fuelling civil unrest in Chile, driving debates in French and Irish politics, a defining social problem in the United States and a serious issue throughout the Global South. In each of these cases, economic inequality is reported as an objective fact which impacts a range of social issues. Indeed, all of the articles in our sample of tabloid news-papers that mentioned economic inequality as a domestic issue within the United Kingdom, appeared in non-objective genres such as opinion articles.

There are two interesting observations from this sample of tabloid news-paper articles. Firstly, economic inequality appears as an acceptable objective fact when reporting on overseas nations in hard news items. However, it only appears as part of the domestic news agenda in opinion pieces. Secondly, the voices of those living in poverty are entirely absent from this sample. In terms of global journalism ethics these publications are far from the ideal of adopting a global perspective.

One logical suggestion is that news gathering practices, rooted in norms of objectivity, serve to eliminate economic inequality from the domestic news agenda with the only exception being found in opinion pieces. Although more ethnographic approaches are needed before we can underpin this suggestion, the systematic results already suggest that some of these limitations may be down to the nature of the tabloid press in the United Kingdom, which has a long tradition of vilifying the working class and ignoring 'structure' as the cause for poverty, even in those cases that identify themselves with progressiveness (such as *The Mirror*).

Having said that, the patterns were also identified in our analysis of the broadsheet sample. For example, the *Daily Telegraph* discusses economic inequality as a hard news topic which exists outside of the United Kingdom. Articles report economic inequality as: a problem for the European Union, a key factor in Australian electoral politics, and a catalyst for civil unrest in Chile. However, when economic inequality is reported in a domestic context, it is only in the form of opinion columns by writers who defend the existence of economic inequality. In fact, the main difference between coverage in the *Daily Telegraph* and the tabloid press is the notable increase in the volume of opinion columns. In one example, columnist Charles Moore compares wealth to a seed, arguing that 'the essential thing is that as many people as possible should be free to plant as many seeds as possible and profit from whatever plants flourish. Inequality will certainly result, but so will a much wider prosperity' (something that reflects the notion of 'Trickle-down economics).[1] Similar arguments are put forward in two opinion pieces written by Ryan Bourne, a scholar at the Cato Institute, a US-based libertarian think tank. Bourne argues that 'we should not care about inequality at all' by analysing the weaknesses of inequality measures such as the Gini coefficient.[2] Another opinion piece from the same author asserts that the link between economic inequality and a wide range of social problems is based on 'very weak evidence'.[3] In other words, while this news-paper does incorporate inequality in its news content it only does so in terms of opinion, not hard news, and in a very bias neoliberal manner.

Coverage of economic inequality in *The Times* follows a similar pattern although its overall approach is more nuanced because the articles dedicated to the topic have some variation in their perspectives. Hard news items about economic inequality in *The Times* are usually reserved for discussing its impact overseas. These articles examine the impact of economic inequality in France, Colombia, Ecuador, Germany, Ireland, Japan and the USA. Indeed, 57% of the articles in *The Times* focused on manifestations of inequality outside the UK. Nevertheless, *The Times* does occasionally report the effects of economic inequality as a hard news topic. One brief news article describes a study which claims that 'Economic inequality in Britain could lead to higher rates of suicide and drug and alcohol-related deaths on a similar scale to the opioid crisis in the US'.[4] In another article discussing global economic inequality *The Times* examines its impact 'From Latin America through Europe and the Middle East to Hong Kong'; the article specifically references the link between economic inequality and populism in Britain as well as countries such as Chile, Lebanon, China, France, Turkey, Russia, Iraq, Spain, Ecuador, Bolivia and the USA.[5] Economic inequality and austerity cuts are also cited as possible factors in scaling back life expectancy projections in the UK.[6] These examples were rare and the majority of articles in *The Times* about economic inequality within the United Kingdom were found in opinion pieces. These articles explicitly argue that economic inequality is worth the cost for the benefits of the free market[7] or that it is not a serious issue. For example:

> *Why are so many people raging about a non-existent income inequality crisis instead? Do we blame social media for making the super-rich more*

visible? Do we blame the real earnings squeeze for leaving everyone with an economic hangover? My theory is we're still digesting the after-effects of Britain's last genuine inequality crisis. In the 1980s all sorts of factors, from changes in the international monetary system to Thatcherite benefit cuts to the decline of trade unions, pushed up inequality very sharply. The rich really did get richer and the poor, poorer. Britain went from being one of the world's most equal economies to one of the least equal. This was such a big shift it might plausibly take a few decades to absorb. [8]

There was one single example of an opinion piece which made the case for tackling economic inequality in this sample. The piece was written by the director of the Institute for Fiscal Studies, a centrist think tank. The author argued that 'differences in health and life expectancy are undoubtedly among the most dramatic and worrying manifestations of economic inequality'.[9] This piece suggests a slightly more ideologically diverse approach to selecting commentators than was evident at the *Daily Telegraph*. Nevertheless, *The Times'* sample follows a similar pattern to the one observed in the *Daily Telegraph* and the two tabloid newspapers. Economic inequality is a hard news item overseas but rarely appears in domestic news coverage. When economic inequality in the UK does appear in a domestic context its impact is most often disputed by commentators writing opinion pieces. However, *The Times* does demonstrate a broader view on economic inequality by occasionally publishing exceptions to both of these rules.

While the previous two broadsheet newspapers share a conservative perspective, the *Guardian* has an ideologically left-leaning or liberal outlook. The combination of broadsheet style and political outlook perhaps explain why the *Guardian* accounted for the largest number of articles in our sample that address the issue of inequality. Only 25% of the articles in the *Guardian* were in 'non-objective' genres as they were the only publication whose output contained more editorials and opinion pieces than news items. Hard news items about economic inequality often focus on its manifestation overseas. These reports focus on economic inequality in the United States, Australia, Chile, Ireland, France, Germany, Mexico, South Africa, Bolivia, Brazil, the Bahamas, Italy, Israel, Norway, New Zealand, China, India and Russia. Domestic news articles containing the phrase 'economic inequality' were rare. One example of a hard news piece on government borrowing adds a comment from the Equality Trust who are introduced as an organization that 'campaigns to reduce economic inequality'.[10] The phrase also appears in a news report about a survey of the 1% highest earners in the UK who reportedly feel the effects of economic inequality because of the disparity in earnings between themselves and their peer group.[11]

Another news article on the same subject describes how there has been a regulatory failure in terms of tackling excessive executive pay; this piece cites the High Pay Centre think tank describing how polling regularly shows public support for measures to curb executive pay and address economic inequality.

The piece reports that policies such as 'caps on top pay and worker repre-sentation on company boards' have a popular appeal amongst the UK popula-tion.[12] These articles that examine domestic economic inequality in the UK appear more often in the *Guardian* than in the other newspapers in our sample. However, the pattern remains that economic inequality as a hard news story most often features overseas nations. Nevertheless, the subject does appear in opinion columns in this newspaper more often than their competitors.

The *Guardian* published a range of pieces from a left-wing perspective, including an extract from left-wing academic Danny Dorling's book on the corrosive impact of economic inequality.[13] Dorling also writes an opinion piece directly challenging the way that the *Daily Telegraph* frames economic inequality by diminishing its impact.[14] A range of opinion pieces are published highlighting the corrosive effects of economic inequality; these are written by a US academic,[15] an Australian Pastor,[16] political figures from the Green Party[17] and the Labour Party.[18] Economic inequality is linked to a range of social issues including the Grenfell Tower tragedy[19] and premature deaths in the North of England. The editorial argues that England has a 'deadly divide' rooted in 'economic inequalities' which causes premature deaths in the North.[20] Further editorials are written in support of the Labour Party's 'radical, sweeping, anti-establishment ideas on economic inequality'.[21] The sample of comment and opinion pieces in the *Guardian* are consistently written from a perspective that assumes that economic inequality is the root cause of a range of social problems and needs to be tackled as a matter of urgency. This perspective was absent from comment pieces in the other broadsheet newspapers, conversely the view that economic inequality was not a serious problem did not appear in the sample from the *Guardian*. However, while the 'non-objective' genres in the *Guardian* clearly tackle economic inequality as a serious social issue; the 'objective' genre follows a similar pattern that has been observed within the other titles in this sample.

The evidence presented here suggests that economic inequality is a contributing factor to civil unrest and a key consideration for covering electoral politics over-seas. However, it is rarely the central focus on news coverage in these contexts. The topic that has news value is the election or civil unrest; in the absence of these events economic inequality loses its news value. This also means that the voices of those affected by economic inequality are largely absent from news reporting on the topic. As a domestic news item, economic inequality is rarely acknowledged by the British press. This is because journalists follow the institutional practice of performing the 'strategic ritual' of objectivity (Tuchman, 1972: 661). This involves reporting news through using quotations from others so as to reinforce the jour-nalists' authority as an impartial observer. Economic inequality as an explanatory framework is contested as being too ideological within their organizations and by the key stakeholders that sustain the political economy of the newspapers (namely, advertisers). A stark contrast to these practices can be found in the 'non-objective' coverage of economic inequality in the British broadsheet press. Conservative newspapers such as *The Times* and the *Daily Telegraph* acknowledge the wider debate on economic inequality in a way that is absent from their news coverage. They entire debate in these papers is about arguing that reducing economic inequality is neither necessary nor desirable. In contrast, the liberal newspaper, the *Guardian* is responsible for publishing a series of opinion-led pieces which accept the need to tackle economic inequality and argue that this must be done as a matter of urgency. The volume of these articles in the 'non-objective' genres in the *Guardian* stand in stark contrast to the fact that the debate is almost entirely absent from their news coverage.

The predictable patterns uncovered in our analysis of legacy news organizations will be of no surprise to anybody familiar with the British press. The shift towards digital publication which is available to a global audience has done little to change the culture of the traditional UK newsroom. The following analysis examines these patterns amongst digital start-ups to see if any new patterns have emerged.

Changes and continuities

Since the expectation was that a new media ecology would create pressures upon the legacy media to change the way it covered poverty it is then logical to expect a distinctive news agenda and aesthetics from the digital-native outlets (created after the emergence of the Internet and only present in digital forms). Is there a significant difference in the way they report poverty and inequality? To answer this question, we took a sample of new digital-native media and carried out a comparative analysis of news coverage of poverty and inequality. Our sample included: *The Bureau of Investigative Journalism; The Canary*; and *The Huffington Post UK*. The organizations that capture a combination of different funding models (advertising supported, subscription supported, donation supported), distribution models (niche vs scale), and editorial strategies (focus on few investigative stories versus a broader range of coverage and a greater output). We replicated the sample for a study conducted by the Reuters Journalism Institute at the University of Oxford under the title Digital-born News Media in Europe (Nicholls, Shabbir, and Nielsen, 2016).

One of the first things to notice is that as a proportion of their overall content, these media outlets tend to publish far more stories on poverty and social exclusion than their legacy counterparts. Mostly, all of these outlets tend to be at the liberal/left side of the political spectrum and, consequently, are assumed to be more committed to having these topics within their news agenda. Over the sample, that we took from 1 November 2019 to 30 January 2020, we found that the average proportion of content dedicated to poverty was less than 8% of the overall news coverage (if one excludes *The Huffington Post UK*, then it is even smaller). This is concurrent with many other studies on news coverage of poverty, which also indicate how little attention the overall news media place upon poverty (Harkins and Lugo-Ocando, 2017; Kitzberger and Pérez, 2008; McKendrick, Sinclair, Anthea, O'Donnell, and Dobbie, 2008).

In addition, our findings suggest that inequality is rarely mentioned in hard news stories. Our content analysis of the same sample indicates that the code for 'inequality' – which mentions the word itself as to other related and synonymous terms – accounted for less than 1% of the words used. Moreover, in only a few cases 'inequality' related to the code for poverty. The same indicates that not only is inequality scarcely present in the news units analysed here but also that in only a few of the cases did it appear to be related to poverty.

This is corroborated by a close reading of a sub-sample of 12 articles, which indicates that inequality is rarely linked to poverty in the development of an explanatory framework or context/rationale for a news story to social exclusion. This was also the case for those news outlets at the left of the political spectrum. Indeed, in a piece on the changes to the benefit system in the UK, which left thousands of people destitute as government help was suddenly cut off, reporter Steve Topple from *The Canary*, one of the leading left-wing outlets, exposed the way that these changes had negatively impacted on the lives of ordinary people living in poverty. His piece concentrates on how people with disabilities had taken the Department for Work and Pensions to court to challenge the changes made by the government. However, as in most of the cases examined in our study, it highlights how the journalists' work about poverty often report the manifestations of poverty rather than its root causes (Lugo-Ocando, 2015). There is no mention in this piece that these changes are part of a wider package of austerity measures that were implemented to reduce a fiscal deficit relating to government debt, created by the decision to mitigate the 2008 financial crisis by bailing out banking institutions. Neither it is mentioned that austerity cuts like this will continue as long as governments fail to clamp down on loopholes in the legal system that permit corporations and individuals to redirect their profits to tax havens. Neither could we find examples where there was a discussion on the monopoly of means of production, incorporation of workers into the board of directors of companies (something that did appear in previous years) or greater access to the banking system and capital. Pieces such as this leave their readers with the impression that the cuts in welfare are just about policy rather than structure.

Through analysing news coverage of poverty and inequality in the UK press though the lens of global journalism ethics we have made a number of observations. Firstly, news coverage of poverty remains scarce and far-in-between. More importantly, despite all of these news organizations now publishing to a global audience via digital platforms, their focus remains strictly parochial and limited to the manifestation of poverty rather than its structural causes. This news coverage is filtered through the concerns of the UK national interest and worldview. Secondly, economic inequality is presented as an objective fact when it is observed overseas; however, it is relegated to the comment pages when it is tackled as a domestic issue in the United Kingdom. Furthermore, much of the content of these comment pages extol the virtue of the free market and makes the positive case for the existence of economic inequality. Only the *Guardian* pointed to economic inequality as an issue that underpins social problems. It is significant that this discussion took place in the comment and opinion pages instead of forming part of the news content. This suggests that economic inequality is not accepted as a fact in domestic news coverage, meaning that discussions about poverty are entirely divorced from their social, political and economic contexts.

Now, these results are not surprising as the legacy news organizations in the United Kingdom do work under a number of constraints which can explain these patterns of news coverage. They are, broadly speaking, attached to business models and production practices that influence their end product. However, the emergence of digital platforms that are free from these constraints has not delivered a critical explanation of economic inequality. Ultimately, this has led to a news ecology that largely erases the voices of those living in poverty in the United Kingdom and beyond while the UK press rarely accept economic inequality as an objective fact in a domestic sense. The objective news agenda in the British press does accept that economic inequality is the root cause of social problems and political unrest overseas. Furthermore, the discussion of economic inequality overseas is restricted to hard news coverage of its negative impact on elite political actors. Overall, there is little wider discussion of the causes of these issues, while the voices of those affected by economic inequality are not featured.

What was really surprising, however, was to find that the digital-native news media also did not change their approach to poverty and that it remained subject to similar patterns encountered among the legacy media. In this sense, the digital revolution has not provided yet a suitable platform for the voices of those living in poverty and it has not shifted the focus of the UK press towards publishing for a global audience or incorporating more structural explanations for poverty. If, as Ward (2008) suggests, we are to widen the conceptual base of journalism ethics, then it is important to understand this news coverage by examining its meaning more broadly. The issues that we examined here do not exist in a vacuum and are not specific to any single country. Patterns of wealth and poverty, economic inequality and tax justice are being played out on a global stage, with wider implications and, therefore, require a global perspective and multilateral actions and solutions. It is in this context of poverty and other urgent themes (such as climate change) that journalism as a political institution needs to revisit its deontology and set values towards not only the guiding principles from the early twentieth century but more adapted to the necessary actions that can actually make this a better world for all. Especially if it intends to remain as relevant to future generations as it was in the past.

Conclusion

The cases above highlight how the aesthetics of news on poverty are profoundly defined by the core normative aspirations to be fact-based, objective and/or impartial. Journalists are reluctant to incorporate structural analysis in their work as they hold strong self-perceptions around their own professional roles that incorporate notions such as impartiality, detachment and objective reporting. Indeed, one of the most remarkable findings of the Worlds of Journalism Study (WJS) research project is the overall convergence of normative claims and deontological aspirations among journalists from all over the world with regards to news values and journalistic ethics (Hanitzsch, 2016; Mellado, 2015; Mellado and Van Dalen, 2017). Although this same research project also highlights that there are important caveats within these normative professional aspirations, cultures and practices, the survey nevertheless conclusively suggests important overlaps regarding ethical aspirations and stances among news reporters across the globe.

This convergence of normative values and aspirations seems closely interconnected to the notion of objectivity, which despite criticism, continues to be paramount in the conceptualization of journalism as a professional and independent field (Maras, 2013; McNair, 2000; Ward, 2015). Indeed, as some of the findings of the WJS project underline, the idea of 'professional autonomy' is strongly associated with detachment and non-involvement, both of which are considered essential journalistic functions by those interviewed across the globe. The journalists surveyed in this project equally value notions such as impartiality, reliability and factualness of information, as well as adherence to universal ethical principles such as accuracy (Hanitzsch, et al., 2011), despite important cross-national and cross-cultural differences.

Objectivity continues to retain a central, if disputed, place in discussions of journalism as a profession that works across national frontiers despite very distinctive historical-national origins (Maras, 2013: 5). Despite a far more sophisticated discussion of what objectivity really means, the practice nevertheless often translates into the normative claim that journalists' work is somehow detached from their own feelings and that it is scientifically objective. Historically speaking and in relation to the news coverage, it meant that journalists' compassion should not cloud the impartiality of reporting poverty.

Over the years this 'illusion of detachment' has played in the hands of the impulse to exclude explicit ideology from the narratives. Structure therefore is not an acceptable element of the discursive regimes that frame and establish the boundaries for the news on poverty. To be sure, the adoption of this aesthetic by mainstream journalism has helped the news media as a political institution to comply with the notion of objectivity, which is central to the prevalent news cultures that shape and define how journalists understand poverty and present it as a news item to the general public. If objectivity is still a contested notion, it nevertheless 'continues to play a central role in media and journalism in linking concepts of truth, accuracy, impartiality and independence' (Maras, 2013: 228) and therefore also continues to shape the representation of poverty in the news.

Our main point then is that despite all the profound and revolutionary changes experienced within the media landscape, journalists have remained anchored to an ideal that limits their own ability to provide a more structuralist explanation of poverty. This ideal, which has proved to be extremely useful to exercise authorial control of what is regarded as truth has, nevertheless, been an impediment to a more contextualized interpretation of poverty and social exclusion in our society. In this sense, the new digital era has so far been unable to bring about a new deontology for journalists, one that can reconcile the aspiration of being credible and factually based with the urgent need to reinterpret truth as social justice. In this sense, from an ethical perspective, news on poverty seems to be travelling the same old dirt roads of the past while the rest of news is already driving through the information superhighway.

Notes

1 Charles Moore, 'Wealth is not like a cake, it is more like a seed', *Daily Telegraph*, 10 July 2017.
2 Ryan Bourne, 'Nobel Prize winner Deaton is right: Leftists do see inequality all wrong', *Daily Telegraph*, 5 January 2018.
3 Ryan Bourne', It's not inequality but the underlying problems that pose the greater risk', *Daily Telegraph*, 17 May 2019.
4 Gurpreet Narwan, 'Economist Sir Angus Deaton warns inequality will damage UK progress', *The Times*, 14 May 2019.
5 Charles Bremner, Stephen Gibbs, Richard Spencer and Graham Keeley, 'From East to West, fury erupts on to the streets; Poverty, inequality and the greed of rulers have unleashed global anger', *The Times*, 26 October 2019.
6 Greg Hurst, 'Deprivation in poor areas cuts years off the lives of newborns', *The Times*, 3 December 2019.
7 Cormac Lucey, 'Socialism won't solve the young's problems; Yes, times are tough but turning against capitalism risks erasing the gains that have pulled millions out of poverty', *The Times*, 8 November 2018.
8 Ed Conway, 'Ignore the 'wealth gap' prophets of doom; The left's obsession with a supposedly yawning gap between rich and poor is wide of the mark', *The Times*, 17 May 2019.
9 Paul Johnson, 'Is it fair to increase the pension age when it's the rich who benefit most? ', *The Times*, 7 August 2017.
10 Angela Monaghan', UK Government borrowing at lowest level since the financial crisis', *The Guardian*, 25 April 2017.
11 Rupert Neate, 'Voices of the 1%; How do Britain's highest earners feel about their income', *The Guardian*, 3 May 2017.
12 Rupert Jones, 'Measures to curb executive pay have flopped, says thinktank', *The Guardian*, 6 May 2019.
13 Danny Dorling, 'Is inequality bad for the environment?', *The Guardian*, 4 July 2017.
14 Danny Dorling, 'Humans are most atrocious when we live under the weight of great inequalities', *The Guardian*, 15 May 2017.
15 Ganesh Sitaraman, 'To rescue democracy, we must revive the reforms of the Progressive Era', *The Guardian*, 30 August 2019.
16 Brad Chilcott, 'Jesus was on the side of the poor and exploited. Christian politicians should remember that', *The Guardian*, 13 April 2017.
17 Caroline Lucas, 'The answer to climate breakdown and austerity? A green new deal', *The Guardian*, 27 March 2019.
18 Faiza Shaheen, 'It's not the "white working class". The real home of bigotry is elsewhere; Poorer people get blamed for everything. But it's actually middle-income earners who are most prejudiced', *The Guardian*, 7 March 2019.
19 Dawn Foster, 'The Grenfell inquiry opens but no one expects justice to be easily won', *The Guardian*, 15 September 2017.

20 Editorial, 'The Guardian view on premature deaths: Inequality kills', *The Guardian*, 9 August 2017.
21 Gaby Hinsliff, 'Labour is finally back in the real world – and taking on the gig economy', *The Guardian*, 11 September 2018.

References

Allan, S. (2004), *News Culture*. Maidenhead: Open University/McGraw Hill Education.
Arquilla, J. and Ronfeldt, D. (1997), *In Athena's Camp: Preparing for Conflict in the Information Age*. Santa Monica, CA: Rand Corporation.
Berkowitz, D. and Beach, D. W. (1993), 'News sources and news context: The effect of routine news, conflict and proximity'. *Journalism and Mass Communication Quarterly*, 70(1), 4–12. doi:10.1177/107769909307000102
Block, F. L. (1990), *Postindustrial Possibilities: A Critique of Economic Discourse*. Berkeley: University of California Press.
Brighton, P. and Foy, D. (2007), *News Values*. Los Angeles: SAGE.
Compaine, B. M. (2001), *The Digital Divide: Facing a Crisis or Creating a Myth?* Cambridge, MA: MIT Press.
Dorling, D. (2011), *Injustice: Why Social Inequality Persists*. Bristol: Policy.
eMediaMillWorks (2001, 20 September). 'Text: President Bush addresses the nation'. *The Washington Post*. Retrieved from: http://www.washingtonpost.com/wp-srv/nation/specials/attacked/transcripts/bushaddress_092001.html
Fukuyama, F. (1989), 'The end of history'. *The National Interest*, Summer 1989 1989, 3–18.
Genro Filho, A. (1987), *El Secreto de la Pirámide*. Caracas: Imprenta Nacional.
Hanitzsch, T. (2016), 'The WJS 2012–2016 study'. Retrieved from: http://www.worldsofjournalism.org/
Hanitzsch, T., Hanusch, F., Mellado, C., Anikina, M., Berganza, R., Cangoz, I. ... and Karadjov, C. D. (2011), 'Mapping journalism cultures across nations: A comparative study of 18 countries'. *Journalism Studies*, 12(3), 273–293.
Harkins, S. and Lugo-Ocando, J. (2016), 'All People are Equal, but Some People are More Equal than Others: How and Why Inequality Became Invisible in the British Press', in J. Servaes and T. Oyedemi (eds), *The Praxis of Social Inequality in Media: A Global Perspective*. London: Rowman and Littlefield, pp. 3–19.
Harkins, S. and Lugo-Ocando, J. (2017), *Poor News: Media Discourses of Poverty in Times of Austerity*. Lanham, MD: Rowman and Littlefield International.
Kapferer, B. (2005), 'New formations of power, the oligarchic-corporate state, and anthropological ideological discourse'. *Anthropological Theory*, 5(3), 285–299. doi:10.1177/1463499605055961
Kim, E. G. and Hamilton, J. W. (2006), 'Capitulation to capital? OhmyNews as alternative media'. *Media, Culture & Society*, 28(4), 541–560.
Kitzberger, P. and Pérez, G. (2008), *Los pobres en papel. Las narrativas de la pobreza en la prensa latinoamericana*. Buenos Aires. https://www.kas.de/c/document_library/get_file?uuid=92ea1eaa-d3ab-955c-dcbf-bc7a2266fabb&groupId=287460
Lansley, S. (2012), *The Cost of Inequality: Why Equality is Essential for Recovery*. London: Gibson Square.
Lenoe, M. E. (2004), *Closer to the Masses*. Cambridge, MA: Harvard University Press.
Lewis, J., Williams, A. and Franklin, B. (2008), 'A compromised fourth estate?'. *Journalism Studies*, 9(1), 1–20. doi:10.1080/14616700701767974

Lugo-Ocando, J. (2015), *Blaming the Victim: How Global Journalism Fails Those in Poverty*. London: Pluto Press.

Lugo-Ocando, J. (2019), 'Poverty in the news media: Continuities, ruptures, and change in the reporting socioeconomic inequality'. *Sociology Compass*, e12719.

Lugo-Ocando, J. and Nguyen, A. (2017), *Developing News: Global Journalism and the Coverage of "Third World" Development*. Abingdon: Routledge.

Lynch, M. (2016), *The Internet of Us: Knowing More and Understanding Less in the Age of Big Data*. New York: W. W. Norton and Company.

Manning, P. (2001), *News and News Sources: A Critical Introduction*. London: Sage.

Maras, S. (2013), *Objectivity in Journalism*. Cambridge: Polity Press.

McKendrick, J., Sinclair, S., Anthea, H., O'Donnell, G. and Dobbie, L. (2008), 'The media, poverty and public opinion in the UK'. Retrieved from: https://pure.ulster.ac.uk/ws/portalfiles/portal/11366740/A_Irwin_JRF_Media_Poverty.pdf

McNair, B. (2000), *Journalism and Democracy*. Abingdon: Routledge.

Mellado, C. (2015), 'Professional roles in news content: Six dimensions of journalistic role performance'. *Journalism Studies*, 16(4), 596–614.

Mellado, C. and Van Dalen, A. (2017), 'Changing times, changing journalism: A content analysis of journalistic role performances in a transitional democracy'. *The International Journal of Press/Politics*, 22(2), 244–263.

Mount, F. (2010), *Mind the Gap: The New Class Divide in Britain* (rev. edition). London: Short.

Nguyen, A. (2006), 'Journalism in the wake of participatory publishing'. *Australian Journalism Review*, 28(1), 143–155.

Nicholls, T., Shabbir, N. and Nielsen, R.-K. (2016), *Digital-born News Media in Europe*. Reuters Institute. Retrieved from: https://reutersinstitute.politics.ox.ac.uk/our-research/digital-born-news-media-europe. Accessed: 29 July 2021.

Norris, P. (2001), *Digital Divide: Civic Engagement, Information Poverty, and the Internet Worldwide*. Cambridge: Cambridge University Press.

Rudin, R. and Ibbotson, T. (2002), *An Introduction to Journalism: Essential Techniques and Background Knowledge*. Oxford: Focal.

Sainath, P. (1996), *Everybody Loves a Good Drought: Stories from India's Poorest Districts*. London: Penguin.

Sanders, K. (2003), *Ethics and Journalism*. London: Sage.

Schudson, M. (2002), The news media as political institutions. *Annual Review of Political Science*, 5(1), 249–269.

Soley, L. C. (1992), *The News Shapers: The Sources Who Explain the News*. New York: Praeger.

Spurr, D. (1993), *The Rhetoric of Empire: Colonial Discourse in Journalism, Travel Writing and Imperial Administration*. Durham, NC:Duke University Press.

Stiglitz, J. E. (2012), *The Price of Inequality*. London: Allen Lane.

Taylor, J. (2005), 'Iraqi torture photographs and documentary realism in the press'. *Journalism Studies*, 6(1), 39–49.

Thurman, N. (2008), 'Forums for citizen journalists? Adoption of user generated content initiatives by online news media'. *New Media & Society*, 10 (1), 139–157.

Tuchman, G. (1972), 'Objectivity as strategic ritual: An examination of newsmen's notions of objectivity'. *American Journal of Sociology*, 77(4), 660–679.

Ward, S. J. (2015), *The Invention of Journalism Ethics: The Path to Objectivity and Beyond* (Vol. 38). Montreal, Quebec: McGill-Queen's Press.

Ward, S. J. (2008), 'Global journalism ethics: Widening the conceptual base'. *Global Media Journal*, 1 (1), 137–149.

Warschauer, M. (2004), *Technology and Social Inclusion: Rethinking the Digital Divide*. Cambridge, MA: MIT Press.

Wilkinson, R. G. and Pickett, K. (2009), *The Spirit Level: Why More Equal Societies almost Always Do Better*. London: Allen Lane.

13 The culture of framing terminologies

Ibrahim N. Abusharif

Introduction

Early Christmas morning, 2020, a man drove a recreational vehicle packed with explosives to downtown Nashville, Tennessee, and parked near an AT&T building. A looped recording emanating from the RV warned residents and passersby to immediately evacuate the area. After an audio countdown, the vehicle was detonated. The explosion shook the city, destroyed or damaged nearby buildings, and killed the driver. As expected, the event was covered extensively by local and national news networks, which invited contributing editors and experts to comment about the event. The experts cautioned against premature conclusions, as they should have done so in journalistic best practices, but they eventually spoke of possible motivations behind an intentional act of public violence. In their conjectures, they employed framing terminologies to describe the potential impetus behind such an event, namely, 'terror' and 'terrorism', as well as problematic and seemingly racialized categories of 'domestic' and 'international' or 'foreign' terrorism. This was well before the details of the driver (a 63-year-old white male, Anthony Warner) were known or revealed.

After nearly three months of multiple-agency investigations, law enforcement authorities concluded that the explosion was not an act of terrorism. Rather, Warner's premeditated act of public violence was motivated by nothing more than his desire to commit suicide – an enormous and carefully choreographed denouement of a person who simply lost the will to live.

There is no known reason to dispute the conclusions of the authorities. However, concomitant queries and commentary populated social media spaces and other forums, as they often do in the wake of the media coverage of public violence. Some of the texts raised a familiar question: had Warner been a Muslim or carried a Muslim name, would 'terrorism' or 'terror' have been part of the choice of descriptors of the event? While it is plausible that the driver's religious identity would not have altered the FBI's conclusions and, a harder argument, would not have changed journalistic coverage, but it is reasonable to give credence to the query because it has legitimacy, supported, in part, by the fact that there has been little, if any, news media push back on the conclusions of the investigations.

DOI: 10.4324/9781003203551-17

Terroristic violence and their news framing terminologies are often unevenly applied in Western news media and seem reserved for racial or religious categories, as research has shown concerning American and European mediascapes and their reportage and narrative-constructions of Muslims and Islam (Pintak, 2019; DeFoster, 2017; Richardson, 2004; Saeed, 2007). Collectively, such imbalanced coverage helps fuel public resentment of Muslims and Islam in the West. Even the very popular British tabloids have trained their legendary and sensationalist ire toward Muslim communities and, in turn, have contributed to anti-Muslim sentiment (Miladi, 2021). A study of Danish media has shown that news media have 'constructed a distorted and negative' image of Islam and Muslims (Jacobson, 2013: 53), with similar results in more traditional British news media (Richardson, 2004). A more recent study of reportage about Muslims between 2007 and 2013 concluded that 75% of prime-time news broadcasts in the United States about Muslims tended to be negative (Media Tenor, 2013).

As Pintak stated concerning US media, the reportage has had 'a long and inglorious relationship with the world's Muslims, characterized by stereotype, distortion and oversimplification' (2006: 30). Pintak added that the negative portrayal has a created

> the frame through which Americans viewed Islam and those who practiced it in the wake of 9/11: dehumanizing Muslims, creating the cultural ground for violence and fueling the subsequent polarization of attitudes between the U.S. and the Muslim world. (2006: 30)

Scholarship on entertainment media (Alsultany, 2013; Shaheen, 2003) and news media are not lacking when it comes to finding patterns in the negative depictions of Muslims and their religion and communities. Thus, a question arises, how to rectify the matter, if there is a will to do so? There is nothing direct or easy about this question, given how deeply embedded narrative-construction is in powerful, hegemonic mediascapes. Nonetheless, this essay advocates that the proposition is indeed critical, especially as the debate about the globalization of journalism ethics accelerates in the digital age. As such, the chapter suggests that to fully address the apprehension surrounding the potential hegemonization of reportage and framing terminologies for acts of 'terrorism', it is necessary to distil and unpack the underlying epistemic postulations about Muslims and Islam in the public sphere. The reason is straightforward: epistemic postulations and pre-modern presumptions (especially) of powerful nations, inform journalistic choices of descriptors and reporting practices. As a social institution and protector of democracy, journalism must also be viewed as part of the power structure of a given nation or groups of nations, who ultimately have, as Appadurai words it, 'taxonomic control over difference' (1996: 39), which I believe applies to journalistic descriptors.

While attending to the usage of terminologies in the style guidelines of newspapers, websites, and other forms of news content is a useful occupation and can tell us much about the hierarchical structures and 'the valence of portrayals of different social groups' (Bleich, Nisar, and Vazquez, 2018), the exercise, however, is incomplete. The reason for this is that editorial choices, headline vernacular and framing guidelines are not entirely intra-journalistic phenomena. While the words of choice in the reporting cache may be established in the contemporary vulgate, but the foundations are, to a good degree, pre-modern in their epistemic and discursive ancestry. Thus, while acknowledging the uneven usage of 'hate crime' and 'terrorism' (and the automatic fear-responses to the words 'Sharia' and 'jihad'), for example, points out immediate concerns of narrative-construction of Muslims and Islam by news media, the foundation is insufficiently considered.

Communication studies often favour content analysis and quantitative approaches in studying news production; however, as van Dijk argues, news structures (in which I include framing terminologies) are best unpacked when linked to 'social practices and ideologies of newsmaking and, indirectly, to the institutional and macrosociological contexts of the news media' (van Dijk, 1988: vii). This approach permits explicit analyses of 'the well-known role of news values and ideologies in the production and understanding of news. Since such values and ideologies are also inherently social, we thus hope to build a bridge between the psychological and the sociological studies of news' (van Dijk, 1988: 2).

Thus, this chapter further suggests that such social practices and ideologies that influence news production and choice of what many believe to be dema-gogic descriptors should not be cordoned off to news studies alone, since recent research has started to take a noticable turn in addressing the 'ideologies' that likely permit and normalize the uneven usages of framing terminologies in contemporary Western journalism.

As such, in the last decade or so scholars and intellectuals have increasingly focused their attention to the forensics of modern media-constructed stereotypes of Muslims. This chapter highlights these efforts and argues along the way that it is essential to address the 'macrosociological' roots of repetitive problematic depictions of a whole people for the nefarious acts of a few. The chapter speaks to a critical mass of Muslim and non-Muslim scholars whose works collectively represent *oppositional discourses* that challenge the heredities of contemporary media practices.

Covering 'Islam': Knowledge production and power

Before examining recent works that challenge the roots of problematic media portrayals of Islam and Muslims, it is important to start with Edward Said. He remains one of the most cited academics in our times for many reasons. Surely one of them is that his scholarship has well-tilled the academic landscape for current studies to flourish – notable studies that seek to address the roots of contemporary knowledge production and media instrumentality. Said has also provided the grammar or vocabulary to critique the intellectual origins of modern discourses in conversation with Oriental scholarship of the past. As such, he was among the first and most convincing intellectuals to have critically evaluated the coverage of Islam and Muslims in a broader contemporary and historical context. In other words, he critically connects the origins of modern journalistic coverage of Islam and Muslims to non-journalistic, pre-modern themes of Orientalism and Medieval polemics. Contemporary scholars and authors addressing the narrative roots of news media, as a result, have followed his lead.

Said gives away the central premise of his book in its title: *Covering Islam: How the Media and the Experts Determine How We See the Rest of the World'*. Said argues that the Western coverage of Muslims/Arabs and nefarious acts associated with them (most conspicuously plane hijackings and bombings, as well as the Iranian hostage crisis) drifts into what ultimately devolves into the coverage 'Islam' itself, a religion essentialized as an incompatible ideology with the West for its perpetual *strangeness* and *otherness*. This practice, according to Said, is 'an unacceptable generalization of the most irresponsible sort, and could never be used for any other religious, cultural, or demographic group on earth' (Said, 1997: xvi). For Said, the discursive traditions of Orientalism cannot be simply historicized as a matter of the past; rather they are active in contemporary knowledge production and the kind of narrative subjugation we see in news media sources.

In *Covering Islam*, Said associates the news judgements and coverage of Muslims and Islam as an extension of Oriental scholarship, translated into descriptors and journalistic interpretation for everyday readers. News media's coverage of 'Islam is a one-sided activity that obscures what "we" do, and highlights instead what Muslims and Arabs by their very flawed nature are' (Said, 1997: xxii). So this ideation of Islam has become entrenched in popular discourse, and, to make his point, Said cites the news reportage and reactions to the Oklahoma City bombing of 1995: 'So inflamed against Islam as the media environment in the United States and the West generally become that when the Oklahoma City bomb attack took place in 1995, the alarm was sounded that the Muslims had struck once again ...' (Said, 1997: xiv). How that takes place – news values and coverage as an indictment of the religion itself – has centuries-old roots, as Said argues, but, from our vantage point now, it has gained renewed resonance after 11 September 2001, years after Said's book was published. The most important chapter in Covering Islam is the last, 'Knowledge and Power.' There he makes the argument that engaging contemporary Islam and, by extension, its coverage, must be dislodged from past ambitions of empire and colonial conquest. He wrote:

> But underlying every interpretation of other cultures – especially of Islam – is a choice facing the individual scholar or intellectual: whether to put intellect at the service of power or at the service of criticism, community, dialogue, and moral sense. This choice must be the first act of interpretation today. (Said, 1997: 172)

The value of the scholarly progeny of Said's works to this day cannot be understated. They have, in part, materialized in the form of articles and monographs published in the last decade or so. They are significant works and will be discussed herein, because, as this chapter argues, they are particularly suitable for inclusion in the larger discussion of the globalization of journalistic ethics, since they introduce critical perspectives beyond the narrow vistas of journalistic practices, style guides and a cacophonous range of journalism ethics. They are perspectives that have led to an acknowledgement that the narratives and rhetorical privileges of the colonial past can be found in the shadows of today's newsrooms.

Opposition discourses: At a critical mass?

With the 'Ground Zero Mosque' controversy of 2009, in which a community of Muslims sought to build an inter-faith Mosque structure and prayer centre in Manhattan (not far from where the World Trade Center Towers stood), an uproar of opposition to the plan ultimately scuttled the project. The mosque centre was never built. Essentially, the project to construct an inter-faith, ecumenical, Muslim-led structure seemed, in isolation, as the appropriate, good-faith initiative and vision to ameliorate post-9/11 tensions. However, the extraordinary backlash the proposal received and its full-throttle mediation in all venues of journalism (print, broadcast, websites, and radio) not only cancelled the project but caused injury to the goodwill of the project and exasperated anti-Muslim sentiment in the country. In other words, when Muslims sought to reach out and offer to engage in constructive dialogue in a systematic and open way, the pre-established images of Islam, as Said described it, overwhelmed the concept and plan with the din of stereotypes and tropes of the past.

In her meticulous analysis of the media coverage of the backlash and the discursive tendencies of the resultant coverage, scholar Ruth DeFoster's research has shown the following:

> In cable news coverage of the Ground Zero Mosque controversy, Park51 was discursively tied to the events of September 11 early on and remained rhetorically connected in all subsequent coverage, to the massive detriment of transparency and truth telling – two central goals of the news media. Many of the arguments and stereotypes that were deployed in the cable news debate represented long-simmering centuries-old tropes about Islam, the East and the West – a clear return to old, well-documented Orientalist rhetoric. (DeFoster, 2015: 77)

Locating 'Orientalist rhetoric' was key to DeFoster's article, and the methodology she employed involved coded context analysis that showed a pattern of language and rhetorical bursts employed to buttress the opposition to the Park 51 project. But her theme is drawn out more in her book, *Terrorizing the Masses: Identity, Mass Shootings and the Media Construction of 'Terror'*

(2017). DeFoster takes high-profile case studies in her book and the media coverage and the terminologies they used in covering various mass shootings. She concluded that the uneven usage of 'terrorism', which appears to be determined by racial or religious identities, renders the descriptor just about 'meaningless, from a policy/scholarship perspective – there's almost no agreement on a national or international scale, to say nothing of scholarly definitions, on how to define the term' (DeFoster, 2017: 3). The disagreement, one may conclude, is not a lexical difficulty; rather it is created by subjective usages of journalistic descriptors.

> Analyses of acts of terrorism (and acts that have been identified as terrorism) during the last couple of decades have consistently found the same result – the answer to the question 'what makes one a terrorist?' is almost always some version of 'it depends'. It depends on whose interests are served by identifying the act as an act of terrorism. It depends on how policymakers decide to define the act, and which legislative definitions were in place at the time. It depends, in media coverage, on the identity of the culprit, especially with regard to his race and religion. (DeFoster, 2017: 3–4)

In the absence of discernible and objective usages of these important terms, it is reasonable to conclude (or at least argue) that another intellectualizing force is at play. She illustrates this with the 2009 mass shooting at Fort Hood, a military base located in Killeen, Texas. The shooter, in this case, was a Muslim, Army Major Nidal Hasan. DeFoster examined the frames used in mainly broadcast journalism's coverage of the shooting, comparing the 'choices made by these media (inclusions, omissions, primary sources) to what we now know about the facts of the event, and the personal history of the shooter, Army Major Nidal Hasan' (DeFoster: 2017).

The coverage of Fort Hood was a strategic and well-founded choice of analysis. The event, according to DeFoster, and the influence the coverage had in

> upholding norms and cultural scripts of the Iraq War period in the first decade of the 21st century – the infallibility of the military (and its role in the aftermath of this shooting as a stand-in for the American people), the framing of the event as an act of 'terror' closely akin to the Oklahoma City bombings or September 11, and the reinforcement and repetition of latently Orientalist 'East vs. West' tropes in coverage that firmly positioned Hasan as an un-American other.

Critical evaluation of the language and themes of news coverage of the Fort Hood event, and surely the broader coverage of other Muslim-linked events, points toward careless usage of 'Orientalist tropes', which is significant for not only what it means for the analytical value of a given study, but for the potential of enriching and expanding a larger discourse about future best practices when it comes to reportage about or in the Muslim world. 'Orientalism', outside the restrictive view of an historical phenomenon, is more readily rendered as a research design, as Jacqui Ewart and Kate O'Donnell argue in their book *Reporting Islam: International Best Practice for Journalists*. 'Contemporary reportage that includes tropes of the swarthy, turbaned Muslim terrorist and the oppressed (veiled) Muslim woman and fails to reject the homogenisation of Islam and Muslims tap into and reinforce this long history of Orientalist discourse' (Ewart and O'Donnell, 2018: 23).

Ewart and O'Donnell make a significant contribution to this discussion about the representation and typecasting of a people because they argue that Orientalism, Islamophobia, and racism (and by extension 'the clash of civilizations') are bona fide conceptional frameworks that inform and systematically evaluate not just content of coverage but their historical roots.

Thus, 'Islamophobia', the word, social spectacle, and framework, is now firmly established in popular and academic discourses. The critiques of the word are well noted, but by all measures, 'Islamophobia' is part of the modern vulgate and, in fact, in the language of American and European politics. Linking media coverage of Islam with Islamophobia has been another rich area of scholarly work that has bourgeoned in the last decade, and, just like Orientalism, the inclusion of Islamophobia in the globalization discussion of journalism and ethics is appropriate. While Islamophobia may not be a fully agreed-upon term, its ascendancy in the public sphere cannot be ignored. Interestingly, works on Islamophobia often overlap and link to contemporary media narratives and Orientalism. To make this point, it is helpful to examine three books that have come out in recent years that draw attention to and examine the roots in the reality of contemporary Islamophobia and Western climes.

Nathan Lean provocatively framed Islamophobia in the West as an 'industry', using the language of economics to suggest a systematic and profiteering tenacity of anti-Muslim angst. *The Islamophobia Industry: How the Right Manufactures Fear of Muslims* is a critical examination of the very purpose of Islamophobia for political gains and its caustic effects on society, particularly Muslim minority communities in the West. For Lean, hostility toward Islam and Muslims has become 'an industry of hate', led by 'bigoted bloggers, racist politicians, fundamentalist religious leaders, Fox News pundits, and religious Zionists' (2012: 10) have developed 'an industry of hate' (2012: 10). Lean singles out a cadre of writers, bloggers, and news pundits who are effectively responsible for the distribution and repetition of anti-Muslim activity in the United States and its mediation streams.

Among the results of repetitious negative portrayals, according to Lean, is the casting of Muslims as a kind of 'monster', a depiction especially popular among the far-right political spectrum and their powerful and sympathetic media venues (2012). Lean's choice of 'monster' is hardly casual. Associating racial or religious groups with monster fantasies encourages irrational fear (or phobia), since monsters cannot be reasoned with or redeemed. As such, their villainy must be defeated, deported, or kept out of the country, and their persons and properties become vulnerable to attacks. On a related note, Todd Green (2018) is confident that calling upon Muslims to condemn the violence and nefarious deeds of a few is ultimately illegitimate, since the assumption behind this unreasonable demand is that somehow the Muslim community has ownership and agency over all of its 1.6 billion people, and, more damning, it assumes that Islam itself is the cause of terrorism (2018). Thus demanding apologies from Muslims is underhanded and contributes to Islamophobia.

> The only show in town [about Islam], it would seem, is the story of violence and terrorism. This story dominates news articles, op-ed pieces, and political speeches. The general consensus is that Islam has a violence problem, an epidemic really, and Muslims need to own up to it. They should make amends for all that is wrong in their religion since the only way to explain terrorist attacks carried out by the likes of al-Qaeda or ISIS is to look to their reputed source of inspiration – Islam. (Green, 2018: xxiii–xxiv)

Attorney and law professor, Khaled A. Beydoun, writes about Islamophobia, in part, through the analytical framework of critical race theory. His approach links growing Islamophobia with a form of official rhetoric. In other words, Beydoun contends that the Trump administration 'was poised to integrate Islamophobia fully into the government he would preside over and to convert his bellicose rhetoric into state-sanctioned policy' (2018: 9). As such, the rhetoric of anti-Muslim bias has become so pervasive in American society, its inclusion in speeches and policymaking became a strategic opportunity to attract electoral capital. Interestingly, Beydoun introduces a section of his book with the phrase 'Dialectical Islamophobia', which he defines as 'the process by which structural Islamophobia shapes, reshapes, and endorses views or attitudes about Islam and Muslim subjects inside and outside of America's borders' (2018: 46).

Beydoun offers a typology of Islamophobia that is meant to avoid a mono-lithic ideation of a complex and evolving phenomenon. His locating of the roots of modern xenophobic trends (as well as his typological work) is valuable to the argument that links mediation with not only the roots of problematic nar-ratives of a people; it also admits into the discourse Islamophobia as changing and evolving concept, which is critical. If the matter at hand has plasticity, then recommendations for amelioration have a better chance of being heard.

As such, Beydoun raised a critical point, that is, grouping Islamophobia with anti-black racism in the United States. There is consonance between these categories of prejudice in the United States, and Beydoun sees this bond in Muhammad Ali, the most well-known Muslim in America.

> His passing came at a very turbulent time in American history, when the rising tide of Islamophobia intersected with a Black Lives Matter move-ment that was already in full swing. This movement condemned the insti-tutional racism and systemic violence inflicted on black bodies with the same ferocity and fight as the champion buried before thousands in Louis-ville and billions more watching at home. Ali, up until his final day, was

unapologetically black and unrepentantly Muslim and spoke out against the bigotry directed at both halves of his identity. (2018: 153)

Some may sardonically see a strategic value in linking these two problematic racial categories, but as Beydoun argues, separating Islamophobia from other bigoted blights of the country (which should include anti-Asian, anti-Semitism, and anti-immigrant vituperative opinions) would ultimately be incomplete, since they all share a common thread: the fear of the 'other'.

Beydoun stated that the assertion that 'Muslims are the new blacks' is problematic, since it 'ignores the extensive history of black Muslims in the United States, and ignores the very existence of black Muslim communities, indigenous and immigrant, today'. In other words,

> Demographics, history, and modern narratives testify to the inextricable relationship between blackness and Muslim American identity. To treat black and Muslim as distinct and divided identities is to make this community even less visible and more vulnerable, at a time when anti-black racism and Islamophobia are not only proliferating, but converging, with vile and violent consequences. (2018: 154)

For other scholars, Islamophobia discourses must include enslaved African Muslims before the very birth of the United States, which ultimately widens the discussion about Islamophobia to include historical racism in America (Mugabo, 2016).

It should be noted that Erik Love situated the very premise of his monograph on legitimating the relationship between Islamophobia and the broader blight of racism in America. He, too, does not separate or sever one form of prejudice in a given nation from its broader anti-racism discourses (Love, 2017).

The synergy between Black Lives Matter and Islamophobia activism was on full display in the wake of the 10 February 2015 murders of three Muslim American students in Chapel Hill, North Carolina. Demonstrations and vigils were held in the United States (as well as in the Arab Gulf) with the newly minted hashtag '#MuslimLivesMatter' trending social media. The hashtag often appeared in many tweets alongside its inspiration #blacklivesmatter. The joint hashtag activism managed to link the Chapel Hill crime with the unrest of Ferguson, Missouri, over the police killing of Michael Brown. The Twitter event linked BLM with Islamophobia in a transnational, unsegregated mediated space.

The search for solutions, though hardly fully agreed upon, should avoid 'Simplified Complex Representations', a phrase coined by Evelyn Alsultany, as she critically evaluates attempts by journalists (and filmmakers) to offer simplistic disclaimers in an attempt to contextualize their reportage (usually) about conflict zones in the Middle East and Southeast Asia. For example, as Alsultany notes, simplified complex representations often come in the form of journalists offering disclaimers in their coverage, such as, 'It is impossible to capture the diversity of the Muslim world' or, more directly, 'These are not Islamic practices'. However, these disclaimers often precede the reportage that eventually presents a seeming 'onslaught of evidence to prove the brutality of Islam' (Alsultanuy, 2013: 166). The disclaimer signals that the journalist is aware of the diversity of Muslim lived experiences and is making an effort to present a semblance of sensitivity and awareness. It's important to note that the often-strange relationship between entertainment and news media may permit journalistic practices to thrive without much comment, even if they are problematic.

While this perspective is not central to the purpose of this chapter, one should consider the plethora of television dramas constructed around 'terrorism' and Middle Eastern culprits. 'Dramatized news fits neatly with the personalization bias. Drama, after all, is the quintessential medium for representing human conflict. Promising psychological release and resolution, drama satisfies emotional release', and more often then we think, journalistic practices at times are acts of scriptwriting (Bennet, 2003: 64).

Circling back to the main point of this chapter, the references and research mentioned here are far from exhaustive and most of them quite recent. They have put forth their nuanced and varied arguments about the breadth of Islamophobia and its influence on the public perception of Islam and Muslims in Western milieus; they spoke about the origins of anti-Muslim angst, and they are in response to uncomfortable Islamophobic trends in the West. But they all mention (fronted or inferential) the role of news media in the negative portrayals of Muslims and their religion. Collectively, these works, in my view, represent a welcome oppositional discourse that confronts in a more comprehensive manner the contemporary escalation of xenophobic, racist and Islamophobic in Western nations.

Concluding remarks: Framing the framers

Islam as *news* is 'of a particular unpleasant sort', Said wrote. He continued to say that the 'media, the government, the geopolitical strategists, and – although they are marginal to the culture at large – the academic experts on Islam are all in concert: Islam is a threat to Western civilization' (Said, 1997: 36). It is an obvious exaggeration to contend that 'all' academic experts view Islam as a threat. The authors mentioned above and their timely research on the roots of Islamophobia and news media narratives demonstrate a scholarly narrative trend, since collectively their work represents a wave of oppositional discourses that actually contest the essentialist narratives about the trope of an 'Islam-threat'. Because of their studies, it has become clearer today – now that we conduct our professional and personal affairs in a highly disruptive age of digital mediation and mediatization – the role of news media cannot be separated from the historical ideological forces and power distribution that help shape a country's presumptions, educational systems and mainstream media practices.

One does not have to look very far to find arguments that suggest that 'Anti-Muslim xenophobia was nothing new; America's fear of Islam was older than the republic itself. Even before Paul Revere rode through Massachusetts warning, 'The British are coming', his compatriots were effectively saying the same thing about Muslims. (Pintak, 2019).

Since the main unit of all mediation is mainly the word – written or broadcast – there is little wonder why scholars stress the importance of media framing and the terminologies they are constructed from. It has been established in journalism studies that media framing (particularly conflict frames) can determine 'the way in which the public and policy-makers perceive the causes, consequences, and importance of those conflicts and where diplomatic and material resources are committed' (Evans 2010). Media frames, in turn, have historical roots and political bearing, such that they carry the capacity to not just describe newsworthy events but offer an interpretation of the event for a given audience for whom the historical roots and bearing resonate (Overholser, 2005). It is for these reasons that this chapter argues that to truly understand the influence of news media and its frames, it is critical to take a deep dive into the intellectual and ideological origins of society and its news structures.

No one has to be convinced of the power of news framing and descriptors; it is something anyone can appreciate, for the simple reason that the 'words we use to name and define things matter, because words are not neutral agents', as Morin states.

> Words do not just describe the world but create it. This is because words in and of themselves have no inherent meanings; rather, they attain meanings in their own historical and discursive settings through a long process of repetitive, selective, and careful usage within specific contexts. (Morin, 2016: 988–989)

In a similar vein, Wagner and Gruszczynski show that media framing links with personal and political opinion-making. 'When framing in communication affects a frame in thought, a framing effect has occurred' (2016: 6). While their work focuses on party politics in the United States, their attention to how framing informs opinion-making is of high value for any framing discussion. One should also consider situating framing in the context of a specific media environment, namely, an environment that has become increasingly partisan (as it has in the United States, for example) and their advocacies in news media ecologies. The contextualization helps us see news content drifting away from moderatism to partisanship (McCluskey and Kim, 2012) – often strident and extreme partisan content.

The language of journalism practice, as cited by Cotter (2010), can be categorized into two categories of 'complaints' (Milroy, 1999) 'legalistic' and 'moralistic'. The former concerns itself with the mechanics (and errors) of journalistic prose, such as grammar and punctuation, and for broadcast, pronunciation is key. What is of keen interest in the context of this chapter is the 'moralistic' rubric, which, according to Cotter, is 'the actual meta-lexical meanings of the words (semantic sleights-of-hand leading to the absence of clarity and honesty)' (2010: 194). While Cotter does not directly associate this taxonomy with framing terminologies and their stylesheet acceptance, but patterns of usages of descriptors, their uneven usages as research cited above conclude, seem to fit more in the moralistic column. When an incendiary word like 'terrorism' is reserved mainly for religious or racial categories, then it becomes tantamount to spin or, more accurately, ideological spin. And if a phenomenon like racism (and all of its permutations) is 'reproduced through discourse, then racism will be evidence at all three "levels" of discursive communication – social practices, discursive practices and the text themselves' (Richardson, 2004: 33).

News frames per se are not the only considerations here. There is something to be said about how enriching and diversifying the experiences and cultures of newsrooms and editorial hierarchies can help address, however incrementally, not just anti-Muslim biases, but all biases. Increasingly in recent years, there has been a significant rise in the number of American Muslim journalists and British Muslim journalists who work in mainstream media organizations of their respective countries: The *Huffington Post, Religious News Service, The Chicago Tribune, The New York Times, The Los Angeles Times, The Washington Post, Foreign Policy Magazine, The Guardian, The BBC, CNN, MSNBC, The Atlantic*, just to name a few, as well as many local and regional news outlets in the US. As a parallel argument, it can be said that to introduce a more inclusive culture in contemporary journalism and to work on the blind spot it may have for Islam-related reportage pivots on greater representations of Muslim journalists and media professionals working in mainstream newsrooms. This observation, while substantiative, is mentioned here in the spirit of propaedeutic considerations. Ethnographic examinations of newsrooms and/or staff of major news organizations would offer greater insight into the influence that a news organization's diversified work culture may have in affecting reportage and framing choices.

Public and academic discussions about racism, Islamophobia and media are not elite deliberations with few consequences. On the contrary, the material stakes are high and the risks faced by the communities affected by it are real:

> Popular discourse over the role of Muslims and Islam in the United States remains fraught, fractured, and deeply problematic, and the worst effects of this larger trend of anti-Muslim discourse are yet to be felt. This Islamophobia is not without significant cost, both to the health of our national discourse and to the human lives it degrades. (DeFoster, 2015: 77)

References

Abusharif, Ibrahim N. (2014), *Parsing 'Arab Spring'*. Occasional Paper Series. Northwestern University in Qatar.

Alsultany, E. (2013), 'Arabs and Muslims in the media after 9/11: Representational strategies for a "post race" era'. *American Quarterly* 65(1), 161–169.

Appadurai, A. (1996), *Modernity at Large: Cultural Dimensions of Globalization*. Minneapolis: University of Minnesota Press.

Bennet, L. (2003), *News: The Politics of Illusion*. London: Longman.

Beydoun, K. A. (2018), *American Islamophobia: Understanding the Roots and Rise of Fear*. Oakland, CA: University of California Press.

Bleich, E., Nisar, H., and Vazquez, C. (2018), 'Investigating status hierarchies with media analysis: Muslims, Jews, and Catholics in the New York times and the Guardian headlines, 1985–2014'. *International Journal of Comparative Sociology*, 59(3), 239–257.

Cotter, C. (2010), *News Talk: Investigating the Language of Journalism*. Cambridge: Cambridge University Press.

Davis, D. K. and Kent, K. (2013), 'Journalism ethics in a global communication era: The framing journalism perspective'. *China Media Research* 9(2), 71–82.

DeFoster, R. (2015), 'Orientalism for a new millennium: Cable news and the specter of the "Ground Zero Mosque"'. *Journal of Communication Inquiry* 39(1), 63–81.

DeFoster, R. (2017), *Terrorizing the Masses: Identity, Mass Shootings and the Media Construction of 'Terror'*. New York: Peter Lang.

Evans, M. (2010), 'Framing international conflicts: Media coverage of fighting in the Middle East'. *International Journal of Media and International Politics*, 6(2), 209–233.

Ewart, J., and O'Donnell, K. (2018), *Reporting Islam: International Best Practice for Journalists*. London: Routledge.

Green, T. H. (2018), *Presumed Guilty: Why We Shouldn't Ask Muslims to Condemn Terrorism*. Minneapolis: Fortress Press.

Hafez, K. (2011), 'Global journalism for global governance? Theoretical visions, practical constraints'. *Journalism*, 12(4), 483–496.

Jacobsen, T. G., Jensen, T. G., Vitus, K., and Weibel, K. (2013), *Analysis of Danish Media Setting and Framing of Muslims, Islam and Racism*. The Danish National Centre for Social Research. Retrieved from: https://pure.vive.dk/ws/files/224036/WP_10_2013.pdf. Accessed: 9 August 2021.

Latif, J. (2018), 'Muslim American cyber contestations between scholars and activists debating racism, Islamophobia and Black Lives Matter'. *Journal of Religion, Media and Digital Culture*, 7(1), 67–89.

Lean, N. (2012), *The Islamophobia Industry: How the Right Manufactures Fear of Muslims*. London: Pluto Press.

Love, E. (2017), *Islamophobia and racism in America*. New York: New York University Press.

Lyons, J. (2012), *Islam through Western Eyes: From the Crusades to the War on Terrorism*. New York: Columbia University Press.

McCluskey, M. and Kim, Y. M. (2012), Moderatism or polarization? Representation of advocacy groups' ideology in newspapers'. *Journalism & Mass Communication Quarterly*, 89(4), 565–584.

Media Tenor (2013), 'US TV primetime news prefer stereotypes: Muslims framed mostly as criminals'. Media Tenor. Retrieved from http://us.mediatenor.com/en/library/sp eeches/download/203_e7b0fd1fe879affa8739882f73c12e27&usg=AOvVa w2g9l6Pdr3Bwfa2I5cZG48n

Miladi, N. (2021), 'The discursive representation of Islam and Muslims in the British tabloid press'. *Journal of Applied Journalism and Media Studies*, 10(1), 117–138.

Milroy, J. and Milroy, L. (1999), *Authority in Language: Investigating Standard English*. London: Psychology Press.

Morin, A. (2016), 'Framing terror: The strategies newspapers use to frame an act as terror or crime'. *Journalism & Mass Communication Quarterly*, 93(4), 986–1005.

Mugabo, D. (2016) On rocks and hard places: A reflection on antiblackness in organizing against Islamophobia'. *Critical Ethnic Studies*, 2(2), 159–183.

Overholser, G. and Hall Jamieson, K. (2005), *The Press*. Oxford: Oxford University Press.

Peng, Z. (2008), 'Framing the anti-war protests in the global village: A comparative study of newspaper coverage in three countries'. *International Communication Gazette* 70(5), 361–377.

Pintak, L. (2006), *Reflections in a Bloodshot Lens: America, Islam and the War of Ideas*. London: Pluto Press.

Pintak, L. (2019), *America & Islam: Soundbites, Suicide Bombs and the Road to Donald Trump*. London: Bloomsbury Publishing.

Rao, S. (2010), 'Postcolonial Theory and Global Media Ethics: A Theoretical Intervention', in S. J. A. Ward and H. Wasserman (eds), *Media Ethics beyond Borders*. New York: Routledge, pp. 90–104.

Rao, S. and Wasserman, H. (2007), 'Global media ethics revisited: A postcolonial critique'. *Global Media and Communication* 3(1), pp. 29–50.

Reese, S. D., Gandy, Jr, O. H. and Grant, A. E. (eds) (2001), *Framing Public Life: Perspectives on Media and Our Understanding of the Social World*. New York: Routledge.

Richardson, J. E. (2004), *(Mis)Representing Islam: The Racism and Rhetoric of British Broadsheet Newspapers*. Amsterdam and Philadelphia, PA: John Benjamins Publishing.

Said, E. W. (1997), *Covering Islam: How the Media and the Experts Determine How We See the Rest of the World*. London: Vintage Books.

Scheufele, D. A. (1999), 'Framing as a theory of media effects'. *Journal of Communication*. 49(1), 103–122.

Shaheen, J. G. (2003), 'Reel bad Arabs: How Hollywood vilifies a people'. *The Annals of the American Academy of Political and Social science*, 588(1), 171–193.

Tsagarousianou, R. (2016), 'Muslims in public and media discourse in Western Europe: The reproduction of aporia and exclusion', in S. Mertens (ed), *Representations of Islam in the News: A Cross-Cultural Analysis*. Lanham: Lexington Books.

van Dijk, T. A. (1988), *News as Discourse*. Hillsdale, NJ: Lawrence Erlbaum Associates.

Wagner, M. W. and Gruszczynski, M. (2016), 'When framing matters: How partisan and journalistic frames affect individual opinions and party identification'. *Journalism & Communication Monographs*, 18(1), 5–48.

Ward, S. J. A., and Wasserman, H. (2015), 'Open ethics: Towards a global media ethics of listening'. *Journalism Studies*, 16(6), 834–849.

14 Tracing securitization of narratives and images in the global media discourse

Abdulfatah Mohamed

Introduction

For several decades, security theory has been in a state of flux since the traditional Realism approach has been ineffective in providing a framework for understanding security issues in the aftermath of the Cold War (Robinson, 2010: 847). Constructivist approaches to security theory have emerged to understand the characterization of problems as security matters by various actors, and the ways in which individuals and groups respond to security challenges (Buzan and Hansen, 2009: 191). For example, the critical security school of thought assumes that both the perception of a threat and the response necessary to deal with the threat are socially constructed and therefore lacking an objective reality. Societal security theory is also rooted in constructivism, positing that societies need to maintain their identity in the face of perceived threats such as migration or globalization (Research Council of Norway, 2011: 3). Risk management security theory adopts a proactive approach to identifying and mitigating security risks. However, it also recognizes that the nature of modern security risks defies rational calculation (Van Munster, 2005: 7).

The Copenhagen Securitization School Theory Framework (CSSTF) provides an approach for understanding how the securitization and de-securitization of an issue occur (Does, 2013: 3.1). Securitization is the process by which political or other actors use rhetoric to characterize an issue as a significant threat to the fundamental values and institutions of a nation, and demand extraordinary powers to contend with the purported threat (Stritzel, 2007: 358). When used together with risk management security theory, the Copenhagen Securitization School Theory Framework offers insights into how the Global War on Terrorism influenced the securitization of Islamic charities. Significantly, both the Copenhagen Securitization School Theory Framework and risk management theory also inform the processes by which Western nations construct a dialectic narrative, creating a clash of identities between Western and terrorist organizations. Such narrative about the threat terror organizations pose, and measures to manage the risk of terrorism, provide the foundations for the securitization of Islamic charities, which Western governments and mainstream media have labelled as funding conduits for terrorism.

DOI: 10.4324/9781003203551-18

Definitions

The definitions necessary to understand security issues and securitization concepts often involve multifaceted, imprecise constructs. Attempts to define terrorism provide an example. Kruglanski et al. (2016: 1) suggests the concept of terrorism can be understood as a group attempting to achieve objectives by using extreme, radical behaviour as understood by the values and norms of a specific society. Since it involves actions that are contrary to the values and norms of a specific society (Kundnani, 2015: 9), the definition of terrorism is amorphous. Actions considered terrorism in one society may not be considered terrorism in another society. Vague definitions, including those used in the legislation of Western nations, make it difficult to understand terrorism as an occurrence in society that can be prosecuted under the law (Sciullo, 2011: 566). An additional problem with the definition of terrorism is the use of the term to characterize social movements that may challenge existing social norms or values (Munson, 2001: 507).

Challenges with 'security' as terminology

The concept of security has vague and imprecise meaning, rendering problematic the use of 'security' as terminology. Security can mean the safety of the state, with military power at the fore, as in the traditional construct as understood in Realism theory (Baldwin 1997: 9). Security can also mean protecting the interests of a group of people or infrastructure deemed by the state to be vital for the operation of society, such as economic interests or transportation infrastructure. Consequently, the concept of security is mutable and depends on the discourse surrounding the issue (Does 2013: 3.1). The concept of security is the product of the historical, cultural, and political environment in a particular place and time (Buzan and Hansen, 2009: 9); furthermore, objective facts or data are often not relevant to the understanding of security. Because of these issues, security is often regarded as a contested concept for which a neutral definition is impossible (Diskaya 2013: 1). The many different understandings of security suggest it is an essentially contested concept, for which no consensus on its meaning can be brokered, regardless of the evidence or persuasive arguments presented (Baldwin 1997: 10). Even this, however, is disputed by researchers in security studies, some of whom argue that security can indeed be clearly defined as a concept.

Sulovic (2010: 2) suggested the concept of security can only be understood through carefully examining the usage of the term in discourse. The term can only be fully understood by assessing it in light of additional, clarifying information such as security for whom, for which values, from which threats and by which means. While security theories attempt to define security as a concept, by examining the specific discourse associated with the speech act leading to securitization, the Copenhagen Securitization School Theory Framework provides a means through which to analyse the context in which the term is used.

There is no generally accepted definition of security because of the inconsistency created by objective and subjective interpretations of the concept. Objective security can mean there are no actual threats to values, while subjective security can mean merely the fear of such threats is absent (Buzan and Hansen, 2009: 32). Since it is impossible to measure objective security, subjective factors necessarily play a substantial role in the understanding of security. Consequently, the term 'security' often refers to the outcome of a subjective process rather than an objective state of protection from threats (Popovic, 2007: 14).

Traditional approaches considered 'security' to be a term synonymous with the military, because of the importance of the military in protecting the state and in projecting power (Robinson, 2010: 847). The concept of security as military power, however, relied on a perception of security that is based on the centrality of the state. Consequently, security was defined as the preservation of the state, with all political, military and civilian actors accepting the premise that the continuation of the state, using military force if necessary, was fundamental to the safety and prosperity of those living within its political boundaries.

The securitization process

Developing a counterterrorism policy requires a working definition of the nature of terrorism and the factors motivating people to use terrorism to achieve their objectives (Kundnani, 2015: 9). However, there is not universally accepted definition of terrorism. A process therefore occurs in which both state and non-state actors define the concept, using discourse representing a specific group as terrorists posing a threat to a value or norm that is fundamental to society (Schlentz, 2010: 6). Connecting the concept of security to discourse and narratives concerning terrorism fosters a sense of legitimacy for representing the object that is external to normal society as terrorism and a threat. Presenting the threat as external in origin means there is less scrutiny of the legitimacy of representing the object as a threat. The process can be described as securitization of an object by linking the object with terrorism and the need to maintain security against the threat this presents.

In practice, a state actor's claim that an incident involves national security becomes the rationale for the use of force or other extraordinary measures. Consequently, the state actor mobilizes resources or exercises extraordinary power that, were usually established in emergency to counter the claimed threat to national security and the audience (Robinson, 2010: 850). From this perspective, a working definition of the concept of securitization is an event or incident leading to the use of force as a means of providing security to prevent a future occurrence of the event. Consequently, securitization is a process with three components: first, the representation of an external threat; second, a demand to take action to mitigate the threat; and third, related actions outside the normal social or political rules (Bonacker et al. 2009: 3).

The need for process

The human condition involves insecurities of various types (Diskaya, 2013: 1). To reduce insecurity, people in the modern era have adopted a rational approach leading to enlightenment, which relies on a systematic approach to understand and protect against insecurity (Horkheimer and Adorno, 2002: 3). Enlightenment is based on rationality and rules. Consequently, anything that does not conform to the rules that reduced insecurity in the past requires the use of extraordinary methods or procedures to reduce insecurity. Deeply rooted in the use of rationality and rules, the process constructs evidence about the source of the insecurity, such as the nature of the threat and the methods necessary to eliminate it. In this context, insecurity involves anything the community identifies as a threat to its survival, including physical threats as well as religious and ideological challenges to values and norms (Kaya, 2009: 8). Identifying the threat generates the need to engage in a process that ensures others understand the nature of the threat and to take measures to address it.

Securitization actors

The individuals who identify the existence of a threat and use speech acts to convince others the threat is real and imminent are actors in the development of security policy (Walker and Seegers, 2012: 27). The actor exerts influence over others to accept the proposition of an existing threat and the need for extraordinary action to protect against it. Such actors are typically political leaders, although they can also be community, religious or other types of leaders. An actor's senior position in the political and social hierarchy bolsters perceptions of their authority and increases their ability to influence others. However, the actor attempting to securitize an issue using speech act can have an agenda they hide from those they aim to persuade (Kaya, 2009: 8).

Speech act

Securitization involves speech or discourse, which is necessary to communicate information about the existence of a threat and the actions that the speaker believes are necessary to mitigate the danger (Robinson, 2010: 851). The way in which the nature and source of the threat is presented significantly influences the public's understanding and their willingness to accept the use of extraordinary powers deemed necessary to counter the threat. Such speech is also often framed in terms of traditional Realism theory, in which the threat is presented as an objective reality threatening the survival of the state, rather than to the well-being of the people living within the state. In using a speech act presenting an object as constituting a threat, the actor in effect constructs the security issue. They expect the discourse resulting from the speech act to motivate others to accept the need for actions to address the threat (Schlentz, 2010: 6). The constructs contained in the speech act, however, are a securitizing move or effort to securitise an issue. The speech act itself does not lead to securitization of the issue that occurs only when members of the group accept the premise that the issue indeed represents a threat (Bonacker et al. 2013: 3).

The discourse surrounding terrorism demonstrates how the speech act operates to ultimately securitise an issue in Western nations. The official narrative contends that terrorism is the product of extremist ideology (Kundnani, 2015: 8). The way the speech actor constructs the official narrative, however, is the product of the methods which are culturally appropriate to Western nations in presenting a narrative (Maan, 2015: 80). The narrative-construction has a linear quality intended to assign meaning to an event. It begins with a description of the event, moves on to discuss the agency behind the event, and then offers some resolution to the problem the event created. People often uncritically accept such a narrative because the discourse enables them to understand the event and the effect it will have on their lives. A persuasively constructed narrative has the quality of a foundational myth, which resonates with cultural norms and values. From this perspective, the acceptance of the official narrative of terrorism as the product of extremist ideology depends on the way in which the narrative has been constructed.

The discourse concerning terrorism is not solely a phenomenon of Western nations. There also exists an Islamist narrative based on a Salafi-jihadi ideology promoting the use of violence to achieve a utopian vision (Russel and Rafiq, 2016: 7). The Western discourse, however, does not focus on dismantling or undermining the Islamist narrative. As a result, the Western and the Islamist narratives coexist with both narratives serving the purposes of political actors in a specific cultural and social context.

Prioritization and politicization

Once securitized, the group prioritizes the issue concerning the threat, which contains the implicit assumption that the group will lose its identity and freedom of action if the threat is not neutralized (Bonacker et al., 2013: 3). No longer subject to debate as to whether a legitimate security threat exists, this prioritization of a securitized issue can be viewed as conflict escalation. Placing a high priority on a securitized issue also determines the resources a society will invest in addressing or mitigating the threat, as well as the means by which it will attempt to mitigate or manage the threat (Burgess and Jore, 2008: 4).

Designating an act as a security issue is fundamentally a political decision, which results in the politicization not only of the act but also of the discourse concerning the act (Does, 2014: 3.1). Politicization occurs when groups of people articulate their needs in a way they appear to be incompatible. The result is conflict within society as it mobilizes to defend itself against the presumed threat (Marchetti and Tocci, 2011: 51). Once the conflict arises, the politicization of the threat draws new actors into the civil society discourse because of the dangers assumed to the associated with the presumed threat. Consequently, new political forces influence decision-makers, which increases the pressure on political actors to act, including by adopting extraordinary measures to manage the threat. The politicization of the issue also prevents serious debate about whether the issue represents a legitimate or objective threat (Delibas, 2009, p. 90).

The perceived terrorist threat to security in the early stages of the global War on Terror led Western political leaders to prioritize measures intended to reduce vulnerability to terrorism. Compounding the rush to adopt extraordinary measures was the discourse of political actors not normally involved in security issues, such as business organizations and local communities. Contrary to the stated aim to eliminate the root cause of terrorism, the chosen measures were typically protective, focusing on interdicting terrorist attacks. Consequently, Western nations adopted protective counterterrorism methods such the surveillance of Muslims and requiring teachers and youth workers to report suspected terrorist activities. However, the counterproductive approach fostered hostility and resentment among Muslims (Langman and Morris, 2002: 2).

Do audiences have veto power?

Audiences are defined as the listeners and spectators at an event(s). For instance, in a stadium during a football match, the audience is all the people who watch, support and attend the game, which is designed to entertain. The role of the audience is to consume that which the event offers, but they also exert influence on the event, even though their performance may only seem external (Ahmad, 2013: 35). For instance, their roar of approval may motivate the actors in the event to work harder to please the crowd. Some events are crafted to test the reactions they evoke in their audience. The illocutionary act related to securitization, therefore, is performed by audiences.

Securitizing speech can be addressed in two ways: firstly, by identifying the agents of threat at the source, through the speech act; secondly, by ensuring adequate protection objects to which the speech act refers. Securitizing speech acts can help execute statements meant to highlight the position of the actor, or while recognizing the threat and do not require acceptance for their validity. However, this does not mean that relevant objects are not required to dispute securitization acts – merely that their veto power has no influence on whether securitization occurs. For instance, it is sensible that states take care of their citizens, but that does not mean security should be used to justify protecting citizens committing criminal or terrorist acts (Balzacq, 2011: 112). For the most part, every faction has a role to play in ensuring that all people have protection, even if from themselves, to ensure there is no foul play when it comes to security.

The role of the media

The lens the media applies to issues such as globalization and atrocities that occur can conceal the truth from their audiences. For instance, a media outlet with a particular agenda to push can downplay or exaggerate the issues that a society faces. Indeed, the global news houses that dominate the industry have, for many years, been criticized for the role they play at ensuring that people follow their line of thought. This is a common feature in the media landscape in Arab countries, especially in reporting the death of public figures in states such as Iraq and Libya. In both instances, it is the media that was used to push an agenda designed to criticize or reduce the popularity of long-established political administrations. With different factions differing in their opinion on democracy and morality, it is likely that such problems will persist, with their resultant victims and victors. Securitization allows for the global protection of every sovereignty based on what is thought to be moral or immoral.

For instance, the war on terrorism is a battle of images. That is, it all depends on how the media portray the various factors within an action. An example is the 9/11 attacks, which as well as being destructive, were also used to create global speculation that tainted the power and prestige that the United States of America is deemed to have (Hammond, 2003: 17). In retaliation, the US and UK governments ensured that they are conscious of the image they project, and that the media does not undermine that image.

If these states did not consider the potential damage to their image, they may have taken different actions. This highlights that the significance of the media cannot be downplayed, especially regarding the handling of global terror issues. In this instance it may be argued that, devastating though the subsequent course of action was, the media helped to prevent a far worse scenario from occurring. It is also worth noting that the media can be used to the corrupt position in ways that they should not have been in the first place.

Sometimes, war can be used for image generation. The illusions are significant in ensuring that there are factors that are reported and providing the best possible environment for scrutiny and critique necessary to improve accountability. The protection that is received from states and bodies that do not want their issues played out in public is an example of botched purpose for all the work that can be done for various reasons (Halper and Clarke, 2007: 153). In some cases, the media analysis is biased or insufficient, thus misleading those who accept it without question. Individual reporters with a limited view or little knowledge end up doing more harm than good. Propaganda ensures that negative portrayals of events dominate, and it is often difficult for the masses to discern the reality of the situation. For example, after the release of the first video of al-Qaeda in 2001, there were concerns about the wrong 'image' being disseminated to the public, which led to many wrangles. American televisions were advised not to air the original, unedited messages from Osama bin Laden and the Arab outlet Alja-zeera, which aired the video, was compelled to restrain its coverage. These acts reveal the level of securitization of images, to which the media contributes, and the impact of this on media coverage.

It is argued that the initial war on terrorism was supposed to be mostly a covert effort to mitigate an already damaging issue, rather than it is becoming a means by which TV networks and other media platforms gained publicity. Media ethics shall call for the right image to be used rather than dwelling on things that do not have real importance to the people (Morie and McCallum, 2015: 98). It is not necessary for everyone to believe the portrayal with which they are presented, especially by the media, but not every portrayal has negative consequences. Indeed, some portrayals are vital. Coverage of key issues facing the world – including climate change, conflict and famine – raise much-needed awareness and motivate action to resolve these problems (Guan and Liu, 2019: 24). This has been to the benefit of people in war-torn countries, victims of terrorism, natural disasters and other devastating events. The impact of these problems has been reduced, highlighting that when media is used for the globalization and securitization of key issues affecting humanity, it can be a force for positive change.

Nevertheless, there are instances where media outlets have been forced to pay for the damage their influence have caused. With people generally trusting media outlets for news, such outlets hold significant sway over the thoughts and actions of their audiences. For this reason, some outlets have been subject to scrutiny and sometimes even lawsuits. One example is where the British newspaper *The Sunday Telegraph* was forced to pay more than 30,000 Sterling Pounds in defamatory damages after it published a false report describing how a leader at Finsbury Park Mosque had supported extremist violence. The article, which was headlined, "Corbyn and the mosque leader who blames the UK for Isil", was published on 13 March 2016. It included claims that the faith leader, '*blames Britain for the Islamic State of Iraq and the Levant [Isil]*' and had '*called for the destruction of Israel and appeared to praise the recent wave of terrorist stabbings in that country*' (Forsdick, 2020).

The allegations in the article were false, and the court upheld the case brought against the newspaper. However, it is highly likely that many people were influenced by the newspaper report, despite the untruth of its claims. Shockingly, the newspaper did not even offer a formal apology for the harm inflicted upon the maligned faith leader; instead, it simply published a report that stated, 'The Daily Telegraph has accepted an offer to settle the claim by payment of substantial damages and his costs to be agreed'.

Reputational damages faced by Islamic charities

Islamic charities who found themselves associated with terrorist groups, or on designating lists of criminals have been put in extreme situations and faced great deal of challenges. The increased number of mainstream media allegations to charities' reputations is another impact of securitization and the global War on Terror. Reputational threats usually would translate into a wide range of implications for the operations of charitable organizations. For Islamic charities, the risks associated with reputational defamatory damages in mainstream media would extend to an opening of statuary inquiry investigation by a regulatory body of charities or police authority, cease of donations, possible charity's bank accounts and assists freeze, halting of operations and overseas projects into further legal battles and administrative burdens.

Political polarization

The globalization of ideas has become a norm that results in localized securitizations. The political polarization of issues and problems have not helped, due to the consequences, partisan incentives, and democratic, electoral contexts. In one-party societies, the role of the media tends to be minimized and directed to propaganda, but Western democracies have highlighted such digitization, mass polarization and selective media exposure. In the digital epoch and mass media era, the media is the primary mode through which political issues are disseminated to the people in networked and linear ways.

The newer era media channels have more polarizing influence over the people. Polarization can be connoted to dichotomy and incompatibility resulting in partisan affiliation to specific environments, especially those at opposing ends of the extreme, such as liberal or conservative, and right-wing or left-wing (Floyd, 2020: 58). Often, the polarization that the media creates is partisan. The different factions tend to prefer divisive media, and this is especially true of Democrats and Republicans in the United States. A study by the PEW Research Centre on Journalism and Media (2014) revealed that the former prefers television news and avoids talk radio, while the latter would rather listen to a television advertisement, radio news and talk radio. Conservative Republicans tend to avoid news from CNN and the NPR, choosing instead to read online platforms such as Fox News. The opposite is true of the liberal Democrats. It is quite evident that partisan media is leading to more polarization around the globe, and Americans are becoming more partisan due to the influence of the media upon them.

The media continues to play a significant role in image manipulation and the disruption of securitization from a worldwide perspective. Different issues and agendas have been pushed and consumed based on their portrayal in the media. In some cases, portrayals are pure propaganda intended to brainwash particular groups of people. Chinese political space has also been influenced by radical polarization, despite being a one-party state. The country's political culture emphasizes cohesion and internal unity regardless of conflict, disagreements and authorities between the political elites. The media is utilized effectively in a war against issues such as disloyalty and terrorism (Diez, Lucke and Wellmann, 2016: 351). The media sphere in China plays the role of political condensation and discourses between diverse viewpoints in the country.

Mass media and the refugee crisis

Mass media influenced public opinion and political discourse during the refugee crisis of 2014–2015, in which many fled conflict zones such as Syria, Iraq and Afghanistan. Framing the debates around migrants, asylum seekers and refugees based on a set agenda, in the West, mass media has stirred up fear in societies about the security implications of changes in national demographics or identity. This has led European citizens hardening their stances and lobbying their governments or political parties against open borders. Then came media coverage of the death of 3-year-old Alan Kurdi, from Syria. The infant was part of a group attempting to reach the Greek island of Kos by sea. Though the trip from Turkey to Kos is just 13 miles across the Mediterranean, the flimsy dinghy in which they attempted the crossing capsized. The child, along with others, drowned. Mass media broadcast the tragic story, including heartbreaking images of his body washed up on the shore. Though the image gained mainstream media attention and an outpouring of grief and outrage, the impact was short-term and did not yield critical shift at policy levels in Europe. (Mike Berry, Inaki Garcia-Blanco, Kerry Moore, 2015).

Charities are known traditionally for helping needy and poor communities such as refugees and displaced communities. However, the suspicions raised by security agencies seem to have adversely affected the transfer of funds to Islamic charities and other philanthropic organizations. funds sent to Islamic groups are largely held in suspicion and most cases there are many steps to fulfil before due scrutiny is deemed complete. Transactions may be delayed, reversed or denied. Public charities are usually tax-exempt in the US, UK and many other countries with some degree of regulatory framework, varying in its capacities from one country to another. In many societies, charities are valued and considered to be trustworthy institutions deserving public support. Hence the hypothesis for experts in terrorist financing has been that Islamic charities may provide covert platforms and infrastructure to raise and transfer funds, or recruit sleeper cells for terrorist groups who could divert funds to terrorist activities under the cover of a good public image, with very minimal accountability frameworks (Bell, 2008). Even if not serving as a façade for terrorist activities, Islamic charities were therefore perceived to be vulnerable to abuse by terrorist groups. According to the United States' Treasury and other government authorities, there are alleged links between charitable activities and terrorist funding. Terrorism financing is therefore a major concern and area of investigation for US government officials. Western media had painted a negative image of Islamic charities, making it essential to repair their reputation, particularly for those wrongly suspected of financing terror. A strategy is needed to improve the long-term image of Islamic charities, especially those which do not have good relations with the United States.

There have been deep and growing concerns on the long-term consequences of stopping the funding mechanism of Islamic charities. Unfortunately, the media pays little attention to the issue, leaving the public largely unaware of the plight of these charities, the problems they face when they need to work abroad and the continued crippling of the non-profit sector. There is an urgent need for policy changes so that the non-profit sector can escape the quagmire and become as productive as it needs to be to meet the needs of vulnerable people around the world. It is crucial to maximize the positive role of the non-profit sector and help promote national security and the welfare of ordinary citizens.

It is often reported that state actors and other stakeholders such as the media tend to overstate the likelihood or prevalence of infiltration and abuse by terrorist groups. Poorly informed media coverage is exacting a major, detrimental toll on the ability of legitimate organizations to conduct their vital charitable and humanitarian work (The Graduate Institute of International Studies, 2005), and, as ever, it is the world's most vulnerable people who are paying the price.

There are also concerns that statements made by the media and government agencies about the operations of terrorist groups lend weight to the crackdown on legitimate Islamic charities involved in emergency relief services. Undoubtedly, the intensity of the War on Terror has rendered most Islamic charities vulnerable to unfounded allegations of links to terror groups (Robert, 2007: 42). This can profoundly damage their reputations, and by extension undermine their ability to secure funding and partnerships. Ultimately, reputational damage has caused some charity groups to withdraw from their core mission or scale down the level of support offered (Kroessin, 2011), particularly in conflict zones, where their humanitarian interventions are desperately needed.

Conclusion

To conclude, securitization through anti-terrorism frameworks is viewed by many states and non-state actors as a central strategy for influencing public perception and gathering public support. It is essential when states are trying their best to win public support for their political values. The media's role in terrorism, polarization, and securitization is to do what it can so that the public could be better educated through civic values to combat threat of terrorism in local communities. As a result, communities could relate to the authorities' discourse, believing what they have been told about some issues and becoming persuaded to act. Worryingly, as has been established, while the media can do good by ensuring that people are informed about vital issues, the media has also been used to push propaganda and falsehood, which can threaten securitization (Mansell and Raboy, 2015: 201). Heads of State, policy makers and the media have political responsibilities in protecting the liberties and rights of civil society. However, the irresponsible securitization of civil society is in contradiction with that. The media is a force that has its rights to foreign policy processes and international relations. It is used to ensure that issues such as global terrorism are handled in ways that are not too harmful to the public. The advent of social media has, however, decreased the ability of governments to withhold information. By reporting the actions and statements of political leaders, the media plays a significant role in securitization and their effects on other factors such as global terrorism and climate change.

In closing it is quite evident to say that global media has been blended into the securitization process and became a politicized tool that aims to create a polarized narrow view of Islamic charities. Securitization of Islamic charities has produced the growing default view of their automatic and immediate connection with terror groups. Where this has only been an allegation with no concrete proof, the media has managed to influence its audience into believing that the connection is logical. The consequence of these actions by the media and political leaders have been that many Islamic charities were pressured to close their organizations, leaving behind the families that were in desperate need of their aid. The recent refugee crisis post Arab Spring uprisings remains to be one of the most difficult humanitarian challenges facing the global community since the Second World War in the last century.

Securitization of philanthropic civil society comes in the context of other significant challenges and at the cost of the effective management of refugee reintegration and rehabilitation policies. Although there is a recognition of the increasingly robust evidence base on the importance of refugee's reintegration as a long-term developmental issue, policies towards refugee populations globally frequently adopt short-term emergency response models in what is an all-too-often protracted displacement crises. Mainstream media corporations are not holding global leaders and international organizations accountable and advocate strongly for timely solutions to enable the realization of policy changes to the refugee's crisis.

The continuous selective portrayal of news alongside a subjective definition of terrorism and security will eventually work to decrease many viewers' trust in the media that have dealt with Islamic charities and benefit from them. The question remains whether mainstream media corporations would be able to uphold the highest standards of ethics and create any long-term solutions once decided to broaden and deepen the lenses and not politicize the narratives presented to its audiences.

References

Ahmad, J. (2013), 'Book review: Media and terrorism: global perspectives. *Global Media and Communication*, 9 (1), 74–76.

Baldwin, D. (1997), 'The concept of security'. *Review of International Studies*, 23, 9–10.

Balzacq, T. (2011), *Securitisation Theory: How Security Problems Emerge and Dissolve*. London: Routledge.

Bell, L. (2008), 'Terrorist abuse of non-profits and charities: A proactive approach to preventing terrorist financing'. *Kanas Journal of Law and Public Policy*, 17, 450–476.

Berry, M., Garcia-Blanco, I., and Moore, K. (2015), '*Press Coverage of the Refugee and Migrant Crisis in the EU: A Content Analysis of Five European Countries*'. United Nations High Commission for Refugees. Retrieved from: https://www.unhcr.org/56bb369c9.pdf. Accessed: 9 August 2021.

Berschinski, R. G. (2007), *Africom's Dilemma: "The Global War on Terrorism", "Capacity Building", "Humanitarianism and the U.S. Security Policy in Africa"*. Washington, DC: Strategic Studies Institute. Retrieved from: URL:https://www.hsdl.org/?view&did=481206 Accessed: 10 August 2021.

Bonacker, T. and Groth, B. (2013), 'Civil society impact on conflict: A qualitative comparative analysis'. Retrieved from: https://www.un-ilibrary.org/content/books/9789210563406s006-c004. Accessed: 10 August 2021.

Burgess, P. and Jore, S. (2008), 'The Influence of Globalization on Societal Security: The International Setting'. PRIO Policy Brief, 3. Retrieved from: https://www.prio.org/utility/DownloadFile.ashx?id=174&type=publicationfile. Accessed: 10 August 2021.

Buzan, B. and Hansen, L. (2009), *The Evolution of International Security Studies*. Cambridge: Cambridge University Press.

Delibas, K. (2009), 'Conceptualizing Islamic movements: The case of Turkey'. *International Political Science Review*, 30(1), 89–103.

Diez, T., Lucke, F. and Wellmann, Z. (2016), *The Securitisation of Climate Change*. London: Routledge.

Diskaya, A. (2013), 'Toward a critical securitization Theory: The Copenhagen and Aberystwyth Schools of Security Studies'. E-International Relations Students. Retrieved from: http://www.e-ir.info/2013/02/01/towards-a-critical-securitization-theory-the-copenha gen-and-aberystwyth-schools-of-security-studies/. Accessed: 9 August 2021.

Does, A. (2013), *The Construction of the Maras*. Geneva: Open Edition Books.

Floyd, R. (2020), 'Securitisation and the function of functional actors'. *Critical Studies on Security*, 5, 5–15. Retrieved from: https://www.tandfonline.com/doi/full/10.1080/ 2162488. 7.2020.182590. Accessed: 9 August 2021.

Forsdick, S. (2020), 'The Telegraph has paid £30,000 in damages over defamatory article headlined: 'Corbyn and the mosque leader who blames the UK for Isil'. *Press-Gazette* [online]. Retrieved from: https://www.pressgazette.co.uk/the-telegraph-has-paid-dama ges-over-defamatory-article-headlined-corbyn-and-the-mosque-leader-who-blam es-the-uk-for-isil. Accessed: 9 August 2021.

Guan, T. and Liu, T. (2019), 'Globalised fears, localised securities: "Terrorism" in political polarisation in a one-party state'. *Communist and Post-Communist Studies* [online], 53(4), 343–353. Retrieved from: https://www.sciencedirect.com/science/arti cle/abs/pii/S0967067 X19300558. Accessed: 9 August 2021.

Halper, S. and Clarke, J. (2007), *The Silence of The Rational Center: Why American Foreign Policy Is Failing*. New York: Basic Books.

Hammond, P. (2003), 'The media war on terrorism'. *Journal for Crime, Conflict, and the Media*, 1 (1), 23–36. Retrieved from: https://www.researchgate.net/publication/ 26403576_The_. Accessed: 9 August 2021.

Horkheimer, M., and Adorno, T. (2002). *Dialectic of Enlightenment*. Stanford, CA: Stanford University Press.

Kaya, A. (2009), *Islam, Migration, and Integration: The Age of Securitisation*. Basingstoke: Palgrave Macmillan.

Kroessin, M. (2011), 'A genealogy of the Islamic development discourse: Underlying assumptions and policy implications from a development studies perspective. In: 8th International Conference on Islamic Education and Finance'. Retrieved from: www. iefpedia.com/english/wp-content/uploads/2011/12/Ralf-Mohammed-Kroessin.pdf Accessed: 28 October 2017. Accessed: 9 August 2021.

Kruglanski, A., Gelfand, M., and Gunaratna, R. (2016), 'Aspects of deradicalization'. Institute for the Study of Asymmetric Conflict. Retrieved from: https://journals.sagep ub.com/doi/pdf/10.1177/1745691618812688. Accessed: 9 August 2021.

Kundnani, A. (2015), 'A lost decade: Rethinking radicalisation and extremism'. Center of Claystone. Retrieved from https://mabonline.net/wp-content/uploads/2015/01/Claysto ne-rethinking-radicalisation.pdf. Accessed: 9 August 2021.

Langman, P., and Morris, C. (2002), 'Islamic Terrorism: From retrenchment to ressentiment and beyond'. Retrieved from: http://irows.ucr.edu/conferences/pews02/pprla ngman.do. Accessed: 9 August 2021.

Maan, A. (2015), 'The call to terrorism and other weak narratives'. *Narratives and Conflict: Explorations of Theory and Practice*, 2(1). Retrieved from: https://www.

researchgate.net/publication/304697231_The_Call_to_Terrorism_and_Other_Weak_ Narratives_Identification_As_Disruptive_Technique. Accessed: 10 August 2021.

Mansell, R. and Raboy, M. (2015), *The Handbook of Global Media and Communication Policy*. New York: SAGE Publishers.

Marchetti, R. and Tocci, N. (2011), Conflict Society and Human Rights: An analytical framework. In R. Marchetti and N. Tocci (eds), *Civil Society, Conflicts, and the Politicization of Human Rights*. Tokyo: UNU Press, 47–72.

Mitchell, A., Gottfried, J., Kiley, J. and Masta, K. (2014), 'Political polarization & media habits'. *PEW Research Centre Journalism and Media*. Retrieved from https:// www.journalism.org/2014/10/21/political-polarization-media-habits.   Accessed: 9 August 2021.

Morie, J. and McCallum, K. (2015), *Handbook of Research on the Global Impacts and Roles of Immersive Media*. New York: SAGE.

Munson, Z. (2001), 'Islamic mobilization: Social movement theory and the Egyptian Muslim Brotherhood'. *The Sociological Quarterly*, 42(4), 487–510. Retrieved from: https://pdfs.semanticscholar.org/ceba/813f90caaa3eac1b55856d28d2b1a0410f98. Accessed: 9 August 2021.

Popovic, G. (2007), *Securitization of EU Development Policy*. Lund University. Retrieved from: https://lup.lub.lu.se/student-papers/search/publication/1321231.   Accessed: 9 August 2021.

Research Council of Norway. (2011), *What We Know about Societal Security: Results from the Programme*. Research Programme on Societal Security and Risk – SAMRISK. Retrieved from: https://www.forskningsradet.no/servlet/Satellite?cid= 1253967007671&pagename=VedleggPointer&target=_blank. Accessed: 9 August 2021.

Robinson, D. (2010), 'Critical security studies and the deconstruction of realist hegemony'. *Journal of Alternative Perspectives in the Social Sciences*, 2(2), 846–853.

Russel, J. and Rafiq, H. (2016), 'Countering Islamic extremist narratives: A strategic briefing'. *Quilliam Foundation*, 1–20. Retrieved from: http://www.quilliamfoundation. org/wp/wp-content/uploads/ publications/free/countering-islamist-extremist-narratives. pdf. Accessed: 10 August 2021.

Schlentz, D. (2010), 'Securitization of asylum and immigration in the European Union in the period 1992 to 2008'. *Refugees Study Centre*, 56. Retrieved from: https://www.rsc. ox.ac.uk/files/files-1/wp56-did-911-matter-2010.pdf. Accessed: 10 August 2021.

Sciullo, N. (2011), 'The ghost in the global war on terror: Critical perspectives and dangerous implications for national security and the law'. *Drexel Law Review*, 3, 561–582.

Stritzel, H. (2007), 'Towards a theory of securitization: Copenhagen and beyond'. *European Journal of International Relations*, 13(3), 357–383.

Sulovic, V. (2010), 'Meaning of security and theory of securitization'. Belgrade Centre for Security Policy. Retrieved from: http://www.bezbednost.org/upload/ document/ sulovic_(2010)_meaning_of_secu.pdf. Accessed: 9 August 2021.

The Graduate Institute of International Studies, Geneva. (2005), *Proceedings of the Workshop Religion, Politics, Conflict and Humanitarian Action Faith-Based Organisations as Political, Humanitarian or Religious Actors*. Geneva, Switzerland. Retrieved from: https://s3.amazonaws.com/berkley-center/06ReligionPoliticsConflictHumanitaria nActionFaith-BasedOrganisationsPoliticalHumanitarianReligiousActors.pdf.   Accessed: 10 August 2021.

Van Munster, R. (2005), *Logics of Security: The Copenhagen School, Risk Management, and The Logics of Security*. Odense, Denmark: Syddansk Universitet. Retrieved from: https://www.sdu.dk/~/media/Files/Om_SDU/Institutter/Statskundskab/Skriftserie/ 05RVM10.as. Accessed: 10 August 2021.

Walker, R. and Seegers, A. (2012), 'Securitisation: The case of post 9/11 United States Africa policy'. *South African Journal of Military Studies*, 40(2), 22–45.

15 Decolonizing African journalism ethics
From Afriethics to Afrokology

Winston Mano

Introduction

The chapter argues for decolonizing journalism ethics from an Afrokological standpoint. Afrokology first underpins a critical engagement that not only pushes back on irrelevant colonial epistemes but also unmasks the incompleteness of dominant global North journalism ethical frameworks. Secondly, Afrokology as heuristic tool is mobilized to centre African journalism ethics from an African standpoint, unapologetically positioning African journalism ethics or 'Afriethics' within a decolonial African/global South perspective that speaks truth to power. Unlike with the previous efforts, African journalism ethics in this chapter are informed by key Afrokological building blocks based on conviviality, incompleteness and relational accountability, with an emphasis on centering African lived experience in a pluriverse (Mano and milton, 2021). The main objective is to develop a more relevant and responsive ethical framework of values and behaviour for African journalism, from an African vantage point. Afrokology is equally against insular and narrow ideas and beliefs in African ethics as the continent is evidently dynamic and diverse. The chapter critically builds on and excavates from relevant African epistemes such as Francis Kasoma's (1994, 1996) concept of "Afriethics" and Colin Chasi's (2021) *Ubuntu for Warriors*. The chapter locates the discussion of African journalism ethics within decoloniality and in terms of Afrokology.

Journalism ethics in this chapter are defined in terms of situations and issues relating to what journalists should do both in 'micro' and 'macro' contexts, given their role in society (Ward, 2008: 139). Crucially, journalism requires ethical codes:

> Codes are documents that are useful in pinning down the tenets of good journalism practice, just like other sectors which have a strong linkage with the public sphere (e.g. lawyers, police force, civil service). Codes of ethics or conduct do provide a reference for acceptable behaviour but they should ideally be adopted after consultation with the public, with regular updates to respond to the needs of the day ... once the codes are adopted,

DOI: 10.4324/9781003203551-19

compliance has to be ensured so that they do not remain as mere window-dressing actions. (Chan-Metoo, 2013: 43)

Journalism ethics encompass issues such as limits of free speech, accuracy and bias, fairness and privacy, the use of graphic images, conflicts of interest, the representation of minorities and the role of journalism (ibid.). Some scholars from postcolonial perspectives have argued that journalism 'ethical concepts are interpreted, applied and given meaning within specific, concrete, geo-historical contexts' (Wasserman, 2011: 793). Human lived experience in specific historical context is seen as particularly important by decolonial scholars.

There is a tension between local, national and global media ethics in terms of their relationships and relevance, with some advocating a hybrid of local and global ethics in journalism. This chapter discusses but rejects the add and stir approaches to African media ethics, from an Afrokological decolonial position. It first presents the debates for global ethics and the problems with such a position. Secondly, it considers the trajectory of African journalism ethics driven by local epistemes and how this has met with its own problems. The chapter is ultimately against those who have maintained that the global South ethics have value only 'because of their grounding in the cultural and historical conditions of the West' (Rao and Wasserman, 2007: 31). The first position sees journalism ethics and values as global (Northern) with capability to transcend cultural, geographic or religious experiences in which they originate, with room to 'fit', 'insert' or 'incorporate' other concepts from the global South into global ethics. Mano and milton (2021), have specifically argued against such a pro-global Northern position as the normal order, expressly speaking against incorporating other paradigms as mere add-ons in ways that continue to position African (and other so-called non-Western/global South ethics) approaches as minor appendages or mere corollaries. Afrokologized journalism ethics, as will be discussed below, engenders the methodology of the oppressed and champions media ethics that centres African epistemes to underpin ethical relational accountability and values from own vantage point (milton and Mano, 2021).

The chapter argues for decoloniality to be applied in journalism ethics from an African standpoint and African lived experiences, respecting African epistemes in their own right rather than as appendages or mere add-ons to global ethics. In the African context there is 'tension between dominant normative theories of journalism that demand of journalists professional independence and detachment, and the conflicting loyalties to cultural and ethnic communities' (Nyamnjoh, 2013: 7). This has necessitated dual critiques of on the one hand, ethnicized and politicized media in democratization as well as coming to terms with 'limitations of liberal democracy in a context where people are obliged or ready and willing to be both citizens and subjects' (ibid). For Nyamnjoh (2013:12), 'African Journalism is like swimming upstream most of the time, given all the hurdles journalists and the media face in our various countries'. Crucially, the circumstances and lived experience of African journalists required own ways of knowing and thinking that resonate with the circumstances.

In this chapter, decoloniality is generative of alternative media ethics to counter and de-link from global ethics which valorize the provincial foundations of Western journalism ethics and accumulation of knowledge as universal (Ndlovu-Gatsheni, 2018). After formal end of colonialism, Africa embark on decolonization but coloniality remains a problem. On the one hand, 'Decolonization is about the creation of a new symbolic and material order that takes the full spectrum of human history, its achievements and its failures, into view' (Maldonado-Torres, 2004: 36). On the other hand, decoloniality involves liberating of 'culture, the psyche, mind, language, aesthetics, religion, and many others have remained colonized' by matrices of power (Ndlovu-Gatsheni, 2018: 485). In terms of decolonial Afrokology, this involves unsilencing and positioning African journalism ethics (Afriethics), in their own right, as an important affirmation of decoloniality. It means centering African worldviews and normative ethical frameworks in ways that resonate with African lived experience (Kasoma, 1994, 1996; Ronning and Kasoma, 2002; Christians, 2004; Nyamnjoh, 2005; Mfumbusa, 2008; White, 2010). As is noted by Banda (2009: 240), Afriethics as a foundation for journalism in Africa could be applicable if first debated and interrogated by African journalists, academics and other stakeholders.

In line with Afrokologized decolonial epistemes, the chapter invokes Chasi's (2021) innovative reworking of the moral philosophy of Ubuntu to include a counter hegemonic dimension to African media ethics that can empower the struggle for media freedom by African journalists seeking enhanced relational accountability with its key stakeholders. A decolonial Afrokological standpoint centres such African journalism ethics in ways that are more responsive to African democratic citizenship and empowerment in the digital age. Afrokology unapoletically centres African epistemes in their own right in a pluriverse.

The problem with global media ethics

Those who push for universal or global media ethical values are motivated by the news media transformation and its impact on the ethics of news journalism. Observing such changes, Nyamnjoh (2013) describes African journalism as becoming more partisan, highly politicized and in some cases playing a militant role in Africa. He argues the ongoing transformation has seen Africa's journalist play a more divisive role with explicit party-political leanings, ideologies, regional, cultural or ethnic belonging. Part of the problems arise from coloniality. In such an environment there are questions about the extent to which journalists can be ethical, honest, fair and neutral professionals. Meanwhile, Dube (2017), for instance, investigated how new digital technologies have radically transformed the face of journalism in general and photo journalism in particular, making it easier for photo journalists to obtain images and to transmit them quickly to newsrooms and consumers across the globe. The added opportunities for photo manipulation raise new questions about the profession in Africa, including about authenticity and the availability of national media ethics to deal with the resultant ethical dilemmas. Needless to state that the issues raised by Dube (2017) equally apply to other contexts, leading others to openly push for global or universal media ethics. From a postcolonial framework Wasserman (2011: 791), for example, asks whether such 'a global media ethics is possible, and what it could look like' as well as how 'to account for a diversity of ethical perspectives globally, while avoiding cultural relativism'. He, however, finds that 'media ethics codes globally agree, at least denotatively, on the centrality of concepts such as media freedom, truth-telling, independence and responsibility' (ibid.). The need for global journalism ethics arise from how varied news formats driven by technologies and structural changes to journalism are now impacting local and global contexts in similar ways:

> A significant trend in media ethics is the attempt to construct an ethics for media that are global in reach and impact ... globalization has been responsible for major transformations in the structures of media production and reception. As media worlds get rearranged, it becomes necessary to focus on the ethical principles that underlie media practices and content around the world. (Rao, 2011, n.p.)

The above argument for a 'universal' journalism as well as 'global media ethics' order are therefore a response to perceived shifts in the structure and processes underpinning news media. There are shared factors seen as influencing media ethics, new media and codes of ethics across many societies. Stephen J. A. Ward, a member of the Global Media Ethics project, outlines the rationale for global ethics:

> We need to construct a global media ethics because we live amid a media revolution that blurs geographical, cultural, and temporal boundaries. Urgent global issues and the power of global communication point to the need for a media ethics that is global in its principles. With global reach comes global responsibilities. (ibid.)

The argument here is that most codes of ethics contain standards for news organizations and are too specific to countries. What is needed is a 'global code' applicable to all, including for coverage of international events. According to Ward:

> The idea of a global media ethics arises out a larger attempt change, improve or reform the global media system to eliminate inequalities in media technology and to reduce the control of global media in the hands of minority of Western countries. This attempt to re-structure the media system have been controversial, often being accused of being motivated by an agenda to control media or inhibit a free press. The debate continues today. (Ibid.)

The focus on the globalization of media process builds on the wider issues of 'globalising' political, economic and technological factors that have been under discussion for a long-time. Sparks (2000: 78–79) sees globalization as mainly aiding a 'bureaucratic rationalisation' of foreign capital which is facilitating the takeover of 'local media' and the emergence of 'predators' who buy and dominate media globally. What is also instructive here are two observations by Sreberny (2005: 607) about, on the one hand, 'global' not meaning 'universal' but rather processes that foster and give more power to actors and media operations from a specific part of the global North. On the other hand, the so-called 'local'/ 'national' being not that 'clean' or uncontaminated because of contacts with other societies, including coloniality. These critical insights are key to how, from a postcolonial critical perspective, Wasserman (2011: 792) argues that 'grand and totalizing schemes for global media ethics have to make way for more nuanced understandings of the specific cultural and political histories within which ethics are interpreted and operationalized, especially in various settings outside the Northern metropolitan centers'. For Wasserman (2011: 792), the route to global media ethics is to introduce non-Western perspectives into a 'global' in a non-superficial, patronizing or tokenistic manner so that so that global ethics do not result in validating the hegemony of existing dominant frameworks. The problem of asymmetries in the global knowledge and cultural arenas has seen persistent challenges to the hegemony of values from the global North, as evidenced by the 1970s demands for a New World Information and Communication Order (NWICO) (Thussu, 2000). In spite of grandstanding by global leaders, structural, technological and ideological imbalances exist in world information and communication. Afrokology from a decolonial standpoint pushes from social justice and a pluriversal epistemological framework that challenges the universal stance. This chapter is aware of these problems which have characterized debates about globalization and hence advances Afriethics.

News processes are changing in ways that impact on news regulation and ethics. Crucially, as Wasserman and Rao (2008: 167) contend, globalization wields 'influence on the level of professional ideologies, ethical frameworks and practices of media workers'. There are two main reasons put forward for the urgent need for global ethics of journalism. Firstly, a non-global ethic is no longer able to adequately address the new problems that face global journalism, and secondly, in ethical terms, there is urgent need to attend to new global responsibilities that come with global impact and reach of media (Ward, 2021 n.p). Global ethical journalists would serve as agents of a global sphere and as loyal and engaged citizens of the world. They would be a bulwark against parochial news coverage by pursuing objective and nuanced reports from an international perspective. The media failures behind the 1994 Rwandan genocide have seen others call for an International Media Alert System to monitor media contents in areas of conflict: 'Once the perpetrators of crimes against humanity are brought to justice, it usually is too late for the victims. It is, therefore, of utmost importance that public expressions of elimination beliefs are spotted – and exposed! -as early as possible' (Hamelink, 2008: 82). In regards to this, Wasserman and Rao (2008: 163) argue for glocalization of journalism ethics, using a 'global-to-local theoretical matrix of resignification in the local arena'. Using findings from South Africa and India, they argue for a 'genuine' two-way relationship between global and local epistemologies and practices. Apart from the obvious practical challenges of implementing this in terms of global ethics, the chapter does find this approach in inadequate as it perpetuates the hegemony of the epistemes from the global North. The Rwandan genocide revealed problems with continued coloniality which created tensions and competition among fragmented African communities. With decolonization, we have moved 'from a period of "global colonialism" to the current period of "global coloniality"' (Grosfoguel, 2007: 219). It is useful here to invoke Afrokology as decolonial heuristic tool that is collaborative, convivial and transdisciplinary in its conversation with other forms of knowledge (Mano and milton, 2021). Afrokology fosters insights from postcolonial theory but also from decoloniality. 'Decoloniality and postcolonial theory converge and diverge. On the convergence side, they both aimed at dealing with the colonial experience … Decoloniality and postcoloniality provide a range of critiques of modernity. But they diverge in their intellectual genealogy' (Ndlovu-Gatsheni, 2015: 490). The 'decolonial turn' involves the freeing cultural knowledge and epistemes, such as media ethics, from coloniality.

The dilemmas for African media have seen Wasserman (2011) and others question the extent to which on the one hand African media can negotiate the space between its own ethical norms and practices and globalized ethical discourses laying claim to universal validity, on the other hand:

> As several case studies from Africa … have made clear, the circumstances under which African journalists work are often so radically different from those in the North, that a wholesale importation of Northern ethical frameworks would be unsuitable for these conditions. More recent scholarly concerns with 'global media ethics' run the risk of again (albeit inadvertently) imposing Northern norms under the guise of universalism, as postcolonial critics have argued. (Wasserman, 2011: 794)

Clearly, global media ethics are not a one size fit all. However, 'It must be emphasised from the onset that ethics is not the law but that its use and application help enhance the quality of journalism and push for greater responsible reporting' (Chan-Metoo, 2013: 32). What is required a decolonized ethical approach that resonates with a specific context in terms driven by interests of all stakeholders. Hence from an Afrokological perspective what is needed is to decolonize existing approaches to journalism ethics and to empower locally relevant ethics. It requires the centring of African journalism ethics in their own right within a pluriverse.

The push for African ethics

African epistemes and experience have been marginalized and misrecognized in media and communication (Mano and milton, 2021). In the area of journalism ethics, there is need to undo this misrepresentation and work towards Africa-centred moral and ethical codes in journalism to avoid frequent direct intervention and control by governments and other vested interests.

> While the risk exists that codes of ethics could lead to the temptation of excessive highbrow morality, this is still not a sufficient argument to simply not have any framework for a common agreement as to what is acceptable or not in the way news are sourced, treated and put into the public arena. (Chan-Metoo, 2013: 33)

From a decolonial Afrokological standpoint this section unsilences and relexicalizes African ethics applicable to journalism. This means taking seriously Kasoma's attempt to define and position 'Afriethics' as a viable alternative to failing Western journalism ethics invited sharp criticism. The foundations of Kasoma's (1996: 109–112) African ethics for journalism emphasize learning from the community and society; morality of African journalism for the fulfilment of obligations to society and to the journalistic corps; emphasis on societal as opposed to individual morals; need for dialogue (informed by African cultural heritage) among media people so that the practice of mass communication becomes a democratic and participatory; treating journalism as 'a communal profession in which the wrongs of an individual journalist have a capacity to tarnish the image of every one who practices it'; 'ethicality of the individual acts of the journalist should be first and foremost measured against whether or not they serve the wider community and the journalism profession; erring journalists or media houses should, in the true African spirit, be counselled by the other journalists; Journalists must cultivate a deep sense of solidarity and oneness of voice. These African values could help put reshape African journalism in ways that resonate with society. African journalists should show respect for their predecessors (i.e. learn from the experience of others) (Banda, 2009). In Africa, the problem is further compounded by perpetuation of media ethics and standards from the colonial era:

> Some African journalists even claim that the Northern standards they follow are world journalism standards which every media person should observe. They refuse to listen to any suggestions that journalism can have African ethical roots and still maintain its global validity and appeal. (Kasoma, 1996: 95)

The necessary curative according to Kasoma (1994: 8–19) is to take 'into account the African approach to life' with provision for principles and values from elsewhere. Afriethics should take into account the material conditions within which African journalists work, including poor pay that make them susceptible to bribes. Afriethics foster a communal rather than individual orientation:

African society, drawing from its humane approach to life, can inspire its recalcitrant journalists to bring some sanity into African journalism and with it redeem the disintegrating world press, and the African press in particular. Perhaps African journalists can bring in some fresh air into their journalism by making it once more a society-centred rather than a money and power-centred profession which always wants to have the last word on issues and hardly admits any wrong-doing. (Kasoma, 1996: 96)

The 'African world view' implied in the above is 'active' in African cultures and could form the basis for professional service and a shared commitment to serve common good among journalists (Mfumbusa, 2008).

The above emphasis on African ethics has been criticized. Tomaselli (2009) is critical of Afriethics not just on the basis on his perception of Kasoma's contradictory professional attitudes to state and private press but also his narrow notion of national identity rooted in traditional African culture, which exists severally across Africa and cannot be extrapolated to all contexts. Even though Kasoma warned against uncritical stance to national unity, Tomaselli (2009: 430) suggests that under African norms media would serve the role of a 'guidedog' rather than 'watchdog'. In his critical overview of Kasoma's (1994, 1994) work, Banda argues that the 'communalistic values and ethics that Kasoma presents in his Afrie-ethics thesis are based on a romantic reconstruction of the pre-colonial situation and a frozen view of harmony in rural Africa' (2009: 233). However, Banda (2009: 240) also posits that Afrie-ethics 'can only become acceptable once it is fully debated and interrogated by African journalists, academics and other stakeholders'. For Banda, Afriethics can be acceptable if it 'explicitly incorporates notions of democratic citizenship and empowerment' (ibid.).

The other main accusation against Kasoma's Afrie-ethics is that it idealizes African society as well as essentializes aspects of African culture. For some African media ethics are problematic:

> Media ethics in Africa can, therefore, be seen as contested terrain. Various normative frameworks continue to co-exist and compete for dominance over media ethical discourses. These ethical frameworks also have a political dimension, as they may support conflicting visions of who African media owe their primary responsibility to, and what their degree of freedom should be. It should not be taken for granted that the use of central ethical concepts such as media freedom and social responsibility in African media contexts necessarily correspond with the way these terms are used elsewhere. Nor should it be assumed that these ethical values are understood in the same way across various African contexts or even between different sections of the media in African countries. (Wasserman, 2011: 794–795)

The above critique, pitched from a global ethics standpoint, arguably throws away the baby with the bathwater when it comes to African journalism ethics. There has not been debates about forms and structures and exactly how to make such ethics work in Africa. What is a required is a nuanced balance in the regulation framework, between statutory regulation (imposed by law) and independent voluntary self-regulation by the industry (without any state intervention). The reported instances of unethical reporting should not result in one-sided direct government intervention and control as that would undermine and threaten media freedom. This chapter argues for open debates about African ethics, making it clear that they are not unlike those in other places. What is required is open thinking and inclusion of all stakeholders in the construction of relevant ethics. That African ethics can be positioned and contextualized in a more relevant manner is not out of question.

From a decolonial Afrokological perspective, African media ethics can be relexicalized in a more relevant and applicable manner to journalism on the continent if they are centred and shared. The infusion and valorization of relevant African moral and ethical ideas could help strengthen African democratization and development. As Gazibo (2019, 8) observes, 'Africans are not so different from other people around the world when it comes to the degree to which they value democratic ideals and principles'. In terms of African ethics, these should be defined in ways that characterize what is good or bad among Africans, 'constituted by the deeds, habits, and behaviour patterns considered by the society as worthwhile because of their consequences for human welfare' (Gyekye, 2011, n.p). Given the problems with today's African journalism, some respectability for journalists 'lie in once again in going back to the primordial ethical checks and balances that have always existed in African society and ensured reasonably good moral order' (Kasoma, 1996: 95). Crucially, such African ethics are necessarily 'embedded in a human community, the individual person has a *dual* moral responsibility: for him or herself as an individual and for others as co-members of the community with whom she shares certain basic needs and interests' (Gyekye, 2011, n.p). African ethics are 'humanitarian ethics, the kind of ethics that places a great deal of emphasis on human welfare' (ibid.). Although circumstances are diverse and different, African ethics emphasize a shared duty to others and to the community. There are relational moral responsibilities and obligations that are underlined and motivated by a concern for the interests of others:

African humanitarian ethics spawns social morality, the morality of the common good, and the morality of duty that is so comprehensive as to bring within its compass what are referred to as moral ideals (such as love, virtue, compassion), which are considered supererogatory in Western ethics. But central or basic to the African morality is character, for the success of the moral life is held to be a function of the quality of an individual's personal life. A moral conception of personhood is held in African ethics, the conception that there are certain basic moral norms and ideals to which the conduct of the individual human being, if he is a person, ought to conform. (Gyekye, 2011, n.p.)

While these ethical norms and values appear perfect, the challenge the extent to which they can inform Africa journalists so that they can serve as agents of African national or global spheres.

In Africa, part of the challenge is identified by Kasoma when he states that:

> The African press has increasingly become the 'accuser', 'the jury' and 'the judge' ... as it pounces on one victim after the another in the name of press freedom and democracy and refuses to be held accountable for the harm it causes to society both individually and collectively. (1996: 95)

As stated above, what is urgently needed are ethics, standards and regulations developed to respond to local problems in order to promote public interest and uphold relevant normative values. In regards to the need for a regulatory and ethics, Schudson (2008: 4) argues that '... no human institution seems worth our fidelity if it does not provide for its own monitoring, criticism and revision'. Curran and Seaton (1997: 4) similarly argue that 'Something which daily intrudes into our lives in ever more sophisticated ways needs to be, itself, the subject of continual public surveillance' especially that it (media) wields such a massive power, a power that is often exercised without responsibility'. There is need for media accountability but self-regulatory bodies are not always ineffective in bringing the press to account. A good example is a review of findings from a workshop on ethics in the practice of journalism held in October 2012 in Mauritius, with participants from Seychelles and Mauritius:

> The issue is that few journalists seem to know the content of the above codes and obviously very few actively refer to such codes in their daily practice. More importantly, there is very little awareness among the public of the existence of such codes and thus limited possibility to interpellate the press for any breach to their own code of ethics. (Chan-Metoo, 2013: 34)

From an Afrokological decolonial standpoint, the chapter offers Ubuntu as an example of an African philosophy that can be dated and expanded by stakeholders of Afriethics. For Chasi (2021: 1–2) Ubuntu is a moral philosophy developed by Bantu-speaking Africans. The word 'ubuntu' is extant in different forms in various Bantu languages. Broadly speaking, it relates to a notion of 'humanness/humanity' which I argue can undergird journalism ethics. Metz (2015) argues that Ubuntu can be a shared and connective moral theory with an African pedigree that can be used to judge contemporary social controversies, including the area of media: Ubuntu is conceived as a 'foundational moral theory with an African pedigree, which is intended to rival Western theories such as Kantianism and utilitarianism ... [with] a unified account of an array of duties of various agents with respect to the news/opinion media' (Metz, 2015: 74) It is an African moral theory that can be useful in accounting for issues such as proper content, investigative ethics and freedom of speech. Ubuntu draws from African lived experience focusing on interdependence and relationships that underpin African life even though it does not apply to all African contexts in the same way. In his work on global media ethics, Christians (2015) states that while there is not yet a 'world ethical theory' as it remains undeveloped, Ubuntu could be 'inserted' in it:

> As an ethics of being, Ubuntu interacts with its intellectual counterparts North and South, while it establishes its domain of relevance for media professionals on the ground. Obviously, this does not mean a homogenized treatment of African media policies and practices as if it were a monolith without vast differences among countries, regions, and media industries. (Christians, 2015: 72)

The above is acceptance of Ubuntu as an innovative ethical approach is echoed in the work of Chasi and Gumede (2017) who explored *Ubuntu journalism and nation-building magic*. They make the argument that by 'invoking ubuntu as an underlying ethos for a reporting ethic and practice, the news media could contribute to a magical idea of nationhood and nation-building in South Africa' (2016: 728). Ubuntu could inform a shared public morality that could inform solidarity with others. 'This is particularly pertinent to ideas of media ethics, and is often inscribed in codes of conduct and ethical guidelines, emphasising that the news must show empathy with, minimalize harm done to, the people about whom they report' (Chasi and Gumede, 2017: 737). In the construction of nationhood, Rodny-Gumede (2015) ironically discovered that most South African journalists seem wary of not being dictated to in terms of how they should do their job under the premise of Ubuntu. Part of the evidence include the controversies from the retraction and apology offered by *City Press* for a picture on its website of Brett Murray's painting *The Spear*, depicting the then President Zuma with his genitals exposed. There were questions raised over outrage it caused on the ruling ANC, particularly issues about 'dignity' Chasi and Rodny-Gumede argue that Ubuntu seen in this way 'is used to propagate the vision and supposed reality of leadership that is able to magically use communication to create realities it desires ... fundamental to how postcolonial and post-apartheid elites gain legitimacy' (2017: 740).

In regards to the media, Fourie (2008: 63) argues that the moral philosophy of Ubuntu can apply to African media ethics because it gives emphasis to both community and collectivism:

> Ubuntuism moves beyond an emphasis on the individual and individual rights, and places the emphasis on sharing and individual *participation in a collective life* ... Ubuntuism therefore places a high premium on negotiation, inclusiveness, transparency and tolerance ... ubuntuism acknowledges individuality not in service of the self, but service of others and the community. (Ibid.)

See in this way Ubuntu ethics would facilitate freedoms at different levels. Fourie (2008: 69) also argues that 'ubuntism or any moral philosophy can easily be misused or hijacked for ideological and political agendas'. He warns about danger of intolerance; danger of indigenizing theory and the danger of political correctness. Fourie (2008: 73) realizing that the questions raised in postcolonial criticism of dominant Western-biased normative media theory could be raised against ubuntuism, among other questions asks the extent to which Ubuntu as a moral philosophy is universal and how it can avoid an ethnocentric bias (73). These are no doubt important questions. However, decolonial Afrokology thinking seeks the centering of African epistemes rather than their universal application (Mano and milton, 2021).

From a decolonial Afrokological standpoint, Afriethics and Ubuntu in particular could be reinterpreted in ways that show dynamism and responsiveness of African epistemes to lived experience. There is urgent need to deal with the unfortunate situation where the state and the press in Africa

> are constantly at daggers' end with regular threats of tough media laws on the one hand and insidious partisan political reporting on the other. The public is a mere standby witness of the feud and its members often are helpless victims of unethical, biased, sensationalist reporting. (Chan-Metoo, 2013: 44)

In his book *Ubuntu for Warriors*, Chasi (2021: 13) critically re-evaluates Ubuntu's standing as a moral thought that values humanity in relation to how it has a dual aspect whereby it 'can burn and harm, or can cook up a good thing or two!' Crucially, Chasi goes beyond simplistic humanistic notions of Ubuntu which have been abused by colonial officials to pacify Africans as 'harmonious collectivists who cannot fight for their interests' (p. 13). Chasi's (2021: 4) is excavating the 'figure of the warrior, seeing the warrior character as a locus of moral agency in the ways in which it has and continues to direct action in African societies'. Fitting in with decolonial Afrokology, Chasi (2021) innovatively reinterprets Ubuntu moral philosophy beyond its commonly well-rehearsed insights that value harmony centre the 'figure of the warrior that expresses the capacity of the people to secure survival by means of abilities to fight, destroy and protect' (p. 4). It is a pushback on how colonial discourses completely misrecognized and erased the 'figure of the warrior from African history'.

> I am taking the stance that people who espouse ubuntu fight to produce good lives and to elaborate social conditions for lives to be lived well. This includes seeking to appropriately valorise the ideal of the warrior who practices ubuntu. Care, though, must immediately be taken to ensure that the values that relate to the figure of the warrior are adopted in ways that are conducive to justice.

Chasi's (2021) radical reworking of Ubuntu could inform the project of centering African epistemes. Rather than try to emulate global or Eurocentric models of journalism ethics, Africans could draw inspiration from African ethics, especially the redefined Ubuntu. As Chasi (2021: 18) notes, 'If we are to have a chance of acting with a good sense of common purpose towards the good, we must articulate with wisdom the moral line that should guide our warriors'. Emphasizing an interest in life projects, relational living, and how we our entangled with others, Chasi openly invites thinkers who are interested in questions to do with Ubuntu to follow the traditional route of testing the attractiveness of their thinking, for example, by valuing the life projects of people, when thinking of just war and peace. Seen in this way, Ubuntu warrior journalism ethics can renew commitment to public engagement and collaboration as a mode of intellectual production. Journalists and stakeholders would deploy emic-etic participatory methodological techniques that also engage with lived experience on the basis that 'the good is an expression of excellence that is perceptible and tangible in relation to people's practices, experiences and situations. On this view, Ubuntu is a culturally and situationally relative and fluid set of moral values' (Chasi, 2021: 63).

In line with Afrokology, it can be seen as unapologetically arguing for an African standpoint and from a decolonial perspective (Mano and milton, 2021). Chasi ultimately argues that Ubuntu is premised on the right relations with others:

> The Ubuntu of the future should be concerned with how communities and their members can relate to others who may or may not value harmony. It should articulate how just war should be fought and how just peace should be made with enemies within, and with enemies who are strangers. (Chasi 2021: 186)

This emphasis on relational accountability and conversation with others is at the heart of Afrokology as it fosters that which contributes to unlocking marginalized ontological and epistemological nuances that can help inform being African in the world. African journalism ethics can benefit from this orientation. It could engender journalism ethics informed by the set of multiple relations that one has with the pluriverse (milton and Mano, 2021).

Afrokology could help underpin the centring of African journalism ethics as it fosters conversation with other knowledges to counter ethical foundations of global North concepts as the normal or universal order in media and journalism. Such a stance is in line with ongoing decolonial debates in knowledge and cultural production which are challenging the coloniality of knowledge as well as recognizing previously marginalizing epistemes (Ndlovu-Gatsheni 2018). Centring local ethics in journalism is an attempt to rescue postcolonial cultural institutions, including the media, by using alternative ethical values because those rooted on the global North are not 'always applicable to Africa' (Mano, 2009: 278). The problem with coloniality is not only that it has emptied 'the minds of African subjects of their knowledges and memories, but has also played a part in implanting foreign ways of knowing and remembering'

(Ndlovu-Gatsheni, 2018: 95). Afrokology is invoked in a decolonial sense to push back on coloniality and to excavate and build connections with relevant ethical and moral orders that have evolved in Africa based on lived experience (Mano and milton, 2021). Africans are not unlike other societies in valuing positive virtues such as truthfulness and all that can bring peace, justice and respect within society. Engendering local vantage points within a more responsive ethical journalism, based on previously marginalized African epistemes and values, could help advance integrity and relational accountability, helping journalists develop a better sense of professionalism. With a more relevant approach, journalists' sense of what is right or wrong could be driven by African public interest rather than vested interests. Good ethical journalism, as elsewhere, could be replenished by relevant African social norms, even though these could be variously defined and contested. The chapter has shown that by reviewing and critiquing arguments for global or universal media ethics. The chapter has also reviewed problems with global media ethics and analysed the debates to reconceptualize Africa media ethics derived from African epistemologies and moral foundations (Christians, 2004; Fourie, 2008; Kasoma, 1996; White, 2010, Ndlovu and Sibanda, 2020). It builds on Kasoma's crucial observation that 'in its haste to clean up society of its scum, the African press and indeed the world press, has often forgotten or simply ignored the fact that it also badly needs cleansing' (1996: 95). Ultimately, the chapter emphasizes the fact that Africa needs to develop its own journalistic ethical values 'informed by underexplored, characteristically African ideas about morality', based on an approach different in important ways from approaches such as libertarianism, Kantianism, utilitarianism, and Aristotelian virtue ethics that dominate media ethical discussion in the English-speaking world (Metz, 2015:). Crucially the chapter argues for centering African ethics in journalism, driven neither by Eurocentrism nor Afrocentrism, but rather a critical mobilization of concepts and research tools that we as Africans deem most appropriate in the African context to rehumanize the profession on the continent (Nyamnjoh 2020, 29). What is needed are not global media ethics but African journalism ethics and an account of African morality for the media that speak to the lived experience of Africans in the pluriverse.

Conclusion

In anchoring Afrokologized journalism ethics, the chapter also calls for a commitment to social justice that translates into action by invoking decolonial ethics for African journalists. Ubuntu warrior journalists could act ethically in the public interest when speaking truth to power or when engaging with the marginalized based on a shared lived conditions and what needs to change. In line with decolonial Afrokology, the chapter pushed back on global ethics and rather centred African ethics within a pluriverse. It reviewed Chasi's (2021) subversive reinterpretation of Ubuntu moral philosophical, to emphasize the role of Ubuntu warrior journalism driven by ethics of justice. Such journalism takes adversarial but caring role performed by 'warrior' advocacy journalists interested in confronting the root causes of conditions that are preventing human dignity in Africa. Afrokologised ethics will both unsilence the marginalized and empower journalists in ways that could bring war and peace. Ubuntu warrior journalism can inspire African journalists to deal with the root causes of problems, with news media playing not just a monitorial role but a primary facilitative role to deal with pressing issues that threaten the African society in the digital age. From a decolonial Afrokological perspective, African-focused moral philosophy for journalism could refine duties for various stakeholders in ways that advance public interest.

References

Banda, F. (2009), 'Kasoma's Afriethics: A reappraisal'. *International CommunicationGazette*, 71(4), 227–242.

Chan-Metoo, C. (ed.) (2013), 'Ethics in Journalism: Why and How?', in C. Chan-Metoo (ed.), *Media Ethics and Regulation: Insights from Africa*. Cameroon: Langaa Research & Publishing CIG, pp. 31–46.

Chasi, C. (2021), *Ubuntu for Warriors*. Trenton/London: Africa World Press.

Chasi, C. and Rodey-Gumede, Y. (2017), 'Ubuntu journalism and nation-building magic'. *Critical Arts*, 30(5), 728–744.

Christians, C. (2004), 'Ubuntu and communitarianism in media ethics'. *Ecquid Novi: African Journalism Studies*, 25(2), 235–256.

Christians, C. (2015), 'Introduction: Ubuntu for journalism theory and practice'. *Journal of Media Ethics*, 30, 61–73.

Christians, C. and Nordenstreng, K. (2004), 'Social responsibility worldwide'. *Journal of Mass Media Ethics*, 19(1), 3–28.

Christians, C., Rao, S., Ward, S. J. and Wasserman, H. (2008), 'Toward a global media ethics: Exploring new theoretical perspectives'. *Ecquid Novi: African Journalism Studies*, 29(2), 135–172.

Curran, J. and Seaton, J. (1997), *Power Without Responsibility: The Press and Broadcasting in Britain*. 5th edition. London and New York: Routledge.

Fourie, P. (2008), 'Ubuntuism as a framework for South African media practice and performance: Can it work?'. *Communicatio: South African For Communication Theory and Research*, 34(1), 53–79.

Fourie, P. (2011), 'Normative Media Theory in a Changed Media Landscape and Globalised Society', in N. Hyde-Clarke (ed.), *Communication and Media Ethics in South Africa*. Cape Town: Juta, pp. 25–45.

Gazibo, M. (2019), 'Democracy and the question of its feasibility in Africa'. *Oxford Research Encyclopedia*. doi:10.1093/acrefore/9780190228637.013.702

Grosfoguel, R. (2007), 'The epistemic decolonial turn'. *Cultural Studies*, 21(2–3), 211–223.

Gyekye, K. (2011), 'African ethics'. *The Stanford Encyclopedia of Philosophy* (Fall 2011 edition), ed. Edward N. Zalta Retrieved from: https://plato.stanford.edu/archives/fall2011/entries/african-ethics/

Hamelink, C. J. (2008), 'Media between warmongers and peacemakers'. *Media, War & Conflict*, 1(1), 77–83. doi:10.1177/1750635207087627

Kasoma, F. P. (1994), *Journalism Ethics in Africa*. Nairobi: ACCE.

Kasoma, F. P. (1996), 'The foundations of African ethics (Afriethics) and the professional practice of journalism: The case for society-centred media morality'. *Africa Media Review*, 10(3), 93–116.

Maldonado-Torres, N. (2004), 'The topology of being and the geopolitics of knowledge'. *City*, 8(1), 29–56.

Mano, W. (2009), 'Re-Conceptualizing Media Studies in Africa', in D. K. Thussu (ed.), *Internationalizing Media Studies*. Abingdon: Routledge, 277–293.

Mano, W. and milton, v. c. (2021), 'Afrokology of Media and Communication Studies: Theorising from the Margins', in Mano and milton (eds), *Routledge Handbook of African Media and Communication Studies*. London: Routledge, pp. 19–42.

Mboti, N. (2015), 'May the real Ubuntu stand up?'. *Journal of Media Ethics*. 30(2), 125–147.

Metz, T. (2015), 'African ethics and journalism ethics: News and opinion in light of Ubuntu'. *Journal of Media Ethics*, 30(2), 74–90.

Mfumbusa, B. F. (2008), 'Newsroom ethics in Africa: Quest for a normative framework'. *African Communication Research*, 1(2). 139–158.

milton, v. c. and Mano, W. (2021), 'Afrokology as a Transdisciplinary Approach to Media and Communication Studies', in Mano and milton (eds), *Routledge Handbook of African Media and Communication Studies*. London: Routledge, pp. 256–275.

Ndlovu, M. and Sibanda, M. K. (2020), 'Ubuntuism as a foundation of media ethics in Zimbabwe? Journalists' perspectives and discontents'. *Communication*, 46(2), 44–63.

Ndlovu-Gatsheni, S. J. (2015), 'Decoloniality as the future of Africa'. *History Compass*, 13(10), 485–496.

Ndlovu-Gatsheni, S. J. (2018), *Epistemic Freedom in Africa: Deprovincialisation and Decolonisation*. London: Taylor & Francis.

Nyamnjoh, F. B. (2013), 'Africa's Media: Between Professional Ethics and Cultural Belonging', in C. Chan-Metoo (ed.), *Media Ethics and Regulation: Insights from Africa*. Cameroon: Langaa Research & Publishing CIG, pp. 5–13.

Nyamnjoh, F. B. (2020), *Decolonising the Academy: A Case for Convial Scholarship*. Basel: Basler Afrika Bibliographien (Namibia Resource Centre & Southern Africa).

Rao, S. (2011), 'The "local" in global media ethics'. *Journalism Studies*, 12(6), 780–790.

Rao, S. and Wasserman, H. (2007), 'Global journalism ethics revisited: A postcolonial critique'. *Global Media and Communication*, 3(1), 29–50.

Rodny-Gumede, Y. (2015), 'An assessment of the public interest and ideas of the public in South Africa and the adoption of 'Ubuntu journalism'. *Journal of Mass Media Ethics*, 30(2), 109–124.

Schudson, M. (2008), *Why Democracies Need an Unlovable Press*. Cambridge: Polity Press.

Sparks, C. (2000), 'The Global, the Local and the Public Sphere', in G. Wang, J. Servaes and A. Goonasekera (eds), *The New Communications Landscape: Demystifying Media Globalization*, London: Routledge, pp. 74–95.

Sreberny, A. (2005), 'The Global and the Local in International Communications', in G. Durham and D. M. Kellner (eds), *Media and Cultural Studies Keyworks*. Malden, MA: Blackwell, pp. 604–626.

Tomaselli, K. G. (2009), 'Afri(ethics), communitarianism and libertarianism'. *International Communication Gazette*, 71(7), 577–594.

Ward, S. J. A. (2008), 'Global journalism ethics: Widening the conceptual base'. *Global Media Journal*, 1(1), 137–149.

Ward, S. J. A. (2013), *Global Media Ethics Problems and Perspectives*. Malden, MA: Wiley-Blackwell.

Wasserman, H. and Rao, S. (2008), 'The glocalization of journalism ethics'. *Journalism: Theory, Practice Criticism*, 9(2), 163–181.

Wasserman, H. (2011), 'Towards a global journalism ethics via local narratives'. *Journalism Studies*, 12(6), 791–803. doi:10.1080/1461670X.2011.614819

White, R. A. (2010), 'The moral foundations of media ethics in Africa'. *Ecquid Novi: African Journalism Studies*, 31(1), 42–67.

Zhang, Y. and Meng, L. (2021), 'Constructive Journalism and Poverty Reduction in China: The Targeted Poverty Alleviation Campaign', in S. L. Borden (ed.), *The Routledge Companion to Media and Poverty*. New York: Routledge.

Index

Page numbers in **bold** refer to figures, page numbers in *italic* refer to tables.